Deleuze, Guattari and the Art of Multiplicity

Edited by Radek Przedpełski and
S. E. Wilmer

EDINBURGH
University Press

Edinburgh University Press is one of the leading university presses in the UK. We publish academic books and journals in our selected subject areas across the humanities and social sciences, combining cutting-edge scholarship with high editorial and production values to produce academic works of lasting importance. For more information visit our website: edinburghuniversitypress.com

Edinburgh University Press Ltd
The Tun – Holyrood Road
12(2f) Jackson's Entry
Edinburgh EH8 8PJ

First published in hardback by Edinburgh University Press 2020

Typeset in 10/12 Times New Roman by
Servis Filmsetting Ltd, Stockport, Cheshire

A CIP record for this book is available from the British Library

ISBN 978 1 4744 5765 1 (hardback)
ISBN 978 1 4744 5766 8 (paperback)
ISBN 978 1 4744 5767 5 (webready PDF)
ISBN 978 1 4744 5768 2 (epub)

Contents

List of Illustrations

Acknowledgements

This book has been inspired by a conference on 'Deleuze and Art' we co-organised in 2016 and a symposium on 'Deleuze, Guattari and the Art of Multiplicity' in 2018 at Trinity College Dublin. We want to express our gratitude to all those who helped with these two events and particularly the Long Room Hub, its director Jane Ohlmeyer and the generous support we received under their Research Incentive Scheme, Digital Arts & Humanities PhD Programme, Trinity Association and Trust, the Visual and Performing Arts Fund, the Faculty of Arts, Humanities and Social Sciences Events Fund, the Alliance Française, the Turkish Embassy, the Visiting Professorships and Fellowships Benefaction Fund, the Arts and Social Sciences Benefactions Fund, the Science Gallery, the Samuel Beckett Centre, the School for Creative Arts, the Arts Technology Research Lab and the Hugh Lane Gallery. We would also like to thank Orla McGinnity for proofreading the text, and Carol MacDonald at Edinburgh University Press for her advice and encouragement. Finally, we would like to express our gratitude to Magdalena Mazik at MOCAK and Karina Garstecka at FSO for their kind assistance with image reproductions. Radek would like to thank his Digital Arts & Humanities PhD Programme for their generous support; special thanks go to Matthew Causey, Poul Holm and Jo D'Arcy for their inspiring leadership and kind help.

List of Contributors

Mieke Bal is a cultural theorist, critic, video artist and occasional curator. She works on gender, migratory culture, psychoanalysis and the critique of capitalism. Her forty-one books include a trilogy on political art: *Endless Andness* (on abstraction), *Thinking in Film* (on video installation), both 2013, and *Of What One Cannot Speak* (on sculpture, 2010). Her early work comes together in *A Mieke Bal Reader* (2006). *In Medias Res: Inside Nalini Malani's Shadow Plays* was published in 2016, followed by *Emma & Edvard Looking Sideways: Loneliness and the Cinematic* in 2017. This accompanied the exhibition she curated for the Munch Museum. Her video project *Madame B*, with Michelle Williams Gamaker, is widely exhibited. After her most recent film and installation *Reasonable Doubt*, on René Descartes and Queen Kristina (2016), she made in 2019 and is currently exhibiting a sixteen-channel video installation *Don Quijote: Sad Countenances*, an attempt to stage trauma not as event but in form, soliciting empathy. <www.miekebal.org>

Burcu Baykan is an Assistant Professor of Visual Communication Design with a specialism in Contemporary Art Theory and Practice at Bilkent University, Turkey. Before coming to Bilkent, she was a graduate fellow at Trinity Long Room Hub Arts & Humanities Research Institute at Trinity College Dublin, where she earned her PhD in 2017. Her doctoral dissertation is a Deleuze-Guattarian investigation of the non-human transformations in contemporary visual arts, including performance art, video art, installation, sculpture, bio-art and the interdisciplinary collaborations within these fields. She has been published in various edited collections and journals, most recently co-authoring the chapter entitled 'The Floating Consciousness and the Embodied Reality in *Altered Carbon*', with a forthcoming article that uses the theoretical insights of Deleuze, Haraway and Bennett to explore the US-based Turkish media artist Pınar Yoldaş's work on speculative post-human biologies.

Gary Genosko is Professor of Communication and Digital Media Studies at the University of Ontario Institute of Technology in Toronto. His books include *Critical Semiotics: Theory, from Information to Affect* (2016), *When Technocultures*

Collide (2013), *Remodelling Communication* (2012), *Baudrillard: The Masters of Implosion* (1999), *The Guattari Reader* (1996) and *Baudrillard and Signs* (1994). His latest books are *The Reinvention of Social Practices: Essays on Félix Guattari* (2018) and *Back Issues: Periodicals and the Formation of Critical and Cultural Theory in Canada* (2019).

Barbara Glowczewski is a Polish-born French anthropologist, with a professorial research tenure at the National Scientific Research Center, and member of the Laboratory of Social Anthropology (<http://las.ehess.fr/index.php?1716>) at the Collège de France, teaching at the EHESS. She has been working with Indigenous Australians since 1979. She currently looks at political alliances connecting Indigenous struggles for environmental justice and French activism for alternative ways to inhabit territories. She has authored many books, including *Warriors for Peace: The Political Situation in Australia as Seen from Palm Island* (2010, <http://eprints.jcu.edu.au/7286/>), *Desert Dreamers* (2015 transl.; 1st edn 1989), *Totemic Becomings* (2015) and *Indigenising Anthropology with Guattari and Deleuze* (2020), and was awarded Special Mention of the Jury Möbius Prize in 1998 for her pioneering multimedia work.

Eugene W. Holland, Professor Emeritus of Comparative Studies at the Ohio State University, is author of the *Bloomsbury Readers Guide to A Thousand Plateaus* (2013), *Nomad Citizenship: Free-Market Communism and the Slow-Motion General Strike* (2011), *Deleuze and Guattari's Anti-Oedipus: Introduction to Schizoanalysis* (1999) and *Baudelaire and Schizoanalysis: The Sociopoetics of Modernism* (1993), along with numerous essays on the political philosophy of Deleuze and Guattari. He also co-edited *Gilles Deleuze: Image and Text* (2009).

Adi Louria Hayon is an Assistant Professor in the Art History Department at Tel Aviv University. She completed her doctorate at the University of Toronto. Her research focuses on the tripartite connection between art, philosophy and sound. Tuned to problems of representation in the intersections of contemporary art and philosophical thought, she is currently writing a book dedicated to the problems of scepticism and epistemology in the work of Bruce Nauman (forthcoming from De Gruyter). She was recently a research fellow at the Scepticism Centre in the Maimonides Institute for Advanced Studies, Hamburg University.

Laura U. Marks works on media art and philosophy with an intercultural focus. Her most recent books are *Hanan al-Cinema: Affections for the Moving Image* (2015) and *Enfoldment and Infinity: An Islamic Genealogy of New Media Art* (2010). With Dr Azadeh Emadi she is a founding member of the Substantial Motion Research Network, <substantialmotion.org>. She is Grant Strate Professor in the School for the Contemporary Arts at Simon Fraser University in Vancouver. <www.sfu.ca/~lmarks>

Radek Przedpełski received his PhD in Digital Arts and Humanities from Trinity

College Dublin, where he presently lectures in interactive digital media, visual arts and critical theory. His dissertation explored metamorphosis and multiplicity in Eastern European neo-avant-garde intermedia and their entanglements of animality, technology and the earth, in dialogue with Deleuze, Guattari and their philosophical interlocutors. Radek's research interests include contemporary (post-)digital artistic practices in the Anthropocene, approached at once as a geomediation and as media technologies of the cosmos. He recently published articles on animism in contemporary post-cinema and performance, as well as on radical contingency in Stanisław Lem's *Solaris*. He also collaborated with the art collective Slavs and Tatars as a researcher. Radek is also a sound artist and freelance photographer. <www.radekprzedpelski.com>

Daniela Voss is Associate Lecturer in the Department of Philosophy at the University of Hildesheim. Her fields of research include the philosophy of Gilles Deleuze and Félix Guattari, post-Kantian philosophy, early modern philosophy and, more recently, philosophy of technology. She is the author of *Conditions of Thought: Deleuze and Transcendental Ideas* (2013) and co-editor with Craig Lundy of *At the Edges of Thought: Deleuze and Post-Kantian Philosophy* (2015). Her journal publications include those in *Angelaki, Australasian Philosophical Review, Continental Philosophy Review, Deleuze and Guattari Studies, Parrhesia* and *Philosophy & Social Criticism*.

James Williams is Honorary Professor of Philosophy at Deakin University. His latest work is on the sublime (*The Egalitarian Sublime*, 2019) and on signs (*A Process Philosophy of Signs*, 2016). He has co-edited a new volume on Deleuze and Guattari's *A Thousand Plateaus*, with Henry Somers-Hall and Jeffrey A. Bell (*A Thousand Plateaus and Philosophy*, 2019). James's current and past work can be accessed at <www.jamesrwilliams.net>.

S. E. Wilmer is Professor Emeritus of Drama at Trinity College Dublin, and was recently a Research Fellow at the Research Centre for 'Interweaving Performance Cultures' at the Freie Universität Berlin. Formerly Head of the School of Drama, Film and Music at Trinity College Dublin, he has been a Visiting Professor at Stanford University and the University of California at Berkeley. He has written and edited twenty books and written more than ten plays. His latest book, *Performing Statelessness in Europe*, was published by Palgrave Macmillan in 2018, and he is currently serving as editor-in-chief of the *Nordic Theatre Studies* journal.

Audronė Žukauskaitė is Chief Researcher at the Lithuanian Culture Research Institute. Her recent publications include the monographs *From Biopolitics to Biophilosophy* (2016, in Lithuanian) and *Gilles Deleuze and Félix Guattari's Philosophy: The Logic of Multiplicity* (2011, in Lithuanian). She also co-edited (with S. E. Wilmer) *Interrogating Antigone in Postmodern Philosophy and Criticism* (2010), *Deleuze and Beckett* (2015) and *Resisting Biopolitics: Philosophical, Political and Performative Strategies* (2016).

Introduction

Radek Przedpełski and S. E. Wilmer

Western philosophy has habitually privileged notions of identity, essence and static existence. The importance of Deleuze and Guattari is that they critically interrogate this pattern, and instead favour multiplicities. In this way, they expose the political implications of traditional metaphysics, which undervalues flux, difference, diversity and the possibilities of becoming other. Guattari joins in Deleuze's project of reversing Platonism, understood as a firm opposition between essence and appearance, by unleashing the differential powers of the simulacrum, which is neither the original nor the copy, and neither the one nor the many (see Smith 2012a). Deleuze and Guattari embark on the Nietzschean project of immanent becoming, conceptualised as the eternal return of difference. Rather than asking the 'big' questions about the essence of a thing, 'what is . . .', a question which seeks to ground a thing in a transcendent point of reference, Deleuze and Guattari launch a becoming-minoritarian of philosophy by asking minor, problematic and illegitimate questions such as 'which', 'who', 'how many', 'to what degree', 'how', 'when' and 'where'.

The radical proposition of Deleuze and Guattari, which makes it particularly relevant nowadays, lies in their notion of change as difference in itself – as an intensity, an in-betweenness which cannot be accounted for by a fixed point of departure or destination. At the heart of the Deleuzoguattarian philosophical and political project is the concept of multiplicity which runs counter to representation and 'tolerates no dependence on the identical in the subject or in the object' (Deleuze 1994: 91). Multiplicity 'do[es] not allow any positing of an essence as "what the thing is"' and is instead bound up with 'events and singularities' (ibid.).

Multiplicity as a Concept

Deleuze's process philosophy of difference can be encapsulated by one simple yet problematic equation that Deleuze and Guattari (2005: 20, original emphasis) introduce in *A Thousand Plateaus*, namely: 'PLURALISM = MONISM'. As Smith (2012b: 42) points out, the formula expresses the identity between 'equivocity of difference' and 'univocity of Being'. Responding to the ancient philosophical problem of the one and the many, Deleuze and Guattari argue that a qualitative variety of beings nonetheless taps into a single plane of immanence that admits no dialectical opposition between one separate entity grounding or founding another. Consequently, a representation, a phantasm or a theory of a thing is an event itself, contemplating and affirming a single ontological plane. Deleuze introduces the theme of the paradoxical equation of pluralism and monism in *Difference and Repetition*, as encapsulated in what he (1994: 36) calls the 'nomadic distribution' of diverse entities in an open space, pointing out (1994: 37) that 'it is not a matter of being which is distributed according to the requirements of representation, but of all things being divided up within being in the univocity of simple presence (the One–All)'.

According to Éric Alliez (2004: 91), the 'pluralism = monism' formula, encapsulating the Deleuzian differential ontology, can be understood in terms of the Deleuzian-Bergsonian concept of multiplicity. In fact, as the philosopher Audronė Žukauskaitė (2014: 75) reminds us, Deleuze repeatedly framed his entire philosophical project precisely in terms of 'a logic of multiplicities'. The concept of multiplicity – and the distinction between qualitative continuous and quantitative discrete multiplicities as developed in Deleuze's 1966 *Bergsonism* – has fundamental ontological implications for Deleuzoguattarian philosophy because it replaces the oppositional dialectics of the one and the multiple. As DeLanda (2002: 9–10) summarises, Deleuze conceived the notion of multiplicities as a novel way of giving a non-totalisable, immanent characterisation of things via the 'morphogenetic process that gave rise to [them]'. Such a characterisation should be distinguished from the traditional metaphysical notion of essence understood as a set of defining characteristics that are transcendent, timeless and immutable and constitute the unified static identity of a thing. As Bergson explains (2001: 222–3, original emphasis), multiplicities, unlike essences, dynamically 'unfold in time and constitute *duration*'. Therefore, their character, or 'nature', cannot be determined in advance. As Žukauskaitė (2014: 75) succinctly summarises, 'the multiplicity is never given all at once and appears in a form of progressive differentiation'.

Developing the Notion of Multiplicities

In *Bergsonism*, Deleuze first invokes the Bergsonian distinction between two types of multiplicities. These two types are exemplified by the physical configuration of objects in space and duration associated with qualitative differences in conscious states. As Deleuze explains (1988: 38, original emphasis),

> one is represented by space . . . : It is a multiplicity of exteriority, of simultaneity, of juxtaposition, of order, of quantitative differentiation, of *difference in degree*; it is a numerical multiplicity, *discontinuous and actual*. The other type of multiplicity appears in pure duration: It is an internal multiplicity of succession, of fusion, of organization, of heterogeneity, of qualitative discrimination, or of *difference in kind*; it is a *virtual and continuous* multiplicity that cannot be reduced to numbers.

Deleuze subsequently plots the Bergsonian distinction on to the differential geometry of Riemann. As Smith points out (2012c: 303), Riemann builds on Gauss's use of differential calculus to approach 'curves and surfaces in a purely intrinsic and "local" manner, that is without any reference to a "global" embedding space', elaborating 'a non-Euclidean geometry (showing that Euclid's axioms were not self-evident truths) of a multi-dimensional, non-metric, and non-intuitable "any-space-whatever," which he termed a pure "multiplicity" or "manifold"'. According to Deleuze (1988: 39), Riemann posited multiplicities as 'those things that could be determined in terms of their dimensions or their independent variables', subsequently distinguishing between *discrete multiplicities* and *continuous multiplicities* whereby

> the former contain the principle of their own metrics (the measure of one of their parts being given by the number of elements they contain). The latter found a metrical principle in something else, even if only in phenomena unfolding in them or in the forces acting in them.

Drawing on, and conflating, ideas of Bergson and Riemann, in *Bergsonism*, Deleuze (1988: 42) develops the notion of virtual multiplicity, later on also called intensive multiplicity, defined as that which 'does not divide up without changing in kind, [that which] changes in kind in the process of dividing up'. It entails qualitative differentiation along divergent lines (Deleuze 1988: 43) and concerns the problem of change in itself, beyond the extensive metrics of time and space. The virtual multiplicity cannot be separated from its movement of actualisation; 'it is virtual insofar as it is actualized, in the course of being actualized, … inseparable from the movement of its actualization … , creat[ing] … differences in kind by virtue of its own movement' (Deleuze 1988: 42–3). In other words, such multiplicity 'divides into elements that differ in kind; … [but at the same time], these elements or these parts only actually exist insofar as the division itself is effectively carried out' (ibid. 81).

The concept of virtual multiplicity, also cast as *intensive quantity*, is subsequently elaborated in *Difference and Repetition*. As Deleuze (1994: 237) explains, 'an intensive quantity may be divided, but not without changing its nature. In a sense, it is therefore indivisible, but only because no part exists prior to the division and no part retains the same nature after division.' Furthermore, the word 'multiplicity' should not be understood as an attribute or property of the one, and hence as predicated upon an already constituted prior thing, but, writes Deleuze (1994: 182), as a 'substantive noun' that designates 'an organisation belonging to the many as such, which has no need whatsoever of unity in order to form a system'. The opposition between the one and the many, the general (and abstract) and the particular (and concrete), is also at work in the representational logic of Kantian aesthetics that for Deleuze (ibid. 68) is split into two domains: 'the theory of the sensible which captures only the real's conformity with possible experience; and … the theory of the beautiful, which deals with the reality of the real in so far as it is thought'. Thinking with multiplicity, Deleuze puts forward a vision of aesthetics in which 'the two senses of the aesthetic become one, to the point where the being of the sensible reveals itself in the work of art, while at the same time the work of art appears as experimentation' (ibid.) One might say that 'the art of multiplicities = the multiplicities of art'. Multiplicities in *Difference and Repetition* also receive a more strict Riemannian formulation as 'an n-dimensional, continuous, defined multiplicity' whereby

> dimensions . . . [designate] the variables or co-ordinates upon which a phenomenon depends; . . . continuity [designates] the set of relations between changes in these variables; . . . [while] definition [designates] the elements reciprocally determined by these relations, elements which cannot change unless the multiplicity changes its order and its metric. (Ibid. 182–3)

Multiplicities in *A Thousand Plateaus*

The above formulation of multiplicity provides consistency with later Deleuzoguattarian thought developed in *A Thousand Plateaus*. *A Thousand Plateaus* marks an important movement in the development of the Deleuzian logic of multiplicities. This 1980 publication, following on from their earlier work *Anti-Oedipus*, unfolds from Deleuze's encounter with the activist and psychoanalyst Félix Guattari. The encounter is described in the introduction (Deleuze and Guattari 2005: 1–5) as the generation of an asignifying, impersonal intensive multiplicity. Such multiplicity is not acting in a vacuum, but it is deployed as a machine of resistance set in motion against the oppressive, stratifying axiomatic logic of the capitalist state it is enmeshed in. Whereas *Difference and Repetition* could still be said to be *about* multiplicities and the corresponding method of transcendental empiricism, *A Thousand Plateaus* actually composes a rhizomatic multiplicity. The book's chapters ('plateaus') – at once philosophical and immediately political in their content – make up its dimensions. As Žukauskaitė (2014: 76) points out, in *A Thousand Plateaus* the Bergsonian-Riemannian (intensive) multiplicities are plotted on to psychic, biological and socio-political planes. Those 'weaponised multiplicities', as we shall call them, are important for Deleuze and Guattari, because they engender qualitative change, embodying difference in itself. For Žukauskaitė (2014: 85–6), *A Thousand Plateaus* probes 'the tension between the capitalist axiomatic and the potential for revolutionary change' while at the same time rethinking the Bergsonian distinction between intensive and extensive multiplicities through a series of paired concepts such as arborescent schema/rhizomatic flows; strata/becoming; territorial assemblage/deterritorialisations; organism/body without organs (BwO); apparatus of capture/war machine; the molar/the molecular; and striated space/smooth space. What is at stake here is not a dialectical opposition between static essences but a dynamic relation between a tendency towards change and a tendency towards its capture, organisation, signification and subjectification. The two tendencies engage, to use here the Deleuzoguattarian understanding of BwO, 'pure matter, a phenomenon of physical, biological, psychic, social, or cosmic matter' (Deleuze and Guattari 2005: 165).

It is in *A Thousand Plateaus* that Deleuze and Guattari (2005: 8–9) put forward the seminal notion of *rhizomatic multiplicities*. They point out that multidimensional multiplicities are, however, *flat multiplicities* in the sense that they lack an additional higher dimension that could ground them. Rhizomatic multiplicities are 'flat' because they do not have a pivot-point that could be used to establish an anchor for their subsequent unification and totalisation, akin to the arithmetic '1' as the founding unit of the metric principle. Continuing with the theme of arithmetics, Deleuze and Guattari (ibid. 6) in fact suggest that the formula for creating a *rhizome* as multiplicity is to 'subtract the unique from the multiplicity to be constituted; write at $n - 1$ dimensions'. One of the avatars of rhizomatic multiplicities is the functioning of viruses which exemplify for Deleuze and Guttari (2005: 10–11, original emphasis) an 'anti-genealogic[al]' '*aparallel evolution* of two beings that have absolutely nothing to do with each other' which proceeds through 'transversal communications between different lines'. As Deleuze and Guattari (ibid. 10) explain, 'under certain conditions, a virus can connect to germ cells and transmit itself as the cellular gene of a complex species; moreover, it can take flight, move into the cells of an entirely different species, but not without bringing with it "genetic information" from the first host'. Furthermore, Deleuze and Guattari (ibid. 10–11, 237–9) view zoonotic viruses, i.e. transmitted to humans by non-human (vertebrate) animals, as effectuating a becoming-animal understood as a molecular interspecies alliance.

In the Nomadology chapter of *A Thousand Plateaus*, Deleuze and Guattari ponder the mystery of the mutual co-implication of intensive and extensive multiplicities in the metallurgical-artisanal process of machinic modulation of the *machinic phylum*. The latter is understood at once as matter in a state of ongoing variation and as a singular technological lineage. Elsewhere in *A Thousand Plateaus*, intensive multiplicities are conceptualised as defined by a variable number of dimensions stretched towards their mobile borderline zones of potential, which under auspicious conditions may serve as a threshold where change happens (see 2005: 243–52).

The Deleuzoguattarian logic of multiplicities and the notion of intensive multiplicity in particular have fundamental implications for art. Art itself, as it is conceptualised in the Capitalism and Schizophrenia project encompassing *Anti-Oedipus* and *A Thousand Plateaus*, arises as a problem that affirms the logic of multiplicities. It is a question harnessing or capturing imperceptible cosmic forces and rendering them perceptible in deterritorialised materials (2005: 342–4). At the same time, art also immediately invests and qualitatively changes the social; it functions in a transversal and contingent manner as an 'abstract machine [which] operate[s] within [a] concrete assemblage' (ibid. 510). If art engenders the potential for change, this potential arises under the specific conditions of a concrete social assemblage of matter.

Multiplicities, Art and Politics

The present era of environmental degradation, the novel coronavirus (COVID-19) pandemic, stark social inequalities, forced migration, stigmatisation of otherness, illiberal democracies, societies of control and surveillance, and the extension of the state's biopower into what Achille Mbembe (2019: 92) calls *necropolitics*, i.e. 'contemporary forms of subjugating life to the power of death', necessitates seeking new paradigms of art, and exploring their ethical and political potential. Western philosophy grounded upon identity and static essences contributes to stigmatisation and the exclusion of those labelled as the other, the different or the undesirable, who do not conform to a specific idea of the self. Mbembe (ibid.) speaks of the current phenomenon of 'borderization' which he understands as 'the process by which world powers permanently transform certain spaces into impassable places for certain classes of populations'. 'What is it about', asks Mbembe (ibid.), 'if not the conscious multiplication of spaces of loss and mourn-ing, where the lives of a multitude of people judged to be undesirable come to be shattered?' The aim of this volume of academic articles is to examine the work of Deleuze and Guattari and make it resonate with new dimensions of artistic practice. The publication provides alternative aesthetic and conceptual means, which crystallise out of an array of case studies, to address contemporary issues.

Already art theorists such as Kodwo Eshun (1998), Stephen Zepke (2005) and Simon O'Sullivan (2006) have been using Deleuzoguattarian philosophy to approach artistic practice, while Anne Sauvagnargues [2005] (2013) has provided a pioneering exposition of Deleuzoguattarian aesthetics. Rather than suggesting a new global art studies, such as 'the project of global art history' which 'calls for a balanced materialist treatment of artifacts and a unified approach that emphasizes questions of transcultural encounters and exchanges as circulations' whereby 'transnational, global history [is approached] through the study of circulations in a historical materialist perspective' (DaCosta Kaufmann et al. 2016: 1), this book takes a different, complementary path. Engaging with the Deleuzoguattarian conceptualisation of change in terms of *multiplicity*, the contributors to this book take their work further by offering novel approaches to art, advancing at once cultural, political and aesthetic aims in what Isabelle Stengers (2015) has called 'an ecology of practices'. Such ecology, writes Stengers (ibid. 186), 'aims at the construction of new "practical identities" for practices, that is, new possibilities for them to be present, or in other words to connect. It thus does not approach practices as they are – physics as we know it, for instance – but as they may become.'

Transcendental Empiricism and Schizoanalysis: Art against Interpretation

The philosophical method of transcendental empiricism that Deleuze developed in *Difference and Repetition* (1968) is preoccupied with the idea that 'something in the world forces us to think. This something is an object not of recognition but of a fundamental *encounter*' (Deleuze 1994: 139). It is an encounter of 'difference, potential difference and difference of intensity as the reason behind qualitative diversity' (ibid. 57). The object of the encounter is 'not a sensible being but the being *of* the sensible. It is not the given but that by which the given is given' (ibid. 140). The task of (art) philosophy is to deduce the implicit, imperceptible virtual potentialities making possible the emergence of a new state of affairs. Transcendental empiricism is preoccupied with the problem of an experimental contact with something that can only be sensed (ibid. 236). Such contact – in its constitutive, creative relation with an excessive force – composes at the same time a work of art. As Deleuze explains (ibid. 56), 'the work of art leaves the domain of representation in order to become "experience", transcendental empiricism or science of the sensible'. Deleuze's critique of the paradigm of re-cognition and re-presentation developed in *Difference and Repetition* was further elaborated in the Deleuzoguattarian schizoanalytic critique of the tendency to explain art away by recourse to significance and interpretation, enriched by Guattari's experience with psychotic patients at La Borde clinic. Launched in *Anti-Oedipus* (1972), whose preoccupation with literature culminates in their case study titled *Kafka: Toward a Minor Literature* (1975), the critique continues all the way through *A Thousand Plateaus* (1980), spanning a wide array of social and artistic practices, until their last co-authored work *What Is Philosophy?* (1991). The critique of art analysis grounded upon interpretation resonates in Guattari's *Schizoanalytic Cartographies* (1989), *The Three Ecologies* (1989) and *Chaosmosis* (1992). It also ripples in a range of Deleuze's sole-authored works produced in the 1980s and revolving around a single medium – painting (*Francis Bacon: The Logic of Sensation*, 1981), cinema (*Cinema 1: The Movement-Image*, 1983; *Cinema 2: The Time-Image*, 1985) and Baroque intermedia (*The Fold: Leibniz and the Baroque*, 1988).

For Deleuze and Guattari, the representational paradigm is a mode of gaining knowledge about art by identifying and comparing it with a prior, fixed essence. Such operation fails to attend to the intensive process of change; it only ever reveals art as a given, constituted in linear time and metric space as the relation between a determinate subject and a quantifiable object. If interpretation falls back on a transcendent, external point of reference (economic base, hidden symbolism, Oedipal structures, etc.), Deleuze and Guattari offer an immanent account of art bound up with encounter and experimentation, which nonetheless coexists with the social field as its contingency. Art is immediately real, ontogenetic and functioning as the animal act of staking out a territory, of establishing a house that captures chaotic forces in affective materials (Deleuze and Guattari 1994: 183). This minimal structure can be also understood as functioning in the manner of an apparatus such as a sieve, a membrane or a resonance box. What this means for art analysis is attending to art as an experimentation both selecting and engendering really acting forces, always resonant with the world in the infinity of its differential unfolding, and not as a way of representing or reflecting some transcendent, prior agency and anterior narrative about art. Such formulation corresponds to Guattari's (1995: 90) understanding of performance art as the 'extraction of intensive, atemporal, aspatial, asignifying dimensions from the semiotic net of quotidianity'. Performance art epitomises Guattari's (ibid.) understanding of art as 'a machinic processuality' ensuring that 'every aesthetic decentering of points of view ... passes through a preliminary deconstruction of the structures and codes in use and a chaosmic plunge into the materials of sensation', engendering in the process 'a proliferation not just of the forms but of the modalities of being'. Art does not stage 'a return to an originary orality' but entails something 'artificial, constructed, composed' (ibid.) One might say that for Deleuze and Guattari, art performs a kind of phase shift, (trans)mutation or transduction. It does not open itself up to the vital forces of the universe without changing in kind and thus co-constructing the world. In this sense, Deleuze and Guattari's vision affirms the art of multiplicities as both aesthetic and ontogenetic.

The Art of Multiplicities = The Multiplicities of Art

The aim of this publication is to explore the notion of multiplicity in Deleuze and Guattari and its relevance to various dimensions of artistic practice. While the volume opens with a series of philosophical encounters with the concept of multiplicity, re-accentuating and extending in different ways, or even constructing, the multiple lineages that make up this fundamental concept (*the art of multiplicities*), the second section investigates the relevance of Deleuzoguattarian conceptualisations for specific artistic processes and practices and points to the potentialities circulating in various media (*the multiplicities of art*). The division of the book has only a pragmatic significance, and it is far from being clear-cut. In fact, all the contributions constitute ecologies of practices that go beyond the theory/application hylomorphism. Rather than resolving their mutual differences, the volume seeks to extend a productive, problematic field that incorporates many voices. There is no explicating the Deleuzoguattarian concept of multiplicity without simultaneously implicating it in a system of resonances that jointly articulate a speculative proposal for the ethical future of art. The articles of the volume are at once a work of 'practical philosophy' in the Deleuzian sense and also a polyphonic artwork.

The first section in the book seeks to attend to multiple trajectories and lineages that the notion of multiplicity engages. James Williams builds on multiplicity in order to develop his processual philosophy of signs which thinks affect 'as manifold changes of emotional intensities distributed among long-lasting conscious and unconscious thoughts, acts and environments named by a dominant tone' while dispensing with the notion of expression. In turn, Audronė Žukauskaitė demonstrates that 'the Deleuzian theory of multiplicity is indebted to Simondon's distinction between the pre-individual and the process of individuation, and Ruyer's distinction between equipotentiality and the actual process of morphogenesis'. Žukauskaitė's exploration of multiplicity in terms of philosophies of biological life varies from Daniela Voss's critique of machinic phylum. On Voss's reading, the Deleuzoguattarian notion of machinic phylum conceived as fundamentally metallic constitutes a 'vitalist materialism' that obliterates the many nuances of

Simondon's 'informational materialism', and in particular his subtle distinctions between individuation in physical and in biological systems. In turn, Eugene W. Holland brings multiplicity to bear on 'the dynamics of axiomatisation that Deleuze and Guattari consider constitutive of the capitalist mode of production and crucial to their understanding of contemporary politics'. Holland's sustained focus on multiplicity as a logic of the Deleuzoguattarian 'anti-capitalist politics' generates productive difference with Mieke Bal's understanding of multiplicity as affirming those forms of contemporary art that 'make art politically powerful by avoiding any expected "politics"', 'allud[ing] to narrative without deploying it'. Bal's perspective of the 'mobile relationality' between '*analysing* and *making*' that she sees at play in her collaboratively elaborated practice of '*thinking* in film' '*unthinkable* without Deleuze' provides a link to the second section of the book that demonstrates how the concept of multiplicity resonates with various media and their impact on society.

The second section extends the Deleuzoguattarian formulation of multiplicities to new fields and frames of natural-cultural and artistic production. It surveys a play of multiplicities in various media, processes and practices. Such 'weaponised multiplicities' are affective weapons of social change. Gary Genosko investigates 'the social and inter-relational uses of [portable tape] recorders' in the work of David Wojnarowicz. The magnetic medium functions not only as a technical device for stitching together Wojnarowicz's autofiction but, more importantly, as an operator and diagram of processes of subjectivation. The 'magnetic field of marshalled particles', extended by Wojnarowicz's tape recorders, resonates with the metallic intensities associated with *steppe cosmotechnics*: a mode functioning in Scytho-Siberian Early Iron Age metallurgical art, which Radek Przedpełski sees as at work in the neo-avant-garde intermedial performance and sculptural instal-lations of the Warsaw-based artist Marek Konieczny. Przedpełski's investigation of Eastern European neo-avant-garde geo-media preoccupied with living with, and enduring, inhuman change finds many commonalities with Burcu Baykan's encounter between the concept of the BwO and 'the bodily mutations at play in the Australian visual artist Patricia Piccinini'. For Baykan, Piccinini's sculptural installations affirm the 'potential for corporeal plasticity' implicit in contempo-rary biotechnology. In turn, the social dimension of Piccinini's sculptures, and in particular their preoccupation with living ethically with others, connects them to Steve Wilmer's examination of Théâtre du Soleil's theatrical production of *Le Dernier Caravansérail* (*Odyssées*) in terms of their nomadic multiplicities. Wilmer's inquiry draws attention to the ways in which both the functioning of this theatrical group and the play under scrutiny 'open up ways of seeing and thinking differently about refugees and nomads, and awakening their audiences to the pos-sibility of change'. Wilmer's preoccupation with both 'nomadic mobility' and 'the need for refuge' of the refugees resonates with Barbara Glowczewski's field notes which explore Indigenous ritual both in its virtual becomings and in its relation to the need of compensation. Glowczewski examines Indigenous cosmopolitical ritual in Australia and Brazil with its attendant logics of *Jukurrpa* (Dreamings) and *Orixá* incorporations, respectively, in terms of multiplicity understood as 'the crossing of the threshold from the actual back to the virtual'. In turn, Adi Louria Hayon's contribution investigates ripples of musical serial transformations across Deleuze's reading of Kant's differential interval, musical compositions of Boulez, as well as the geometrical spatial compositions of Bruce Nauman. Hayon sees Deleuze's philosophy as a sonorous project where 'the Boulezian series of transformations . . . reverberate the multiplicity of the synthesis of time'. Hayon's technique of mapping out the many ripples of sonorous serialism resonates with Laura U. Marks's practice of media archaeology, looking at talismanic magic in the Islamic Neoplatonist tradition in order to identify a certain 'talisman-image' which transhistorically accounts for practices and technologies of contemporary art. Marks's vision of *talisman-image* as an interface that 'intervenes in the order of the cosmos by folding it and drawing the folded points into contact with the body' frames our publication. In this way, multiplicity is affirmed as a certain media technology of the cosmos.

The ecology of practices put forward in the present volume does not only function as a qualitative diversity of genres, media and contexts. Most importantly, it works through inchoate pre-individual potentialities, guiding development of tactical proposals for uncommon and untimely futures, cosmologies and cosmogonies; construction of speculative scenarios for emergence and techniques of individuation; as well as the forging of unlikely alliances. The contributions in the present book therefore stretch the thought of Deleuze and Guattari in new, unforeseen directions. Thinking with multiplicity, they push Deleuzoguattarian philosophy towards a becoming-other and they bring about another multiplicity.

References

Alliez, Éric (2004), *The Signature of the World, or, What is Deleuze and Guattari's Philosophy?*, trans. Eliot Ross Albert and Alberto Toscano, London and New York: Continuum.

Bergson, Henri [1913] (2001), *Time and Free Will: An Essay on the Immediate Data of Consciousness*, trans. Frank Lubecki Pogson, New York: Dover Publications, Inc.

DaCosta Kaufmann, Thomas, Catherine Dossin and Béatrice Joyeux-Prunel (2016), 'Introduction: Reintroducing Circulations: Historiography and the Project of Global Art History', in Thomas DaCosta Kaufmann, Catherine Dossin and Béatrice Joyeux-Prunel (eds), *Circulations in the Global History of Art*, London and New York: Routledge, pp. 1–22.

DeLanda, Manuel (2002), *Intensive Science and Virtual Philosophy*, London and New York: Continuum.

Deleuze, Gilles (1988), *Bergsonism*, trans. Barbara Habberjam and Hugh Tomlinson, New York: Zone Books.

Deleuze, Gilles (1994), *Difference and Repetition*, trans. Paul Patton, London: Athlone Press.

Deleuze, Gilles (2003), *Francis Bacon: The Logic of Sensation*, trans. Daniel W. Smith, London and New York: Continuum.

Deleuze, Gilles and Félix Guattari (1994), *What Is Philosophy?*, trans. Graham Burchell and Hugh Tomlinson, New York: Columbia University Press.

Deleuze, Gilles and Félix Guattari (2005), *A Thousand Plateaus: Capitalism and Schizophrenia*, trans. Brian Massumi, London and Minneapolis: University of Minnesota Press.

Eshun, Kodwo (1998), *More Brilliant Than the Sun: Adventures in Sonic Fiction*, London: Quartet Books.

Guattari, Félix (1995), *Chaosmosis: An Ethico-Aesthetic Paradigm*, trans. Paul Bains and Julian Pefanis, Bloomington and Indianapolis: Indiana University Press.

Mbembe, Achille (2019), *Necro-Politics*, trans. Steven Corcoran, Durham, NC, and London: Duke University Press.

O'Sullivan, Simon (2006), *Art Encounters Deleuze and Guattari: Thought Beyond Representation*, New York: Palgrave Macmillan.

Sauvagnargues, Anne [2005] (2013), *Deleuze and Art*, trans. Samantha Bankston, London and New York: Bloomsbury.

Smith, Daniel W. (2012a), 'The Concept of the Simulacrum: Deleuze and the Overturning of Platonism', in *Essays on Deleuze*, Edinburgh: Edinburgh University Press, pp. 3–26.

Smith, Daniel W. (2012b), 'The Doctrine of Univocity: Deleuze's Ontology of Immanence', in *Essays on Deleuze*, Edinburgh: Edinburgh University Press, pp. 27–42.

Smith, Daniel W. (2012c), 'Mathematics and the Theory of Multiplicities: Deleuze and Badiou Revisited', in *Essays on Deleuze*, Edinburgh: Edinburgh University Press, pp. 287–311.

Stengers, Isabelle (2005), 'Introductory Notes on an Ecology of Practices', *Cultural Studies Review*, 11(1): 183–96.

Zepke, Stephen (2005), *Art as Abstract Machine: Ontology and Aesthetics in Deleuze and Guattari*, New York and London: Routledge.

Zourabichvili, François (2012), *Deleuze: A Philosophy of the Event together with The Vocabulary of Deleuze*, trans. Kieran Aarons, Edinburgh: Edinburgh University Press.

Žukauskaitė, Audronė (2014), 'Intensive Multiplicities in *A Thousand Plateaus*', in Paul Ardoin, S. E. Gontarski and Laci Mattison (eds), *Understanding Deleuze, Understanding Modernism*, London and New York: Bloomsbury, pp. 75–89.

Part I

Philosophical Compositions of Multiplicity

1

Distributed Affects and the Necessity of Expression

James Williams

What is an Affect?

On the walk up the Royal Mile to Edinburgh Castle, just before the first gatehouse, there is an actor in full Braveheart costume, collecting for charities by posing for photographs with passers-by. Tourists practise expressive faces with him, showing combinations of resolve, anger, pride, doubt, burden and vengefulness, as their friends photograph them.

The tourists are creating affects for themselves and for a wide audience. They tailor expressions and the Braveheart story to what they want to portray, whether it is a courageous struggle for independence or revenge-crazed spirit. In doing so, they give us clues as to the nature of affect as distributed individual and social event, rather than isolated psychic, neural, somatic or behavioural state. An affect is mobile, 'complex, episodic, dynamic and structured' (Goldie 2000: 12). It is individual and social, dominated by a particular emotion, but implicating many others. Each affect extends into the actions it is played out in.

I define an affect as *manifold changes of emotional intensities distributed among long-lasting conscious and unconscious thoughts, acts and environments named by a dominant tone*. Hate is an affect because its changes in intensity cover and reveal other emotional differences in intensity – in fear, revenge and love, for instance. Yet for it to be hate rather than any other affect, hate has to be the dominant tone, the one whose changes in intensity articulate others.

My definition expands an emotion into a complex affect. These affects are implicated in one another; they slide into each other when the dominant tone shifts. Affects are about degrees within multiple relations. We do not jump from hate to fear across a clear divide. They aren't separate states or phenomena. There is instead a re-alignment of continuous and multiple intensities such that love can become the dominant tone in a pattern once characterised by hate.

Influenced by Deleuze and Guattari's manifesto for multiplicity in *Anti-Oedipus*, the definition does not take an affect to be a totality or an unchanging unit, but rather something that 'goes beyond the multiple as well as the One' (1972: 50).[1] There aren't individual affects that can be combined into totalities of multiple fragments: 'We no longer believe in those false fragments that, like pieces of ancient statues, wait to be glued together and completed in order to compose a unity that is also their unity of origin' (ibid.). An affect is a multiplicity in a continuous and indivisible sense, neither made of parts nor countable as a part.

An affect should be seen as an unstable pattern of shadings of emotional intensities, bleeding into and across one another with no clear boundaries. It is not a placeholder in a table of distinct phenomena determined by exclusive predicates. The determination of affects is closer to the way we might distinguish a purple dominant and green minor in subtly different shimmerings of the Northern Lights. Affects are defined tonally, as individuals belonging to loosely defined and evolving processes.

Affects, Acts and Environments

Not only do affects merge into one another, they also include thoughts and actions. Changes in emotional intensities are accompanied by conscious reflection on how to live with them, as well as unconscious repercussions and preparations, not only for the individual, but for those who have to witness affects and undergo their consequences.

Thoughts around affects are played out in actions that are themselves dependent on environments. The affect of hate only attains its full reach when the blow accompanies the anger in a particular situation, a milieu. For Deleuze and Guattari, faces expressing affects only appear as multiplicities in relation to milieux (1980: 211). The affect is individual and collective because, as emotional event, it takes hold in an individual but this grip spreads through groups of thinkers, acts and environments. When a fearful child becomes a problem for family and school, the affect of fear is distributed across family and school.

The preliminary reason I give for this distributive quality of affects is that they are misunderstood without this disseminated play with other affects, with effect on thoughts, with the way subconscious processes shape the distribution, with its development in acts and with the influence of environment on its evolution and character.

Robert Solomon captures some of the motivation of the move to affect as distributive in his response to work on cognition and emotion as short-lived and somatically located ('more or less over and done with after 120 milliseconds') by LeDoux, Panksepp and Damasio: 'I am interested in processes that last more than five minutes and have the potential to last five hours or five days (or five weeks, months or even years)' (2003: 179).

Jealousy takes on different forms dependent on whether it is related to love or to envy. It tends to be more destructive of self and others for the former – such as Othello's terrible violence and obsessiveness, distributed in deathly fashion among his loves and friendships, changing 'trifles light as air' into 'confirmations strong as proofs of holy writ' (*Othello*, III, iii, 332). Jealousy is partly determined in its strength, by whether it hinders all thought or sets off fantasies of revenge. It can appear to be waning when in fact it is gaining unconsciously, only to surprise us when it re-emerges. It's these fluxes in intensity and their relation to a struggle between appeals to identity – as well as the challenge of becoming adequate to an affect – that Deleuze and Guattari have most to teach us about.

Acts determine jealousy by modulating its power – in an act of forgiveness, say. These acts and jealousy itself depend on environments, because the setting for the act has an effect on how it can unfold – hence the horror of societies that compound the violence of jealousy by condoning it or reinforcing it with fantasies of male honour and the reality of unjust possession. The subsequent course of events conditions the intensities of the affect. An attempt to forgive might be thwarted by recurring memories of loss. The affect of vengefulness depends on how revenge is taken.

Why is an affect necessarily distributed through these things? Couldn't we think of an independent affect that enters into wider causal relations, such that jealousy is a well-determined and located emotion that then changes and has effects through wider causal interactions? An affect might well alter in different environments, but this does not mean that it is fully dependent on them.

The answer is that when an affect is defined in abstraction its multiple changes in intensity cannot be explained due to the absence of other affects and of thoughts, unconscious processes, acts and environments. This is because abstraction from its distribution misses the nature of affect as modulation of intensities in these distributed fields. Thoughts, acts and environments determine the intensities of affects.

Jesse Prinz poses two problems for the philosophy of emotions. There is the problem of parts, which encourages us to look for the right component to attribute to emotion among a number of linked processes: 'There are thoughts, bodily changes, action tendencies, modulations of mental processes such as attention, and conscious feelings. But which of these *is* the emotion?' (Prinz 2004: 3). There is the countervailing problem of plenty. Rather than seeking to find the right component they are all taken to matter, but this raises the difficulty of how 'they all hang together as a coherent whole' (ibid. 18). Deleuze and Guattari's work on affects and their wider philosophies reject the problem of parts and instead seek to answer the problem of plenty when it is combined with the concept of affects as multiplicities interacting with other multiplicities and individuations. How do affects work as dynamic processes through feelings, thoughts, the unconscious, acts and environments?

This question is technical, in the sense of responding to the problem of how we can individuate an affect without depending on a form of identity, without appealing to clear and distinct boundaries, and without relying on a set of predicates. It is also political in seeking to answer the question of how to stop an affect taking over and becoming a destructive personal and political force, in hatred of others or extreme jealousy, for instance.

The insight to take from Deleuze and Guattari is that since affects are complex multiplicities, the problems of identity (of individuation) and of destruction through violent and repressive dead-ends can only be overcome by taking account of interlinked multiplicities and their twin tendencies to negative reliance on identity and the positivity of creative becoming. They define those negative ends and 'black holes' and 'micro-fascisms' leading into more general state-based fascisms (Deleuze and Guattari 1980: 261). Counters to fascisms take place thanks to cautious experiments on the fine balances of the directions, tones and intensities involved in any affect. These trials are already part of popular wisdom – in the ways wise advice and practice seek to balance out hatred through applications of sadness and love, with degrees dependent on cases and environments.

In *A Thousand Plateaus*, Deleuze and Guattari consider the problem of violence and affects in the potential of romantic music to engender affects leading to terrible political movements and disastrous individual outcomes. The question is how to balance out this catastrophic potential with the more positive work of romantic music on affects, where a people is constituted as multiple and mobile, and where individuals are given new and affirmative lines of escape, not a force of destruction but rather one of inclusive multiplicity, resistant to the destructiveness of identity politics. How can the power of romantic music avoid giving rise to destructive sentimentality and instead release positive affects? To make their argument Deleuze and Guattari work through a series of distinctions: between Earth and People, One-Whole and One-People, groups of powers and the individuation of groups, and between the Universal and the Dividual (1980: 420).

The concepts of process and balance are critical to any understanding of these distinctions. They aren't based on a logic of exclusion – either, or – but rather a logic of co-implication – both, and. For Deleuze and Guattari, in romantic music the relation of orchestration to voice is a balancing act around affects connected to processes linked to the harnessing of forces of the Earth – an appeal to history, soil and identity – and forces of a people to come – an appeal to shared new directions, potentials and fleeting unity and power. Music and affect always have these twin directions: confirmation of historical belief and the spark of the new.

In turn, once the affect has been tuned towards historical roots and identity, it is also turned more towards identity as a finished totality, embodied by nationhood, homeland and subjects determined by a shared (if false) universality. Whereas, once the turn is towards a people to come, there is no finished whole but rather the fleeting unity of a people as an ongoing and changing direction, an experiment on new ways of living with and through affects.

The forces of the Earth and of the whole depend on groups of powers. They rely on the harnessing of pre-existing forces (military and bureaucratic, for example) to reinforce and prosecute a form of identity while repressing and seeking to eliminate its foes, its others, out-groups to its identity politics. In contrast, the efforts of a people to come are directed and (only ever partly) achieved by individuating a group around an affect.

This people to come could be an emergent commune or a movement responding to a new hope or to a new challenge defined by a shared affect, for instance love, but perhaps also outrage and hope, a yearning for equality, or a will to heal. The difference is between an obsessive grouping, driven by the desire to protect an identity and eliminate its enemies, and the coming together of a people around a common affect such as empathies for fellow sufferers and the determination not to be defined by pre-established rules, morals and expectations.

Deleuze and Guattari's distinction between Universal and Dividual is introduced to avoid having to define the people to come in relation to the predefined and unchanging – Universal – identity of subjects. Instead, complex and multiple affects bring together an equally multiple crowd – a Dividual – where 'a crowd must be fully individuated, but through group individuations that cannot be reduced to the individuality of the subjects that compose it' (Deleuze and Guattari 1980: 421).

According to Deleuze and Guattari an affect does not make sense as a transforming passion, where it is defined by way of an abstract entity with independent effects, because the transformation is continuous and multiple across fields that include the affect. Its power is not through an operation on things external to it, but rather within fields implicating and shaping it.

My definition of affect as distributive follows from these features of Deleuze and Guattari's work on affects. The core of the following analysis depends on interpretative work by Daniel S. Smith and by Anne Sauvagnargues on Deleuze, Guattari, signs and affect (Smith 2012; Sauvagnargues 2006, 2009). The idea of sign is important for the definition of affect because changes in emotional intensity are signs for lines of conscious and unconscious thought and action. The affect is not only an event; it is also a sign.

This reference to signs should not be seen as aligning Deleuze and Guattari's work on affects with works that define emotions as judgements (Nussbaum 2001). It is exactly the opposite. The distributive form of affect precedes and denies their organisation according to values and flourishing because the affect is a complex and shifting problem before it can be reduced to a specific judgement and morality.

For Deleuze and Guattari, the affect is always a becoming rather than a property or predicate we could use as a basis for judgement and moral life. They frequently make this point through readings of minor literature, for instance, in Kleist as different from Hegel as thinker of state and majority. Again, the most important feature here is opposition to the interiority and identity of a subject, replaced by a 'form of exteriority' individuated by the affect (Deleuze and Guattari 1980: 440).

For an affect as becoming, 'feelings are torn from the interiority of a "subject"'. The subject loses control because of the affect. Once this begins, identity is lost. The subject's remnants are 'violently projected into an environment of pure exteriority, giving affects an astonishing speed, the force of a catapult'. When this happens, 'love and hate are no longer feelings but rather affects' (Deleuze and Guattari 1980: 440). This speed is the extreme intensity of the affect, making it something beyond what we know and beyond how we ought to act – as defined by morality, state, society or family. The affect as great speed runs before existing values and practices, calling for new acts and new groupings – the forming of a people to come through a common affect rather than a common identity.

The linking of affects and signs has wide implications for the definition of the sign and understanding of its operation. The technical question I want to pursue is whether we should describe affects and signs as necessarily involving expressivity. The Braveheart example seems to support this view. The facial poses are expressive of the emotional complexity of the event. That's how they become a sign for others.

Against this account of the interaction of expression, affect and sign, I want to make a pragmatic and structural argument for a wider definition of the sign as process (Williams 2016). Accordingly, expressivity is not necessary for affects or for thinking about signs. This is because I define signs as multiple processes where the idea of expression is replaced by a process of selection that names the sign and a series of competing diagrams mapping its effects as it runs through an environment. The affect and sign are given by a selection of elements and then described by different accounts of process. Expression can be one such description, but not the only one. In my definition of the affect, intensive multiplicity is therefore situated on a single plane, rather than between different ones of expressed and expressive.

A face need not express a disembodied virtual power of, for instance, the affect of rage. Instead, the face and perceived emotions and actions, and the flows of intensities around them, are selected in different ways as signs. The concept of expression is a way of characterising this selection, but it should not be taken as the only way.

Deleuze describes affect as multiplicity and its relation to signs and time in *Cinéma 2*. Flashbacks in film renew sense because they work at 'bifurcations in time'. In a flashback, time splits not only between past and future but also into multiple perspectives around events and circuits in time because a flashback is individual rather than objective: 'The multiplicity of circuits is given another sense. It is not only that many people have flashbacks, but also that each flashback occurs to many people' (Deleuze 1985: 67).

The important point is that multiplicity is constitutive of the sign as flashback, thereby setting up relations between individuals that cannot be reduced to a single objective viewpoint, memory or time. A sign and an affect are forms of relational ambiguity requiring further acts and interpretations – at which cinema excels where time is concerned. Deleuze and Guattari couch this sign and manifestation structure in terms of expression, but I don't think that is necessary. It might even be damagingly restrictive, when compared to a more open and permissive account of a further multiplicity of diagrams of effects following on from a sign.

According to my account of process signs such structures can be named by characteristic selected sets and a suite of diagrams (Williams 2016), such as the fear set and its accompanying changes in intensities as represented on at least one diagram of the effects of fear running to and from its environment. For this definition of the sign and affect, more than being an expressive art, cinema proposes diagrams following on from signs and affects and producing new ones, themselves requiring further diagrams – for instance, in another film or a critical essay, or a life influenced by the film. The dominant tone of an affect would be part of its characteristic set. So though expressivity might be one feature of the set and of the diagram, it is not necessarily so. The wider point is to avoid some of the metaphysical and aesthetic presuppositions of Deleuze and Guattari's accounts –

as found in their appeal to powers, types of becoming and subjects – in order to allow for a more speculative and open model.

Affect as Read by Daniel S. Smith

In *Essays on Deleuze* (2012), Daniel S. Smith supports the distribution of affect away from the emotion of a subject to a pre-subjective process running from emotion right through to action. He also endorses the expressive structure proposed by Deleuze. In line with the account of affect given in Deleuze and Guattari, the background to Smith's analysis is the 'dissolution of the subject' in favour of the concept of a mobile and disparate individual: 'An individual is a multiplicity, the actualization of a set of virtual singularities that function together, that enter into symbiosis, that attain a certain consistency' (Smith 2012: 202).

Deleuze develops this idea of multiplicity in *Difference and Repetition* through a discussion of Leibniz in contrast to Hegel. To underwrite the resistance of multiplicity to identification any multiplicity brings into line singularities that are themselves impossible to identify, 'the remarkable points and differential elements of a multiplicity' (Deleuze 1968a: 72). A multiplicity is determined by the 'convergence' and 'divergence' of series, concepts picked up again much later in Deleuze and Guattari's concept of the Dividual and in their twin concepts of territorialisation and deterritorialisation (ibid. 73).

The first thing to note is the use of the idea of a *set* of things or a *series* of singularities, similar to my use of 'set' in the definition of the sign. This reference to sets will be repeated in Smith's definition of an affect. The second thing to mark out is the nature of the set. It is made up of virtual singularities. Why only virtual? The third thing to notice is how the set is formed: by actualisation which brings about a degree of consistency. How does it bring about the consistency that forms the set?

Virtual singularities allow for the definition of a pure affect, that is one that has no actual components dependent on an actual subject for their full being: 'This "something" is what Deleuze calls a pure affect or percept, which is irreducible to the affections or perceptions of a subject' (Smith 2012: 203). However, expressivity is essential to this definition, even of the pure affect, because as a complex entity the set only comes together when constructed by a process of expression in the actual.

In their last book, *What Is Philosophy?*, Deleuze and Guattari retain this role for expressivity as the necessary transition from pure percept to the material of art: 'It is under this condition that matter becomes expressive: the composition of sensations is realised in the material, or the material passes into the composition, but always to be situated on a properly aesthetic plane of composition' (1991: 185).

This use of expression is an example of what can go wrong in the adoption of a model of expression when it is restricted to different operations according to different fields. *What Is Philosophy?* divides art, science and philosophy away from each other, as shown in the phrase 'properly aesthetic', a wording inconsistent with the continuity and open multiplicity of earlier definitions of affect. A further concern is whether the concept of purity is already problematic for definitions of the affect as a multiplicity in bringing in a sense of absolute into affects that only allow for degrees rather than any summit or *ne plus ultra*.

Returning to Smith's reading, the structure for the expression of the virtual is perplexing, since it involves an external process on a field claimed to be pure. How can it remain pure if it depends on the action of something else for its constitution and consistency? Isn't it touched, and hence imprinted, and hence tainted by its expression through the actual and by the work the pure affect does in return on the actual?

Smith goes on to explain the detailed structure of expression in a reading of Deleuze's *Cinema 1* where, in close-up shots, virtual singularities are said to dissolve the face as belonging to a well-defined subject: 'The organization of the face is undone in favour of its own material traits . . . which become the building material, the "*hyle*," of an affect, or even a system of affects' (Smith 2012: 205). The process is itself complex and distributed. It is divided into a material decomposition into traits, then a virtual purification into non-subjective singularities, and then a virtual collection and composition.

Expression is not only from the actual to the virtual, as process of dissolution, but also from the virtual to the actual as process of selection or determination. That expression is necessarily a two-way process can be shown by answering a question about sufficient reason. What is the sufficient reason for any particular set rather than no set at all or any other particular set?

The answer is that expression is the sufficient reason for the creation of an affect defined according to a determined set: 'what Deleuze calls an affect is precisely the "complex entity" that, at each instant, secures the virtual conjunction of a set of such singular qualities or powers (the brightness, the terror, the compassion)' (Smith 2012: 205). It is the affect as expressed that 'secures' the set, as shown in Smith's particular selection of brightness, terror and compassion.

In Smith's description of stills from Dreyer and Pabst, film shots give life to an affect as complex set by dramatising it – for instance, in a series of close-ups. This does not mean that the film takes a pre-existing emotion, in order to then communicate it. It is rather that the affect comes to life with the film. As selected complex, it does not pre-exist the film, even if all its singularities do in a potential virtual state.

It is a mistake to understand this expression as involving stages, separated according to potential, realisation and value. When flour and water are mixed together to make glue, there is a stage of separate potentials (flour and water) and a stage where these potentials are realised as glue. This stage is said to hold greater value, since it is only in this one that flour and water work as adhesive. The latter stage is also separate from the earlier one, since the glue no longer contains the independent potentials; they have been exchanged for the real predicate of stickiness.

Against this image of realised potential, the Deleuzian meaning of expression can be deduced from this statement by Smith: 'Art does not actualize these virtual affects; rather, it gives them "a body, a life, a universe"' (2012: 205). When art dramatises affects, it does not actualise them in the sense of bringing them into reality. It is rather that the staging brings the pure affect together with an ever-wider series of folding and unfolding actual and virtual processes. These processes resonate with one another: they form a life. The body – say, the face in the close-up – connects the pure affect to an actual thing and thereby determines the virtual affect as a set of singularities corresponding to the features drawn together on the face without a subject.

This unsteady union of virtual and actual comprises a life. This is not the life of a particular subject. It is the interaction of a virtual pure affect and a process of becoming in the individual. This is a transformation of the subject beyond its particular characteristics into ones that are imperceptible from a subjective point of view: 'Thought in percepts and affects disengages the virtual from corporeal experience and then embodies it in materials that render the imperceptible perceptible' (Bogue 2003: 195). This process then extends – the affect is distributed – to form a universe across the actual and the virtual, where actual boundaries are crossed and where a singular universal is formed by actual and virtual processes.

The paradoxical idea of the singular universal is designed to capture the idea that each affect is singular, because it is different not only with each actual expression, but also as a singular coming together of other singularities which resist repetition as the same. So we do not have a universal in the sense of a thing (an affect) that is the same in each of its instantiations. We have a singular universal that is not only unrepeatable, but also unidentifiable through its components. Nonetheless, it is universal in the sense of untouched by particular instantiations as it is at work in each of them. The affect has no stable parts and does not occur in the same way across different events, while occurring in all of them.

Smith's interpretation brings together four different methods and an important principle. First, his close reading draws as much as possible from all the ramifications of specific passages in Deleuze's work. Second, he connects across Deleuze's work whenever this allows for a deeper explanation of the sense of Deleuze's concepts and arguments. Third, since Deleuze is always in debate with historical positions, Smith tracks back to Deleuze's sources, such as Spinoza and Leibniz. Fourth, the frame for Smith's analysis is a logical one, aiming at logical consistency at the level of philosophical structure; so not simply logical in the sense of agreed premises and attention to specific syllogisms, but rather logical in the sense of a system that accords well.

Finally, there is the counter-intuitive but essential principle for any interpretation of Deleuze: we should look for the becoming or transformation of concepts, rather than for their stable core across arguments and texts. This principle fits with the idea of the singular universal. For Deleuze, thought does not work through stable concepts repeated reliably, but rather through changes between a concept and its context, and within the concept itself.

The reference to affects and 'a life' crosses between Deleuze's *Cinema 1*, his work on the actual and the virtual in *Difference and Repetition*, his work on Stoic time and event in *The Logic of Sense*, his later book *What Is Philosophy?*, written with Félix Guattari, the second volume of their *Capitalism and Schizophrenia*, *A Thousand Plateaus*, and Deleuze's last publication 'Immanence: A Life ...' (1995).

The concept of life is played out between two planes. The primary plane is '*an immanent plane of consistency* that knows only relations between affects and percepts, and whose composition, through the creation of blocks of sensation, takes place in the indefinite and virtual time of the pure event (*Aeon*)' (Smith 2012: 207). The pure event does not occur in chronological time but rather happens in the past and future at the same time as something that has always happened and is always to happen (Bowden 2011: 21–2).

This means that, as virtual, a life is the coming into consistency of pure affects that aren't happening at a particular time but rather draw all affects from the lost past and non-actual future together. As such, life is a disembodied potential that can be expressed in different ways at different times. The 'here and now' of chronological time – the event as happening – is restricted to the secondary plane of the subject: 'A "subject" is constructed on the transcendent plane of organization that already involves the development of forms, organs, and functions, and takes place in a measured and actualized time (*Chronos*)' (Smith 2012: 207). From the point of view of the primary plane the plane of the subject involves an illusion, since its organisation involves the denial of virtual processes of becoming that explain the evolution of its organs and functions.

However, though secondary and involving commitments to illusory entities, the plane of the subject is also necessary: 'affects and percepts presuppose at least a minimal subject from which they are extracted, or as an envelope that allows them to communicate' (Smith 2012: 208). This presupposition is fundamental to answering the questions about the constitution of affects as sets.

It is through processes of extraction and enveloping that affects become complexes of other affects and percepts. This explains why there is an affect rather than an indistinct chaos or nothing, and why there is a particular affect rather than any other. Expression as extraction and enveloping on the plane of the subject is essential to Deleuze's account. This raises two further questions. How exactly do the two planes involved in expression come together and have effects on one another? Can sets be constituted in other ways, if we dispense with the distinction between actual and virtual?

Force in Sauvagnargues' Work on Deleuze and Art

Anne Sauvagnargues' two books on Deleuze, *Deleuze: l'empirisme transcend-antal* and *Deleuze et l'art*, are, respectively, the most rigorous study of Deleuze as a new kind of transcendental philosopher and the most extensive philosophical study of the place of art as critical and clinical practice in Deleuze's philosophy.

One way of understanding Deleuze's solution to the independence of the virtual from its actualisation – a key theme of Sauvagnargues' book on transcendental empiricism – is through the idea of the event. For Deleuze, an event is dual. First, each event involves an actualisation in the present. The main example for this process is a wound, as given in Deleuze's very moving work on Joë Bousquet in *The Logic of Sense* (Williams 2008: 153–7).

In terms of feelings, mind and emotions, it is worth noting that this duality of the event shifts discussions of affect and emotion beyond questions of the embodiment of mind as feeling (Damasio 2006: 252) to questions about the disembodiment of both mind and body towards a virtual realm of pure affects. Deleuze's philosophy is consistent with theses about embodiment and somatic explanations, but it then expands upon them by distributing affect much more widely (Protevi 2009: 99–100).

As event, a wound actualises a series of pure affects, such as 'to be cut'. A way of understanding this abstract move to the infinitive is through the great variety of ways it can be expressed – for instance, in the many different ways we prepare for, experience, behave under and react to the dentist's drill. The phrase 'to be under the drill' allows for a great many different expressions such that we should think of it as a pure affect that can be actualised in many different ways.

Second, the event involves a virtual dissolving or abstraction away from that actualisation. This means that actual events – their subjects and objects – are set in motion by potential pure changes that have happened and will happen. To express 'to be cut' is to be changed with that expression. The actual event involves transformations of its components such that we cannot say there is a reliable subject or series of objects involved.

I am one of those Oliver Hardy people who injure themselves in moments of frustration. If the repair on a window hinge is going badly, I am as prone to jam my fingers in the frame as to calmly arrive at a good mend. What's important for understanding Deleuze is that the actual squishing of the fingers is not the whole event. It is one concentrated side of it – concentrated deep into the urgency of the present event, as anyone who has flattened their fingers knows only too well.

Why so? Because the jamming is a factor of much wider, abstract affects and forces such as frustration, impatience, clumsiness, hopefulness, despair, haste and confusion. For Deleuze, the howl of the injured DIY enthusiast is not simply pain; it is the concentration of the turmoil of pure emotions, like the fury of the bike rider with another puncture, or the despair of the painter before another ruined canvas: 'The scream is a social act, the rendering visible of forces. It poses the problem at the level of sensation, rather than resolving it' (Ruddick 2010: 38).

These emotions are abstract because they appear through a life and in the lives of others. We can consider them as pure potentials hovering in the past and in the future, appearing like ghosts whenever we approach a complicated mechanism with trepidation and optimism. The finger jam is an actualisation. My propensity to be confused and enraged is expressed in it. It is also a counter-actualisation. The banal actual event is drawn into an infinite array of those pure propensities.

Each actual event is an expression of pure abstractions and it expresses them in a singular way – for example, where I feel my frustration increasing or becoming more dangerous in a specific accident. The difficulty is the following: why doesn't that particular expression have an effect on the abstraction, on the pure virtual affect, thereby denying its purity and calling back into a particular actual event and set of predicates in the here and now?

Why does Deleuze call the work of the pure affect our destiny, which can only be reckoned with, rather than chance, which can be forestalled and bent to our will? Justifying what Deleuze calls the neutrality or impassibility of the event to its actualisation, Sauvagnargues' solution turns on the event's irreducibility to a series of actual happenings.

The independence of the virtual side of the event, indicated by the ideas of neutrality and impassibility, follows from the 'bifurcation' of the event (Sauvagnargues 2009: 349). On the one hand, there is the pure event as 'having happened' and 'to happen', where the tenses indicate the non-actual and potential aspects of the pure event. On the other hand, there is the event as present occurrence, as mere happening, where the tense indicates how everything is condensed into the present occurrence as moment of accomplishment and action. What is the reason for this impassibility?

The answer is that the pure and potential side of the event is not exhausted by its actualisation because it is in excess of the happening, in the sense of retaining its purity in being expressed. What's retained is a power to always be expressed differently. For an affect, this means that it withholds itself in each actualisation, to the extent that when it is actualised again it is a different version of the actual side of the affect. It is a new rage each time.

This sense of excess is different from but related to the more traditional sense of excess in an affect or emotion, such as excessive lust or desire (Blackburn 2004: 24). It is different because it is a formal excess, neither good nor bad in itself, so it does not necessarily have to take on the negative meaning that Simon Blackburn discusses in his study of lust and desire. It is related because this formal excess explains how actual affects always have the potential to change and exceed what is taken to be wise or appropriate.

This implies that each expression brings something new into the actual side of the event: 'artistic events which renew the past' (Boljkovac 2013: 27). This novelty is not drained, or even altered, by its actualisation. It therefore remains to be expressed again – with no trace of earlier expressions. Sauvagnargues lays out the argument in the physical language of cuts: 'The impassibility [of the event] does not consist in transcendence but in an untouched power to bring about a cut in the present of bodies' (2009: 349). The virtual affect is pure even when it is expressed because its power remains untouched each time it is applied.

Put in terms of time, the actualisation of the virtual is the reason for a cut in the actual present that does not depend on being present: 'Not-yet and always already, it is never in the present, but divides time into past and future: it cleaves time and subverts the present' (Sauvagnargues 2009: 349). The full argument is that there is absolute novelty in the present. That's why there are events rather than a determined causal unfolding. The reason for the recurrence of novelty is that the source of novelty is a virtual side to the event. The purity of this side explains both the occurrence of the new and the impassibility of the virtual, that it is untouched by its expression in the novel actual event.

Destiny and compulsions are good ways of understanding the argument. If a family suffers from a tragic destiny, or an individual suffers from a deep compulsion, what explains the concurrence of the following apparently contradictory properties? First, we cannot escape the compulsion or destiny. Second, destiny and compulsion keep erupting into actual lives in novel ways which we can act upon. If destiny is part of our actual lives, why can't our acts change it?

The answer is that, as pure, a destiny or compulsion is not altered by its occurrence. It interferes in lives but also remains pure potential. However, exactly because it is pure and ungraspable, when it does occur it is as unpredictable and different: a powerful and inexhaustible reserve of misery and joy. That's why destiny and compulsions cannot be described *in vivo*; they must instead be expressed indirectly.

However, if we move from a principle of sufficient reason allied to transcendental arguments to materialist and physical explanations, reference to the idea of power, as in Sauvagnargues' phrase 'untouched power', shows the extent to which the underlying problem has not been resolved. Deleuze provides us with a complicated and seamless philosophical system where each demand for a reason or explanation for a feature appears to find its satisfactory response somewhere else in the system. Yet this satisfaction is limited when we turn to material conditions.

It is fine to speak of sufficient reasons within discussion in physics, for example, when trying to accommodate sufficient reason and quantum mechanics (Stapp 2011). It is not fine to speak of sufficient reasons based on transcendental arguments whose reasons contradict physical ones, because no matter how satisfactory a philosophical explanation might seem within a particular system, it can be negated by an empirically based counter. For example, the untouched yet effective power of the virtual contradicts the second law of thermodynamics, since the impassibility of the virtual implies there is no energy transfer from the virtual to the actual. If there was such a transfer then we could speak of depletion of the virtual and that would contradict the concept of impassibility.

The answer to this critical point could be that what Deleuze is describing is nothing like a physical process. However, that will not do, because the actual side of the event is a physical process, whether it is the expressive power of increasing redness of cheeks or the fist thrown in the grips of anger. The difficulty remains in describing how these processes interact with pure virtual ones. A transcendental and explanatory account might be good at giving us the architecture of reasons, but it is poor at giving us the detail of exact causes or motivations.

This is where a different approach taken from Sauvagnargues' earlier work on art is helpful. Its sources are not Kantian or transcendental but rather come from the combination of science and philosophy found in Spinoza, Nietzsche and Simondon. This connection between art and affects has been made by others, notably Simon O'Sullivan in terms of art practice (2006: 157). Deleuze's major Spinoza book must be seen as the most important early source for this concept of expression (1968b).

The idea of expression is not to be thought in terms of conditions, but rather in terms of signs, powers and forces. The change is important, because expression now involves power in the actual: the power to affect and be affected. These changes are explained through the concepts of force and power as expressed in signs of art (Sauvagnargues 2006: 58).

The combination of power and force is essential to Sauvagnargues' argument, since expression involves both a change in power and the work of forces. We might think that the concept of force would be enough, in the idea that in expressing something we capture a force from it that we can use elsewhere – for instance, in the way we are sometimes enjoined to channel anger. This would be to miss the more profound point that expression does two things at the same time: it alters powers and works through forces. Power and force cannot be reduced to the same thing. But why can't they?

As an aside, it is important to stress the Spinozist rather than Cartesian roots to this appeal to forces. For Sauvagnargues and for Deleuze forces are of the body and the mind, rather than strictly of the body, to then be controlled by a separate soul, consciousness or mind. So when Descartes 'allocates passions to the body' (James 1997: 259) he misconceives the reach of the force of an affect. They tug right into the sphere of judgement and will, which are themselves directly in the making of passionate forces.

Sauvagnargues' answer to the question of the difference of force and power depends on following Deleuze in distinguishing longitude and latitude in the composition of forces in an actual event. This composition is its haecceity or mode of individuation – all the processes that come together to make it this event rather than any other. Here is Sauvagnargues' account of composition, explained in relation to art:

> Deleuze thinks of art as the composition of relations of material forces, and of this composition as haecceity, according to the longitude of a relation of forces, or speed, and the latitude of power or affect. The group of material elements belonging to a body under relations of motion and rest, speed and slowness, are its longitude. The group of intensive affects that this body is capable of, under this or that power or degree of power, are its latitude. (2006: 60; my translation)

Even if we only consider material forces, a distinction can be made between two related states. There is a direct relation where forces apply to each other such that their speeds are altered. When I put two hands on your shoulders and hold you back to teach you about the effect of resistance there is an effect on the speed of your movements. It is a very broad direct effect working on ideas – a quickening of understanding – right through to growth – a strengthening of muscle.

In addition to this direct work, there is also an indirect effect on what a body can do; this is its power to affect and be affected (for a discussion of affects and powers of the body that contrasts with Deleuze's, see Pethick 2015: 18ff). You might become more powerful in some ways. Your increased understanding is transferable to other situations. Your greater strength and feel for the nature of resistance allows you to apply your strength more effectively. However, this is a very complex and mobile change. There could be debilitating sadness in being pushed back or forced to exercise strength in disaccord with your nature, or what passes for strength might turn out to be weakness in new situations.

Sauvagnargues uses the distinction between longitude and latitude to explain the difference between ontology and ethics in Deleuze's account of affect. There is an ethical aspect to the experimental practice of seeking to increase power through the deployment of forces taken ontologically.

We can have a secure understanding of the forces and still have to appeal to a mobile and uncertain ethology in manipulating them to change power. It is here that signs are important because affects work between force and power and are only open to a critical and clinical symptomology: a reading of changes in power and pure affects with no direct control or access.

The distinction between longitude and latitude goes further than arguments for the openness of affects based on novel encounters and it can stand as a further justification for them. When Paola Marrati claims that 'encounters, when they take place, create new affects, just as real as they are unassignable from a physiological or organic point of view', she invites the criticism that we cannot know that there will be new encounters of this type (2006: 320). The answer is that every encounter is new in this way, but to different degrees and depending on different problems of power.

How does the distinction between longitude and latitude of forces help to answer the critical questions put in the course of this discussion? It is that expression and signs are not at work immediately between the actual and virtual, but rather there is an expressive relation between longitude and latitude, that is, between force and power.

It is also that the affect remains pure because its changes in intensity relate to power and not to force. So if the distinction between power and force is valid, then it justifies the impassibility of virtual affects. The direct play of forces does not bear on the intensity of pure affects because this intensity plays a role through changes in power which do not involve the same physical laws as forces.

Conclusion: From Expression to Undetermined Selection

In *Cinéma 1*, Deleuze gives a definition of affect as 'a grouping of an immobile reflecting unity and intense expressive movements'. When we are given a close-up of the curl of a lip – a dismissive sneer of rebellious confidence, for example – the wider life surrounding the curl is the immobile reflecting surface brought together and expressed by the lip as it arches. The curl is an expression of an intensity of forces that cannot be traced directly to the reflecting unity but that nonetheless draw them together.

The lip expresses two fields: an actual and a virtual one. In turn, these fields comprise relations of forces and power associated with the affect, its expression and its virtual singularities. The reflecting unity should therefore be read in the sense of 'a life', that is, as the unity of forces, intensities of power and virtual affects that go beyond a given actual life. The curious use of the adjective 'immo-bile' corresponds to the impassibility of virtual affects and indirect power.

If we take the affect of disdain, as expressed by a sneer, the curl of the lip might express different forces of fear, mistrust, superiority, rebellion, humour and hate. This relation of forces is itself a product of power, that is, the intensity of the forces depends on the intensity of virtual affects we do not have access to. We can only experiment with them in a practical sense, to see what a body can do. Sometimes a sneer and disdain will be a sign of immense creativity (Elvis at the beginning of his career); at other times it will be a sign of great fragility of will (James Dean in *Rebel Without a Cause*).

Deleuze introduces the emotional aspect of affect by defining the physical movements we usually ascribe to emotions, such as a snarl of fearful contempt, as the expression of pure virtual movements defined as pure affects. The expressive snarl conveys changes in the intensities of the pure affects abstracted from par-ticular actual cases. Expression connects to collective reflection in an expressive event, studied through many different types of close-up by Deleuze in *Cinéma 1* but also in Deleuze's work on Francis Bacon, where figures such as a scream express pure forces and changes in power in an abstract diagram (1981: 39–44).

Against this definition, my conjecture is that the idea of expression is not essential to the main critical and creative features of Deleuze and Guattari's work on affects. This is because the grouping Deleuze describes can be achieved by the simpler concept of an undetermined selection of a set open to differ-ent competing interpretations. The sense of intense relations working through expression can be retained thanks to the idea of intense relations put into play by the selection. It is not necessary to see the selection itself as an expression. We can select a set that includes expressive relations, but they are not necessary for any given selection.

A close-up of lip-curl creates a sign as a selected set with many different elements brought together in a mutual transformation. The problem with viewing this as essentially expressive in terms of reciprocal determination between a vir-tual and neutral surface and an expressive actual gesture is that this unnecessarily limits what affects and signs can be. We do not require the dual structure of the event and of expression to have all the critical and creative benefits of the idea of a process sign or the idea of a wide variety of constructed affects that are complex and distributed.

What matters in Deleuze and Guattari's definitions of affects is the grouping rather than the paradoxical independence-yet-connection of reflective unity and affective movement. Deleuze explains the grouping through the concept of direct unity in a two-fold structure: '[Compact and continuous series of close-ups] instead arrive at a new reality that we could call Dividual, directly uniting an immense collective reflection to the particular emotions of each individual, finally expressing the unity of power and quality' (1983: 131).

The emotion or affect is never limited to a particular place. It is rather in the unity of movements that express an infinitely distributed series of pure affects. Direct means two things here. First, the process is not mediated – for instance, through a grid of possible meanings. It is direct interaction. Second, the affect cannot be taken as the addition of one aspect to the other. It is instead a process of direct transformation implicating them together.

We could have thought that an affect worked because a unity was detached from the expressive gesture – for instance, as anger given as social meaning and anger as gesture. What Deleuze and Guattari show is that every affect is a singular event, running through 'a life' as an individuating process. Affect then becomes unique and yet shared in the sense that different manifestations of it fold into one another. There is an overlap between different manifestations of anger. My point is that we can have the distribution, singularity and individuation afforded by affect as event, but that the dual expressive structure is superfluous and limiting.

For Deleuze, the reflective surface is not uniform, like a single-tone blank slate or *tabula rasa*. It is not simply receptive to the expression of pure emotions. On the contrary, the surface is unification as multiplicity. It is a bringing together of features by the expressive movement, like the faces in a crowd halted for a moment by a loud and frightening sound or first attenders at a distressing emotional breakdown. It is this unification that Smith stresses when he connects the affect to 'a life'. As a concept, though, unification does not require expression. Other processes can unify in this way, from a chance collage, to a conscious gathering, to a collective endeavour. The idea of expression limits the ways in which unity can be created.

Against ideas of pre-set values applying to stable and recognisable affects, Deleuze shows how affects create the group they occur with; they draw it together not as a preformed receptor but as an extended collective thought process, haunted by the pure emotional changes expressed in the affect. The affect is uncertain as pure emotional multiplicity, as intense expression and as collective reflection.

Deleuze gives his most enigmatic but also most significant account of the uncertainty and infinite extension of multiplicity and affect when he connects multiplicity to Nietzsche's eternal return as never allowing the return of the same but only of difference: 'Eternal return is a power of affirmation, but it affirms all of the multiple, all of chance, *except* that which subordinates them to the One, to the Same, to necessity, *except* the One, the Same and the Necessary' (1968a). Affect as multiplicity puts all things in movement through difference. It never stays still. It must always be different and never necessary. An affect is a changing event calling for becoming. It is always open and always uncertain.

However, this uncertainty or openness can be achieved without having to resort to the distinction between force and power described by Sauvagnargues. It can simply be posited and subsequently argued for according to whichever process is deemed to have brought about unification. The importance of the simpler model of undetermined selection is that it allows for many different speculative and pragmatic diagrams of the way different elements are changed in their relations by the selection. One such explanation could be expression as understood by Deleuze, but there can be many others. The great advantage of undetermined selection is that it avoids the metaphysical baggage of expression – for example, in the uses of force and power studied by Sauvagnargues.

Against this view, it could be objected that expression is essential for Deleuze due to the importance of the face and body for his account of affect. The movement-affect is a reprise of Deleuze's work from Proust, for instance, in the world and affect as expressed by Albertine (Deleuze 1970: 14), and from *Difference and Repetition*, for the definition of the ethical as capture, in the idea of the reflection of an unseen field in the terrified face of the other (Deleuze 1968a: 334–5). Here, Deleuze's theory of forces seems vulnerable to well-known difficulties in reliably tracking from the face to wider causes – for example, in the screams of Beatlemania that cannot be easily explained on Darwinian grounds (Deigh 2004: 23).

This objection only confirms the limitation of the expressive model. Why couldn't the rustle of cloth or the shuffling of steps or the jarring idiosyncrasies of a style or the intonation of a musical piece convey affect? They do so not because they necessarily express something else, but because they allow certain things to be brought together that count as emotion and affect. We can dispense with expression in a theory of affect, because manifold changes of emotional intensities accompanied by conscious and unconscious thoughts and acts in the affect only require that they be selected together. This selection is the condition for subsequent and contingent accounts of expression.

Note

1. All references to Deleuze and to Deleuze and Guattari are to the French editions; the English translations are mine.

References

Blackburn, Simon (2004), *Lust*, Oxford: Oxford University Press.
Bogue, Ronald (2003), *Deleuze on Music, Painting and the Arts*, New York: Routledge.
Boljkovac, Nadine (2013), *Untimely Affects: Gilles Deleuze and an Ethics of the Cinema*, Edinburgh: Edinburgh University Press.
Bowden, Sean (2011), *The Priority of Events: Deleuze's Logic of Sense*, Edinburgh: Edinburgh University Press.
Damasio, Antonio (2006), *Descartes' Error*, London: Vintage.
Deigh, John (2004), 'Primitive Emotions', in R. Solomon (ed.), *Thinking about Feeling: Contemporary Philosophers on Emotions*, Oxford: Oxford University Press, pp. 9–27.
Deleuze, Gilles (1968a), *Différence et répétition*, Paris: Presses Universitaires de France. Trans. Paul Patton (1994), *Difference and Repetition*, New York: Columbia University Press.
Deleuze, Gilles (1968b), *Spinoza et le problème de l'expression*, Paris: Éditions de Minuit. Trans. Martin Joughin (1990), *Expressionism in Philosophy: Spinoza*, New York: Zone Books.
Deleuze, Gilles (1969), *Logique du sens*, Paris: Éditions de Minuit. Trans. Mark Lester and Charles Stivale (1999), *The Logic of Sense*, New York: Columbia University Press.
Deleuze, Gilles (1970), *Proust et les signes*, Paris: Presses Universitaires de France. Trans. Richard Howard (1972), *Proust and Signs*, New York: George Braziller.

Deleuze, Gilles (1981), *Francis Bacon: Logique de la sensation*, Paris: Éditions de la Différence. Trans. Daniel W. Smith (2003), *Francis Bacon: The Logic of Sensation*, Minneapolis: University of Minnesota Press.

Deleuze, Gilles (1983), *Cinéma 1: L'Image-mouvement*, Paris: Éditions de Minuit. Trans. Hugh Tomlinson and Barbara Habberjam (1986), *Cinema 1: The Movement-Image*, Minneapolis: University of Minnesota Press.

Deleuze, Gilles (1985), *Cinéma 2: L'Image-temps*, Paris: Éditions de Minuit. Trans. Hugh Tomlinson and Robert Galeta (1989), *Cinema 2: The Time-Image*, Minneapolis: University of Minnesota Press.

Deleuze, Gilles (1995), 'L'Immanence: une vie . . .', *Philosophie*, 47: 3–9.

Deleuze, Gilles and Félix Guattari (1972), *L'Anti-oedipe*, Paris: Éditions de Minuit. Trans. Robert Hurley, Mark Seem and Helen R. Lane (1983), *Anti-Oedipus*, Minneapolis: University of Minnesota Press.

Deleuze, Gilles and Félix Guattari (1980), *Capitalisme et schizophrénie tome 2: Mille plateaux*, Paris: Éditions de Minuit. Trans. Brian Massumi (1987), *A Thousand Plateaus: Capitalism and Schizophrenia*, Minneapolis: University of Minnesota Press.

Deleuze, Gilles and Félix Guattari (1991), *Qu'est-ce que la philosophie?*, Paris: Éditions de Minuit. Trans. Hugh Tomlinson and Graham Burchell (1994), *What Is Philosophy?*, New York: Columbia University Press.

Goldie, Peter (2000), *The Emotions: A Philosophical Exploration*, Oxford: Oxford University Press.

James, Susan (1997), *Passion and Action: The Emotions in Seventeenth-Century Philosophy*, Oxford: Oxford University Press.

Marrati, Paola (2006), 'Time and Affects', *Australian Feminist Studies*, 21(51): 313–25.

Nussbaum, Martha C. (2001), *Upheavals of Thought: The Intelligence of Emotions*, Cambridge: Cambridge University Press.

O'Sullivan, Simon (2006), *Art Encounters Deleuze and Guattari: Thought Beyond Representation*, Basingstoke: Palgrave Macmillan.

Pethick, Stuart (2015), *Affectivity and Philosophy after Spinoza and Nietzsche: Making Knowledge the Most Powerful Affect*, Basingstoke: Palgrave Macmillan.

Prinz, Jesse J. (2004), *Gut Reactions: A Perceptual Theory of Emotions*, Oxford: Oxford University Press.

Protevi, John (2009), *Political Affect: Connecting the Social and the Somatic*, Minneapolis: University of Minnesota Press.

Rebel Without a Cause, film, directed by Nicholas Ray, USA: Warner Bros, 1956.

Ruddick, Susan (2010), 'The Politics of Affect: Spinoza in the Work of Negri and Deleuze', *Theory, Culture & Society*, 27(4): 21–45.

Sauvagnargues, Anne (2006), *Deleuze et l'art*, Paris: Presses Universitaires de France.

Sauvagnargues, Anne (2009), *Deleuze: l'empirisme transcendantal*, Paris: Presses Universitaires de France.

Shakespeare, William (2016), *The Arden Shakespeare: Othello*, rev. edn, London: Bloomsbury.

Smith, Daniel S. (2012), *Essays on Deleuze*, Edinburgh: Edinburgh University Press.

Solomon, Robert C. (2003), *Not Passion's Slave: Emotions and Choice*, Oxford: Oxford University Press.

Stapp, Henry P. (2011), 'Retrocausal Effects as a Consequence of Quantum Mechanics Refined to Accommodate the Principle of Sufficient Reason', *Foundations of Physics*, <http://escholarship.org/uc/item/1bm0k7b7> (last accessed 5 March 2020).

Williams, James (2008), *Gilles Deleuze's Logic of Sense: A Critical Introduction and Guide*, Edinburgh: Edinburgh University Press.
Williams, James (2016), *A Process Philosophy of Signs*, Edinburgh: Edinburgh University Press.

2

Multiplicity as a Life: Deleuze, Simondon, Ruyer

Audronė Žukauskaitė

Multiplicity is one of the crucial notions in Deleuze and Guattari's philosophy. Multiplicity can be related both to the mathematical term 'manifold', developed in the differential geometry of Friedrich Gauss and Bernhard Riemann, and to the philosophy of biology, developed by Gilbert Simondon and Raymond Ruyer. In this chapter I will examine to what extent the Deleuzian theory of multiplicity is indebted to Simondon's distinction between the pre-individual and the process of individuation, and Ruyer's distinction between equipotentiality and the actual process of morphogenesis. I want to argue that these insights helped Deleuze to formulate his idea of double different/ciation: to conceptualise a living being as potentially or virtually containing multiple differences *in itself*, without a privileged point of view, and also to define the living being in its multi-phased actual development and its capacity to differ *from itself*. In this sense Deleuze formulates a very dynamic theory of life, which explains multiple forms, and the unlimited variations of living beings.

Multiplicity in *Difference and Repetition*

The notion of multiplicity appears in Deleuze's *Bergsonism* (1988/1991) and *Difference and Repetition* (1968/2004), and later is reinterpreted by Deleuze and Guattari in *A Thousand Plateaus* (1980/2004) and *What Is Philosophy?* (1991/1994). However, the most systematic description of the notion of multiplicity is given in *Difference and Repetition*, where Deleuze defines multiplicities as Ideas:

> every idea is a multiplicity or a variety. In this Reimannian usage of the word 'multiplicity' . . . the utmost importance must be attached to the substantive form: multiplicity must not designate a combination of the many or the one, but rather an organisation belonging to the many as such, which has no need whatsoever of unity in order to form a system. (2004a: 230)

Deleuze points out that 'the art of multiplicities' is the art of grasping its double dimension: first, multiplicities refer to the dimension of problems and Ideas, which incarnate themselves in things, and, second, multiplicities refer to things, which can be seen as incarnations, or solutions for these problems. In this sense multiplicity implies both *n*-dimensionality, the presence of at least two different dimensions, and a relation, a change or a transformation, which connects them into a continuum.

Deleuze defines three conditions upon which multiplicity emerges. First, multiplicities are indeterminable in the sense that they imply no prior identity which could determine them in advance. Multiplicities are made of a potential or a virtuality, which contains a certain 'problem', and of actual incarnation, providing a 'solution' in the form of differentiation. Second, multiplicities are made not of bounded identities or individuals but of intrinsic relations. 'In all cases the multiplicity is intrinsically defined, without external reference or recourse to a uniform space in which it would be submerged' (Deleuze 2004a: 231). In other words, multiplicity excludes identity as a prior condition: multiplicity is made not of inter-relations between bounded identities but of intra-relations between incomplete entities which are reciprocally determining each other. And third, multiplicities are defined as the passage from virtual structure to actual genesis:

> genesis takes place in time not between one actual term, however small, and another actual term, but between the virtual and its actualisation – in other words, it goes from the structure to its incarnation, from the conditions of a problem to the cases of solution, from differential elements and their ideal connections to actual terms and diverse real relations which constitute at each moment the actuality of time. (Deleuze 2004a: 231–2)

Thus Deleuze describes multiplicity both as a virtual/potential and an actual entity, and as a passage from virtual structure to actual genesis.

We can better understand the novelty of the Deleuzian approach by pointing out that the concept of multiplicity is opposed to the metaphysical concept of identity or essence. As Manuel DeLanda asserts, the term 'multiplicity' is closely related to that of 'manifold', coming from the differential geometry of Friedrich Gauss and Bernhard Riemann. Riemann suggested a new approach to space by examining *n*-dimensional surfaces or spaces, which were defined through their intrinsic features and without embedding them into the global extrinsic higher-dimensional (N+1) space. Deleuze takes these main features of the manifold and extends them into a universal theory of multiplicity. As DeLanda points out, 'a Deleuzian multiplicity takes as its first defining feature these two traits of a manifold: its variable number of dimensions and, more importantly, the absence of a supplementary (higher) dimension imposing an extrinsic coordinatization, and hence, *an extrinsically defined unity*' (2002: 12). Thus the Deleuzian multiplicity can be understood as made of many different dimensions, but still keeping its continuity and carrying the potential for change. The metaphysical tradition used to conceive things as being unified, timeless and eternal, whereas the concept of multiplicity defines things as being differential, unfinished and continuous. Moreover, the identity or the essence of a thing is given all at once, whereas the multiplicity is never given all at once and appears in a form of progressive differentiation. DeLanda makes a distinction between essences, which are always abstract and general, and multiplicities, which are concrete and universal:

> unlike essences, which as abstract general entities coexist side by side sharply distinguished from one another, concrete universals must be thought as *meshed together into a continuum*. . . . Unlike a transcendent heaven which exists as a *separate dimension* from reality, Deleuze asks us to imagine a continuum of multiplicities which *differenciates itself* into our familiar three-dimensional space as well as its spatially structured contents. (2002: 21–2)

This means that multiplicities as Ideas are not transcendent but immanent to the material processes, and that they can initiate changes or progressive differentiations *in medias res*, without any external intervention.

What is important to understand is that the Deleuzian theory of multiplicities can be considered as a model corresponding to different regions of reality. As Deleuze points out,

> there are Ideas which correspond to mathematical relations and realities, others which correspond to physical laws and facts. There are others which, according to their order, correspond to organisms, psychic structures, languages and societies: these correspondences without resemblance are of a structural-genetic nature. (2004a: 232)

These correspondences are not resemblances but analogies, which enable the examination of different regions of knowledge. Thus, Deleuze refers to linguistic multiplicity, which contains both a virtual system of reciprocal relations between phonemes and their actual incarnations in language, or to a biological multiplicity of genes, which together with other genes constitute a potentiality or a virtuality, and which are later incarnated in actual organisms and species. In the same manner Deleuze refers to 'the psychic multiplicities of imagination and phantasy, the biological multiplicities of vitality and "monstrosity", the physical multiplicities of sensibility and sign' (2004a: 243). In other words, multiplicities can be compared not on the basis of what they are but on the analogy of their operations. In this respect Deleuze is very close to Simondon's method of the analogy of operations called 'allagmatics'. Simondon argues that we should make comparisons not between completed structures but between processes or operations. He suggests a new type of analogical paradigmatism, 'allowing us to pass from physical individuation to organic individuation, from organic individuation to psychic individuation and from psychic individuation to the subjective and objective transindividual' (Simondon 2009: 11). Following Simondon, Deleuze creates a theory of analogical differentiations, allowing a comparison between different kinds of multiplicities.

However, it is important to point out that multiplicities correspond to each of these faculties or regions of knowledge, but do not introduce any common sense, any generalisation or unification. Rather, every multiplicity, regardless of the specificity of the region, expresses a tension between a virtual problem and an actual solution. In *Difference and Repetition* Deleuze defines a model of double multiplicity: he refers to the virtual mode of differentiation, charged with internal differences, and the actual process of genesis, which incarnates these differential traits into actual beings.

> We call the determination of the virtual content of an Idea differen*t*iation; we call the actualisation of that virtuality into species and distinguished parts differen*c*iation. It is always in relation to a differen*t*iated problem or to the differen*t*iated conditions of a problem that a differen*c*iation of species and parts is carried out, as though it corresponds to the cases of solution of the problem. It is always a problematic field which conditions a differen*c*iation within a milieu in which it is incarnated. (Deleuze 2004a: 258)

In other words, virtual multiplicity is defined by differential elements and relations and is named as a structure: a structure contains multiple differences in itself, and organises them without any privileged point of view. At the same time, it creates a tension, a problematic field, consisting of these 'unprivileged' differences, which is resolved by the actual process of genesis. 'Whereas differen*t*iation determines the virtual content of the Idea as problem, differen*c*iation expresses the actual-isation of this virtual and the constitution of solutions (by local integrations)' (Deleuze 2004a: 261). Actualisation as differenciation creates differences and divergences, qualities and extensions which do not presuppose any prior identity in the form of a logical possibility. A logical possibility is something that already exists and later is only realised according to the rules of resemblance and limita-tion, whereas virtual potential creates different and new forms of existence, which correspond to but do not resemble virtual multiplicities. 'The virtual possesses the reality of a task to be performed or a problem to be solved: it is the problem which orientates, conditions and engenders solutions, but these do not resemble the conditions of the problem' (Deleuze 2004a: 264). However, the question is how the virtual Idea is determined to incarnate itself into different qualities and extensities. What determines the differential relations coexisting within the virtual structure to differentiate themselves into different entities? Or, as Levi R. Bryant has pointed out, Deleuze never gives a clear explanation of why the virtual actualises itself at all (Bryant 2011: 104).

Gilbert Simondon: The Pre-Individual and the Process of Individuation

As many commentators have pointed out (Bowden 2012; Sauvagnargues 2009, 2012; Grosz 2012b), the Deleuzian distinction between different modalities of multiplicity could be traced to Simondon's theory of ontogenesis and his distinction between the pre-individual and the process of individuation. The pre-individual is a state of being prior to individuation: it is not a substance or an entity, but *a condi-*

tion of individuation. Simondon takes the hypothesis about the pre-individual from physics, namely, from the thermodynamic notion of metastability. Metastability is a state which is neither stable nor unstable but is charged with potentials for becoming, and which contains enough potential to 'produce a sudden alteration leading to a new equally metastable structure' (Simondon 2013: 317). As one of many examples of metastability, Simondon discusses the duality of a photon, which can be regarded as both a particle and a wave, or as both a physical entity and a certain amount of energy capable of potential change. Thus, metastability can be considered as a reservoir of potential, which conditions transformation and engenders the process of individuation. However, as Simon Mills has argued, 'for Simondon potential does not mean the same as possibility or the virtual but something wholly real that is indicative of the potential energy inherent in metastability' (2016: 36). In other words, the potential designates a physical energy, which has the capacity to undergo a phase shift. For example, under a certain temperature, water can undergo a phase shift and turn into ice or a gas. Thus, as Simondon explains,

> becoming is a dimension of being corresponding to a capacity of being to fall out of phase with itself, that is, to resolve itself by dephasing itself. *Pre-individual being is being in which there is no phase*; the being in which individuation occurs is that in which a resolution appears through the division of being into phases. This division of being into phases is becoming. (2009: 6)

In other words, for Simondon being has two modalities: the pre-individual potential, charged with tension between different 'orders of magnitude', and the reality of change or becoming which is called individuation.

Simondon's favourite example of individuation is that of the crystal: in the metastable state the supersaturated mother liquid is rich in potential, but when it encounters a seed – a piece of dust – it loses its metastability and starts a process of crystallisation:

> A crystal that, from a very small seed, grows and expands in all directions in its supersaturated mother liquid provides the most simple image of the transductive operation: each already constituted molecular layer serves as an organizing basis for the layer currently being formed. . . . The transductive operation is an individuation in progress. (2009: 11)

In other words, the process of crystallisation is a transductive operation, which structures and individuates a certain domain in which it appears. Transduction expresses the tension, the heterogeneity that occurs between a certain condition and its possible solution. It is important to stress that transduction is not a relation which is established between two already existing entities; rather, transduction is a process or a propagation from which something new emerges – it is a change, which simultaneously creates something new. As Simondon points out,

> by transduction we mean an operation – physical, biological, mental, social –

by which an activity propagates itself from one element to the next, within a given domain, and founds the propagation on a structuration of the domain that is realized from place to place. (2009: 11)

In this sense the notion of transduction challenges the classical hylomorphic scheme, which explains any change as an interaction between a passive matter and a transcendent form: 'Instead of the idea that form is imposed on matter from without, the notion of transduction describes the process by which form arises in, as well as the manner by which it is amplified throughout, a domain' (Mills 2016: 38). Simondon argues that physical, biological, mental or social domains are driven by self-forming active forces.

Deleuze, who seemingly read only Simondon's book *L'individu et sa genèse physico-biologique*, published in 1964,[1] wrote a review of it. Here, Deleuze points out that Simondon created a profoundly original theory of individuation that presumes the existence of a metastable system, which entails a disparation of at least two orders of magnitude, and a process of individuation, which solves this tension by undergoing a phase shift. Simondon's theory of individuation helps Deleuze give an answer to the question: what makes differences to differentiate? For Deleuze the answer lies in intensive quantities:

It seems to us that Simondon's perspective can be reconciled with a theory of intensive quantities, since each intensive quantity is a difference in itself. ... Like any metastable system, it is a structure (not yet a synthesis) of the heterogeneous. (2001: 44)

Difference here refers to the heterogeneity appearing between two orders of magnitude, between different potentials, which create a tension or a 'problem'. This tension is resolved by shifting into another system, which is now seen as different from the previous one. In this sense difference refers both to difference in itself and to difference between different phases. As Deleuze points out,

what Simondon elaborates is an entire ontology, one in which Being is never One: as pre-individual, it is a metastable more-than-one, superimposed and simultaneous to itself; as individuated, it is again multiple because it is 'multiphasic', it is a 'phase of becoming' that will lead to new operations. (2001: 49)

In other words, Simondon creates an ontology of life where a living being is defined as potentially multiple in its pre-individual state and also multiple or 'multiphasic' in the process of its individuation.

In *Difference and Repetition* Deleuze makes this point more explicit by pointing out that

intensity is the determinant in the process of actualization. It is intensity which *dramatises*. It is intensity which is immediately expressed in the basic spatio-temporal dynamisms and determines an 'indistinct' differential relation in the Idea to incarnate itself in a distinct quality and a distinguished extensity. (2004a: 306–7)

It is intensity which initiates the spatio-temporal dynamisms, and expresses itself in extensities and qualities. In this respect Deleuze traces his notion of intensive quantities to Simondon's notion of individuation, and the notion of virtual Ideas to Simondon's concept of the pre-individual:

The essential process of intensive quantities is individuation. Intensity is individuating, and intensive quantities are individuating factors. . . . Gilbert Simondon has shown recently that individuation presupposes a prior meta-stable state – in other words, the existence of a 'disparateness' such as at least two orders of magnitude or two scales of heterogeneous reality between which potentials are distributed. . . . In all these respects, we believe that individuation is essentially intensive, and that the pre-individual field is a virtual-ideal field, made up of differential relations. (2004a: 307–8)

However, the pre-individual in Simondon expresses the tensions that are simply given and does not create any structure (for example, the tension between the supersaturated mother liquid and the seed, or between the cell and its environment), whereas for Deleuze the virtual is defined by differential relations within the structure. For example, mathematical differential relations or biological gene relations have significance and function only within a structure. Also we can argue that for Simondon the pre-individual metastability is forced to resolve the tension by necessity, whereas for Deleuze the virtual-ideal field is not driven by any necessity. The virtual may or may not come to actualisation by contingency. For example, a specific gene may or may not be actualised, depending on the specific circumstances of living conditions.

Thus, if different/ciation is not incited by any physical necessity, then, as Bryant pointed out, why does the virtual actualise itself at all? Deleuze has an answer: the virtual incarnates itself in things because of a specific agent, which *differentiates the differential*. The virtual is fully differential in itself (as in the case of mathematical differential relations, or in biological gene relations), before it is dramatised: differential relations are differentiated through intensities, which are nothing other than the difference of difference, or a second degree of difference. Intensities create the correspondences between different kinds of differences and involve them into the process of actual differenciation. As Deleuze points out in his 'Method of Dramatization',

This role is filled by what is called an *obscure precursor*. A lightning bolt flashes between different intensities, but it is preceded by an *obscure precursor*, invisible, imperceptible, which determines in advance the inverted path as in negative relief, because this path is first the agent of communication between series of differences. (2004c: 97)

An obscure precursor incites the dramatisation of spatio-temporal dynamisms, which form the sequences of actualisations, and invent qualities and extensities, species and parts. An obscure precursor also creates the communication between sequences or series and in this sense provides a certain coherence or continuity of individuation.

> If it is true that every system is an intensive field of individuation constructed on a series of heterogeneous or disparate boundaries, then when the series come into communication thanks to the action of the obscure precursor, this communication induces certain phenomena: *coupling* between series, *internal resonance* within the system, and *inevitable movement* in the form of an amplitude that goes beyond the most basic series themselves. (Deleuze 2004c: 97)

These spatio-temporal dynamisms can be imagined as the 'dynamic of the egg', where unspecified matter starts folding and unfolding with the help of cellular migrations, invaginations, stretches, couplings, forced movements. In other words, the world is an egg, where the folding and unfolding of life processes take place, and the drama of life begins and ends.

However, defined in this way – as the differenciator of differences – the obscure precursor looks like a transcendent cause, initiating the process of individuation. As Alberto Toscano points out in *The Theatre of Production* (2006), the notion of the obscure precursor in Deleuze works as a totalising structural principle and in this respect compromises the notion of multiplicity (2006: 173–4). However, we can argue that the obscure precursor functions not as the *principle* of production, as Toscano suggests, but as a set of *conditions* which make individuation happen. As Manuel DeLanda points out, the obscure precursor functions as a quasi-causal operator, which links causes and effects not by necessity but by contingency, which Deleuze names as 'destiny' (2002: 52, 101). The virtual or potential object does not require any *principle* or form to be actualised; it is actualised by a creation of divergent lines, which establish a correspondence between the virtual and the actual. However, it is also important to point out that the process of differenciation is not unilateral and that it can be accompanied by the process of counter-actualisation, as described in *The Logic of Sense* (1969/2004) and *A Thousand Plateaus*. This is what clearly separates the Deleuzian virtual from the Simondonian pre-individual: for Simondon the shift from the pre-individual to the process of individuation is necessary, unilateral and irreversible, whereas for Deleuze the transition from the virtual to the actual can be followed by counter-actualisation, effected by quasi-causal 'destiny'.

Raymond Ruyer: Equipotentiality and Morphogenesis

As many researchers have pointed out (Bogue 2009, 2017; Grosz 2012a, 2017; Roffe 2017), Deleuze acquires a very similar inspiration from Raymond Ruyer's books *Neofinalism* (1952/2016) and *The Genesis of Living Forms* (1958/2020). Deleuze was fascinated by Ruyer's theory of morphogenesis, which explains the development of every living being in terms of a formative melody or theme. According to Ruyer, morphogenetic development proceeds according to a certain melodic theme, which is at the same time 'vertical' and 'horizontal'. A 'vertical' theme is trans-temporal and trans-spatial. It is like a score potentially containing all melody in advance, whereas a 'horizontal' sequence is the actual development of this melody. However, the living being undergoing this actualisation is not simply repeating the pre-existing form, but is performing and creating its own material existence, just as a musical performance is much more than the repetition of scores. For example, an embryo has a certain memory of how to make itself into a fully grown-up organism but in the process of its development it is open to variations, improvisations and adjustments. In other words, Ruyer makes a distinction between the 'vertical' melodic theme and the 'horizontal' temporal sequence which takes place in the process of development.

Ruyer's distinction between the 'vertical' melodic theme and the 'horizontal' temporal sequence resonates with the Deleuzian idea about two types of different/ciation elaborated in *Difference and Repetition*. Ruyer's melodic or mnemic theme resembles a virtual Idea or multiplicity, whereas a morphogenesis or development reminds one of the series of actualisations. As Deleuze points out in *Difference and Repetition*, Ruyer 'profoundly analysed the notions of the virtual and actualisation. His entire biological philosophy rests upon them along with the idea of "the thematic"' (2004a: 279). In this regard we can argue that the Deleuzian notion of different/ciation not only rests on a biological notion of morphogenesis but also introduces it into his ontology of becoming. In this sense, not only does every organism perform its own self-creation and development, but the entire ontological field is explained in terms of creative morphogenesis. As Deleuze points out,

> embryology shows that the division of an egg into parts is secondary in relation to more significant morphogenetic movements: the augmentation of free surfaces, stretching of cellular layers, invagination by folding, regional displacement of groups. A whole kinematics of the egg appears, which implies a dynamic. (2004a: 266)

Following Ruyer, Deleuze describes the entire world as an egg, creating its spatio-temporal dynamisms, and thus inciting the dramas of life.

> When a cellular migration takes place, as Raymond Ruyer shows, it is the requirements of a 'role' in so far as this follows from a structural 'theme' to be actualized which determines the situation, not the other way round. The world is an egg, but the egg itself is a theatre: a staged theatre in which the roles dominate the actors, the spaces dominate the roles and the Ideas dominate the spaces. (2004a: 269)

In this respect Ruyer's notion of biological morphogenesis explains the actual differenciation not only in living beings but in any kind of multiplicity.

It is important to understand that even the 'vertical' melodic theme pre-exists its actual development; it is not a transcendent idea or a pattern but a phenomenon immanent to the processes of development. The melodic theme exists as a virtual multiplicity and can be actualised in many different ways. As Elizabeth Grosz observes,

> the trans-spatial theme pervades all of time, to the extent that it constitutes the melody, the rhythm, through which each thing forms itself. Primary form appropriates themes that have already been laid out for it in advance, not a priori like a command, but more like the musical performance of a score, which preexists and to some extent directs but does not determine each performance. Ruyer understands the mnemic theme as the inherited potential of each form of material organization . . . (2017: 226)

In other words, the trans-spatial theme contains the virtual potential of primary forms, which is actualised and developed according to a disparate series of differenciation. As Grosz points out,

> the theme that each living being performs is its potential (or, in Bergson's terms, its virtuality, in Simondon's its preindividual charge), the form-bestowing heritage it must use to make itself. This is a reserve of dynamism, a direction for growth, the orientation to which each individual body and its immediate self-proximity . . . is directed as it creates itself . . . (2017: 216)

Thus the notion of spatio-temporal dynamism, as discussed above, can be understood as the potential residing in a living being, as a material agent, striving to actualise its self-forming activity.

Another important insight coming from Ruyer is his concept of equipotentiality. The notion of equipotentiality can be discussed in several aspects: first, equipotentiality means that a part can stand for the whole in the same organism. As Ruyer points out, 'there is an ordinary "equipotentiality" in countless adult tissues: we can live with a single lung, a single kidney, and even with a fragment of a lung, which is in this sense equivalent to the whole' (2016: 60–1). At this point the part takes the role of the whole, and continues to play the mnemic theme of development. The second aspect of equipotentiality implies that, in the early stage of organisation, embryonic cells are capable of developing in multiple ways (today we speak about pluripotent stem cells). As Bogue points out,

> early in the embryological studies, researchers found that grafting cells from one sector of an embryo into another . . . did not necessarily disrupt normal morphogenesis. If the graft was made early in development, the cell often simply assumed the function appropriate to its new location in the embryo. If, however, the graft was made later in development, the grafted cell developed as if it were in its old position. This suggested that initially embryonic cells

were 'equipotential', capable of developing in a number of ways ... and that as development proceeds, cells are becoming more specific in their function. (2009: 309)

Ruyer's equipotentiality, which in some respect echoes the Deleuzian notion of virtuality, can be thought of as organic memory, which guides the organism or different species according to a certain melodic theme. However, even if initially the cells are capable of (virtual) equipotentiality, later in the process of development they are deprived of it. As Ruyer points out, 'primitive embryonic equipotentiality thus disappears progressively; it is distributed in more and more limited areas. The theme of organs, by taking shape, ceases to be a theme to become a structure' (2016: 70). The cells have to become more and more specific in order to obtain a defined and organised structure. Nevertheless, a certain degree of equipotentiality still persists in every organism and its parts, especially in the brain which never stops changing.

The third aspect of equipotentiality is related to the early experiments in embryogenesis, which prove that a certain degree of equipotentiality is still prevailing even in cells which were grafted into another organism. For example, German embryologist Hans Spemann transplanted the dorsal lips of the blastopore on to the embryonic cells of tritons, and thus managed to change the host embryo. As Grosz explains,

> Ruyer understands these early experiments in embryogenesis as demonstrating the force of the mnemic theme in directing embryonic development long before there is a subject or even a body to be directed. The transplanted blastopores were still living elements or fragments that invoke a mnemic theme other than that which regulates the host species, bringing into being a chimera that nevertheless obeys the overall form of the host. (2017: 233)

The grafted cells still retain their potentiality and develop according to the specific site where they are grafted on:

> The embryonic host performs its melodic theme: the graft, while now located in the embryonic host, continues to play its own melody, create its own form according to its theme, even as the embryo continues to play its own mnemic theme, with which the graft must now, in its own way and through its own inventiveness, harmonize. (Grosz 2017: 234)

In other words, both the host and the graft have to inter-relate with each other and form a certain chimeric multiplicity.

Even if there is a certain analogy between embryonic and cerebral equipotentiality, there are some important differences. When the organism finishes its development, its form remains irreversible, whereas the brain still retains its capacity to change and reverse its form. However, every living being – from molecules to human brains – follows its internal goal or finality. At this point we can discern a clear distinction between Ruyer's notion of equipotentiality and Deleuze's notion of virtuality. As Bogue points out,

> ultimately, it is Ruyer's finalism that sets him apart from Deleuze and from Deleuze and Guattari. Ruyer's trans-spatial is virtual, but it is never without a purposive developmental theme. A living form is a consciousness-agent working through memory and creativity towards a goal. (2017: 534)

The notion of equipotentiality means that a living being may develop in many different ways, but it still seeks a certain finality, whereas the notion of virtuality does not necessarily seek an actualisation. For Deleuze the virtual may or may not become actual without losing any qualifications of its virtuality. By contrast, Ruyer's notion of equipotentiality always seeks a certain organic actuality and can be seen as a dynamic agent, initiating the spatio-temporal dynamisms in actual multiplicities.

Ruyer's influence on Deleuze and Guattari can be felt in *What Is Philosophy?*, where the notion of multiplicity reappears again and this time is named as a concept. The concept here is to be understood not as a semantic unit or a category but as a virtual multiplicity, which may or may not be actualised in the states of affairs or percepts and affects. Thus the locus of virtual multiplicities is the brain, which refers not only to human subjectivity and consciousness but to any living activity. In this regard Deleuze and Guattari follow Ruyer's idea of primary or organic consciousness which is shared by all living beings and is defined by an immediate contact with itself or self-survey. By introducing the notion of self-survey, Ruyer argues that perception is not a perception of an external object but an intensive sensation that takes place inside the organism. If external perception takes place in a geometrical space and can be divided, measured and so on, the capacity for self-survey takes place in an inner space and is indivisible. It is a unity of forces, a structuring activity. Defined in this way, primary or organic consciousness is characteristic to all living beings: as Ruyer points out, 'there is at bottom only a single mode of consciousness: primary consciousness, form-in-itself of every organism and at one with life' (2016: 98). The primacy of organic consciousness over cerebral consciousness implies that all living beings share the same self-forming activity and take equal part in the process of morphogenesis. As Bogue asserts,

> every form, from atoms to molecules, viruses, bacteria and more complex organisms, is a self-sustaining configuration of forces of connection. Each of these forms, according to Ruyer, is a consciousness. (2009: 304)

Deleuze and Guattari refer to Ruyer when they argue that a concept (a multiplicity) is in a state of self-survey and in immediate contact with all its components. Thus cerebral activity for Deleuze and Guattari is not a property of a subject but a characteristic of any living being: 'it is the brain that thinks and not man – the latter being only a cerebral crystallization' (1994: 210). The brain for Deleuze and Guattari is a self-forming organism, which is capable of creating new connections, new cerebral pathways. In this sense cerebral activity can be thought of as a self-surveying and consistent multiplicity, which creates a continuity between different life forms. As Deleuze and Guattari point out, 'not every organism has a brain, and not all life is organic, but everywhere there are forces that constitute microbrains, or an inorganic life of things' (1994: 212–13). The brain for Deleuze and Guattari expresses the vital activity which characterises and organises both organic and inorganic matter. This activity establishes the continuity of different parts of multiplicity, its self-awareness and the ability to follow its own change and condition; second, it establishes the relationship with other multiplicities. In other words, in *What Is Philosophy?* Deleuze and Guattari define the concept as a qualitative multiplicity, and philosophy as a virtual cerebral activity, which surveys these multiplicities and connects them into a coherent continuum.

The Deleuzian Philosophy of Life

To summarise, the Deleuzian theory of multiplicity is very much indebted to Simondon's distinction between the pre-individual and the process of individuation, and Ruyer's distinction between equipotentiality and actual morphogenesis or development. These insights help Deleuze to formulate his idea of double different/ciation: to conceptualise a living being as potentially or virtually containing multiple differences *in itself*, and also to define the living being in its multi-phased actual development and its capacity to differ *from itself*. The double articulation of different/ciation helps to explain the emergence of qualitative change and the plasticity of every living being. In this context multiplicity can be defined as virtual potential, which may or may not be actualised in different forms of organic and inorganic life, and as actual morphogenesis, which is capable of self-survey and consistency. This capacity for self-survey, self-organisation and self-forming activity is the main feature of multiplicity. It means that any living entity is immanent to itself and does not require any recourse to a global embedding space and time. In this sense Deleuze and Guattari extract from biology those features of multiplicity that were found in discussing Riemann's differential geometry: first, multiplicities have a variable number of dimensions; and second, these dimensions do not require any supplementary dimension which would impose on them extrinsically defined coordinates. As Bryant argues,

> for through enabling us to think the *internal structure* of a space without reference to a *global embedding space*, the concept of multiplicity also enables us to think the being of an individual substance *independent* of its relations to other substances or its exo-relations. . . . As an additional consequence of this concept of multiplicity, the Kantian conception of space and time as *containers* must here be abandoned as well in favour of a model of space and time arising from substances. (2011: 107)

Although this may seem an exaggeration, it wouldn't be incorrect to say that multiplicities have a space and time of their own, which allows them to be defined as autonomous and self-referential entities. Similarly, the biological concept of self-survey helps to define multiplicities of life as an inner space of self-forming activity, which is not divisible and which is defined by qualitative change. In this respect the multiplicity of life is in immediate contact with itself and also in immediate contact with the environment, which is collected into a world continuum.

Note

This project has received funding from the Research Council of Lithuania (LMTLT), agreement No S-MIP-17-32.

1. Simondon's doctoral thesis 'L'Individuation à la lumière des notions de forme et d'information' appeared as two separate works: the first part was published under the title *L'individu et sa genèse physico-biologique* by Presses Universitaires de France in 1964, and the second part was published under the title *L'individuation psychique et collective* by Aubier in 1989. The doctoral thesis was published in its entirety by Jérôme Millon in 2005 (later edition in 2013).

References

Bogue, Ronald (2009), 'Raymond Ruyer', in Graham Jones and Jon Roffe (eds), *Deleuze's Philosophical Lineage*, Edinburgh: Edinburgh University Press, pp. 300–20.

Bogue, Ronald (2017), 'The Force that Is but Does Not Act: Ruyer, Leibniz and Deleuze', *Deleuze Studies*, 11(4): 518–37.

Bowden, Sean (2012), 'Gilles Deleuze, a Reader of Gilbert Simondon', in Arne De Boever, Alex Murray, Jon Roffe and Ashley Woodward (eds), *Gilbert Simondon: Being and Technology*, Edinburgh: Edinburgh University Press, pp. 135–53.

Bryant, Levi R. (2011), *The Democracy of Objects*, Ann Arbor: Open Humanities Press.

DeLanda, Manuel (2002), *Intensive Science and Virtual Philosophy*, New York and London: Continuum.

Deleuze, Gilles (1991), *Bergsonism*, trans. Hugh Tomlinson and Barbara Habberjam, New York: Zone Books.

Deleuze, Gilles (2001), 'Review of Gilbert Simondon's *L'individu et sa genèse physico-biologique*', *Pli: The Warwick Journal of Philosophy*, 12: 43–9.

Deleuze, Gilles (2004a), *Difference and Repetition*, trans. Paul Patton, London and New York: Continuum.

Deleuze, Gilles (2004b), *The Logic of Sense*, ed. Constantin Boundas, trans. Mark Lester and Charles Stivale, London and New York: Continuum.

Deleuze, Gilles (2004c), 'The Method of Dramatization', in *Desert Islands and Other Texts, 1953–1974*, ed. David Lapoujade, trans. Michael Taormina, Los Angeles: Semiotext(e), pp. 94–116.

Deleuze, Gilles and Félix Guattari (1994), *What Is Philosophy?*, trans. Graham Burchell and Hugh Tomlinson, London and New York: Verso.

Deleuze, Gilles and Félix Guattari (2004), *A Thousand Plateaus: Capitalism and Schizophrenia*, trans. Brian Massumi, London and New York: Continuum.

Grosz, Elizabeth (2012a), 'Deleuze, Ruyer and Becoming-Brain: The Music of Life's Temporality', *Parrhesia*, 15: 1–13.

Grosz, Elizabeth (2012b), 'Identity and Individuation: Some Feminist Reflections', in Arne

De Boever, Alex Murray, Jon Roffe and Ashley Woodward (eds), *Gilbert Simondon: Being and Technology*, Edinburgh: Edinburgh University Press, pp. 37–56.

Grosz, Elizabeth (2017), *The Incorporeal: Ontology, Ethics, and the Limits of Materialism*, New York: Columbia University Press.

Mills, Simon (2016), *Gilbert Simondon: Information, Technology and Media*, London and New York: Rowman & Littlefield.

Roffe, Jon (2017), 'Form IV: From Ruyer's Psychobiology to Deleuze and Guattari's Socius', *Deleuze Studies*, 11(4): 580–99.

Ruyer, Raymond (2016), *Neofinalism*, trans. Alyosha Edlebi, Minneapolis and London: University of Minnesota Press.

Ruyer, Raymond (2020), *The Genesis of Living Forms*, trans. Jon Roffe and Nicholas B. de Weydenthal, London and New York: Rowman & Littlefield.

Sauvagnargues, Anne (2009), *Deleuze: l'empirisme transcendantal*, Paris: Presses Universitaires de France.

Sauvagnargues, Anne (2012), 'Simondon, Deleuze, and the Construction of Transcendental Empiricism', *Pli: The Warwick Journal of Philosophy* (Special Volume: Deleuze and Simondon), 1–21.

Simondon, Gilbert (2009), 'The Position of the Problem of Ontogenesis', trans. Gregory Flanders, *Parrhesia*, 1(7): 4–16.

Simondon, Gilbert (2013), *L'Individuation à la lumière des notions de forme et d'information*, Grenoble: Éditions Jérôme Millon.

Toscano, Alberto (2006), *The Theatre of Production: Philosophy and Individuation between Kant and Deleuze*, Basingstoke: Palgrave Macmillan.

3

Modulating Matters:
Simondon, Deleuze and Guattari

Daniela Voss

This chapter will look at simple materials such as clay, wood and metal, and propose that 'handling' them will help distinguish three types of materialism: one that Simondon rejects because it does not take information into account, then Simondon's informational materialism, and finally Deleuze and Guattari's vitalist materialism, which is sketched out in *A Thousand Plateaus*. The aim is to show the subtle differences between Simondon on the one hand and Deleuze and Guattari on the other.

First I will present Simondon's seminal critique of hylomorphism, the view that form determines matter. His examples of brickmaking and woodcutting will help define a concept of matter and improve our understanding of technical operations: not as moulding, the imposition of form on inert matter, but as 'modulation'.

In *A Thousand Plateaus*, Deleuze and Guattari make use of Simondon, especially his critique of hylomorphism, in support of their own construction of a new materialism, which culminates in the notion of the 'machinic phylum'. As Muriel Combes puts it: 'Deleuze and Guattari's *A Thousand Plateaus* draws a great deal more from Simondon's works than it cites from them' (2013: xxi). There are, however, significant differences that this chapter will bring into focus. Where Simondon follows a case-by-case approach, ascribing the artisan an irreducible role as operator within the technical ensemble, Deleuze and Guattari are driven by extrinsic philosophical and political concerns toward a vitalist materialism and the conception of '*Nonorganic Life*' (1988: 411).

Simondon: Implicit Forms, Information and Dynamic Systems

Simondon's doctoral thesis 'Individuation in the Light of the Notions of Form and Information', finalised in 1958, was published in two parts over a period of more than thirty years. In 1964, the first part, titled *Individuation and its Physical-Biological Genesis*, appeared; the second part, *Psychic and Collective Individuation*, was released in 1989. Only in 2005 was a complete edition published; as of now there is no full translation available in English.

In this book Simondon develops a theory of individuation by analysing dynamic material systems, in which individuals (such as bricks, crystals or living beings) come to exist. He seeks to explain individuation through processes of structuration and operations of integration and differentiation. He strongly opposes simply projecting the actual individual form back on to an anterior principle of individuation. Aristotle's model of hylomorphism would be an example: departing from the distinction between form and inert matter, it assumes that form actively determines matter, which remains passive.

The hylomorphic model has proven powerful, reproduced from philosophy (the Kantian distinction between *a priori* forms of intuition and sensible matter) to biology (the idea that the genetic code controls the development of the individual being) and anthropology (the idea that material culture is created through the imposition of human forms upon the environment). Simondon claims that hylomorphism and its modern versions have a 'technological origin' (2013: 39), meaning that a technical operation served as the paradigm example.[1] The forming of a brick might be considered an exemplary case for the hylomorphic relation: on the one hand, there is matter (an undifferentiated mass of clay), on the other hand, there is a form which imposes a geometrical figure on to the clay. However, according to Simondon, this way of thinking is an abstraction that only seems plausible outside the manufacturing site: 'The hylomorphic schema corresponds to the knowledge of a person who remains outside the workshop and only takes into consideration what goes into it and what comes out' (2013: 46). As Simondon argues, the outsider does not see that the malleable clay and the mould are results of previous technical operations, the ends of two technical half-chains then brought together in the brick-forming activity. The individuating operation takes place in 'a zone of medium or intermediary dimension' (2013: 59), between form and matter.

The notion of a technical chain (*'chaîne opératoire'*), or technical sequence, is taken from the French palaeontologist André Leroi-Gourhan, who became known for his structural analyses of prehistoric cave art, his studies of technical development, and his methods of archaeological excavation.[2] His two-volume book *Gesture and Speech* (*Technique and Language*, 1964, and *Memory and Rhythms*, 1965) presents human evolution as a series of successive liberations, the most significant of which were the liberation of the hand from the requirements of locomotion, the skull through the acquisition of erect posture, and the mouth from the prehension of food (1993: 25, 36–60, 117–18). This book has been a landmark in the French intellectual landscape and had an impact on many French philosophers (such as Derrida, Deleuze and Guattari). For Leroi-Gourhan, *chaîne opératoire* is a key theoretical concept that designates the sequence of operations, which produces the technical artefacts of material culture. He particularly looks at the fabrication of prehistoric lithic artefacts, such as the chopper, the biface or the 'Levalloisian point', which were not products of an arbitrary striking of stones but a precise sequence of technical operations (1993: 90–103).

Taking up this notion of the technical chain, Simondon shows, with regard to brickmaking, that the clay and the mould are the result of precisely two operational half-chains: the clay is extracted from swamps or marsh lands and initially contains gravel, fine roots and other plant materials. It must be dried, ground, sieved, immersed in water and kneaded for a long time until it yields a homogeneous, malleable substance. As Simondon says, 'the clay is not only passively malleable, it is an actively plastic [mass] because it is colloidal' (2013: 41) – where 'colloidal' means that tiny inorganic and organic particles or colloids are dispersed within the amorphous clay. According to Simondon, *the prepared clay is already a source of form*; it contains *implicit forms* due to the distribution and arrangement of microparticles and macromolecules. This accounts for the quality of the clay, its consistency and plasticity, and helps prevent the occurrence of air bubbles or cracks in the nascent brick. Moreover, the mould likewise must be prepared. Although essentially solid, its walls have to allow for at least a minimal flex or bending. Furthermore, the mould has to be provided with an inner coating so that the brick can be easily removed. Clay and mould are the results of a series of technical operations and their conjunction in the act of moulding is only one stage in a process that has begun much earlier.

We can see now why Simondon criticises the abstract duality of matter and form. In fact, the material already carries implicit forms and the form itself is material. Instead of imposing a form on matter, there is instead a process of reciprocal exchange or communication between the mould and the implicit forms of the material. The technical operation is not one of moulding, but rather of *modulation*. Taken from information theory, this term is used by Simondon to designate processes of transforming energy into structure. The clay carries a potential energy, a plastic force of deformation, actualised only when it is pressed into the mould. The mould becomes effective not as a whole geometrical form, but point by point through the structure of its walls as a reactive force: it limits and stabilises the expansion of the clay and the pressure exerted by the worker. The mould functions as the topological limit of the energy system.

This complex interaction of potential energy and tensile strength puts the material (the prepared clay) into what Simondon calls 'a state of *internal resonance*', the condition for the process of individuation (the moulding of the brick) taking place. Internal resonance, for Simondon, is the state of an energy system characterised by communication between two different orders of magnitude: in this case, a microphysical order involving the molecular encounters and movements of the clay as well as a macrophysical order concerning the whole dynamic 'system mould-hand-clay' (2013: 42).

Matter, for Simondon, is not passive and inert but already contains implicit forms. These are given by nature and are necessary conditions for the technical process of taking on form. As Simondon says, 'they are information, the power to modulate the different operations in a determined manner' (2013: 55). He emphasises that they are not to be confused with qualities: implicit forms are 'real and exist objectively' (ibid.), whereas qualities are the results of technical operations that select and rest on implicit forms.

It might be objected that the term 'implicit form' is not a fortunate choice, especially if one wants to dismantle hylomorphism. The term information, however, is reserved for the process of coupling different orders in a dynamic material system. So Simondon comes up with another term for these natural properties: he talks about the 'ecceity' of matter (2013: 52), which Deleuze and Guattari in their own work will replace with Duns Scotus's term of 'haecceity', the 'thisness' of a thing, which characterises a certain mode of individuation distinct from the fixed form of an actual thing.

For Simondon, there are three levels on which an ecceity manifests itself. He takes the example of a pine trunk: 'this tree here, this trunk, has an ecceity as a whole and in each of its parts, up to a very small scale' (2013: 52). The first type of ecceity, which affects the whole, can be considered the phenotype of the trunk: the way it is straight or bent, cylindrical or conical, with sections more or less round or flattened. This ecceity determines the selection of the trunk, for instance, when it is chosen for a beam. It requires a 'trained eye' to identify the right tree: 'the carpenter', Simondon says, far from remaining at his workbench, 'went into the forest' (2013: 52) . . .

The second level where ecceity manifests itself pertains to the cells and fibres of the pine trunk that determine the behaviour of the wood when so-called green woodworking techniques, such as cleaving, are used. This is not the case when one uses instead a circular saw or bandsaw. As Simondon states:

> the difference is that the metallic saw cuts the wood *abstractly* according to a geometrical plan, without respecting the gentle undulations of fibres or their torsion in form of a stretched helix: the saw cuts the fibres, whereas the wedge separates them in two half-trunks: the cleaving respects the continuity of fibres, curves around a knot, follows the heart wood, is guided by the implicit forms, which the wedge reveals. (2013: 52–3)

Artisans or artists, using green woodworking techniques, have long known this. They are not only trained in a habitual praxis of technical gestures, they also learn to recognise, 'by means of the signals that go from the tool to the human being, the implicit form of the material, which acts at the specific point where the tool attacks' (Simondon 2013: 53). 'The implicit forms', Simondon says, 'are information in the operation of assuming form: they modulate the gesture and partially direct the tool, which is exercised by the human' (2013: 53, n. 12). The technical ensemble, which brings together the workable matter, the tool and the human as an operator, also comprises a semiotic dimension, that is to say, sensual and affective signs (hardness, softness, smoothness, flawlessness, and so on).

The third way in which material's ecceity has an effect concerns limits it imposes on the technical operation. For instance, the nature of the wood cells determines what the wood *cannot* be used for: it would be impossible to produce a filter with holes of a magnitude smaller than the wood cells, for instance. As Simondon summarises: 'This is not matter as an inert reality but as a bearer of implicit forms, which imposes prior limits to the technical operation' (2013: 54).

By distinguishing these three levels of ecceity, Simondon specifies to what extent matter actively determines selection and technical operation: the implicit forms of matter act as information. He criticises classical materialism because it regards matter as inert reality and 'does not take information into account' (2013:

159, n. 3). However, '*it is necessary to replace the notion of form with that of information*' (2013: 35). The classical notion of form is too independent from the notions of system and metastability.

Simondon elaborates the notion of information in the context of his analysis of crystallisation, and defines it as a coupling of disparate orders of magnitude, the result of which triggers a change, a mutation of the material system. Information introduces a tension, carried by a seed or 'germ', into a metastable system (an oversaturated solution in the case of the crystal) and initiates a process of structuration, called transduction. This process of structuration depends on the relation between '*informational tension in the structural germ and an unformed, metastable domain* harbouring a potential energy' (2013: 550).[3] The notion of information, taken from the analysis of physico-chemical systems, can also be applied in the cases previously discussed (brickmaking and woodworking), inasmuch as we take the whole dynamic system (for instance, material-tool-hand) into account.

A materialism founded on the notions of form and matter runs into problems around not only the question of individuation, but also the question of evolution (see Chabot 2013: 92–3). It has to explain how highly organised living beings evolve from simple inert matter: how can the superior evolve from the inferior? Firstly, this view frequently implies a value judgement, which valorises the more 'advanced stages' while degrading inert matter, and secondly, it conceals an 'implicit spiritualism' (Simondon 2013: 159), which determines life as a mysterious event occurring at a given moment in the passage from less to more complex forms of organisation. Simondon, on the contrary, argues that physical systems are already highly organised, and organisation neither emerges suddenly nor gets lost; rather, what occurs are transformations of organisational structures, variations of individuating processes. Simondon underlines the fact that it can sometimes be difficult to distinguish matter and life, for instance on the level of the macromolecules, such as viruses, that organic chemistry deals with. This does not mean, however, that there is a simple continuum of physical and living systems – he argues that there are indeed discontinuities and leaps in evolution, but these refer to changes in the organisational structure and individuating operations. They do not point to a categorical distinction between inorganic and organic matter. This is why Simondon is careful to investigate the specificity of chronotopological structures and dynamisms of particular individuating systems.

Deleuze and Guattari:
Machinic Phylum and the Idea of Nonorganic Life

In the chapter 'Treatise on Nomadology – The War Machine', Deleuze and Guattari write an entire section on metal and metallurgy. This is where they develop a new conception of materialism, according to which matter 'is not dead, brute, homogeneous matter, but a matter-movement bearing singularities or haecceities, qualities, and even operations' (1988: 512). Like Simondon, they suggest that, for the carpenter, 'it is a question of surrendering to the wood, then following where it leads by connecting operations to a materiality, instead of imposing a form upon a matter' (1988: 408).

The relations between wood-carpenter-forest can adequately be described by the term 'assemblage': Deleuze and Guattari call 'assemblage' (*agencement*), or 'machinic assemblage', the grouping and co-functioning of heterogeneous parts within an open whole. One of the examples they provide in *A Thousand Plateaus* is the 'man-animal-weapon, man-horse-bow assemblage' (1988: 404), invented by the nomads. But they define the concept so broadly (for example as nomadic war machines, metal mining and metallurgy) that it can span entire 'cultures' and 'ages' (1988: 406). Assemblages can combine materials, tools, weapons, operations and humans alike. They cut into the flow of the machinic phylum, select and extract from it material singularities, and perform operations to coagulate traits of expression and affective qualities. As Deleuze and Guattari say, 'we will call an assemblage every constellation of singularities and traits deducted from the flow – selected, organized, stratified – in such a way as to converge (consistency) artificially and naturally; an assemblage, in this sense, is a veritable invention' (1988: 406).

Acknowledging the role of invention, they say that 'it is thus necessary to take into account the selective action of the assemblages upon the phylum' (1988: 407). In this sense, they appear to follow Simondon in some way, who ascribes the artisan an irreducible role: the artisan is the one who follows the flow of matter, who selects singularities and works on them. He is an inventor not in the sense that he creates solely according to an idea but rather in exchange with the material, which reacts to the technical operations, partially guides the technical gesture and imposes limits. The inventor does not have to be an isolated, single person. On the contrary, Simondon is well aware that invention can be the product of a group of people – very often people that never meet, that live at different times and places. They communicate through their technical inventions, which are crystallisations of creative human thought in the materiality of technical objects. For this reason, Simondon sees technical invention as a nodal point of 'transindividuation': 'An inter-human relation that is the model of *transindividuality* is thus created through the intermediary of the technical object' (2017: 253).[4] Hence there is a dimension in Simondon's notion of technical invention that goes beyond the spatio-temporal limits of an actual site of machinic couplings and material production – it crosses cultures and ages. However, Deleuze and Guattari go even further than Simondon with their notion of a machinic assemblage, in particular with the *machinic phylum*, which is a component part of the assemblage.

The machinic phylum names a flow of matter that entails materials of an already highly technicised nature; for instance, silicon, uranium and steel are outcomes of complex technical operations and are inseparable from the assemblages in which they are produced. However, Deleuze and Guattari also include naturally given matter such as grass, water or herds in the machinic phylum (1988: 410) – basically anything that is 'a kind of nomos matter, or better yet a vagabond materiality' (Deleuze 1979). The 'operative and expressive flow is as much artificial as natural' (Deleuze and Guattari 1988: 406). The dualisms between nature and technics, organic and inorganic, living and dead are thus undercut.

Moreover, the term 'phylum' suggests families or lineages of closely related objects. Deleuze and Guattari may have been inspired again by Simondon here. In his complementary doctoral thesis 'On the Mode of Existence of Technical Objects', Simondon introduces the concept of phylogenetic lineages of technical objects, defined on the basis of functionalities and structures, calling into question the familiar classification of genera and species:

> a steam engine, a gasoline engine, a turbine, and an engine powered by springs or weights are all equally engines, but there is a more genuine analogy between a spring engine and a bow or a cross-bow than between the spring engine and a steam engine; the engine of a pendulum clock is analogous to a winch, while an electric clock is analogous to a doorbell or a buzzer. (2017: 25)

In a similar vein, Deleuze and Guattari distinguish technological lineages by focusing on the operations of a certain lineage and the traits of expressions of the materials included therein. For example, the iron sword, which is forged and quenched, is distinct from a steel sabre, which is cast and air-cooled. They are produced through different technical operations – forging and foundry – and belong to different technological lineages: the sword descended from the dagger, the sabre from the knife, as Deleuze and Guattari assert in *A Thousand Plateaus*. The machinic phylum contains an indefinite number of technological lineages but 'at the limit', they claim, there is 'a single machinic phylum, ideally continuous: the flow of matter-movement, the flow of matter in continuous variation, conveying singularities and traits of expression' (1988: 406). The idea of a continuous flow as a 'subterranean thread that passes from one assemblage to another' (1988: 407) goes beyond Simondon's account of materiality and the evolution of technical objects.

Deleuze and Guattari trace the idea of matter-movement, where movement is inserted into matter, back to Leroi-Gourhan, who 'has gone the farthest toward a technological vitalism taking biological evolution in general as the model for technical evolution: a *Universal Tendency* ... traverses technical and interior milieus that refract or differentiate it' (Deleuze and Guattari 1988: 407). Leroi-Gourhan argues against the common 'cerebral thesis' that technics erupted suddenly due to the inexplicable emergence of intelligence:

> We perceive our intelligence as being a single entity and our tools as the noble fruit of our thought, whereas the Australanthropians, by contrast, seem to have possessed their tools in much the same way as an animal has claws. They appear to have acquired them, not through some flash of genius which, one fine day, led them to pick up a sharp-edged pebble and use it as an extension of their fist (an infantile hypothesis well-beloved of many works of popularization), but as if their brains and their bodies had gradually exuded them. (1993: 106)

The early hominids seem to have fabricated their tools not through an act of reflective intelligence, but rather using a technical skill that was part of their biological make-up. Prehistoric tools, such as the chopper or the biface, were as if 'secreted' from their body and brain or, as Leroi-Gourhan also puts it, 'chopper and biface seem to form part of the skeleton, to be literally "incorporated" in the living organism' (1993: 91, 106) – a hypothesis that helps him to explain the constant form of lithic tools over several hundreds of thousands of years. Considering the plant and animal kingdom at large, one can find forms of 'proto-technicity' throughout, where natural organs are prolonged or exteriorised in artificial organs:

> Oviparous animals (birds), for instance, followed an evolutionary path that externalized the ovum through the action of laying eggs, objects that are half-living (the embryo) and half technological objects (the calcium shell). . . . Later, in the vertebrates, feathers, hair, hooves, nails and teeth, the shells of the turtles and the scales of anteaters will continue this vital flux of proto-technicity. (Smith 2019: 259–60)

As Daniel Smith puts it succinctly, 'technicity was tied to biology' (2019: 263). The 'Universal Tendency', of which Deleuze and Guattari speak and that traverses technical and interior milieus, can be understood as this vital flux of evolution that combines natural and artificial organs, the organic and inorganic, nature and technics.

As to the notion of matter-movement, one could also discern a Bergsonian influence, insofar as Bergson explained movement as the mingling of duration with matter.[5] Matter is always matter-movement, matter-flux or matter-energy. The heterogeneous series of memory and matter, duration and space, intensity and extension are joined in a higher kind of monism. As Deleuze states in his book on Bergson, 'matter is never expanded (*détendu*) enough to be pure space, to stop having this minimum of contraction through which it participates in duration, through which it is part of duration' (1991: 88). Matter is always differentiated according to two tendencies, contraction and dilation, and, as Constantin Boundas puts it, 'the dilations and the contractions of duration are, in the last analysis, contractions and dilations of the Spirit' (1996: 96). While Bergson ends up spiritualising the entire world, Deleuze avoids using the concept of spirit. Yet he speaks of the world as a 'living animal', as Boundas points out, and in *Bergsonism* Deleuze declares that 'duration, to be precise, is called life when it appears in this movement' (Deleuze 1991: 94–5).

All these considerations lead up to the 'idea of *Nonorganic Life*' (Deleuze and Guattari 1988: 411), and Deleuze and Guattari claim that this idea was most clearly conceived in 'the intuition of metallurgy' (1988: 411). They take metal as the paradigm case of inorganic life, where Simondon prefers substances like clay and wood. Indeed, Simondon thinks that 'vegetable and animal products are already structured and specialised through vital functions – like skin, bone, bark, soft wood of branches, flexible creepers'; these 'primary materials are traces of a living ecceity, and this is why they present themselves as already structured, suitable for the technical operation, which only has to prepare them' (2013: 56). With this Simondon appears to equivocate with respect to the classical schema,

distinguishing simple matter from highly organised living systems and associat-
ing the latter with ecceity. Deleuze and Guattari caution against this move:

> Every direction leads us, I believe, to stop thinking in terms of matter-form
> [*matière-forme*]. To such an extent, that we have stopped believing in the
> hierarchy that moves from the simple to the complex, substance-life-mind,
> in it in every domain. We even thought that life would be a simplification of
> matter; one might think that vital rhythms do not find their unification in a
> spiritual form, but on the contrary in molecular couplings.' (Deleuze 2007: 159,
> translation modified)

Deleuze and Guattari's suggestion is to define life as molecular couplings and
vital rhythms, 'pure productivity: therefore in mineral form, and not in vegetable
or animal form' (1988: 411–12). By claiming that life is everywhere, the precise
differences that Simondon discerns between physical and living systems in terms
of chronotopological structures, receptivity to and propagation of information,
power of self-conditioning and invention are entirely lost.[6] But let us consider the
question why the machinic phylum is quintessentially metallic or metallurgical.
It is again Simondon that serves as inspiration, with his argument that metallurgy
best highlights the insufficiency of the hylomorphic model:

> Metallurgy cannot entirely be thought by means of the hylomorphic schema,
> because the primary matter, which is seldom in a pure native state, must pass
> through a series of intermediate states before receiving the so-called proper
> form; after it has received a definite contour, it is again submitted to a series
> of transformations that add further qualities (for example through quenching).
> In this case, the assumption of form is not accomplished in a single instance
> in a visible manner, but in several successive operations; one cannot strictly
> distinguish the assumption of form from the qualitative transformation; the
> forging and quenching of steel is respectively anterior or posterior to what can
> be called the proper assumption of form. (2013: 56)

Metal reveals properties of formlessness, continuous variability, an ability to
alloy and to mix. At no point in the treatment of metal are there two ends of
technical half-chains brought together in an operation that may be mistaken
as the conjunction of pure matter and pure form. Instead there is continuous
modulation; the matter, that is to say, its adaptable structure, varies continuously.
Forging a sword requires that the hot metal is hammered into shape; the ham-
mering alternates with heating phases to prepare it to forging temperature; the
object is air-cooled, ground and polished – the sequence of technical operations
takes more than a day. In one of his lectures, Deleuze argues that the fabrication
of metallic objects, tools and arms never definitively comes to an end: 'There's
always the possibility of beginning again. [Though] certainly not infinite, all the
same there are phenomena of wear, of rust, but you can always remake the ingot'
(1979). Metal is not consumable; it is the ultimate deterritorialised material. This

leads Deleuze and Guattari to see in metal the epitome of a 'life' that is present in all matter:

> In short, what metal and metallurgy bring to light is a life proper to matter, a vital state of matter as such, a material vitalism that doubtless exists everywhere but is ordinarily hidden or covered, rendered unrecognizable, dissociated by the hylomorphic model. Metallurgy is the consciousness or thought of the matter-flow, and metal the correlate of this consciousness. As expressed in panmetallism, metal is coextensive to the whole of matter, and the whole of matter to metallurgy. Even the waters, the grasses and varieties of wood, the animals are populated by salts or mineral elements. Not everything is metal, but metal is everywhere. Metal is the conductor of all matter. (1988: 411)

The privilege Deleuze and Guattari ascribe to metal, however, follows from certain philosophical preferences. The coextension of metal with all of matter, in particular its continuous variation, is reminiscent of Deleuze's conceptualisation of virtual multiplicities on the plane of consistency. As Mark Bonta and John Protevi suggest,

> there is a sense of 'matter in movement' that is 'astride' the intensive and virtual: metallurgical operations (that push matter far-from-equilibrium into 'crisis' so that intensive states cross thresholds of self-organization) limn the machinic phylum, revealing matter (now converted into 'material') as a conveyor of (virtual) singularities arrayed in continuous variation. (2004: 117)

The careful distinction in *Difference and Repetition* between virtual Ideas and intensive spatio-temporal dynamisms seems in *A Thousand Plateaus* to collapse into a single movement-matter, with speeds and affects of haecceities, to constitute a unified plane of immanence that is inorganic life. Matter in general is conceived according to these philosophical requirements, and metal then seems most adequate to highlight this overspilling flow, continuous variability and creation that is life.[7]

But there is a second reason why Deleuze and Guattari privilege metal and metallurgy, and this has to do with their political views. As Proposition VIII in the 'Treatise on Nomadology' makes clear: 'Metallurgy in itself constitutes a flow necessarily confluent with nomadism' (1988: 404). The artisan-metallurgist has relations with the nomads. Although he depends for his sustenance on the imperial agricultural stockpile, he is positioned as a counter-figure to the state apparatus, just as the 'holey space' that he inhabits is outside the sedentary, striated space of the state. Deleuze and Guattari go as far as calling the smith the figure of the 'Other' (1988: 413). Like any artisan, he is '*the itinerant, the ambulant*' (1988: 409), who follows the flow.

> Mines are a source of flow, mixture, and escape with few equivalents in history. Even when they are well controlled by an empire that owns them (as in

the Chinese and Roman empires), there is a major movement of clandestine exploitation, and of miners' alliances either with nomad and barbarian incursions or peasant revolts. (Deleuze and Guattari 1988: 412–13)

One may wonder whether this is a kind of romanticism: mines, at least in our times, are owned by the state or major corporations; they are sites of social domination and the exploitation of labour. Perhaps today Deleuze and Guattari wouldn't claim that '*every mine is a line of flight* that is in communication with smooth spaces – there are parallels today in the problems with oil' (1988: 412). This reference to oil drilling remains unexplained; unfortunately, they also don't give any details as to where they see the political potential in the assemblage of the mine, apart from gesturing to clandestine exploitation and the creation of possibly subversive alliances. It is rather the concept of assemblage itself that suggests a limit or 'critical threshold', where it reaches 'escape velocity' (DeLanda 2016: 7). The possibility of lines of flight, that is, the construction of a plane of immanence or consistency that escapes stratification, enacted by molar aggregates (the state, big corporations), is built into the concept of assemblage.

When Simondon discusses coal mines and metallurgy, as he does extensively in his lecture course 'L'Invention et le développement des techniques' (1968–9), he does so in a historical and almost encyclopaedic spirit (see Simondon 2005: 106–29). He presents the development of tools, machinery, installations and transportation routes to and from the site of the mine from the pre-industrial epoch to the industrial revolution. He shows in what way technological inventions respond to specific problems encountered in the artificial milieu of a mine, such as problems of transportation of materials and workers, ventilation and water depletion. Sometimes a particular invention not only solves an initial problem but also creates the conditions for further inventions thanks to its surplus efficiency (what Simondon calls 'superabundant function'; 2008: 171–4). For instance, the separation of the function of the pulley from the motor function of the winch made it possible to clear the shaft opening that connects the galleries to the open air. The winch, activated by humans or horses, could be moved away from the shaft and was given the space to evolve and expand as, for example, in the deployment of a hydraulic motor or steam engine. The clearance of the shaft opening enabled the installation of equipment for a balanced ascending and descending of buckets, and so on (Simondon 2005: 113).

Simondon reveals the mine as a site of technological invention as well as a reticular technical ensemble: it is a network that comprises a multiplicity of interconnected sub-ensembles, radiating around a centre. In metallurgy, the blast furnace is the centrepiece, the central operation that combines thermal and chemical relations, and determines the flow of materials (pressurised air, iron ore, coke, slag, and so on). Annexed to this centrepiece are loading systems, rail lines to facilitate transport, coking plants, electric power plants, even housing for workers. This whole reticular technical ensemble is a complex industrial system, covering several square kilometres or an entire region (Simondon 2005: 115).

Conclusion

From the foregoing we can see that Simondon's presentation of the mine as a technical ensemble differs considerably from Deleuze and Guattari's philosophical-political concept of the mine as machinic assemblage. More importantly, these differences flow from a deeper and more significant difference in the way that Simondon and Deleuze and Guattari understand 'matter' and indeed 'materialism'. Simondon analyses specific technical ensembles and intends to illustrate the logic of technical evolution along the lines of problems and solutions. He describes processes, operations, the flow of materials; he catalogues tools and machinery; he also sheds light on the human link in these chains of operation. To furnish a better understanding, he provides plentiful illustrative drawings, comparable to the famous plates contained in Diderot and d'Alembert's *Encyclopedia*, which Simondon greatly admired.

Deleuze and Guattari's mention of the mine and metallurgy, on the contrary, serves the purpose of identifying a site for the escape of deterritorialising forces. The machinic phylum entails a '*nomos* matter' or 'vagabond materiality', which is continuous variation and pure productivity (and therefore the emblem of inorganic life), and at the same time is able to pass through nomadic assemblages and war machines (the connection between metallurgist and warrior). These characterisations go beyond anything that Simondon imagined, losing in the process many of the nuanced distinctions he brings to bear. There are thus good reasons to distinguish Simondon's 'informational materialism' from Deleuze and Guattari's politicised form of 'vitalist materialism' – and to wonder which is the more promising for contributing to understanding of the assemblages in which we are caught up today.

Notes

1. All translations of quotes from Simondon's book *L'Individuation à la lumière des notions de forme et d'information* are mine.
2. A succinct summary of his work and biographical details can be found in Audouze 2002.
3. Although Simondon is inspired by information theory, he nonetheless modifies the notion of information: information must not be defined as an absolute, measurable and quantifiable given magnitude transferred from a sender to a receiver, as is done in the context of transmission technologies. Information must not be confused with signals or vehicles of information (Simondon 2013: 35). The Simondonian notion of information is broader, since it describes an operation between disparate orders of magnitude that are not yet entirely individuated. Information and individuation must be considered together, since information only operates under condition of individuation, that is, within a system that affects itself in a process of self-conditioning (see Simondon 2013: 318).
4. Simondon tends to idealise the figure of the technician or inventor, calling him a 'pure individual', one that subtracts himself from the community in which he lives, introducing an instability into the established social order by means of technical invention. The

pure individual thereby acts as a mediator between the community and the unknown, the object to be invented and its implicit universal normativity. The notion of the pure individual can be found in a supplementary text to *L'Individuation à la lumière des notions de forme et d'information*, in an essay entitled 'Note complémentaire sur les conséquences de la notion d'individuation': the second chapter deals with the technician, or inventor, as 'pure individual' (see Simondon 2013: 339–55).

5. In fact, Bergson's book *Evolution créatrice* from 1907 had also influenced Leroi-Gourhan's evolutionary view of technology (see Audouze 2002: 286).
6. As to the precise differences that Simondon discerns between physical and living systems, see Voss 2018.
7. In his essay 'Deleuze and Materialism: One or Several Matters?', John Mullarkey comments on *Anti-Oedipus* and Deleuze and Guattari's attempt at overcoming the tired dualism between mechanism and vitalism. He finds that 'the solution given there is not so much a genuine rapprochement, however, as a sidestepping of the entire issue'. Although he rightly identifies 'desire and its role in machinic production' as the new account, inspired by Spinoza and Nietzsche, that is set against this spurious dualism, he argues that 'life and matter are just states of something else, according to Deleuze, but rather than explaining precisely what this third element is, Deleuze often just continues to describe it with language fusing biological and physical terms. The rationale for this alloy of concepts is missing' (Mullarkey 1997: 453).

References

Audouze, Françoise (2002), 'Leroi-Gourhan: A Philosopher of Technique and Evolution', *Journal of Anthropological Research*, 10(4): 277–306.

Bonta, Mark and John Protevi (2004), *Deleuze and Geophilosophy: A Guide and Glossary*, Edinburgh: Edinburgh University Press.

Boundas, Constantin V. (1996), 'Deleuze-Bergson: An Ontology of the Virtual', in Paul Patton (ed.), *Deleuze: A Critical Reader*, Oxford: Blackwell, pp. 81–106.

Chabot, Pascal (2013), *The Philosophy of Simondon: Between Technology and Individuation*, trans. Aliza Krefetz and Graeme Kirkpatrick, London and New York: Bloomsbury.

Combes, Muriel (2013), *Gilbert Simondon and the Philosophy of the Transindividual*, trans. Thomas LaMarre, Cambridge, MA: MIT Press.

DeLanda, Manuel (2016), *Assemblage Theory*, Edinburgh: Edinburgh University Press.

Deleuze, Gilles (1979), 'Cours Vincennes, 27 February 1979', trans. Timothy S. Murphy, <https://www.webdeleuze.com/textes/186> (last accessed 6 March 2020).

Deleuze, Gilles (1991), *Bergsonism*, trans. Hugh Tomlinson and Barbara Habberjam, New York: Zone Books.

Deleuze, Gilles (2007), *Two Regimes of Madness: Texts and Interviews 1975–1995*, trans. Ames Hodges and Mike Taormina, New York: Semiotext(e).

Deleuze, Gilles and Félix Guattari (1988), *A Thousand Plateaus: Capitalism and Schizophrenia*, trans. Brian Massumi, Minneapolis: University of Minnesota Press.

Leroi-Gourhan, André (1993), *Gesture and Speech*, trans. Anna Bostock Berger, Cambridge, MA: MIT Press.

Mullarkey, John (1997), 'Deleuze and Materialism: One or Several Matters?', *The South Atlantic Quarterly*, 96(3): 439–63.

Simondon, Gilbert (2005), 'L'Invention et le développement des techniques (1968–1969)', in Jean-Yves Chateau (ed.), *L'Invention dans les techniques: Cours et conférences*, Paris: Seuil, pp. 76–226.

Simondon, Gilbert (2008), *Imagination et invention (1965–1966)*, Chatou: Les Éditions de la Transparence.

Simondon, Gilbert (2013), *L'Individuation à la lumière des notions de forme et d'information*, Grenoble: Éditions Jérôme Millon.

Simondon, Gilbert (2017), *On the Mode of Existence of Technical Objects*, trans. Cécile Malaspina and John Rogove, Minneapolis: Univocal.

Smith, Daniel W. (2019), 'André Leroi-Gourhan', in Graham Jones and Jon Roffe (eds), *Deleuze's Philosophical Lineage*, Edinburgh: Edinburgh University Press, vol. 2, pp. 255–74.

Voss, Daniela (2018), 'Simondon on the Notion of the Problem: A Genetic Schema of Individuation', *Angelaki*, 23(2): 94–112.

4

Multiplicities, Axiomatics, Politics

Eugene W. Holland

Deleuze and Guattari contributed two conceptual innovations to our understanding of politics: the introduction of the concept of micropolitics and a redefinition of the concept of minority.[1] They share the concept of micropolitics with Michel Foucault, and since it has been much commented on and often mobilised for political analysis, I will not dwell on it here.[2] Their redefinition of the concept of minority merits closer examination, and involves two moves. The first frees both minority and majority from a purely statistical treatment: minority no longer means to be fewer in number than the majority, but is understood as a deviation from, or a variation on, or – at best – a challenge to, the standard embodied in a 'major' group – ' "today's average, urban European"; or as Yann Moulier says, "the national Worker, qualified, male and over thirty-five" ' (Deleuze and Guattari 1983: 469) – even if the 'major' group constitutes a statistical minority (as is usually the case). The second move, in its use of set-theoretical terminology, is more unusual: minorities consist of 'non-denumerable sets', regardless of how large or small they may be. The relationship between these two components of the concept of minority is not spelled out in *A Thousand Plateaus*, but in light of the distinction Deleuze and Guattari insist on between pre-capitalist societies governed by qualitative codes and capitalist society organised by the axiomatisation of quantitative flows, we should note that the constitution of minorities in relation to a major standard depends on codes, and that it is accompanied and increasingly eclipsed by the constitution of minorities as non-denumerable sets, whose political importance is that they are resistant to capitalist axiomatisation.[3] But as Jon Roffe has shown, Deleuze and Guattari's use of terms from axiomatic set theory is deeply problematic.[4] So in order to advance our understanding of the dynamics of axiomatisation that Deleuze and Guattari consider constitutive of the capitalist mode of production and crucial to their understanding of contemporary politics, I will start by briefly addressing their use of axiomatic set theory, and then put axiomatisation into resonance with other terms from *A Thousand Plateaus*, such as nomad vs. royal science, subject of enunciation and subject of statements, the numbering number vs. the numbered number, smooth vs. striated space, and rigid vs. supple segmentarity. The hope is that Deleuze and Guattari's concept of axiomatisation will gain greater consistency and clarity in this expanded context, in line with their practice of concept-construction in philosophy (a topic that lies well beyond the scope of this chapter). I will conclude by examining the four basic flows lying at the heart of the capitalist axiomatic – investment capital, labour-power, production materials and technologies, and human populations – and the implications of their reconceptualisation of minorities for politics.

After Roffe's painstaking examination, there can be no question that Deleuze and Guattari's use of terminology from axiomatic set theory is either simply wrong, seriously muddled, or at the very least extremely misleading – especially in light of their claim that '[their] use of the word "axiomatic" is far from a metaphor' (1983: 455, cited in Roffe 2016: 136). But Roffe also suggests a possible solution, by philosophically distinguishing *intensive* from *extended* multiplicities in a way that set theory in mathematics does not; as Roffe insists,

> there is no room at all for intensive multiplicity in set theory. As a result, one must either proceed without reference to set theory if the notion of intensive multiple is to be retained (the decision Deleuze explicitly makes in his work elsewhere), or dispense with the category of intensive multiplicity. (2016: 146)

Retaining the notion of intensive multiplicity, he goes on to say, would produce 'not a literal mathematical account, but a *philosophical* theory of the capitalist axiomatic . . . [which] would have to rely upon the authority of the concept alone' (Roffe 2016: 149, original emphasis). In fact, as I intend to show, it is only by keeping the distinction between intensive and extended multiplicities in play, and by also including the distinction between intensive and metric quantities, that we can develop a cogent and comprehensive account of the dynamics of axiomatisation and of the market as the recording surface of the capitalist socius.[5]

Such a focus on the dynamics of the capitalist market should not be taken to entail or imply that for Deleuze and Guattari all politics must be anti-capitalist. On the contrary, as we shall see, they explicitly highlight the importance of political struggles that can be said to take place *within* capitalism without challenging capitalism itself – even if at the same time they insist that the revolutionary struggle against capitalism involves a 'deeper movement' (1983: 472). But in both cases, struggles *within* and *against* capitalism take place in a social formation organised principally by axioms rather than by the codes that organised previous social formations, and the fact of this novel form of social organisation has important consequences for politics. Notably, the subordination of codes to axioms means that what we think and believe ('ideology') is much less important than the implications of what we actually do – and especially the implications of what we do as buyers, sellers and investors on the capitalist market. So for Deleuze and Guattari, any and all politics must take as a point of departure an understanding of capitalism as an axiomatic system.

Although Deleuze and Guattari (followed by Roffe) cite Robert Blanché's book on axiomatics in their most detailed discussions of axiomatisation theory,[6] I propose to approach the question via the reference they make to Bertrand Russell's *Principles of Mathematics* (1903), which occurs in the 'Mathematical

Model' section of the 'Smooth and Striated' plateau (1983: 483).[7] At issue is
the difference between non-metric multiplicities such as distance or depth and
metric multiplicities such as length – and more importantly (especially in light
of our interest in the dynamics of axiomatisation) the *conversion* of non-metric
multiplicities into metric or metricised multiplicities. The difference between
distance and length is sometimes subtle, but of the utmost importance. On the
colour spectrum, for example, we can say that red is at a greater distance from
yellow than orange is, but that distance is non-metric: it cannot be measured; it is
not a length. In much the same vein, standing on a narrow ledge 100 metres high
is not twenty times scarier than standing on one five metres high: it may well be
scarier, much scarier, but the difference is not susceptible to linear measurement.
Having distinguished categorically between distance and length, Russell goes on
to specify how the former can be converted into the latter, by the application of
two axioms: the axiom of continuity (also known as Archimedes' axiom) and the
axiom of linearity, which I will refer to as the axioms of *comparability* and *homogeneity*, respectively.[8] The first stipulates that, given two terms, one will be larger
than the other (more precisely, that a finite multiple of one will be larger than
the other, even though the multiple may be unknown); the second stipulates that
a given quantity can be divided into equal (homogeneous) parts. Thus once we
convert our colour terms into wavelengths of light, we could say that (some shade
of) 'red' (with a wavelength of 700 nanometres) is twice as far from 'yellow' (600
nanometres) as 'orange' (650 nanometres) is, or that 'cyan' (500) is exactly as
far from 'blue' (450) as it is from 'green' (550). An intensive difference between
colours has been converted into a metricised difference between wavelengths.
And this difference between intensive and metric is not just a matter of perception, of the distinction between what have been called 'primary' ('objective') and
'secondary' ('subjective') qualities. Temperature, for example, is both intensive
and objective: $10°$ is not twice as hot as $5°$, and the 10-degree difference between
water temperatures of $-5°C$ and $+5°C$ is completely distinct from the 10-degree
difference between $+5°C$ and $+15°C$; solid $\neq$ fluid; $10° \neq 10°$.

Now one of the great strengths of Roffe's work is to propose treating the
market as an intensive multiplicity like temperature, depth and distance. Thus the
difference between paying \$5 and paying \$10 for one pair of shoes is completely
distinct from the difference between paying \$295 and paying \$300 for a different
pair of shoes: $\$5 \neq \$5$. In a similar vein, no one paying \$300 for a pair of shoes
would buy twenty pairs of shoes costing \$15 each: $\$300 \neq \$300$. And yet, on the
recording surface of the market, one pair of \$300 shoes is evidently the same as
twenty pairs of \$15 shoes: $\$300 = \$300$. So from the perspective of an investor,
in sharp contrast with that of the consumer, \$300 might well equal \$300, whether
invested in high-fashion stilettos or cheap sneakers. It begins to look as though
the market surface under capitalism is asymmetrical and has two sides, one facing
consumers, the other facing investors, only one of which answers to the axiom
of homogeneity whereby a dollar always and everywhere equals precisely one
dollar.

This appearance of equality or equal exchange on the market surface is of paramount importance – the market simply could not function without it – and yet it is at the same time extremely misleading. For, appearances notwithstanding, investors are buyers too, in their own way – and over time, given the vagaries of supply and demand, those twenty pairs of $15 sneakers might turn out to be worth more than a single pair of stilettos that has fallen out of fashion (or, conversely, an investor might buy twenty pairs of sneakers at $15/pair, but only be able to sell ten pairs at that price, meaning that the originally purchased pairs actually turned out to be worth only $150). That is to say, if the market presents an intensive surface to consumers for reasons of subjective evaluation, the surface it presents to investors is equally intensive, but for different reasons: because of the factors of time and risk. Economists from Frank Wright, John Maynard Keynes and Hyman Minsky to those highlighted by Roffe, Nassim Taleb and Elie Ayache, have insisted on the inherent unpredictability of investment outcomes and the resulting impossibility of grounding investment decisions on any practisable calculation whatsoever. And yet the point of departure for such decisions – the only possible existing point of departure – is what Roffe calls the 'state of the market' at a given time, a thoroughly if only punctually metricised surface where homogeneous exchange-value reigns and a dollar everywhere equals precisely one dollar.[9]

This account of the market surface under capitalism as *two-sided* and *asymmetrical* introduces into Roffe's abstract market theory a set of social and historical elements that merit further elucidation. There are, I will argue, four features that distinguish capitalist markets from markets in general or in the abstract. The first such feature is production for the market. Indeed, Deleuze and Guattari propose that it is production for the market that makes capitalism an axiomatic system to begin with (1983: 436). Markets, of course, have existed in various forms for millennia, but production for the market is distinctive of capitalism in both its stages or versions: in so-called mercantile capitalism as well as in capitalism properly so-called (that is, 'industrial' and 'post-industrial' capitalism). The asymmetry of the specifically capitalist market reflects the fact that whereas consumers sell in order to buy, investors buy in order to sell: consumers sell their labour-power in order to buy and consume goods; investors buy goods or factors of production in order to sell goods and accumulate surplus-value.[10]

The second feature enables us to further distinguish mercantile capitalism from capitalism proper, and revolves around the distinction Deleuze and Guattari make between the 'surplus-value of code' characteristic of pre-capitalist societies and the 'surplus-value of flow' characteristic of capitalist society.[11] Well before capitalism emerged, money-mediated market exchange involved counter-actualising one actual product, the one being taken *to* market, in order to eventually reactualise its virtual value, incarnated in money, through the purchase of a different actual product, the one that will be taken *from* the market to be consumed. Money as incarnation of virtual value here represents a local and punctual consensus about the value of exchanged products in a given context at a given time. The basic arrangement remains the same even under what is called 'mercantile capitalism', where an investor (the 'middle-man') starts with money rather than a product, and intervenes between the initial production and the final consumption (both of which are independent of the market and of no concern to the merchant) in order to turn a profit by 'buying low and selling high' – that is, by buying already-produced, actual products for price M at location or time 1 and selling them for M + Δ or M' at location or time 2. This mercantile capitalism produces a surplus-value of code, depending as it does on differences in qualitative evaluation between two locations or times, just as direct money-mediated exchange in the first case depends on a consensus evaluation. Crucially, neither of these markets forms a system.

Properly capitalist markets, by contrast, produce a surplus-value of flow, and form a complete system, because of the third distinctive feature of capitalism: the commodification of labour-power and the metricisation (quantitative determination) of exchange-value by abstract labour.[12] Turning labour-power into a commodity strips all kinds of work of their qualitative specificity and differences inasmuch as they are made equivalent to one another. And it makes not the nature or quality of the work but simply the time spent working – abstract, homogeneous labour-time (what Marx called socially necessary labour-time) – the common measure of exchange-value throughout a single system: the world market. It is the metricisation of value by labour-power that makes it possible to speak of 'the' market in the singular: a single recording surface that now spans the entire globe. Of course, 'the' market is in fact composed of a patchwork of sub-markets: the housing market, national and regional markets, the job market, the derivatives market, emerging markets, the sub-prime market, and so forth. But metricisation establishes the axiomatic *comparability* and *homogeneity* of value across any and all of these sub-markets – and enables investment decisions to be made on this basis.[13] The market thus presents capital with a homogeneous intensive surface – a surface that is real but not actual: a kind of 'virtual reality', if you will – across which it will search for investment opportunities calculated – or rather (since actual calculation is impossible): hopefully projected – to turn a profit.

And not only is value universally commutable in a system metricised by labour-time in this way, but capital can therefore circulate throughout it as well, taking on different forms without ever ceasing to be capital: the liquid/virtual wealth of an investment bank balance is different from the constant capital invested in actual means of production, and from the variable capital expended on the purchase of labour-power, and from the capital incarnated in goods waiting to be sold – yet in all these different forms it remains capital: capital = capital. Production no longer takes place prior to and independent of exchange, as in mercantile capitalism, but is planned, organised and undertaken by the capitalists themselves; and for the capitalist market, consumption itself merely serves to reproduce labour-power and return capital to owners for re-investment (also known as the 'realisation' of surplus-value in liquid form through the sale of commodities): it is therefore no longer independent of the system either. The Δ of the surplus-value of flow no longer arises from context-dependent differences of qualitative evaluation, but from the circulation of value throughout the system itself. With the commodification of labour-power, abstract labour-time provides the homogeneous measure that endows the intensive recording surface of the capitalist market with the appearance of a metric multiplicity. It is (arguably) only in the capitalist system, or perhaps more precisely on the capitalist market, that time = money.

The fourth and final distinctive feature of capitalist markets is, of course, capital itself – which as we have seen changes form as it circulates throughout the capitalist system, without ever ceasing to be capital. But that begs the question of where capital comes from in the first place. Deleuze and Guattari provide one kind of answer in their genealogy of modes of production in chapter 3 of *Anti-Oedipus*: the infinite debt owed to the despot in the 'barbaric' mode of production becomes an infinite debt owed to capital in the 'civilised' mode of production (capitalism). But a more concrete, historical account of the transfer of the infinite debt from despot to capital better suits our purpose here, for which the crucial turning point is 1694: the year of the founding of the national Bank of England, on which practically all subsequent national central banks (including the US Federal Reserve) are modelled.[14] Crucially, instead of being transferred to the modern state itself, the infinite debt gets transferred to a central bank, marking the subordination of what had been a transcendent, despotic state to the interests of private capital, and especially finance capital. Instead of creating money itself, the English government licensed a private bank to do so, thereby enabling the state to prosecute wars to a far greater extent than under preceding money-lending arrangements, but also thereby guaranteeing owners of private capital a return on their loans through the appropriation of a significant share of the government's tax revenue. (The recurrent congressional battles over raising the US debt-ceiling is evidence that 1694 marks an important Event that still haunts us.) Henceforth, the subordinate functions of the state will include limiting the amount of so-called 'fictitious' capital that banks are permitted to create out of thin air to a percentage of the 'real' capital already on deposit (referred to as a 'reserve ratio') and, even more importantly, controlling the money supply.[15] To suit the interest of finance capital, money can be neither so plentiful as to preclude banks from charging interest for loaning it out, nor so tight as to choke off the production and consumption undertaken on the underside of the market in order to generate the funds necessary to pay the loans back.[16] The domination of modern capitalist markets by finance capital has at least three significant consequences.

The first and perhaps most important consequence is that the capitalist market surface is not a *tabula rasa* or an even playing-field, as it were: it has a *slope*; it is slanted by the pressure always to accumulate more capital, both to prevail over rival capitalists and, increasingly and more significantly, to pay back with interest the funds borrowed to make investments in the first place, since banks always loan principal only, never the money to pay the interest. (One result is the absolute requirement that the capitalist economy must constantly grow – with the disastrous environmental consequences we are only now becoming fully cognisant of.) Secondly, the investment decisions determining the distribution of finance capital across the market surface are not qualitative or evaluative but purely ordinal or differential: they are not intrinsically concerned with what to produce, or where, or for whom; all that matters is successfully fighting the slope so as to avoid sliding off the market surface altogether. The basic axiomatic imperative is therefore not just 'buy low, sell high' (an axiom of unequal exchange that applies equally to mercantile capitalism), but rather what we might call the axiom of differential accumulation, which is both abstract (indifferent to content, to what is produced/consumed[17]) and purely differential (strictly relative to the returns of other capitalists and the prevailing interest rates): every capitalist must earn more than the average return, or eventually get acquired or go bankrupt.[18]

Finally, what I have called the asymmetry and slope of the capitalist market are a matter not just of structure, but of force: production and consumption are undertaken on the underside of the market principally in order to generate the funds necessary to pay back the loans issued on the top side. Unlike pre-capitalist markets, in other words, *the primary (axiomatic) function of the capitalist market is not the production, exchange or consumption of goods, but the registration of obligations and the generation of means to repay the infinite debt.* Money, as we have seen, has always been a repository of virtual value, but the power of finance capital is not merely money's ability to appropriate (to actualise as mine) an object that was already produced; it is the ability to actualise production itself. What is crucial is not just that humans produce goods in the imagination before producing them in actual reality; it is that, under capitalism, decisions as to if and what to produce, and as to when and how and where, are all made in the virtual realm, on the intensive surface of the market, before a single dollar is actually invested, before the first factory actually gets built and before the first workers actually get hired; only after that do the goods in all their post-hoc determinacy actually get produced for eventual sale and use, in the hope of turning a better-than-average profit on the initial investment. That is to say, the vast and complex network of actual producers, production facilities, transportation networks, retail outlets and consumers comprising the global capitalist economy comes into being as an *extended* multiplicity only after and as a consequence of calculations or projections based on prices inscribed on the recording surface of the market as an *intensive* multiplicity.

Now to express the political force of this asymmetry, using proto-linguistic terms, Deleuze and Guattari distinguish between investment capital as the subject of enunciation and the extended economy as subject of (or, we might say, subject to) statements – that is, subject to the operative investment-statements made by capital.[19] In more recognisably economic terms, adapting the analyses of Bernard Schmitt, they likewise distinguish between two circuits of money: one of investment capital circulating from banks to productive enterprises and back (with interest), the other of remuneration capital circulating from employers to worker-consumers as wages and back (when consumers buy back from capitalists the alienated products they have produced for them).[20] And in terms adapted from anthropology, they distinguish between rigid and supple segmentation: the former referring to the overcoding of money via the double-pincer of abstract labour and state-regulated currency; the latter characterising the domain of goods actually produced, exchanged and consumed.[21] To this last pair of anthropological terms, however, Deleuze and Guattari add a third term (drawn from a completely different discipline): quantum flows. The feature they are borrowing from quantum physics is the undecidability or indeterminacy of the state of some particles (and Schrödinger's cat) before they are observed or measured. The point they are emphasising is that above and beneath both rigid and supple segmentation are flows that escape segmentation altogether.

The addition of this third term presents a more complete diagram of the capitalist market, with supple segmentation serving as a battleground of struggle between rigid segmentarity on one side, and quantum flows that are impossible to capture in their entirety, on the other. In much the same way that the despot issued currency to capture flows of surplus *goods* converted into tribute payments, capital issues credit money in order to capture flows of surplus *value*. But before being denominated as an actual loan to be invested in factors of production, credit money takes the form of a quantum flow of yet-to-be-measured value, of pure creative potential – which Deleuze and Guattari (1983: 492) refer to as 'smooth capital' to distinguish it from the 'striated capital' that gets denominated and invested in the production of surplus-value, based on correlated segmentations of labour-time, wage payments, production output, commodity prices and other factors of production and consumption (scientific knowledges, technologies, fads, taste, etc.):

> Not only does each line have its segments, but the segments of one line correspond to those of another; for example, the wage regime establishes a correspondence between monetary segments, production segments, and consumable-goods segments. (1983: 212)

On the capitalist market, rigid segmentarity appears in the actions of state-sanctioned central banks, which issue and validate currency; supple segmentation characterises the aggregate of exchanges actually transacted via the medium of money; and supple segmentation in turn depends on the quantum flows of desire for enjoyment in abundance, only some of which get captured and converted into commercial transactions. On both sides of the capitalist market, then, intensive quantum flows – of value on the top side, of desire on the underside – fuel the processes of rigid and supple segmentation comprising the capitalist economy.

So, given that capitalism as a complete system consists of '*a general axiomatic of decoded flows*' (Deleuze and Guattari 1983: 453, original emphasis), we know perfectly well what two of those flows are: 'capitalism forms when the flow of unqualified wealth encounters the flow of unqualified labour and conjugates with it' (ibid.).[22] But to say that the capitalist axiomatic forms a complete system does not mean that it is a closed system. On the contrary, as Deleuze and Guattari insist (drawing perhaps on Lautman's account on the dynamics of axiomatic structuralism in mathematics), supplementary axioms get added to and subtracted from the capitalist axiomatic for a host of reasons, as long as they reinforce the fundamental axiom, the continuing conjugation of liquid wealth and commodified labour, on which capitalism principally depends: 'a single axiomatic seems capable of encompassing polymorphic models' (1983: 455).[23] Off-shore outsourcing is one familiar contemporary example of the flexibility of the capitalist axiomatic

– which Deleuze and Guattari illustrate at one point with the example of an international corporation closing an off-shore factory (that is to say, withdrawing a previously instituted axiom) when its profits prove insufficient (1983: 463–4). We arrive, then, at a picture of the worldwide market as providing a smooth space, an intensive pricing surface, for capital to explore in search of decoded flows to axiomatise in order to accumulate surplus-value and pay back the infinite debt.

Historically, one of the main reasons for adding axioms has been legal limitations placed on the length of the working day: to the extraction of *absolute* surplus-value by forcing workers to work more hours than required to pay their wages is added the extraction of *relative* surplus-value by making the hours they are permitted to work more productive. This entails the transformation of work through the introduction of scientific technology. Although not expressed directly in terms of price, scientific technology metricises intensive flows of matter and energy in its own way, thereby making them susceptible to subsequent axiomatisation as quantifiable factors of production on the market where their cost gets priced. Even with pre-scientific, craft production-technologies, work has always involved attending to intensive properties of matter/energy in order to counter-actualise one actual factor of production (a piece of wood, say) by transforming it into an actual finished product (a salad bowl or sculpture). But prior to the development of capitalist production, this 'attending to the intensive properties' of factors of production meant mobilising capacities, skills and know-how developed immanently in context over time and instilled in labourers through apprenticeships. With the advent of capitalism, two crucial changes occur. First of all, labourers are uprooted from their local context and obliged to work on means of production that are provided by capital from on high and for which they have to be trained anew: the labour-power taken out of context has been decoded, and then recoded depending on the specifics of the means of production furnished by capital – specifics which themselves emerge only after the operative investment-statements to invest liquid wealth in this or that productive enterprise have been made. Secondly, the know-how once embodied in workers is extracted from the workplace and developed in the laboratory into the abstract and supposedly context-free knowledge of royal science, ready to be re-introduced as technology into the production process as another factor of production.[24] (It was Sir Francis Bacon who initiated this process in England, sending around agents of the Royal Academy to extract practical know-how from workshops throughout England in order to transform it into state-sanctioned, abstract scientific knowledge.) With conception increasingly segregated from and elevated above execution for these reasons (with intellectual labour elevated above manual labour), one result is that workers get deprived of agency at the workplace (reaching its nadir, perhaps, in the Taylorist assembly-line) – which they will vainly attempt to reclaim as consumers. Another result is that the distribution of state-sanctioned knowledge-segments among the population gets correlated with the distribution of wage-segments, with higher rates of remuneration generally corresponding with access to greater amounts and/or more specialised segments of scientific knowledge.[25]

For our purposes, however, the most important result of the separation of conception from execution was the development of a state form of thought – revolving around what Deleuze and Guattari call the 'numbered number' – that metricises all of matter and energy by translating 'secondary qualities' (such as colour perception) into 'primary qualities' (for example, wavelengths of light) expressed in strictly mathematical terms. Compared to the form of thought characteristic of 'savagery', this state form of thought mobilises precisely the comparability and homogenisation on which capitalist axiomatisation will depend:

> Instead of traits of expression that follow a machinic phylum and wed it in a distribution of singularities [as in savage thought], the State constitutes a form of expression that subjugates the phylum: the phylum or matter is no longer anything more than an equalized, homogenized, compared content, while expression becomes a form of resonance or appropriation. (1983: 444–5)[26]

Compared to the imperial state, the modern (capitalist) state applies the metrics of the numbered number and context-free royal science to all of matter, no longer only to human populations:

> Arithmetic, the number, has always had a decisive role in the State apparatus: this is so even as early as the imperial bureaucracy, with the three conjoined operations of the census, taxation, and election. It is even truer of modern forms of the State. . . . [Here] this arithmetic element of the State found its specific power in the treatment of all kinds of matter: primary matters (raw materials), the secondary matter of wrought objects, or the ultimate matter constituted by the human population. Thus the number has always served to gain mastery over matter, to control its variations and movements. (1983: 389)

The applied branch of royal science thus ends up mapping intensive properties of matter and energy so that knowledge of them can be fed into the production process to make it more efficient and generate more relative surplus-value.[27] So not just flows of matter and energy, but flows of technology itself get commodified and axiomatised as factors in investment decisions made on the market surface, whether a capitalist enterprise hires and pays its own scientists to produce such knowledge, pays licensing fees to use knowledge produced by others, or buys machinery with the knowledge so to speak already built in.[28]

Turning to the last of the four basic flows comprising the capitalist axiomatic, it must be said that Deleuze and Guattari's discussion of human populations in terms of axiomatisation re-introduces a certain amount of terminological confusion in relation to set theory proper.[29] But here again, I believe the core of their analysis is worth retrieving or reconstructing through careful selection of which features of a given mathematical concept are to be retained and which discarded for the purposes of a political philosophy. We have seen, for example, that segments of state-sanctioned productive knowledge get correlated with wage-segments – and this can be construed as the effect of an axiomatic national education system that, in principle, offers equal opportunity to all members of its student population, even if the effects of other axioms often prevent some such opportunities from being realised or even offered. Similarly, segments of consumer taste get correlated with segments of purchasing-power as an effect of axioms conducted by advertising addressed indiscriminately to everyone, even if these axioms tend to emerge and disappear more rapidly than those of the education system. Finally, one key feature of the modern state is the tenet of equality before the law: in principle, everyone has the same standing and receives equal treatment in the legal system – although here again, effects of other axioms often prevent realisation of the principle.[30]

What these examples have in common is the axiom of homogeneity: human populations are manageable through their treatment as what Deleuze and Guattari call 'denumerable sets' – which is quite different from the metricisation of non-human matter through primary qualities. Denumerable sets are important for two reasons. First, it is only as an undifferentiated (decoded) mass of homogeneous 'equals' that humans can be counted and human populations quantified so that they can be axiomatised, since 'the axiomatic manipulates only denumerable sets' (1983: 470).[31] Even more important, denumerable sets will be contrasted with non-denumerable sets – a contrast that lies at the heart of Deleuze and Guattari's politics, and aligns term-for-term with the distinction between major and minor:

> What defines a minority, then, is not the number but the relations internal to the number. A minority can be numerous, or even infinite; so can a majority. What distinguishes them is that in the case of a majority the relation internal to the number constitutes a set that may be finite or infinite, but is always denumerable, whereas the minority is defined as a non-denumerable set, however many elements it may have. (1983: 470)

But it is here that the terminological confusion arises, for as Roffe has shown, non-denumerable sets in set theory proper are such *only* because of their size ('the [uncountable] continuum'), with non-denumerable sets always being larger than denumerable sets (even when both are infinite).[32] For Deleuze and Guattari, however, what defines a non-denumerable set is not size but what we might call a particular mode-of-belonging[33] – which is completely irrelevant to denumerable sets:

> What characterizes the non-denumerable is neither the set nor its elements; rather, it is the *connection*, the 'and' produced between elements, between sets, and which belongs to neither, which eludes them and constitutes a line of flight. The axiomatic manipulates only denumerable sets, even infinite ones, whereas the minorities constitute 'fuzzy,' non-denumerable, nonaxiomizable sets, in short, 'masses,' multiplicities of escape and flux. (1983: 470)

Members of a denumerable set are homogeneous in that they belong to the set by answering to a common rule or axiom; members of Deleuze and Guattari's non-denumerable sets are heterogeneous and belong to them 'existentially', so to speak, without answering to any rules whatsoever. The axiomatisation of human populations thus involves the conversion of non-denumerable into denumerable sets – for as Deleuze and Guattari stipulate, the axiomatic always and only manipulates denumerable sets (1983: 470). But the stipulation comes with a crucial proviso: the conversion can never be complete, but always entails quantum flows that escape; always leaves, or indeed generates, 'multiplicities of escape and flux' (1983: 470).

And so we arrive at the political implications of Deleuze and Guattari's theory of capitalist axiomatisation. Politics henceforth takes two basic forms: the struggle over axioms *within* capitalism, and the battle *against* the capitalist axiomatic itself. The battle against capitalism, to which we return below, depends on the wager that the force of minor, non-denumerable multiplicities will potentially be greater than the power of major, denumerable multiplicities – that is to say that the *connection* of quantum flows producing minor multiplicities will be stronger than the *conjugation* of segmented flows that comprise the capitalist axiomatic. Under propitious circumstances, according to this view, the connection of flows boosts their intensity and produces a result that is greater than the sum of the parts, and can even become revolutionary. The conjugation of flows, by contrast, reduces their potential, 'performs a general reterritorialization, and brings the flows under the dominance of a single flow capable of overcoding them' (1983: 220). As Deleuze and Guattari put it:

At the same time as capitalism is effectuated in the denumerable sets serving as its models, it necessarily constitutes nondenumerable sets that cut across and disrupt those models. It does not effect the 'conjugation' of the deterritorialized and decoded flows without those flows forging farther ahead; without their escaping both the axiomatic that conjugates them and the models that reterritorialize them; without their tending to enter into 'connections' that delineate a new Land; without their constituting a war machine whose aim is neither the war of extermination nor the peace of generalized terror, but revolutionary movement (the connection of flows, the composition of nondenumerable aggregates, the becoming-minoritarian of everybody/everything). (1983: 472–3, original emphasis)

This focus on the minor battle *against* the capitalist axiomatic does not, however, diminish the significance of struggles that take place *within* the axiomatic, over the nature of the axioms themselves.[34] On the contrary, Deleuze and Guattari explicitly recognise the importance of a whole range of political movements not directly tied to anti-capitalist politics, and even go so far as to assert that the 'molecular escapes and movements [of minor politics] would be nothing if they did not return to the molar organizations to reshuffle their segments, their binary distributions of sexes, classes, and parties' (1983: 216–17). To propose minority as a 'universal figure' and the 'becoming-everything of everyone (*devenir tout le monde*)' (1983: 470), they insist, is not to say that the struggle on the level of the axioms is without importance; on the contrary, it is determining (at the most diverse levels: women's struggle for the vote, for abortion, for jobs; the struggle of the regions for autonomy; the struggle of the Third World; the struggle of the oppressed masses and minorities in the East or West . . .) (1983: 470–1)

Notwithstanding the caricature of their politics as involving little more than schizo-revolutionary posturing, Deleuze and Guattari in their later works (*A Thousand Plateaus* and *What Is Philosophy?*) pay serious attention to more conventional political issues such as democracy and human rights.[35]

In both cases, their interest is not in establishing some ideal model of democracy or universal list of human rights by which to judge contemporary societies, but to assess and support tendencies already at work in those societies that might make them more democratic and extend concepts of human rights in new directions. Thus in the 'Geophilosophy' section of *What Is Philosophy?*, they repeatedly insist that 'there is no universal democratic State' (1994: 102, 106) and highlight instead a process of 'becoming-democratic' (1994: 113) that would involve, among other things, the extension of suffrage, the re-alignment of pre-existing public institutions on new goals and the invention of new rights: 'when one turns to the justice system . . . it's not a question of applying "the rights of man" but rather of inventing new forms of jurisprudence' (Deleuze 2011, 'G as in Gauche').[36] As important as the struggle over axioms may be, however, it has several problems. Capitalist axioms can simply be revoked by capital, as the rapid elimination in the United States of the axioms of Fordism at the turn of the century vividly illustrates; state axioms, by contrast, may tie populations to an acquired status that fails to keep pace with new developments in social life. Most important: in both cases, relying on axioms effectively grants to capital and the state organisational control over fundamental, and often increasing, areas of economic and political life. This is one reason why Deleuze and Guattari, in a more revolutionary vein, claim that 'the power of minority . . . finds its figure or universal consciousness in the proletariat' (1983: 472), inasmuch as the proletariat pursues revolution not to save itself from capitalism but to abolish itself as (variable) capital.[37] Ultimately, as important a 'tactic' (ibid.) as struggling over axioms may be, Deleuze and Guattari insist that 'the struggle around axioms is *most* important when it manifests, itself opens, the gap between two types of propositions, [minor] propositions of flow and [major] propositions of axioms' (1983: 471, emphasis added). For it is the former that are able to escape and challenge the capitalist axiomatic.[38]

Rather than defend an acquired status or recognised identity, then, minor politics at its best defies axiomatisation by fostering deviations from the major standard ('Woman: we all have to become that, whether we are male or female. Nonwhite: we all have to become that, whether we are white, yellow, or black' (1983: 470)) and by becoming unrecognisable (becoming-imperceptible) and/or uncountable (non-denumerable). And minor politics becomes revolutionary by 'construct[ing] *revolutionary connections in opposition to the conjugations of the axiomatic*' (1983: 473, original emphasis) with the ultimate aim of 'smashing capitalism . . . [and] redefining socialism' (1983: 472). Although they would be averse to proposing a blueprint for a socialist society, Deleuze and Guattari mention two possibilities for advancing post-capitalist society. The more familiar one we have already alluded to: it occurs when decoded, non-denumerable flows enter into connections with one another on a plane of consistency that produces what Deleuze and Guattari repeatedly call a 'new Land' or 'new Earth' (1983: 472, 509, 510 and passim).[39] The other possibility is mentioned only once, in a passage immediately following their description of the gap between propositions of flow and propositions of axioms (quoted above): 'the power of minorities', they affirm,

> is not measured by their capacity to enter and make themselves felt within the majority system . . . but [by their capacity] to bring to bear the force of the nondenumerable sets, however small they may be, against the denumerable sets . . . even if they imply new axioms or, *beyond that, a new axiomatic.* (1983: 471, emphasis added)

It is one thing to say that 'deterritorialized and decoded flows [forge] farther ahead [and tend] to enter into connections that delineate a new Land' – for this aligns perfectly with '*the opposition between, on the one hand, a plane of consistency and, on the other, the plane of organization and development of capital and the bureaucratic socialist plane*' (1983: 473, original emphasis). It is quite different to suggest that the force of non-denumerable sets might 'imply . . . a new axiomatic'. What would a new, post-capitalist axiomatic look like?

Unlike the savage socius, where as we have seen 'traits of expression . . . *follow* a machinic phylum and wed it in a distribution of singularities', capital 'constitutes a form of expression that *subjugates* the phylum . . . [which] is no longer anything more than an equalized, homogenized, compared content, while expression becomes a form of . . . appropriation' (1983: 444–5, emphasis added). And where the machinic phylum followed by savage expression is composed of flows of matter and energy on the earth, the equalised, homogenised, compared content subjugated by the capitalist form of expression is composed of flows of matter and energy on the extended multiplicity of the global capitalist socius – decoded flows that, when expressed in terms of prices on the intensive recording surface of the market, get axiomatised for the appropriation of surplus-value to pay the infinite debt. A post-capitalist axiomatic would constitute a very different form of expression for the content of the worldwide market: one that would (1) eliminate what I have here called the slope of the market by cancelling the infinite debt and replacing central banking with credit-union-like forms of credit where debts are mobile, transient and horizontal; and (2) replace wage-slavery and the private appropriation of surplus with collective forms of work and self-valorisation – thereby freeing the production and consumption taking place on the underside of the market surface from any standardisation operating in the service of private surplus-accumulation and from the obligation to continually grow to pay back the infinite debt on the top side. This would amount to eliminating what

I have elsewhere called the power component of capitalism in order to retain the economic component: the consistency of the worldwide market – 'the only thing', as Deleuze and Guattari insist in *What Is Philosophy?* (1994: 106), 'that is universal in capitalism'.[40]

The invocation of a post-capitalist axiomatic near the end of *A Thousand Plateaus* provides an important link between the two volumes of *Capitalism and Schizophrenia*, and has a number of important political implications. Probably most important is that eliminating the slope of the capitalist market would reduce the pressure for continual economic growth that is so deleterious to the environment. Moreover, without the pressure of differential accumulation to pay the infinite debt, money in a post-capitalist axiomatic would serve as an instrument of exchange rather than a means of extracting surplus-value. And as an instrument of exchange, money would foster decoding and thereby promote the world-historical development of freedom from codes and overcodes that Deleuze and Guattari in *Anti-Oedipus* referred to as schizophrenia. *A Thousand Plateaus* recasts schizophrenia in terms of (among other things) non-denumerable sets and minor politics, both of which are by-products of the expanded division-differentiation of labour and leisure made possible by the axiom-based extended multiplicity of the world market. Understanding the intensive and extensive multiplicities entailed in axiomatics thus ends up being crucial not only for analysing and overthrowing capitalism, but also for identifying features of the market that are worth retaining and developing in a post-capitalist future.

Notes

1. Although the term 'micropolitics' first appears in Deleuze and Guattari's book on Kafka (1986), the main source for what follows is their major work of political philosophy, *A Thousand Plateaus* (1983).
2. See for example Krause and Rölli 2008 and Holland 2018.
3. In *A Thousand Plateaus*, the concept of minorities as non-denumerable sets supersedes the term 'schizophrenia', which was central to *Anti-Oedipus* (1980).
4. See Roffe 2015, 2016 and 2017.
5. Here and throughout, I use the terms 'intensive' and 'extended' (rather than intensive and extensive) intentionally: they correspond to what Deleuze earlier called 'virtual' and 'actual'. I thus consider the world market as both an extended multiplicity – consisting of actual factories, workers, stores, consumers, etc. arrayed all over the world – and an intensive multiplicity: a virtual recording surface registering commercial transactions and investment decisions.
6. Deleuze and Guattari 1983: 570, n. 54.
7. Russell first treats the measurement of distance in chapter 21, before returning to the topic in chapter 31 (which is the chapter cited by Deleuze and Guattari). In the footnote reference to Russell (1983: 553, n. 15), they warn that 'The following discussion does not conform to Russell's theory', but this (I would argue) is because their notion of 'intensive' is derived from Bergson as much as or more than from Russell, and therefore differs significantly from Russell's. For an analysis of Deleuze's terminology in relation to both Russell and Bergson, see Mader 2017, especially pp. 263–8.

8. Russell addresses what I am here calling the 'conversion' of non-metric to metric quantities in these terms: 'In order to show that all the distances of our kind . . . can have numbers assigned to them, we require two further axioms, the axiom of Archimedes, and what may be called the axiom of linearity' (1903: 260–1).

9. Roffe 2015: 101–2, 128.

10. Marx presents this distinction between consumers and investors in two well-known formulae: C-M-C vs M-C-M′ – presupposing that those we are here calling consumers start with only their labour-power, which they sell as a commodity (C) in order to obtain money (M) with which to purchase consumer goods (C).

11. See Deleuze and Guattari 1980, especially chapter 3. The difference between surplus-value of code and surplus-value of flow corresponds to the difference between societies that are organised by coding and overcoding and capitalist society, which is organised by axioms.

12. There is some controversy about the extent to which abstract labour-time really does metricise the market; Deleuze and Guattari retain the concept of surplus-value, but explain it systemically rather than in terms of abstract labour alone (Deleuze and Guattari 1980: 237). In any case, all that is required for the world market to function is the punctual appearance of homogeneity on the recording surface, so that at the time of an investment decision $1 equals precisely $1 or (on 13 March 2020 at 2.40 pm EDT) precisely 0.90 British Pounds or 74.11 Indian Rupees.

13. ' "Capital" is not simply another name for means of production; it is means of production reduced to a qualitatively homogeneous and quantitatively measurable fund of value'; cited in Deleuze and Guattari 1983: 453, n. 49, from Emmanuel 1972: 13–14, citing from Sweezy 1942: 338.

14. See Di Muzio and Robbins 2016.

15. There are even serious doubts as to the extent to which so-called reserve ratios really serve as effective limits on the creation of credit money, since private banks tend to turn to the central bank to fund their reserves only *after* loans have already been made.

16. Nor can money be so plentiful as to raise inflation to the point at which it would effectively cancel out the value of the interest charged.

17. Axioms, Deleuze and Guattari say, are rules that deal 'directly with purely functional elements and relations whose nature is not specified, and which are immediately realized in highly varied domains simultaneously' (1983: 454).

18. See Nitzan and Bichler 2009 and <http://www.capitalaspower.com/> (last accessed 26 March 2020). Their perspective makes it clear that capitalism enslaves two populations rather than one (although as far as I know they themselves do not say so): not just wage-slaves, but also return-on-investment slaves.

19. 'In effect, capital acts as the point of subjectification that constitutes all human beings as subjects; but some, the "capitalists," are subjects of enunciation that form the private subjectivity of capital, while the others, the "proletarians," are subjects of the statement, subjected to the technical machines in which constant capital is effectuated' (Deleuze and Guattari 1983: 457).

20. See Deleuze and Guattari 1980: 237–8. It appears likely that Deleuze and Guattari's characterisation of capitalist culture as a mix of cynicism and piety corresponds to these two circuits of money and to what we have referred to as the two sides of an asymmetrical market surface. (It also corresponds to the cultural logics of sadism and masochism, respectively, as I argue in a forthcoming book.)

21. See Deleuze and Guattari 1983, plateau 9: '1933: Micropolitics and Segmentarity'.

22. 'Circulation constitutes capital as a subjectivity commensurate with society in its

entirety. But this new social subjectivity can form only to the extent that the decoded flows overspill their conjunctions and attain a level of decoding that the State apparatuses are no longer able to reclaim: on the one hand, the flow of labour must no longer be determined as slavery or serfdom but must become naked and free labour; and on the other hand, wealth must no longer be determined as money dealing, merchant's or landed wealth, but must become pure homogeneous and independent capital. And doubtless, these two becomings at least (for other flows also converge) introduce many contingencies and many different factors on each of the lines. But it is their abstract conjunction in a single stroke that constitutes capitalism, providing a universal subject and an object in general for one another. Capitalism forms when the flow of unqualified wealth encounters the flow of unqualified labour and conjugates with it' (Deleuze and Guattari 1983: 452–3).

23. 'The immanent axiomatic finds in the domains it moves through so many models, termed models of realization. It could similarly be said that capital as right, as a "qualitatively homogeneous and quantitatively commensurable element," is realized in sectors and means of production (or that "unified capital" is realized in "differentiated capital"). However, the different sectors are not alone in serving as models of realization—the States do too. Each of them groups together and combines several sectors, according to its resources, population, wealth, industrial capacity, etc.' (Deleuze and Guattari 1983: 454).

24. 'What is proper to royal science, to its theorematic or axiomatic power, is to isolate all operations from the conditions of intuition, making them true intrinsic concepts, or "categories . . ."' (Deleuze and Guattari 1983: 373).

25. See Protevi 2013: 107–8.

26. For a striking example of the axiomatisation of matter, see William Cronon's account (1991, chapter 3) of the transformation of wheat into an equalised, homogenised, compared content.

27. Compared to craft know-how, which is situated or context-specific, scientific knowledge of intensive properties is axiomatic (or 'universal') – abstract and able to be inserted into widely different contexts of production.

28. 'Knowledge, information, and specialized education are just as much parts of capital ("knowledge capital") as is the most elementary labour of the worker' (Deleuze and Guattari 1980: 234).

29. See Roffe 2016: 145–7 for an analysis of the confusion.

30. Deleuze and Guattari on the axiomatic nature of the modern legal system: 'The law ceases to be the overcoding of customs, as it was in the archaic empire; it is no longer a set of topics, as it was in the evolved States, the autonomous cities, and the feudal systems; it increasingly assumes the direct form and immediate characteristics of an axiomatic, as evidenced in our civil "code"' (1983: 453).

31. The axiomatisation of human populations in denumerable sets could be compared to what Foucault calls biopower and/or governmentality.

32. At one point (1983: 473), Deleuze and Guattari use the expression 'non-denumerable aggregates', which would have prevented the confusion had they always used it, instead of 'non-denumerable sets'.

33. Such a mode-of-belonging is a key feature of their concept of the rhizome (1983, plateau 1). As Roffe says about Deleuze and Guattari's use of set theory, 'the crucial problem is that there is no possible distinction in kind . . . between different ways of belonging, between (for example) connection and conjunction. For set theory, it is strictly size that matters and nothing else' (2016: 146).

34. On the minor battle against capitalism, see Holland 2014; on struggles taking place within the capitalist axiomatic, see Holland 2016.
35. This caricature, developed most fully but in all seriousness by so-called 'acceleration-ists', is very effectively dispelled by Paul Patton (2008).
36. For a remarkable discussion and illustration of becoming-democratic in a North American public university, see Coles 2016.
37. Deleuze and Guattari adopt the thesis of the revolutionary self-abolition of the prole-tariat from Mario Tronti (1983: 571–2, n. 67): 'as long as the working class defines itself by an acquired status, or even by a theoretically conquered State, it appears only as "capital," a part of capital (variable capital), and does not leave the plan(e) of capital. At best, the plan(e) becomes bureaucratic. On the other hand, it is by leaving the plan(e) of capital, and never ceasing to leave it, that a mass becomes increasingly revolutionary and destroys the dominant equilibrium of the denumerable sets' (1983: 472). For a comprehensive treatment of Deleuze and Guattari's debts to Marx, and to Italian Marxism in particular, see Thoburn 2003.
38. As Deleuze and Guattari explain, 'minorities do not receive a better solution of their problem by integration, even with axioms, statutes, autonomies, independences. Their tactics necessarily go that route. But if they are revolutionary, it is because they carry within them a deeper movement that challenges the worldwide axiomatic' (1983: 472).
39. For a suggestive discussion of the commons as a central element of such a new Land or Earth, see Thorsteinsson 2010.
40. On the power and economic components of capitalism, see Holland 1999, especially pp. 59–60; on strategies for eliminating the power component in favour of the eco-nomic component, see Holland 2011, especially chapter 4 and the conclusion.

References

Coles, Romand (2016), *Visionary Pragmatism: Radical and Ecological Democracy in Neoliberal Times*, Durham, NC: Duke University Press.

Cronon, William (1991), *Nature's Metropolis: Chicago and the Great West*, New York: Norton.

Deleuze, Gilles and Félix Guattari (1980), *Anti-Oedipus: Capitalism and Schizophrenia*, trans. Robert Hurley, Mark Seem and Helen R. Lane, Minneapolis: University of Minnesota Press.

Deleuze, Gilles and Félix Guattari (1983), *A Thousand Plateaus: Capitalism and Schizophrenia*, trans. Brian Massumi, Minneapolis: University of Minnesota Press.

Deleuze, Gilles and Félix Guattari (1986), *Kafka: Toward a Minor Literature*, trans. Dana Polan, Minneapolis: University of Minnesota Press.

Deleuze, Gilles and Félix Guattari (1994), *What Is Philosophy?*, trans. Hugh Tomlinson and Graham Burchell, New York: Columbia University Press.

Deleuze, Gilles and Claire Parnet (2011), DVD, *Deleuze from A to Z*, Cambridge, MA: MIT Press.

Di Muzio, Tim and Richard Robbins (2016), *Debt as Power*, Manchester: Manchester University Press.

Emmanuel, Arghiri (1972), *Unequal Exchange*, New York: Monthly Review Press.

Holland, Eugene W. (1999), *Deleuze and Guattari's Anti-Oedipus: Introduction to Schizoanalysis*, New York: Routledge.

Holland, Eugene W. (2011), *Nomad Citizenship: Free-Market Communism and the Slow-Motion General Strike*, Minneapolis: University of Minnesota Press.

Holland, Eugene W. (2014), 'Deleuze and Guattari and Minor Marxism', in Jernej Habjan and Jessica Whyte (eds), *(Mis)Readings of Marx in Continental Philosophy*, New York: Palgrave, pp. 99–110.

Holland, Eugene W. (2016), 'On/Beyond the Anthropocene', *Deleuze Studies*, 10(4): 564–73.

Holland, Eugene W. (2018), 'Micropolitics and Segmentarity', in Henry Somers-Hall, Jeffrey A. Bell and James Williams (eds), *A Thousand Plateaus and Philosophy*, Edinburgh: Edinburgh University Press, pp. 152–71.

Kerslake, Christian (2015), 'Marxism and Money in Deleuze and Guattari's *Capitalism and Schizophrenia*: On the Conflict between the Theories of Suzanne de Brunhoff and Bernard Schmitt', *Parrhesia*, 22: 38–78.

Krause, Ralf and Marc Rölli (2008), 'Micropolitical Associations', in Ian Buchanan and Nicholas Thoburn (eds), *Deleuze and Politics*, Edinburgh: Edinburgh University Press, pp. 240–54.

Mader, Mary Beth (2017), 'Philosophical and Scientific Intensity in the Thought of Gilles Deleuze', *Deleuze Studies*, 11(2): 259–77.

Nitzan, Jonathan and Shimshon Bichler (2009), *Capital as Power: A Study of Order and Creorder*, London: Routledge.

Patton, Paul (2008), 'Becoming-Democratic', in Ian Buchanan and Nicholas Thoburn (eds), *Deleuze and Politics*, Edinburgh: Edinburgh University Press, pp. 178–95.

Protevi, John (2013), *Life, War, Earth: Deleuze and the Sciences*, Minneapolis: University of Minnesota Press.

Roffe, Jon (2015), *Abstract Market Theory*, London: Palgrave Macmillan.

Roffe, Jon (2016), 'Axiomatic Set Theory in the Work of Deleuze and Guattari: A Critique', *Parrhesia*, 23: 129–54.

Roffe, Jon (2017), 'Form IV: From Ruyer's Psychobiology to Deleuze and Guattari's Socius', *Deleuze Studies*, 11(4): 580–99.

Russell, Bertrand (1903), *The Principles of Mathematics*, Cambridge: Cambridge University Press.

Sweezy, Paul (1942), *The Theory of Capitalist Development*, New York: Monthly Review Press.

Thoburn, Nicholas (2003), *Deleuze, Marx and Politics*, London: Routledge.

Thorsteinsson, Vidar (2010), 'The Common as Body Without Organs', in Marcelo Svirksy (ed.), *Deleuze and Political Activism*, Edinburgh: Edinburgh University Press, pp. 46–63.

5

Movement, Precarity, Affect

Mieke Bal

In the current academic climate shamelessly identified as neo-liberal as if the term meant new and free, what is being destroyed is, in addition to other important things, the imagination. And yet, the imagination is what we need most, for it is our primary task, as academics in this world of regulated violence and misery, to think 'out of the box', and deny the legitimacy of the box's existence and presence. Which is why it is so useful to bring together, in this volume, the imagination with the imaginative thoughts of Gilles Deleuze. Few philosophers have been as productive in promoting creative thinking. And few have been so keen on exploring what they had learned from predecessors – which is what philosophy's primary vocation seems to be. Of my personal sources of inspiration, he wrote a book about each: Spinoza, Leibniz, Bergson.

The interest of this volume is not simply how Deleuzian ideas can help us understand art better, and thus be better art critics. One does not 'apply' his ideas. The difficulty of his prose is actually helpful to avoid their instrumentalisation, just as in the case of Jacques Lacan. The relationship is mutual and multiple. Deleuze's thought itself can be considered artistic in that sense; conversely, it argues and demonstrates that art has cognitive and intellectual contributions to make to our work, including on other things than art. His writings would be a great help to feed what Arjun Appadurai has termed 'the research imagination' (1999). The movement and affect as aspects of the imagination in my title are best suited to deal with the middle term, precarity. This is an example of the relation between Deleuze's thought, art and problem-solving.

Here is just one example of many that demonstrates Deleuzian imaginative philosophy – two short quotations from *Cinema 2: The Time-Image* (1989):

The question is no longer
what we see behind an image but rather,
how we can endure
what we see in it already

(to foreground the artistic quality of the thought I read it like poetry), and

If all the movement-images, perceptions, actions and affects
underwent such a change, was this not first of all because
a new element came onto the scene which was to prevent perception
from being extended into action to put it in contact with thought?

I am not a philosopher, nor a Deleuze specialist. My chapter thinks *with* Deleuze,
rather than being *on* Deleuze. And together, we think 'in film'.

I have learned from Deleuzian thought to appreciate relationality between
domains rather than boundaries, and the simultaneity of the multiple rather than
chronology; between categories and temporalities. I call that mobile relationality
fed by affect *inter-ship*, and try to bring it to bear on our work as intellectuals.
And I don't just mean 'interdisciplinarity'. I want to add another 'inter-ship': that
between *analysing* and *making*, as a way of liberating, expanding and deepening
our insights through multiplicity of levels or forms of activities accumulating. In
this context I present some elements from what I call 'thinking in film' in order to
demonstrate the intellectual contribution of creativity.[1]

Filmmaking shares three areas of activity with analysis, but then on multiple
levels: sharp and imaginative looking, which includes framing and visualising,
or 'imaging'; before as well as during the making, in simultaneous processes,
reading and writing; and thirdly, and most creatively productive, collaborating
with others who each bring their own expertise and focus to the process. This
multiple activity of making and/as analysing with several people began in 2002.
With the small, informal collective Cinema Suitcase, we made a number of
experimental documentaries on migration, identity and cultural citizenship, with
varying members of the collective. From this we learned enormously for an
understanding of the contemporary world. Michelle Williams Gamaker and I took
the next step, and examined if and how fiction-making could even increase that
intellectual yield, stacking, or multiplying, levels and modes of engagement with
social reality. It was a staggering experience, on which space forbids me to dwell.
We then proceeded to make installation pieces, with the hope of understanding
more the different combinations of images and affect in visual interaction. This
resulted in a range of exhibitions, one of which, titled *Facing It*, was held in
Dublin in the Broadcast Gallery. This was so well installed and well received that
I am extremely happy that another work of mine was shown in this beautiful and
historically layered city at the occasion of the Deleuze conference.

Concretely, Deleuze on cinema is *thinking* in film, so that our project is literally
unthinkable without Deleuze – for example, his reflections on kinds of images,
and the fundamental ideas of movement, time and affect. To show the clarity of
these three kinds of images, as well as their relatedness, in spite of Deleuze's
difficult writing I quote Paola Marrati, who writes in a very useful short book on
Deleuze and cinema: 'between a perception, troubling in some respects, and a
hesitant action, what surges is affection' (2008: 35).

Thinking in film turns on the partly overlapping, partly distinct concepts of *performance* and performativity, especially the latter – the use of signs, such as words
and images, that *do* what they say. Well-known and widely used as these concepts

are, they are also in danger of dilution. As is the case with Deleuze's three kinds of images, the distinction between the two is important, but so is the impossibility of maintaining a watertight separation between them. For me, this is the point of multiplicity and the simultaneity it entails. It is the 'inter-ship' so characteristic of Deleuzian thought. Performativity can be a tool for challenging and destabilising the social power of habit. This is a primary function of art. The simpler word 'performance' has yielded an artistic genre that brings together an intense engagement with time, space and the performer's body in a live relationship with, an audience. Time slows down or speeds up; space is transformed into the invisible fictional space of the performance; and the body takes on ritualistic properties, which make the person doing the performance invisible in favour of another body we never saw before. Boldly, the artist steps out of her ordinary self and becomes someone else – not in imitation of an existing other person, but rather someone fictitious, of short duration. Yet in doing so, this other draws out time so that everything changes. If successful, a performance emanates 'performativity': the effect of an act on its recipients.[2]

Performativity is also bound up with affect, a Deleuzian term also at risk of over-use. As I have argued elsewhere (2018), the recent installation work *Palimpsesto* by Colombian artist Doris Salcedo makes a brilliant case for the simultaneity of performance and performativity, bound together by affect. This work deploys slow time, humble materials and forms together to entice affect for political awareness. And, to put a fine Deleuzian point to it, I would say that the work deploys multiplicity to denounce another multiplicity; the multiplicity of singularity must not be obliterated by the multiplicity of the mass. A brief description follows.

Movement, of the smallest, subtlest kind, trembles through an immense plaza consisting of large slabs with a grainy surface of extremely fine pebbles, designed to resist the absorption of water. Nearly effaced names are written on them, in a dark hue. These are written in sand. Overwriting these are other names, in the same size and font, in shallow relief engraved in the slabs. Suddenly, a shiny drop of water appears, rolling towards the relief; then more, until the letters of the name are filled, and the water becomes a convex shiny surface, surmounting the flatness of the slabs. After a few minutes, the water letters start to tremble; then they disappear. Appearance and disappearance: the names keep moving. This is their performance. Moving, as physical instability, and performatively, as emotional effect, produces turmoil. The flat ground on which the visitor must walk; the humble material; and the constant unsteadiness: these are the basic tenets of *Palimpsesto* (2017). The water names nearly overwrite the sand names, which, while being put in the shadow of the water names, remain as a palimpsest, a trace of forgotten people; those who, in search of a liveable existence, drowned in the Mediterranean, due to European callous indifference. By naming them, Salcedo makes them singular; by them all having died, she enhances their multiplicity. Together, these aspects prevent multiplicity from melting into an anonymous mass.[3]

For the *Madame B* project, the first consideration has been of the increasing importance of affect in the economic, and of the economic in culture; the bond between visuality, romantic love and capitalism. Israeli sociologist Eva Illouz's concept 'emotional capitalism' has helped us articulate what we had already realised, namely how urgent a reflection on these connections is. We must understand how we all participate in causing the economic crisis – critically resisting while also acknowledging our complicity. This is, for me, the value of integrating performance and performativity to practise 'thinking in film', irrespective, or disrespectful, of chronology. Layering, or multiplying, not only media but also moments in time, rather than the progressivist ideology inherent in chronological thinking, is the ground of thinking in film.[4]

This perspective places *affect* at the centre of attention and focuses analysis on the resulting interactivity of artworks. Instead of taking what is there to be seen on the painted surface, for example, affective analysis will establish a relationship between that spectacle and what it does to the people looking at it, and, precisely, being *affected* by it. This 'doing' is the common ground between affect, its performance and performativity. Again, it is Deleuze who both complicates and elucidates the relevant aspects of affect. I take *affect* in the Deleuzian sense of intensity. Deleuze defines intensity in *Difference and Repetition* as a 'qualitative difference within the sensible' (1994: 182). Importantly, there is a subtle temporal discrepancy involved here, one between perception and understanding. Deleuze adds that intensity can only be grasped, or felt, *after* it has been mediated by the quality it creates (ibid.). This posteriority defines affect and makes it difficult to grasp, impossible to locate, yet crucial for political art. The definition James Williams proposes in chapter 1 of this volume demonstrates that temporal and emotional multiplicity is key to the effectivity of affect: '*manifold changes of emotional intensities distributed among long-lasting conscious and unconscious thoughts, acts and environments named by a dominant tone*' (emphasis in text).

The temporality of intensity also brings affect in touch with another key concept, *narrativity*. This is not a concept Deleuze has elaborated, although it is, of course, relevant for his cinema books. The combination between affect and narrativity is best seen in the opening sequence of our feature film. The images of the opening credits of *Madame B* posit ruin. Emma is balancing on the threshold of a ruined house; her precarity is poignantly visible. This ruin is the present state; what follows gets us back there, in a circular movement that turns out to be, narratively speaking, a vicious circle. Thus, the opening credit sequence foretells the mode of story-telling: based on circularity, repetition and an undermining of the narrative movement forwards, it posits the multiple moments that build up the story *together*. This circularity proposes the power of *habit*. Rather than deploying narrativity for suspense, the idea was to immerse viewers in affect from the beginning. In our film, we have turned Flaubert's famous ambiguity of narration and the implication of witnessing through focalisation into a beginning image that posits the 'pre-posterous' temporality that makes us all peers of Emma – in an intersubjective multiplicity that implies the philosophical point of fiction.[5]

Emma precariously hovers in the ruined house that stands for her ruined life. But then Deleuzian affect and Flaubertian narrativity join forces. After some thirty seconds, when the title *Madame B* shifts into it, the image becomes slightly wobbly, indicating a hand-held camera. That typical cinematic feature signifies the presence of others. These others – in the novel, the inhabitants of the village who gossip about and despise Emma, but also the contemporary viewers – witness, with relish, when the image hints at spying, meddling, but also possibly empathising others. The hand-held camera creates the 'nous', the 'we', of Flaubert's opening sentence: 'We were in study-hall when the headmaster entered, followed by a new boy not yet in school uniform and by the handyman carrying a large desk' ('Nous étions à l'Etude quand le proviseur entra, suivi d'un *nouveau* habillé en bourgeois et d'un garçon de classe qui portait un grand pupitre').[6]

While, narratively speaking, our image of ruin occurs at the end of the fabula, we use it to introduce the 'nous' of witnessing, asking viewers to determine their own attitude. This affect is a condition for what 'thinking in film' can do, because it helps viewers watch with a delicate balance of empathy, hence understanding, and critical distance at the same time. For the emotional content of affect is also multiple, and since this is how ambivalence, complexity and change of opinion are possible, it is important to propose this through artistic form. We aimed to make the destructive power of habit affectively tangible. To make this more directly understandable we displayed in Dublin the installation *Precarity*, and screened the film. The role of narrativity is very different in each work. I hoped this would advance the audience's insights, including affectively.

It is time for some examples. In school, Emma dreams away during classes about reality, but is the best student in the singing class; she takes extra-curricular lessons in art and deportment, for elegance. She is talented enough, but she lacks commitment to the present, the world, and the social reality in which she lives. As a result, she is ostracised by others. She is radically alone. How to explore this cinematically, in a way that makes it, say, philosophically understandable and affectively effective, while staying in touch with the literary masterpiece on which our film is based? Deleuze's concept of *affect image*, so effectively explained by Marrati, is very helpful, not only for analysis but also for actual filmmaking. For this, and to explore what performativity can do for understanding, we staged particular kinds of looks to which social behaviours are bound and judgements frequently attached. This combination ensures the power structure of social life – for which no one in particular is held responsible. We tried to create a visual form of encounter where the kind of look determines both the beginning of a relationship and the inequality that structures it.

In an audio-visual medium, looking is a self-reflexive issue. In the large, nineteen-screen installation we made parallel to this film, we staged these looks on two opposing screens. In order to hamper looking from a distance, the screens are so close as to make the viewing experience slightly uncomfortable, and to make it impossible to see both sides at the same time. Flaubert staged this discomfort within his own medium. It is that discomfort, not the exact literary means he used, that, we felt, had to end up in our film. This is how Deleuze's cinema books are crucially important for a cinematic aesthetic that triggers affective response, neither as political one-liners nor as binary oppositions, but, in the words of

Williams in this volume, as a 'pattern of shadings of emotional intensities, bleed-ing into and across one another'.

It is the task of the humanities to understand, analyse and explain the impor-tance and relevance of art and its thought – from the past as well as the present – for the *contemporary* world. I am interested in movement as an integration of physical and emotional movement, the trajectories of affect and perception. When I try to convince readers of the point of 'making and analysing in one' – for me, an important 'inter-ship' – it is to foreground this double movement. Deleuze is with us, now through his Spinozism, then his *Bergsonism* – another multiplicity. And we need all three braids of thought to get more out of Deleuze's taxonomy of kinds of images, which are distinct and interconnected at the same time.

To reiterate once more: Bergson's book *Matter and Memory* states that percep-tion is not a construction but a *selection*. The perceiving subject makes that selec-tion in view of her own interests, as a form of *gathering in duration*. Perception is an *act*, *of* the body and *for* the body. This selection takes place in the present. Not only the interests of the perceiver motivate it, but also her memories. Charles looks at Emma, Emma at Charles, because, even before seeing each other, they each had an interest – say, to escape boredom. But the viewer, too, has interests. And viewers bring their own memories, different for each, to the combination of recognition and newness that the experience of art is, if, and only if, the art succeeds in its performativity.[7]

When points of convergence occur, a beginning of cultural citizenship emerges. At the end of the book, Bergson writes:

> In concrete perception memory intervenes, and the subjectivity of sensible qualities is due precisely to the fact that our consciousness, which begins by being only memory, prolongs a plurality of moments into each other, contract-ing them into a single intuition. (1991: 219)

That coexistence of a multiplicity of moments the memories embody binds viewers to what they see and thus draws them out of what I once called their 'cultural autism'. That binding, not the value judgement about a work of art, is aesthetic. The story may be fictional; the contact with it is real. Spinoza had already suggested that conclusion. Affect cannot be discarded from this con-fluence of times in the act of perception, because, as Bergson makes clear, the materiality of the body is implicated.[8]

Bergson considers the body to be a material entity, and he consequently sees perception as a material practice. This makes Bergson's conception of the *image* parasynonymous with the *moving image*. As a video artist, I consider this a particularly useful insight that mitigates the commonly assumed and technically meaningful distinction between moving and still images. But there is a deeper level on which images move; it comes closer to affect. The image itself – not its support – is both moving and material. It implies that it is multiple and functional – it *does* something. This is how, as I have argued above, it is performative. That something it does can be individual, but also social; then the image becomes politically effective. Spinoza explains what Deleuze will elaborate. In the words of Australian philosophers Gatens and Lloyd:

> Understanding doesn't happen in isolation. The complex interactions of imagination and affect . . . yield this common space of *intersubjectivity* . . . and the processes of imitation and identification between minds which make the *fabric of social life*.
>
> The awareness of actual bodily modification – *the awareness of things as present* – is fundamental to the affects; and this is what makes the definition of *affect* overlap with that of *imagination*. All this gives special priority to the *present*. (1997: 82–3, paraphrasing Spinoza; emphasis added)

In 1907, Bergson coined the term 'creative evolution' to account for this aspect of movement in the image.[9]

This occurs when the perception image, as Deleuze called it, morphs into an affect image and makes the perceiver develop a *readiness to act*. This readiness – not the potentially resulting actualisation – lies at the heart of the political potential of art and brings Spinoza back to the present. It implies endorsing responsibility as Spinoza saw it (I have edited the passage for brevity):

> 'Spinozistic responsibility,' instead, is derived from the philosopher's concept of self as social, and consists of projecting presently felt responsibilities 'back into a past which itself becomes determinate only from the perspective of what lies in the future of that past – in our present.' Taking seriously the 'temporal dimensions of human consciousness' includes endorsing the 'multiple forming and reforming of identities over time and within the deliverances of memory and imagination at any one time.' (Gatens and Lloyd 1997: 81)

'Affect' helps make connections on behalf of the cultural force of art. Through the old sense of *aesthetics* as binding through the senses, affect connects the aesthetic quality of artworks to forging a contemporary politics of looking. Deleuze understood that we need a concept of perception different from the usual sense of that term, where perception is seen as either a somatic processing of the reality confronting the eye, or an interpretive construction of an image on the basis of visible elements.

That the performativity of an image depends on the look one casts on the other means that the ontology of the visual is fundamentally *dialogic* and *performative* – the performative success of which depends on the endorsement of multiplicity. The two kinds of looks staged in our dual projection on floating screens of the first visual encounter between Emma and Charles are flirtatious (Emma) and voyeuristic (Charles). Both are subject to judgement, of the kind announced by the hand-held images of the opening credit sequence. But the performativity makes such judgements uncomfortable. That is the political effect. Discomfort vitalises and ruptures habit.

In Flaubert's novel, written at a time when nobility was already obsolete, yet still quite present in the socio-cultural multiplicity that, after Deleuze, we cannot ignore, Emma's final moment of illusion that her marriage can make her happy, is the ball at the Vaubyessard Castle. This is a key moment: an experience of almost-belonging, but not quite, and afterwards, definitely not. A contemporary equivalent, it seemed to us, would be a reception given by a commercial power, the association of pharmaceutical companies. This is a fourfold *allusion*, simultaneously invoking a combination of 'pensive' threads: (1) to emotional capitalism; (2) to Homais, the pharmacist; (3) to the idea that today, Emma would be taking anti-depressants; and (4) to our previous work, on madness, where we opposed psychoanalytic treatment to the currently popular and devastating treatment with drugs.[10]

Emma is excited; her first reaction is to ask her husband if she can buy a new dress. She falls into the claws of capitalism. She over-dresses, and the dreamt-of event in the Glamorous World turns into a nightmare. The other guests freeze when they see her – a visual allusion to Maya Deren's avant-garde film *Ritual in Transfigured Time* (1946). They do not admit either Charles or Emma into the small circles of their conversations, and everything Emma does in seeking the limelight is slightly out of place. She has an awkward conversation with an attractive man, then dances with him, and that's it: more loneliness, isolation and shame. This is the image of *not* belonging. Awkwardness is the expression of that denial. The power to deny belonging may well be the strongest affective power of social life. Think of bullying in schools, and, increasingly, bullying by mediocre scholars who take on administrative jobs to hide their lack of academic output and gain bullying power instead.[11]

This scene concerns moods. Moods impact on viewers and make them accept the propelling movement of narrative, but they can also counter that movement, and instead hamper linear progress, make viewers stop, and thus create circles of thought in multiplicity, and maintain a tense, unstable balance between a critical view of Emma and an empathetic one – as precarious as is Emma's situation in the opening credits.

Moments of painful awkwardness occur in consequence of this moment of truth where Emma is confronted with her out-of-placeness. First, facing their ostracism together, the couple soon end up alone, when Emma dances and Charles tries not to look, and then when Emma over-eats to compensate for her frustration. In keeping with our conception of narrative as circular, and also in keeping with Flaubert's deployment of symbolic prediction in the scene of the ball, we hint at the overdosing of powder sugar, and later we have Emma appear as a ghost, unseen by the others, including Charles. I call this '*the politics of allusion*'. The fourfold allusion I mentioned above, in the updating of the Castle to an industry, was one example. The ghost appearance is another. To see these allusions to the ending we must be willing to give up on narrative streamlining and, in conjunction with Deleuzian multiplicity, consider the image as double by definition. Allusions operate not on an 'either/or' structure but on an inclusive model of 'both . . . and' or 'as well as'. To use a Flaubertian word, they imply '*frémissement*' or '*tressaillement*' – a kind of trembling, the nano-movement in multiplicity that, for Flaubert, was a requirement he put to his prose.

Another Deleuzian necessity is *anachronism*. For us, the key was the contemporary critique that speaks 'in film'. We wanted film to help us understand our contemporary society better through understanding Flaubert's novel in relation to *its* time – the one through the other. And with Deleuze and his Bergson: in the durational present tense. For Flaubert, Donizetti's *Lucia di Lammermoor* represented the romanticism he saw all around him. When, in the 1850s, the character Madame Bovary went to the opera, she got distracted from the music by the appearance of a prospective lover. Was it due to *Lucia di Lammermoor*'s romantic lure, or was it something else, which could happen today as well? To make our film contemporary, we chose instead William Kentridge's opera *Refuse the Hour* from 2012. This opera ridicules political issues, especially colonialism, through foregrounding the unification of time. Only when we set the mid nineteenth century in its own time, and ours in our own, can we grasp the significance of Flaubert's prophetic vision. The fundamental issue is that Emma does not manage to be an active cultural citizen of her time. That time is, quite profoundly, NOW.

She is not part of a community of women, nor of any kind of people. Instead of celebrating a City of Women, I must, alas, deplore a fundamental lack of community. And this is what Emma and Léon don't understand. Hence, we espoused Flaubert's interest in misunderstanding while using an opera that was vastly different from his, not only thematically and artistically, but also in its own layering of multiple moments into the present. This is the counter-power of anachronism – a kind of anachronism that is a form of historical thinking, rather than the unreflected projection from the present to which historians are rightly allergic.

There are many films, 'historical costume dramas', based on *Madame Bovary*. In its attempt at historical fidelity, this genre ruins the contemporaneity of the historical artwork, denies that problems persist in the present, even if in a different guise, and hampers the cinematic thought that is at the heart of cinema. Instead of a narrative, a performative film is in the present tense. For example, the long section of the film that alternates Emma's meetings with her lover Rodolphe, dinner time with Charles, interference from the outside world, and her love affair with commerce posed the challenge that faces all translations of, or rather, responses to, literature in film: how to *show routine*, even when it is disguised as exciting novelty? This concerns the Deleuzian question of difference and repetition. This section stages the tension between event and routine in Emma's failing attempts to break the latter, through romance and through acquisition of luxury goods, whether or not she needs any of these. After the seduction, once he 'has' her, Rodolphe soon tires of her constant attempts at closeness and passion; her increasing demands on him. In the routine of the affair and caught in the romantic lure of seeking a logically impossible permanent excitement, Emma slowly understands that the man is not interested in the long-term commitment she seeks.

The men in her life – her husband and her two lovers – are too alike. The mediocrity so frequently assigned to Charles but also to the other two men is one aspect of the link between them. On the other hand, the problem also lies with Emma herself. She is in love with the idea of love, not with any man in particular.

This is why we cast the same actor to play the three men. Yet we made him look different enough in the three roles so that viewers can and do mistake them for different men – and understand Emma from within. Another case of difference and repetition, which becomes repetition in, or in spite of, difference.

The boredom of routine is difficult to audio-visualise. My example here is a sonic image, outside of story time, that becomes the source of the power, even the power to kill, by words and voice alone. This is an 'imaging' of the famous sentence: 'La conversation de Charles était plate comme un trottoir de rue' ('Charles's conversation was flat like a pavement'). This sentence needed including as a narrative expression of a non-event. This implicates another short narrative sentence that resonates with the comparison: 'C'était surtout aux heures des repas qu'elle n'en pouvait plus' ('especially during mealtimes she couldn't stand it anymore'). A narrative summing up follows this sentence: 'toute l'amer-tume de son existence lui semblait servie sur son assiette' ('it seemed to her that the entire bitterness of her existence was served to her on her plate'). Conflating the three short sentences into a rather extensive audio(-visual) image had to do justice to the effective although failed 'dialogic' nature of Charles's monologic conversations.

Instead of Flaubert's concise economy of words, to explore the difference between literary and cinematic narrative, we made an extended sequence, with entirely improvised acting, where Thomas Germaine developed four topics of utter boredom and futility: the weather, the lack of taste of the garden-grown raspberries, a neighbour, and making cherry jam. This is the thematic equivalent of the casting of the three men as one actor: the topics may seem different, but they are mired in the same affect of boredom. It gives a sense of how boredom and the resulting horror are the product of unwitting collaboration. Like the emerging contact out of two socially dubious looks in the scene of the first encounter, the two characters produce the boredom, ending in horror, together. The spectator, seeing and feeling the horror, allows the boredom to become visible. Deleuzian affect is not *in* a person but *between* people, or things and people, as a force of intensity that makes emotion possible, just as abstraction according to Deleuze makes form possible. This is how affect images are literally *engaging*. In the social field where one can be lonely, but is never alone; where we are surrounded by Deleuze's three kinds of movement-image, in duration, with responsibility; and in the present tense of images that bear the memories of the multiple past moments that were once present, and can become so again, in difference-with-repetition; if necessary, with the help of the imagination.

So far, I have primarily discussed the productivity of Deleuze's work, espe-cially his 'thinking multiplicity', for filmmaking, and in particular the way a film can respond to a literary text with a loyalty but not fidelity. I would like to end on an important methodological consequence of Deleuze's multiplicity in the practice of analysis his work enables. In this chapter I have insisted a few times on the need to deploy concepts with precision and nuance. Too often, a concept that gains purchase in academic work becomes vague, sometime even abusively so. I am thinking of the concept of 'trauma', which is not a Deleuzian one;

another is the very Deleuzian one of affect. But Deleuze also resists the desire for monosemic clarity in concepts. Too much clarity tends to be reductive. Too little clarity dilutes concepts into slogans. Here may well lie the motivation or motor of the difficulty of Deleuze's writing.

For Deleuze, concepts are the essence of philosophy; for me, concepts are the indispensable tools for the practice of cultural analysis. This is why, as a non-philosopher, I venture to claim a certain Deleuzianism for that approach in the humanities. This is particularly visible in the concept of multiplicity, which is in itself multiple. Especially what Deleuze calls 'qualitative multiplicity' is helpful to probe, and affectively understand, the complexity of art as the primary object of study in the humanities. Qualitative multiplicities are virtual, subjective and intensive, and as Williams explains, intensity itself is multiple and mobile. Such multiplicities are experienced in the present of lived time, and they differ in kind, such as the critical and the empathetic views of Emma's behaviour. They help grasp the elusive singularity of each society, language, politics or individual, without losing sight of the multiplicity that also defines them.[12]

In a study on the political nature of Deleuze's thought, the eminent Deleuze specialist Paul Patton phrases the inherently political nature of philosophy as follows:

> Philosophical concepts ... fulfil their intrinsically political vocation by counter-effectuating existing states of affairs and referring them back to the virtual realm of becoming. (2000: 139)[13]

The notion of 'counter-effectuating' turns concepts from stable dictionary entries into performative agents. Like images, concepts have the power to act because they make alternative states of affairs thinkable and thus promote their becoming – to invoke that keyword that runs through Deleuze's work and instates the inevitable multiplicity it implies. A concept can be seen as a fluid, 'becoming' point of coincidence, a condensation, an accumulation of its own components. The submerged stones in the brilliant photograph that served as the logo for the Dublin conference, which is part of Radek Przedpełski's 2015 *Chi-Rho [Folio 2001r]/ Away* series (see the front and back cover of this volume), are a visual-imaginary emblem of how I see concepts, linked by the water's ripples. Hence, a concept is both absolute (ontologically) and relative ('pedagogically', in its power to demonstrate possibility). Furthermore, while it is syntactic, according to Deleuze and Guattari, a concept is not discursive, for it does not link up propositions (1994: 22). This is why Przedpełski's photograph is so suitable to perform what concepts are. This may be precisely why concepts maintain the flexibility and multiplicity of meaning that fully fledged theories, discursively elaborated, inevitably lose. To understand, then, what the 'actions' are of which images consist, I invoke the philosophers' statement that concepts are centres of vibrations, each in itself and every one in relation to all the others (1994: 23): they resonate rather than cohere. There is no more adequate description of culture than that.

Notes

1. On intership, see Bal 2017b; on 'thinking in film', see Bal 2019b.

2. On performativity, see Austin 1975 and the early books by Judith Butler (1990, 1993, 1997). There is a lucid explanation in Culler 2007. For a short explanation of performance art, see Appel 2015. For the difference and mutual indispensability between performance and performativity, see the relevant chapter in Bal 2002.

3. For more on the work of Salcedo, see Bal 2010. For an in-depth analysis of *Palimpsesto*, see Huyssen 2018. For more on *Palimpsesto*, see my article on affect, Bal 2019a.

4. Eugenie Brinkema has initiated a resistance against the vague use of the term in her book *The Forms of the Affects* (2014). For a lucid explanation of affect, see Alphen 2008. Alphen and Jirsa 2019 is a collection of essays on the potential of the concept for analysis.

5. Flaubert's ambiguous mode of story-telling has been masterfully analysed by Jonathan Culler (2006). The term 'pre-posterous', which implies Deleuze's posteriority of affect, is the key term of my book (Bal 1999) in which I allege the need to understand contemporary art for an understanding of old-master art, rather than the usual converse chrono-logic.

6. Given the many different editions and translations of this novel, I will not refer to page numbers. On the beginning, a favourite of Flaubert critics, see Raitt 1986 and González 1999.

7. On Bergson's vision of images as it pertains to *Madame B*, see Bal 2017a: 40–1 and throughout. This book accompanied the large exhibition in the Munch Museum in Oslo, where I was invited to integrate Flaubert's and our video work with paintings by Edvard Munch. For extensive documentation, see <http://www.miekebal.org/artworks/exhibitions/emma-edvard-love-in-the-time-of-loneliness/> (last accessed 10 March 2020).

8. The polemical phrase 'cultural autism' came to me in an interview on the occasion of the exhibition of the videos on migration in the Museum of the History of Saint Petersburg in 2011. For information see <http://www.miekebal.org/artworks/exhibitions/towards-the-other/> (last accessed 10 March 2020). It was the most effective way to succinctly explain my call for a look and an interest in what I don't like to call 'otherness'. Needless to say, I don't mean this in the pejorative sense in which people with neurologically diverse particularities have been typecast. On a more open perspective on forms of autism, see Erin Manning's 2016 book *The Minor Gesture*, and various activities by Australian scholar Jill Bennett.

9. For more on the relevance of Spinoza for a contemporary, Bergson-inspired, Deleuzian view of images that includes affect and can be politically effective, see the fictional appearance of Spinoza in my film on Descartes, *Reasonable Doubt*, <http://www.miekebal.org/artworks/films/reasonable-doubt/> (last accessed 10 March 2020). Abel Streefland plays the young Spinoza. Staging the encounter enabled me to imagine a dialogue between the two philosophers, rather than a chronological line of 'influence'.

10. See <http://www.miekebal.org/artworks/films/a-long-history-of-madness/> (last accessed 10 March 2020) for this project, devoted to the theoretical question of whether psychosis can be remedied analytically, instead of through pharmaceutical means.

11. For a varied range of views on Deren's films, see the volume edited by Bill Nichols

(2001). Bullying in our very own 'neo-liberal' universities is so widespread that most readers of this volume will recognise it.
12. My 2002 book is devoted to such conceptual-methodological issues in cultural analysis. For an extremely succinct presentation of it, see a three-minute video at <http://www.miekebal.org/about/> (last accessed 10 March 2020).
13. For a succinct argument about the conceptual nature of metaphors, see Patton 2006.

References

Alphen, Ernst van (2008), 'Affective Operations of Art and Literature', *RES: Journal of Anthropology and Aesthetics*, 53/54: 20–30.

Alphen, Ernst van and Tomáš Jirsa (eds) (2019), *How to Do Things with Affects: Affective Triggers in Aesthetic Forms and Cultural Practices*, Leiden: Brill.

Appadurai, Arjun (1999), 'Globalization and the Research Imagination', *International Social Science Journal*, 160: 229–38.

Appel, Mervi (ed.) (2015), *Helinä Hukkataival: Space between Ritual and Carnival*, Heidelberg: Kehrer Verlag.

Austin, J. L. [1962] (1975), *How to Do Things with Words*, Cambridge, MA: Harvard University Press.

Bal, Mieke (1999), *Quoting Caravaggio: Contemporary Art, Preposterous History*, Chicago: University of Chicago Press.

Bal, Mieke (2002), *Travelling Concepts in the Humanities: A Rough Guide*, Toronto: University of Toronto Press.

Bal, Mieke (2010), *Of What One Cannot Speak: Doris Salcedo's Political Art*, Chicago: University of Chicago Press.

Bal, Mieke (2017a), *Emma and Edvard Looking Sideways: Loneliness and the Cinematic*, Oslo: Munch Museum/Brussels: Mercatorfonds; Yale University Press.

Bal, Mieke (2017b), 'Intership: Anachronism between Loyalty and the Case', in Thomas Leitch (ed.), *The Oxford Handbook of Adaptation Studies*, New York and Oxford: Oxford University Press, pp. 179–96.

Bal, Mieke (2018), 'Y-cidad: los múltiples sentidos de "y"', *Versants*, 65(3), fascículo español, 187–207.

Bal, Mieke (2019a), 'Affectively Effective: Affect as an Artistic-Political Strategy', in Ernst van Alphen and Tomáš Jirsa (eds), *How to Do Things with Affects: Affective Triggers in Aesthetic Forms and Cultural Practices*, Leiden: Brill, pp. 179–99.

Bal, Mieke (2019b), 'Thinking in Film', in Jill Bennett (ed.), *Thinking in the World*, London: Bloomsbury, pp. 239–80.

Bergson, Henri [1907] (1983), *Creative Evolution*, trans. Arthur Mitchell, Lanham: University Press of America.

Bergson, Henri [1896] (1991), *Matter and Memory*, trans. Nancy Margaret Paul and W. Scott Palmer, New York: Zone Books.

Brinkema, Eugenie (2014), *The Forms of the Affects*, Durham, NC: Duke University Press.

Butler, Judith (1990), *Gender Trouble: Feminism and the Subversion of Identity*, New York: Routledge.

Butler, Judith (1993), *Bodies that Matter: On the Discursive Limits of 'Sex'*, New York: Routledge.

Butler, Judith (1997), *Excitable Speech: A Politics of the Performative*, New York: Routledge.

Culler, Jonathan [1974] (2006), *Flaubert: The Uses of Uncertainty*, Aurora, CO: Davies Group.

Culler, Jonathan (2007), 'The Performative', in *The Literary in Theory*, Stanford: Stanford University Press, pp. 137–65.

Deleuze, Gilles (1989), *Cinema 2: The Time-Image*, trans. Hugh Tomlinson and Robert Galeta, London: Athlone Press.

Deleuze, Gilles (1994), *Difference and Repetition*, trans. Paul Patton, London: Athlone Press.

Deleuze, Gilles and Félix Guattari (1987), *A Thousand Plateaus: Capitalism and Schizophrenia*, trans. Brian Massumi, London: Athlone Press.

Deleuze, Gilles and Félix Guattari (1994), *What Is Philosophy?*, trans. Hugh Tomlinson and Graham Burchill, London: Verso.

Gatens, Moira and Genevieve Lloyd (1997), *Collective Imaginings: Spinoza, Past and Present*, London and New York: Routledge.

González, Francisco (1999), *La scène originaire de Madame Bovary*, Oviedo: Universidad de Oviedo.

Huyssen, Andreas (2018), 'A Palimpsest of Grief: Writing in Water and Light', in Honey Luard (ed.) *Doris Salcedo* (exhibition catalogue), London: The White Cube, pp. 4–11.

Illouz, Eva (2007), *Cold Intimacies: The Making of Emotional Capitalism*, Cambridge: Polity Press.

Manning, Erin (2016), *The Minor Gesture*, Durham, NC: Duke University Press.

Marrati, Paola (2008), *Gilles Deleuze: Cinema and Philosophy*, trans. Alisa Hartz, Baltimore: Johns Hopkins University Press.

Nichols, Bill (ed.) (2001), *Maya Deren and the American Avant-Garde*, Berkeley: University of California Press.

Patton, Paul (2000), *Deleuze and the Political*, New York: Routledge.

Patton, Paul (2006), 'Mobile Concepts, Metaphor, and the Problem of Referentiality in Deleuze and Guattari', in Maria Margaroni and Effie Yiannopoulou (eds), *Metaphoricity and the Politics of Mobility*, Amsterdam and New York: Rodopi, pp. 27–46.

Raitt, Alain (1986), 'Nous étions à l'étude . . .', in Bernard Masson (ed.), *'G. Flaubert (2): Mythes et religions (1)'*, Paris: Lettres Modernes, pp. 161–92.

Part II

Multiplicities across Different Artistic Media

6

The Magnetic Medium:
David Wojnarowicz and Tape Machines

Gary Genosko

Take a walk along any river in any country and you can see that the machine is almost defunct; God is rusting away leaving a fragile shell . . .
(Wojnarowicz in Guattari 1990a: 76)

Introduction

Félix Guattari wrote short catalogue essays on a number of artists, including painter-poet-sculptor Jean-Jacques Lebel, painter George Condo, and painters Toshimitsu Imai and Yayoi Kusama, as well as longer essays on individual artists such as Balthus. He went beyond visual art to write substantive essays on the architecture of Shin Takamatsu, and the performances of Stanisław Witkiewicz. His short reflection on David Wojnarowicz, however, belongs to the more casual, short form he sometimes adopted in response to requests to comment on work with which he was not already familiar. When writing about Lebel, for instance, Guattari's tone is familiar and laudatory, in keeping with their long personal association; in the case of Condo, he is responding to a packaged press release, and plays the role of interpreting the critical panic unleashed by Condo's unclassifiable style and the buffoonery of his paintings, with their numerous references to canonical works. Guattari enlists one or two concepts with which to rethink the challenges posed by the works in question, referring to Lebel as a painter of transversality since he crosses so many practices in engaging multiple materials of expression. In both cases Guattari is focusing on the roles of creativity and differentiation in the actualisation of virtual impulses, and the mutational role played by new technologies (video and photography) (Guattari 1988a), and how he reflexively refused an easy recourse to the postmodern label. In his Condo essay Guattari introduced the polyphony of stylistic periods, rather than attempting a period breakdown of creative process, and without reducing the citational extravagance to a postmodern 'plastering of quotations' (1990b: 12).

Guattari paid close attention to what he called the personal methods of the artists he admired, and Wojnarowicz's tape recordings and notebooks filled with dreams fascinated him; Guattari was also a collector of dreams, those from Kafka's letters and notebooks. The social-poetic-personal are intertwined in Wojnarowicz's production of paintings-writings, and these consist partially of exhortations to social action, but are not reducible to an exclusive focus on political action during the AIDS crisis, nor to the downtown New York art scene (sometimes known as the East Village scene) of the late 1970s and early 1980s. Guattari did not want to trap Wojnarowicz in single categories such as AIDS activist or queer artist, but he did respect him for his courage and public engagements. Guattari's modest catalogue essay, invited by his friend and collaborator Marion Scemama, is important for scholars because it reflects a new reality in Guattari's writings and interviews about homosexuality as the 1980s came to a close. Much of what Guattari wrote about the links between desire and sexuality, semiotic-sexual ruptures and the subversive overflowing of homosexual desire[1] dates from the 1970s, which cannot be mythologised simply as a pre-AIDS era.[2] Guattari's sense of concern about the pandemic not only grew through the 1980s, but by the year of his death in 1992, his public statements increased alarmingly to suggest an equivalence between finding a cure for AIDS and the future of humankind: 'Biological sciences and medical technology will win the battle with this illness or, in the end, the human species will be eliminated' (1996: 268). Readers of Guattari know that he considered the 1980s to be a period of greyness and political reaction, and he saw in the formidable mutations of subjectivation brought about by pandemics, computerisation, global ecological events and capitalism's breaking of the Berlin Wall, challenges to be addressed through a renewal of democracy, ethics and collective intelligence. Indeed, he participated in discussions in the pages of *Gai Pied Hebdo*, whose role in promoting AIDS/HIV awareness was important before the magazine's demise in 1992, and spoke of the importance of recognising a multiplicity of subjectivities within what is called a self, that is, of finite embodied experience in a fragile existential territory, one of Guattari's four functors (Territories, Universes, Fluxes, Phyla) referenced to Universes of value from a given culture and time.

Elsewhere, in my essay 'In this Sleep: A Dream Pragmatics for David Wojnarowicz' (Genosko 2018), an expanded version of a French translation that appeared in Deleuze and Guattari's journal *Chimères* (Genosko 2016), I addressed the question of personal methods of aesthetic production and dream collection as transversal practices modelled on Guattari's own approach to Kafka (2007), via Freudian dream interpretation. This essay presented a psychoanalytic Guattari, as he makes love to a certain Freud, for the sake of Wojnarowicz. Although such Guattarian concepts as transversality helped to put an end to lingering attachments to interpretation in the thinking of literature, what comes after interpretation does not put an end to psychoanalytic approaches to art nor to dream interpretation. The mythic narratives of Freud survive, not as primary reference points, but despite their limits, as inventive worlds of concept creation that Freudianism later petrified.[3]

Thinking about Guattari's Wojnarowicz brings to an uncertain closure Guattari's experience of a bohemian New York that he first encountered during the Semiotext(e) Schizo-culture conference in 1975, where French theory rubbed shoulders with subversive American fiction (William Burroughs, Kathy Acker and Allen Ginsberg) and music (John Cage and Patti Smith). This is a trajectory mapped by Sylvère Lotringer, for whom 'schizo-culture, equals New York' (Lotringer 2016; Deleuze and Guattari 1987: 19). The reference to Patti Smith in *A Thousand Plateaus* is attributed to this event and the myriad of meetings that took place.[4] For Lotringer (2016), 'Deleuze quotes Patti Smith because he came to the States for the Schizo-Culture convention, and then met Smith and Allen Ginsberg.' Lotringer would eventually converse at length with Wojnarowicz and his collaborators, following this line of flight deep into a now highly mythologised moment in an earlier bohemian America.

In terms of art writing, New York rapidly recedes into the background in relation to Tokyo. Guattari developed both personal and critical interests in a number of Japanese artists including Buto dancer Min Tanaka and photographer Keiichi Tahara. More generally, Guattari had a sense of the singularity of Japan's 'mutant creationism' during his visits there over the course of the 'bubble economy' of the 1980s up to its collapse in the early 1990s. Guattari visited Japan at least eight times during the period between 1980 and 1992. These visits can be clarified in the following manner: early visits involved dialogues with media theorist Tetsuo Kogawa (autumn 1980 and spring 1981) and translator Kuniichi Uno (University of Kyoto in 1983 and Uno's La Borde visit in 1984–5); mid-decade dialogues with Min Tanaka (summer 1985) as well as appearances at Radio Homerun and a literal pilgrimage to Sanya in Tokyo in honour of the assassinated documentary filmmaker Mitsuo Sato (attended by many artists and counter-cultural figures), followed by a February 1985 visit to Tokyo and a June 1986 visit to the Yayoi Kusama show to which he contributes a catalogue essay in anticipation of the major Centre Pompidou exhibition the following year of *Japon des avant-gardes* (staging a dialogue with postmodernist Akira Asada); the later visits become strange as they are sponsored by the Seibu department store (1987), and the large-scale Japan Institute of Architects event (encompassing Guattari's dialogue with Takamatsu and the Nagoya urban planning presentation), followed in the same year by the Keiichi Tahara exhibition and catalogue essay in Paris. There was one more visit in the summer of 1992 as Guattari's old friend painter Toshimitsu was hospitalised for leukaemia treatment (he passed away in 2002), and the film he planned with photographer Tahara never materialised. Guattari passed away in August 1992. Guattari's interest extended to the novels of Abé Kobo. By the mid-1980s Guattari had a wide-ranging knowledge of the Japanese arts, electronic music (Yellow Magic Orchestra), fashion and performance scenes, and he used this knowledge to help co-organise visits to Paris of many Japanese artists and writers through his involvement in the Centre Georges Pompidou. During the 1980s, Japanese translations of Guattari's single-authored books began to appear, as well as documents of his activities in Japan. Masaaki Sugimura is a key figure in these translation efforts. Guattari's repeated visits to Japan were immersive experiments into a machinic interconnectedness striated by animist tendencies that he deployed in a panoply of interfaces – 'collaborations' and different kinds of writing (short pieces for fashion magazines, film scripts, art criticism) for likely and unlikely audiences. During his visits to Japan, Guattari participated in transits and blendings of machinic components of subjectivation (subjectities and objectities) and joined some of their assemblages through his engagements, trying to understand the machinic eros of Japanese culture, that is, the desire to be in the thick of things, in the pop cuteness of Harajuku, and stuck in refrains of pachinko, anime, manga and baseball. A book of Guattari's writings on art would be skewed towards Japanese materials, short articles, interviews, catalogue essays, fashion magazine essays, and the reception of his work through its translation (the Kyoto Guattari Studies Group, for instance, at Ryukoku University).

C30/C60/C90: Cassette Ethos

There is no definitive collection of Guattari's writings on the arts – such would be vast and wildly heterogeneous. Indeed, I have not even mentioned the dialogue he staged with Italian script writer, film director and visual poet Sarenco (Guattari 1988b) on the themes of horses and pianos in his cinematic works, in one of which, *En attendant la troisième guerre mondiale* (1985–6), he appeared; so any preliminary attempt to focus on a single artist or group of artists will be partial. Here is where Wojnarowicz comes to the fore. Wojnarowicz's life and work is undertheorised. There is something curious about the Sarenco discussion, as it is noted that a third participant (Jacques Donguy) is lying on a couch holding a tape recorder, undoubtedly a cassette device given the date. The once near ubiquity of portable tape decks is not yet forgotten. This is just before the breakthrough public moments of the boombox revolution and the birth of rap culture. While Wojnarowicz kept many notebooks, he regularly used his cassette recorder. At first he recorded the stories he heard when hanging out with Beat godfather Hubert Huncke and his companion Louis Cartwright, in anticipation of publishing them, a project that never came to fruition; he did publish transcripts of monologues of people he encountered on the waterfront and in the streets of his neighbourhood, but his ambition was for something beyond monologues (Wojnarowicz 1982).[5] Wojnarowicz was bewitched by Cartwright's tales:

> David had begun taping Louis Cartwright's stories. Here was another lost voice from the margin – an important one, in David's opinion. A monologue wouldn't be enough. Cartwright deserved a full book. After all, he'd ridden a bike over the twisting mountain roads of Nepal, visiting monasteries 'where they worshipped love and light on one side, death and darkness on the other.' He'd passed a winter in Kabul, sleeping on a rope bed for five cents a night. He'd learned how to press powder into hash from 'rogue Afghanies.' He'd take drugs so pure people died from them. David transcribed one of the tapes and labeled it 'an excerpt from *Morpheus*, a book forthcoming from Redd Herring Press.'
>
> David never actually set up Redd Herring, nor did he finish the project. But the taping went on for several months. (Carr 2012: 87)

As a young man Wojnarowicz was a collector of stories. He continued visiting Huncke and Cartwright until the heavy drugs at play became frightening. Small technical machines populated Wojnarowicz's life in the late 1970s and early 1980s: portable tape recorders, manual typewriters sourced from flea markets or borrowed from friends, Super 8 cameras, cans of spray paint, slide machines, stencils, screens for printing, cigarette machines, eye glasses, notebooks, zines, hypodermic needles. By the early 1980s magnetic media in the form of cassettes would be nudged aside by the CD. Yet tape's materiality, its literal minerality written in metal oxide particles, remained part of Wojnarowicz's world, as if in a looped homage to William Burroughs and his tactile methods. Or, just as well, the minerality of a face exposed to the street and the unfiltered particulates of vehicles and industry.

The recently published 'tape journals' provide an account of Wojnarowicz's diaristic use of the tape recorder to record his dreams, commentaries and reflections on his friends, family, lovers and art. While this chapter focuses on the social and inter-relational uses of recorders, it is worthwhile to consider a few places where the device itself breaks through the solitary monologue. For instance, Wojnarowicz says in November 1988: 'I just woke up. Waking up every hour or less, I don't know, three or four hours? And I want to start talking into this tape recorder, talking about the things I see' (2018: 73).[6] Likening this intimacy to his days as a heroin user in the 1970s when he would talk into his recorder until he fell asleep, the machine finds a place in his bed once again. At the time he was living at Peter Hujar's apartment, and had just been diagnosed with Aids-Related-Complex (ARC). Comfort with the device, even in his bed, is not guaranteed. Wojnarowicz says in the same period: 'I just can't stand my self-consciousness when I talk into this thing' (2018: 78). On one occasion he used a tape that contained a short interview he had given a few years earlier, and when he listened to it, he was surprised at how awkwardly he answered questions about his lover and mentor Hujar (2018: 99–102). Wojnarowicz confessed that he used an automatic camera because he could not master a manual one. He abandoned the instruction manual since, for him, readers of such books become our rulers. A portable cassette recorder is a simple device. It doesn't require many instructions. It is manual, but does not need to be set (knowing how to calculate the f-stop). He resigned himself to the randomness of either understanding or misunderstanding machines. But he did not discuss tape recorders in his reflections on machines. He simply used a recorder to capture his reflections on the rusted shells (fossils) of former inventions. As for instruction manuals, the reader can only surmise that they belong to the pre-existing world and its systems of control. Only imagination can break through such control, Wojnarowicz believed (2018: 119). Despite his moments of self-consciousness, a cassette recorder was for him a device for capturing and carrying subversive voices.

Analytic Tape Recorder

Describing his background in an interview on the occasion of the publication of *Anti-Oedipus*, Guattari ended with a fourth kind of formation: 'I had sort of a schizoid background or discourse, I'd always liked schizophrenics, been drawn to them. You have to live with them to understand this. Schizophrenics do at least, unlike neurotics, have real problems. My first work as a psychotherapist was with a schizophrenic, using a tape recorder' (Deleuze and Guattari 1995: 14–15). Let's first look at the distinction between neurosis and psychosis, then the linkage between multiplicities and machines, before turning to the role of the tape recorder in analysis.

For Deleuze and Guattari, 'a schizophrenic out for a walk is a better model than a neurotic lying on the analyst's couch'; this was an early lesson of *Anti-Oedipus* (1977: 2). A peripatetic schizo is much preferred, and the authors borrow from Georg Büchner's novella *Lenz* (1836): one in movement in relation to social life, who has a body that is in hyper-contact with non-human phenomena: snowflakes, stars, mountains. The human/nature dichotomy cannot get a foothold in a machinic coupling of mutual production: 'the self and the non-self, outside and inside, no longer have any meaning whatsoever' (Deleuze and Guattari 1977: 2). This is a way around a tired 'descent into madness' interpretation. Psychosis confronts molecular multiplicities (crowd phenomena); it lives in the midst of machinic fluxes (flows flee by means of devices such as swaddled tape recorders), including lunar phases, photosynthesis: 'everything is a machine' (ibid.).

A machine is not only a mechanical device, although such a thing is a machine, albeit a technical one, like Beckett's bicycles, horns, rowboats. A mouth on a breast; a stone sucker, anus sunbeam constricter. A body has many sphincter muscles beyond the anus. It also has thousands of pores: 'Comparing a sock to a vagina is OK, it's done all the time, but you'd have to be insane to compare a pure aggregate of stitches to a field of vaginas: that's what Freud says' (Deleuze and Guattari 1987: 27).

Proliferation separates neurosis from psychosis. An organised body is suscep-tible to analysis and the application of psychoanalytic concepts. Oedipus belongs to neurosis. The issue is containment and whether the concept takes. Whereas the investments of desiring-production are social and technical and produce reality. The schizophrenisation of the neurotic is achieved by drawing out the potential for connectivity trapped in the Oedipal triangle and other representations of desire as anti-production, the transformation of the neurotic into a group-subject in which transference is not focused on individuation and identity. Indeed, Guattari would later write in *Chaosmosis*: 'Psychosis thus not only haunts neurosis and perversion but also all the forms of normality' (1995: 79). The project of schiz-ophrenising neurosis is not random: in clinical practice, there is no real neurosis that is not paired with some form of psychosis. Machines are bridges across the divide between neurosis and psychosis. Since neurosis is linked with impasses and dislocations arising from the distresses of individuation, a schizoanalytic approach instead turns toward open collective processes rather than ready-made personological containments, such as the triangulation known as the Oedipus complex: Mummy-Daddy-Me, the familial relation through which schizo break-throughs are made along lines of flight. Do not fetishise anybody's precious tape recorder.

What about that tape recorder? Guattari is referring to his work with a patient known as 'R.A.', one of the few so-called case studies published during his lifetime in the collection of early writings *Psychoanalysis and Transversality*. In this 'Monograph on R.A.', Guattari explains the role of a tape recorder:

> With Dr. [Jean] Oury, we decided that my conversations with R.A. would take place in the presence of a tape recorder. Ostensibly, I started the recording when the dialogue entered what I considered to be an impasse, or when something 'bothered' me. It was then as if a third person had appeared in the room . . . an objectivation of the situation took place that had the effect, most often, of deviating, if not blocking the dialogue. (2015: 37–8)

From the outset of the monograph, playback is an issue. R.A. runs away from the clinic and 'replays' a teenage event. Generally, he was non-communicative and intractable, unengaged, until a group of patients adopted him and got him involved in some activities, including playing a role in a film. Guattari explains that he got along well with R.A. but didn't want to subject him to a transference analysis, as the rotation of duties at La Borde meant that the analyst's role would change with the turning of the wheel, as it were, and thus he 'would take on an entirely different attitude with the subject' (2015: 37). Hence, the tape recorder would be turned on when the dialogue faltered or presented something to analytic listening that made, to use a Freudianism, 'evenly-floating attention' impossible. The tape recorder assisted the dialogue in either deviating from or ending it. It was a 'third person' in a way. What this third person heard could be replayed. One of R.A.'s problems was that he could not carry on dialogues with other members of the clinic. Months later he was able to do so, and even share a text he had written. In a sense, the tape recording didn't work. But in not working, it forced something to happen. Part of Guattari's method was to play back the recordings to R.A. during their sessions. Guattari would then erase the tapes. They were not permanent records but ephemeral inscriptions embedded in a dialogical situation. However,

> During the first sessions, when we listened to the tape . . . R.A. lost his temper. The opposition that he had turned against the world, the 'what?' and 'hunh?' etc., he now turned against himself. The recorded voice, the drawling tone, the hesitations, the breaks, the constant incoherence revolted him, and he took me as a witness that he must have truly fallen 'lower than everything' to end up speaking like that. From there, it was easy for me to have him recognize that it was absurd to persist in claiming that the cause of his illness was Dr. Oury, electroshocks, etc. (Guattari 2015: 38)

It was viewing himself in the aforementioned film, in accompaniment with the tape, that allowed R.A. to regain a sense of bodily integration, and his passage through a doubly visual and aural mirror stage was jubilant but fraught with episodes of self-harm; Guattari once tried to pinch R.A. hard enough to make him cry in order to get him to abandon his insensitivity toward others. The results were, then, tentative. Persisting, Guattari made a further attempt with a 'third term' outside him to help shift R.A. to regain his lost ego, and this was to have him copy out Kafka's *The Castle* (R.A. was likened in a number of ways to Kafka by Oury and Guattari). R.A. enjoyed this task. At this point in the dialogue, R.A. began to speak more coherently about his situation, and 'after a certain time, the tape recorder had conditioned the situation of our dialogue to the point that I almost did not need to turn it on' (Guattari 2015: 40). Instead, Guattari wrote in a notebook, to which R.A. would also contribute, and he encouraged R.A. to write certain things down. In this way Guattari became a tape recorder (and a mirror) and would replay or repeat R.A.'s statements to him so he could remember them. In addition, R.A. also became a recording device ('the machine'), and the tape device was in this manner 'disautomatized'. Unfortunately, this did not last long, as a relapse took place that Guattari attributes to a failure in love that R.A. replayed in the clinic, replaying the same volatile teenage period noted above. Eventually, Guattari had him recopy the notebook they had shared, and R.A. made it his own. He began writing on his own and inviting others to read what he had written, and this changed his relation to his illness. The inevitability that he would end up like his father was no longer an abiding obsession. By then the tape recorder was no longer part of the equation.

Wojnarowicz as an Ethno-Analyst

The long chapter 'The Suicide of a Guy Who Once Built an Elaborate Shrine over a Mouse Hole' in *Close to the Knives* (Wojnarowicz 1991: 165–276) is a work of punk ethnography. It begins with an extended journal entry but shifts into fieldwork in the club Wojnarowicz worked at as a busboy, the Danceteria, where he met his local informants in American marginality and despair. It was his collaborator on the zine *MURDER*, Johnny, who introduced him to Dakota, the builder of the mouse shrine in a room in an uptown welfare hotel. Wojnarowicz became curious about Dakota's voodoo-themed collages and used his tape recorder to interview Johnny, also a lab worker, about Dakota's art. The chapter begins with an 'author's note' explaining that the goal was to include excerpts from letters to Wojnarowicz from Dakota but the latter's family would not grant permission following his death. The transcripts of taped discussions are noted in Wojnarowicz's 'memoir' and Dakota's uplifting spiritual influence on Johnny is explained. Wojnarowicz then switches back to his journal entries, introducing another friend, Joe, who published Dakota's collages in his zine *Addict Magazine* and included him in his gory Super 8 films. The next transcript is with Joe. The subject is still death, Dakota's artistic preoccupation, shared by members of this small fraternity and evident in Wojnarowicz's mid-1980s installation work with Richard Kern and film work with Tommy Turner. Wojnarowicz probes how Dakota utilised his employer's state-of-the-art Xerox machine to produce and mail Joe's zines (long before Dakota fell on hard times). Then readers are sent back to Wojnarowicz's journal, reflecting on his lack of fear of death, televisual hypnosis and heroin, and the war on drugs of Reagan's America.

Transcript follows transcript, punctuated by journal entry, and a few telephone calls. Each investigation concerns depression, bearing insults, serial murder, drug addiction, giving up, and the crushing pressures of normality. In the mid-1980s Wojnarowicz and Joe both reflect on their belief that Dakota had committed a murder, around the same time he began to attempt suicide. Wojnarowicz excavates Dakota's story, exposing in another transcript Joe's revelation that Dakota was in love with him, and his unrequited love precipitated his decline. Dakota's further suicide attempts are discussed by Joe. Johnny returns and describes how he found out that Dakota stole money from him to buy drugs. The elaborate details of how Dakota planned to stab a drug dealer are exposed. At one point in a detailed discussion of the murder, the tape runs out (Wojnarowicz 1991: 223). The recorder asserts its presence through a break/flow. A recalled phone call is included. Wojnarowicz narrates the death of mentor-friend-lover Peter Hujar. More transcripts follow, this time David and Joe talking about the dark psyche of America. Dakota had returned home to his parents in Texas. Around the same time Wojnarowicz began noticing lesions on his legs. A journal entry explains that a letter arrived without a return address explaining that Dakota had committed suicide. The transcripts continue: Johnny, Joe, Sylvia, Beth (David's friends). The focus is Dakota, why he may have killed himself. Dakota's friend Beth thinks he knew what he was doing. He would never fit in because the structures he built had no place in the larger scheme of things. He simply could not adapt. He never visited her, although he lived close. He lied to his employer, reverted to alcoholism, spent some time as a day patient at an asylum. He suffocated himself with a gasoline-filled bag. His cremated ashes were kept by his parents. Another transcript featured Johnny interrogating the relationship between suicide and reincarnation: are they mutually reinforcing? It turns out that Johnny's heart had stopped beating at least three times. His near-death experiences were not revelatory. Joe is jealous of Dakota's murder. Johnny is saddened, and is certain that Dakota was guilt-ridden. Joe is less certain. Wojnarowicz continues, as Joe describes how he tried to staunch the steady stream of communications from Dakota. Wojnarowicz cannot let go of the suicide. The long chapter ends with a 'Postscript' of disconnected memories and dreams.

What role does the tape recorder play in a decentred memoir/diary? It is a select tool among others in an elaborate autofiction in which the subject stitches together and manipulates media of capture (notebook, tape, telephone, dream, memory, testimony) and contents derived from a number of sources. The stitching metaphor is borrowed from D. A. Beronä's analysis of the use of a plastic Frankenstein figure in the comic book *Seven Miles a Second* by James Romberger and Wojnarowicz to explain the 'compilation of real life experiences—sometimes personally experienced and other times second hand stories—and dreams that are sewn together to make a whole person' (Beronä 2008). The Frankenstein figure also expresses for Beronä Wojnarowicz's reflection on reanimation following an HIV+ diagnosis. This critical turn to autofiction does not address the adjacency of the subject in machinic subjectivation. What would it mean to think about a diary with a displaced diarist? A memoir with a decentred memoirist? The stronger the decentring, the less subjective and heterogeneous the subjectivation.

A tape recorder is neither a passive device nor an objective record of events. It gives shape to events and changes the environment. 'To anyone who asked David what instrument he played in 3 Teens Kill 4, he always replied, "tape recorder"' (Carr 2012: 168).[7] His brief post-punk exploits and other sound-based experiments with cassettes indicate that tape recorders are instruments. These were once characterised as 'lowbrow sampling' (Lotringer in McCormick 2006: 11). As Guattari reminds us, even devices that are broken and not activated can have a productive connectivity. A recording is a highly constructed object: always already a monster. The stitches that hold together Frankenstein's monster's poached body parts and tape splices bear some relation. Canadian pianist Glenn Gould reminds listeners that splices are not only for rectifying mishaps and should not be dismissed as dishonest disruptions of some abstract conception of a unified performance, but post-taping editorial control expands the field of the technically informed performer, and opens on to a new participatory listener whose home devices and tape-editing options are often as powerful as the tools once found only in studios (1984).

In the field the very presence of a tape recorder is enough to constitute an audience. This is another kind of power. As Edmund Carpenter wrote of his fieldwork in New Guinea in the late 1960s in *Oh, What a Blow That Phantom Gave Me!*: 'setting up a tape recorder here is enough to attract a crowd of teenagers, each anxious to be recorded' (1973: 83). Carpenter was a sophisticated thinker of media and recognised that the tools of the anthropologist's trade were far from neutral. They are part of the colonialist project of anthropology because media *conquer all cultures*. Although Deleuze and Guattari quote Carpenter in *A Thousand Plateaus* to support their conception of smooth space (1987: 557, n. 56), Carpenter concludes above that the portable tape recorder is striating: recording is an extractive industry. Despite its instability, the connection of tape recording with the smooth body without organs is taken up by Janne Vanhanen in Deleuzian sound studies:

> It would appear that one can construct a sonorous Body without Organs with the tape recorder. . . . The tape recorder has no focus of attention and becomes the Inorganized Ear that listens deeply. (2017: 177)

The sonorous BwO is referenced to both American composer Pauline Oliveros's and John Cage's experiments, unfocusing and decentring listening from a subjective centre through devices such as microphones and tape recorders and modified instruments that unleashed molecular multiplicities. The inorganised ear is without organs, that is, it is disorganised, and it is opened to new capacities to listen, to feel sound, in ways that are not predetermined. Tape recorders assist in de-subjectivation, even if this attachment to a technical device does not exhaust the question of the machine since 'everything is a machine' (Deleuze and Guattari 1977: 2).

In Conclusion: Wojnarowicz's Last Tape

'David's forte was dealing with tapes,' fellow band member Julie Hair remembers about his contributions to 3 Teens Kill 4. One of his random recordings of a radio broadcast captured in a vehicle on the way to the studio made it into the final mix of a recorded song (Hair 2006: 19). Coupled with Wojnarowicz's insertion of lengthy interviews with friends in his own memoirs, the artist as focal subject becomes less a meaning-giving nucleus and more a residual spare part. The artist's identity is unmoored. Even catalogue essayists who make the connection between Wojnarowicz's *Arthur Rimbaud in New York* (1978–9) (Fig. 6.1) photographic pieces and the famous formulation from 1871, *Je est un autre*, are reluctant to permit him to stray too far from coherence, or 'manifold unity' of continuities and discontinuities. These works are basically thought of as self-referential (self-portraits, self-mythologies, despite the fact that a number of different people appear in the photographs wearing the Rimbaud mask) (Bordowitz 2018: 50). Perhaps a little more should be expected of this phrase after Deleuze's analysis of its pure Aristotelianism as *Je* is the 'moulding of a matter [abstract form and abstract matter]', by contrast to a Kantian 'infinite modulation' of phenomena (appearances) *in and by time* undertaken as a synthesis by *un autre* (Deleuze 1984).[8] Change is permanent yet, as Deleuze says, the self uses *Je* to

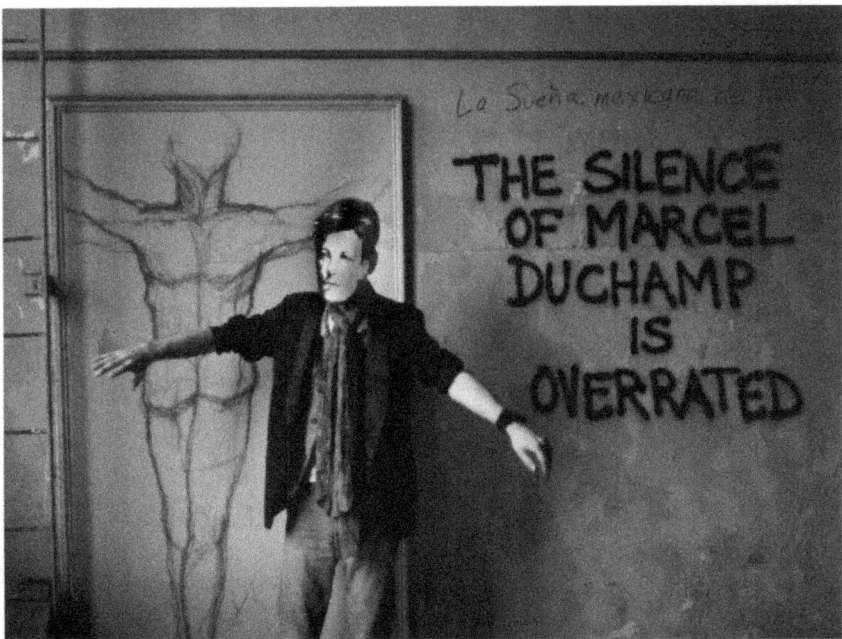

Figure 6.1 David Wojnarowicz, *Arthur Rimbaud in New York (Duchamp)*, 1978–9. Silver print, 11 x 14 in., 27.94 x 35.56 cm.
Courtesy of the Estate of David Wojnarowicz and P·P·O·W, New York.

represent itself as an other that is affected by it, and is 'stitched together by [the thread of] time'. The movement from mould to modulation is decisive. Unity persists in a time that never ends even as it splits us apart. Still, let's reinsert modulation into technical machines like tape recorders and all of the operations at work in recording in magnetic media. These considerations break down the hylomorphism that Deleuze identified in Rimbaud's famous phrase. But that is not all. The tape recorder is embedded in a context of recording but also listening, of bodily gestures, stillness and postures, not to mention the transfer of libidinal energy that it extracts from the warm bed and that is then transcribed and transmitted forward in print and in other replays and relays (archival, curatorial, editorial, digital).

Beckett's *Krapp's Last Tape* is a good example. It engages a tape reel, to be sure, but it is also a study in listening by a body encountering an older version of itself. There are, to be cute, two tracks: the tape's recorded messages and the memories and reactions associated with the content; but there is also Krapp's reception and listening practices: 'leaning forward, elbows on table, hand cupping ear towards machine, face front' (Beckett 1960: 13). Not only do these get tangled, he is in addition interventionist in regularly winding the tape forwards and backwards, and sometimes pausing, especially when he is annoyed at his earlier self and the sound of his own voice: 'The voice! Jesus!' Memory is complicated by listening to himself. Yet the tape does not run out. It continues in silence. As Paul Hegarty reflects:

> Krapp, and tape, Krapp and tape, and the playing of tape, the playing of Krapp and the listening of Krapp combine into something more or, significantly less, than a subject (Krapp) listening to an object (his voice, the tape) through another machine (the recorder/player). (2007)

Undifferentiated: Krapp becoming tape. The body without organs is a giant tape – 'a surface for the recording of the entire process of production of desire' (Deleuze and Guattari 1977: 11) – laying down in the metal powder by the recording head the sound signals converted into memorable magnetic fluxes. Where is the subject? Such a subject is in a position of adjacency, a part among parts, and a part with parts of its own, without a fixed personal identity. *Subject*ities are componentially heterogeneous and largely asubjective, coated in exhaust soot, toxins, unsettled urban miasma of the sewers, spilt coffee, spittle, urine and dog shit, arrayed across an energetic band. Subjectivation is a process through which contingent identities are continuously formed and deformed: a permanent work in progress involving both human and ahuman components. Spooling and unspooling. Playing and pausing. Converting energy back and forth from signals into a magnetic field of marshalled particles (ferric oxide, most likely) in metastable assemblages around machinic nuclei that inexorably turn to rust. It is well known that recordings are made on a rusty ribbon of tape. Rust is the destiny of the machine, yet, as Wojnarowicz warned us in an anti-Oedipean spirit, it continues to work.

Notes

1. Paul Eliot devotes a few pages to Guattari's Wojnarowicz essay in his book *Guattari Reframed* (2012: 112–14).
2. An example of Guattari's construction of homosexual becoming from the mid-1970s is 'Une sexualisation en rupture' (1975).
3. On this point see O'Sullivan 2012: 106.
4. 'The American singer Patti Smith sings the bible of the American dentist: Don't go for the root, follow the canal . . .' (Deleuze and Guattari 1987: 19).
5. See also a selection of his spoken performance with Ben Neill, *ITSOFOMO* from 1989 at The Kitchen, NYC, included in *Tellus* 25 (1991). *Tellus* was a cassette/audio magazine established in 1983. I am grateful for co-founder Joseph Nechvatal's assistance in this matter.
6. The publication of this collection follows closely upon the major retrospective exhibition *David Wojnarowicz: History Keeps Me Awake at Night*, in the late summer/autumn of 2018 at the Whitney Museum of American Art in New York. My chapter is inspired by the exhibit, but is not a review of it in any sense of the term.
7. The short-lived post-punk band 3 Teens Kill 4 was formed in the early 1980s in New York's East Village. Wojnarowicz left the band shortly after the release of *No Motive* in 1982.
8. See also Deleuze 1997: 30–1.

References

Beckett, Samuel (1960), *Krapp's Last Tape and Other Dramatic Pieces*, New York: Grove Press.

Beronä, D. A. (2008), 'A Renegade of Expression: David Wojnarowicz's Autofiction in Comics', *Image & Narrative* [e-journal], 22, <http://www.imageandnarrative.be/inarchive/autofiction2/berona.html> (last accessed 11 March 2020).

Bordowitz, Gregg (2018), 'Multiple Selves, Singular Self', in *David Wojnarowicz: History Keeps Me Awake at Night*, New Haven: Yale University Press, pp. 41–53.

Carpenter, Edmund (1973), *Oh, What a Blow That Phantom Gave Me!*, New York: Holt, Rinehart and Winston.

Carr, Cynthia (2012), *Fire in the Belly: The Life and Times of David Wojnarowicz*, New York: Bloomsbury.

Deleuze, Gilles (1984), 'Vérité et temps Cours 60 – 17/04/1984 – 3', *La voix de Gilles Deleuze en ligne*, <http://www2.univ-paris8.fr/deleuze/article.php3?id_article=345> (last accessed 11 March 2020).

Deleuze, Gilles (1997), 'On Four Poetic Formulas that Might Summarize the Kantian Philosophy', in *Essays Critical and Clinical*, trans. Daniel Smith and Michael Greco, Minneapolis: University of Minnesota Press, pp. 27–35.

Deleuze, Gilles and Félix Guattari (1977), *Anti-Oedipus: Capitalism and Schizophrenia*, trans. Robert Hurley, Mark Seem and Helen R. Lane, New York: Viking Press.

Deleuze, Gilles and Félix Guattari (1987), *A Thousand Plateaus: Capitalism and Schizophrenia*, trans. Brian Massumi, Minneapolis: University of Minnesota Press.

Deleuze, Gilles and Félix Guattari (1995), 'On Anti-Oedipus', in Gilles Deleuze, *Negotiations*, trans. Martin Joughin, New York: Columbia University Press, pp. 14–24.

Eliot, Paul (2012), *Guattari Reframed*, London: I. B. Tauris.

Genosko, Gary (2016), 'Félix Guattari et David Wojnarowicz: Essai de schizoanalyse', trans. Anne Querrien, *Chimères*, 88: 187–96.

Genosko, Gary (2018), 'In this Sleep: A Dream Pragmatics for David Wojnarowicz', in *The Reinvention of Social Practices: Essays on Félix Guattari*, London and New York: Rowman & Littlefield International, pp. 63–77.

Gould, Glenn (1984), 'The Prospects of Recording', in Tim Page (ed.), *The Glenn Gould Reader*, Toronto: Lester & Orpen Dennys, pp. 338–40.

Guattari, Félix (1975), 'Une sexualisation en rupture' [Interview by Christian Deschamps], *La Quinzaine littéraire*, 215: 14–15.

Guattari, Félix (1988a), 'Jean-Jacques Lebel: Painter of Transversality', trans. Melissa McMahon, *GLOBE*, 8, <http://www.artdes.monash.edu.au/globe/issue8/jjltxt.html> (last accessed 11 March 2020).

Guattari, Félix (1988b), 'La lettre oubliée: Entretien avec Sarenco', in *Sarenco: Le Triptyque du cinéma mobile 1983–87*, Paris: Henri Veyrier, pp. 7–23.

Guattari, Félix (1990a), 'In the Shadow of Forward Motion: David Wojnarowicz', *Rethinking Marxism*, 3(1): 75–84.

Guattari, Félix (1990b), 'Introduction', in *George Condo*, Paris: Daniel Templon, pp. 5–9 and 10–12.

Guattari, Félix (1995), *Chaosmosis*, trans. Julian Pefanis and Paul Bains, Bloomington: Indiana University Press.

Guattari, Félix (1996), 'Remaking Social Practices', in Gary Genosko (ed.), *The Guattari Reader*, Oxford: Blackwell, pp. 262–72.

Guattari, Félix (2007), *Soixante-cinq rêves de Franz Kafka*, Paris: Lignes.

Guattari, Félix (2015), 'Monograph on R.A.', in *Psychoanalysis and Transversality*, trans. Ames Hodges, South Pasadena: Semiotext(e), pp. 36–41.

Hair, Julie (2006), 'Interview with Sylvère Lotringer', in G. Ambrosino (ed.), *David Wojnarowicz: A Definitive History of Five or Six Years on the Lower East Side*, New York: Semiotext(e), pp. 19–25.

Hegarty, Paul (2007), 'The Hallucinatory Life of Tape', *Culture Machine* (Special Issue on Recordings), 9, <https://culturemachine.net/recordings/the-hallucinatory-life-of-tape/> (last accessed 11 March 2020).

Lotringer, Sylvère (2016), 'Sylvère Lotringer: Interview with D. Grau', *Purple Magazine*, 26, <https://purple.fr/magazine/fw-2016-issue-26/sylvere-lotringer/> (last accessed 11 March 2020).

McCormick, Carlo (2006), 'Interview with Sylvère Lotringer', in G. Ambrosino (ed.), *David Wojnarowicz: A Definitive History of Five or Six Years on the Lower East Side*, New York: Semiotext(e), pp. 11–18.

O'Sullivan, Simon (2012), *On the Production of Subjectivity*, London: Palgrave Macmillan.

Vanhanen, Janne (2017), 'Learning to Listen: Inorganization of the Ear', in Pirkko Moisala, Taru Leppänen, Milla Tiainen and Hanna Väätäinen (eds), *Musical Encounters with Deleuze and Guattari*, London: Bloomsbury, pp. 169–87.

Wojnarowicz, David (1982), *Sounds in the Distance*, ed. J. Pennington, London: Aloes Books.

Wojnarowicz, David (1991), *Close to the Knives*, New York: Vintage.

Wojnarowicz, David (2018), *Weight of the Earth: The Tape Journals*, ed. Lisa Darms and David O'Neill, South Pasadena: Semiotext(e).

7

Steppe C(ha)osmotechnics:
Art as Engineering of Forces in Marek Konieczny and Beyond

Radek Przedpełski

This chapter investigates intensive multiplicities in works of Marek Konieczny (b. 1936, Sosnowiec), an under-researched construction-engineer-turned-artist associated with the Warsaw neo-avant-garde of the 1970s who since 1974 has pursued a singular artistic idiom called 'Think Crazy'. In particular, it interrogates Think Crazy between 1974 and 1980.[1] 1980 marks a certain threshold of intensity – the emergence of the Solidarity movement,[2] an independent labour union committed to social change, which Guattari, after his 1982 visit to People's Republic of Poland, deemed a *molecular revolution*[3] in the collective production of subjectivity (see Guattari and Rolnik 2007: 219, 230). Solidarity played a central role in delegitimising the Communist government. As I aim to demonstrate, Think Crazy affirms the molecular revolution Guattari saw in Solidarity as a solidarity with inhuman and ahuman materials.

My departure point is a close (re)reading of the Deleuzoguattarian concept of the *machinic phylum*. Thinking with the machinic phylum, I shall argue that Think Crazy has a past-future orientation which operates as a transversal, technological and specifically metallic lineage. This metallic line connects (1) aspects of seventeenth-century art and culture of the Polish-Lithuanian Commonwealth (*Sarmato-Baroque*); (2) the Early Iron Age metallurgical art of the Great Steppe investigated in the '1227: Treatise on Nomadology – The War Machine' plateau (henceforth 'Nomadology') (*steppe c(ha)osmotechnics*); and (3) the wider perspective of inhuman planetary and cosmic changes (*unfeeling rocks*). All these different dimensions connected on the basis of metallic singularities, operations and affects enter resonance and make one another become something else – converging in a case study of Konieczny's 1979 *Unfeeling Rocks with Self-Portrait*, which will also serve as a conclusion of this chapter.

The chapter launches a media-archaeological inquiry defined by Parikka (2012: 2) as 'a way to investigate the new media cultures through insights from past new media, often with an emphasis on the forgotten, the quirky, the non-obvious apparatuses'. Furthermore, for Parikka (2015: viii) processes of mediation engage the earth, and as such can be conceptualised as a 'media geology'. My chapter aligns itself with a strand of such speculative and mutant media archaeologies/ geologies which in response to the region's political instrumentalisation of history deterritorialise the zones of 'Eastern Europe', 'Eurasia', 'Central Asia', 'Siberia' or 'Mongolia'.[4]

1000 BCE: Machinic Phylum as a Steppe C(ha)osmotechnics

In what follows, I am going to present an overview of the problem of the *machinic phylum* in Deleuze and Guattari, and subsequently develop its understanding in terms of what I shall call 'a steppe c(ha)osmotechnics' in an attempt to recover on the one hand its Eurasian formulation, frequently omitted in its discussion, and its ungrounding connection to the cosmos, on the other.

The Deleuzoguattarian (2005: 404–15) concept of the machinic phylum developed in Nomadology draws a vision of becoming pertaining to matter. Simply put, the term 'machinic phylum' refers to matter in the process of change. Deleuze explained the concept during his 1979 lecture at Vincennes where it is also called 'metallic line' and 'metallic synthesis'. As defined in Nomadology, the machinic phylum signifies at once 'matter-movement' and 'technological lineage', the two aspects ontologically inseparable. Such coupled formulation affirms the logic of multiplicity, responding to the fundamental Deleuzoguattarian (2005: 20) problem of 'PLURALISM = MONISM'. As we shall see, machinic phylum can be understood in terms of qualitative (intensive) multiplicity, which Deleuze (2002: 42) defines in *Bergsonism* as that which 'does not divide up without changing in kind, it changes in kind in the process of dividing up'.[5]

Matter-movement, also termed 'matter-energy' (Deleuze and Guattari 2005: 407), designates non-hylomorphic and natural-artificial flow of destratified matter in continuous variation and laden with energetic potentialities. Matter-movement bears singularities (implicit forms) enabling operations (events of deformation and transformation) and variable expressive traits (affective qualities) (ibid. 406–7). It is 'a single phylogenetic lineage' (406) that cuts across assemblages as their 'subterranean thread' (407).

Technological lineage, in turn, refers to phylum's differentiation into distinctive lines, for example a cast steel sabre, each with its own singularities, operations and affects. These differentiated lineages correspond to the operations of cutting and selecting the phylum by technical assemblages (ibid. 406–7). An assemblage 'deducts' – that is, it selects, organises and stratifies – the phylum's singularities so as to lend them consistency (406), while being simultaneously selected and destratified by the phylum's machinic functioning. Phylum is a force of differentiation by which an assemblage selects and is selected.

Drawing on their reading of Simondon's conceptualisation of genesis and evolution of technical objects (Simondon 2017: 26), Deleuze and Guattari distinguish between *phylogenetic* and *ontogenetic lines* depending on whether a line is viewed from the point of the phylum or the assemblage. The former 'travel long distances between assemblages of various ages and cultures', whereas the latter are 'internal to one assemblage and link up its various elements or else cause one element to pass . . . into another assemblage of a different nature but of the same culture or age' (Deleuze and Guattari 2005: 407). 'Cultures' and 'ages' imply here names of archaeological cultures and periods determined by technological developments such as the use of a particular material or artefact, as in 'Iron Age' or 'Pit Grave Culture'. In this respect, Nomadology mentions '*battle-ax* people, who came in off the steppes like a detached metallic branch of the nomads' (ibid. 414).

The machinic phylum is conceived as fundamentally metallic, given the metals' conductivity and ubiquity (the latter also in the expanded sense of minerals) (ibid. 411). It is thus correlated with metallurgy understood as 'thought of the matter-flow', 'thought . . . borne . . . from metal' (ibid.). The metallurgist brings to the surface material singularities through operations of selection which produce intensive qualities. Artisanal operation cuts the phylum but simultaneously 'follows the connections between singularities of matter and traits of expression' (ibid. 369). For example, the crucible (cast) steel sabre, 'oft short and curved' (ibid. 404), is produced through operations of melting iron at high temperatures and its successive decarbonations, which assign specific traits of expression (affects) to this composite material. These include the banded pattern corresponding to the structure of the cast steel, its sharpness and hardness (ibid. 406) enabling 'side attack with the edge of the blade' (404), and the possibility of always reusing it by melting it down into an ingot (411). These operations harness singularities of the crucible steel, itself an alloy of iron and carbon, such as the carbon's low melting point or its ability to confer hardness upon the composite material. Metallurgy is the art of manipulating the steel's carbon content. In fact, Nomadology expressly mentions 'the chemistry of carbon' viewed as a singularity of the phylum (ibid. 406–7).

Deleuze and Guattari (ibid. 410–11) conceive the metallurgical process not as a single, instantaneously completed operation of taking form occurring between determinate thresholds constituted by the matter prepared for the operation and the form to be imposed upon it, but as a process of taking form in several successive operations that straddle the determinate thresholds, whereby assuming form is inseparable from quantitative transformation.

The synthesis of matter encapsulated in metallurgy does not only harness such metallic affects as conductivity and ubiquity but also harnesses the power of metals to consolidate an assemblage. As Deleuze (1979) explains, 'there's no assemblage that doesn't include a metal bit [*bout*]. Metal is the fundamental procedure by which every assemblage is consolidated. The man-horse unit is fastened together with the stirrup.' The process of consolidation, framed in *A Thousand Plateaus* also in terms of the Monodian 'molecular engineering', consists in (1) the insertion of an element into matter in order to make it even more heterogeneous (*intercalary events*); (2) 'distribution of inequalities' (*intervals*); and (3) 'a superimposition of disparate rhythms' (*superposition*) (Deleuze and Guattari 2005: 328–9). As I see it, the operation of consolidation consists in intensifying connectivity, puncturing it and opening up the resulting membrane to its cosmic outside. Such paradoxical gestures at once hold material aggregates together and deterritorialise them. This is exemplified in reinforced concrete (Fr. *béton armé*, lit. 'armed concrete') where 'iron is intercalated following a rhythm' (ibid. 329). The '*self-supporting* [reinforced concrete] *surfaces* form a complex rhythmic personage whose "stems" have different sections and variable intervals depending on the intensity and direction of the force to be tapped (armature instead of structure)' (ibid.). As structural engineering demonstrates, through the addition of metal such as iron or steel, concrete is able to endure tensile forces resulting in elongation, beside its innate ability to withstand compressive loads resulting in reduction of volume. Such composite materials enable construction of extremely thin, lightweight curved roof structures (so-called (*thin-*)*shell* structures) able to cover large spaces without the traditional intermediate supports (Kobiak and Stachurski 1991: 9). Metal has the power of consolidation and deterritorialisation of heterogeneous assemblages that cuts across the distinction between the physical and the biological domain. Just as concrete can be 'armed', metal also has the power to consolidate a masochist assemblage. For Deleuze and Guattari (2005: 155, 260), a becoming-horse of the masochist – alongside its transmissions, conversions and redistributions of human and non-human, innate and acquired forces – is made possible through operations performed on a harness that includes metal elements.

The phylum is encapsulated in the invention of weapons (sabre) and other technological elements (stirrup, harness) by nomadic peoples of the Great Steppe, during 'the ages of metal' (Deleuze and Guattari 2005: 404), that is, the Copper, Bronze and Iron Ages. Invention is inseparable from adaptation and diffusion, as was the case with the Scythians who adapted and propagated the cast steel sabre invented by itinerant metallurgists (ibid. 404–5). Such technical elements both occasioned and presupposed new assemblages; for example, the stirrup brought about its associated man-horse-stirrup assemblage (ibid. 399, 404). The concrete assemblages are linked to the socius and presuppose different modes of its functioning. As demonstrated by the stirrup, 'readapted to the sedentary conditions of feudalism' (399), 'the social or collective machine, the machinic assemblage . . . determines what is a technical element at a given moment', and in particular whether the technical element is a tool presupposing the mode of work associated with the capture of the state apparatus, which overcodes and semiotises activity), or a weapon presupposing a *war machine* correlated with nomadism (397–402). The nomad war machine strives to 'ward off' the advent of the proto-state implicit in 'primitive, segmentary societies' (ibid. 357–61, 393–4). In other words, 'the phylum simultaneously has two different modes of liaison' (ibid. 415): the arborescent operations of forming or coding corresponding to the sedentary assemblages, and the rhizomatic operations of consolidation corresponding to nomadic assemblages.

The machinic phylum is 'a *body* without organs' (ibid. 411) (henceforth, 'BwO'), the latter diagrammed as an embryo (164), that is, in terms of mobile distributions of embryonic cells (54) that belong to the ontogenesis occurring before the determinate organisation of the body and cell specialisation. Such formulation points towards the unformed dimension of intensive transformations prior to, and cutting across, the biological and the physical domains. Furthermore, the machinic phylum co-opts the model of biological evolution, something that

Nomadology expressly identified in Leroi-Gourhan's 'technological vitalism' (ibid. 407), but stretches it towards the '*Nonorganic Life*' that Worringer saw in the 'Northern, or Gothic line' (411). Phylogeny ceases to designate evolutionary species development limited to organic life and diagrammable as a genealogical tree whose common root branches out against the benchmarks of chronological time into an ever-increasing complexity of subgroups, which marks a descent from the least to the most differentiated. Instead, it becomes a line of differentiation that unfolds in a transversal and transhistorical rhizomatic becoming between heterogeneous terms (see Deleuze and Guattari 2005: 47–9, 237–9 on this creative 'neoevolutionism', and ibid. 10–11 on 'anti-genealogic[al]' 'aparallel evolution' diagrammed by viral contagion). Machinic phylum thus confronts the arborescent thinking at play in Haeckel's recapitulation doctrine, which he also called the 'biogenetic law', that stated that 'ontogeny is nothing other than a short recapitulation of phylogeny' (Haeckel qtd in Richards 2008: 148). Transposed to art history, artwork-as-phylum does not so much recapitulate the history of its technical medium and genre as qualitatively change them. Such an approach is capable of addressing the problem of art's untimely operation beyond the art-historical focus on linear periodisation (see discussion on periodisation in Kaufmann 2010) and the notion of influence (see Baxandall 1985).

Is the phylum earth-bound or cosmic? The problem revolves around Deleuze and Guattari's many varied, differently accentuated engagements with Simondon's notion of modulation. These multiple readings exhibit a twofold tension. On the one hand, they reveal a tension between a view of modulation in terms of continuous moulding and a view of modulation that accentuates its energetic transformations. On the other hand, in the Deleuzoguattarian body of work there is also a tension between an understanding of modulation as pertaining to the earth and another view that links it to the cosmic.

At Vincennes, Deleuze approached the metallic synthesis, which he identified in both Varèse's music and metallurgy, as the Simondonian modulation defined as 'moulding in a continuous and variable manner' and entailing 'continuous development of the form and continuous variation of the matter itself' (1979). Nomadology understands the phylum in the same way: as a 'continuous development of form, and . . . a continuous variation of matter' shared by metallurgy and music (Deleuze and Guattari 2005: 411). However, the Nomadology plateau also draws attention to another, hidden aspect of modulation intimated by Simondon: ' "the existence, between form and matter, of a zone of medium and intermediary dimension," of energetic, molecular dimension' (ibid. 409). In turn, the preceding chapter of *A Thousand Plateaus*, '1837: Of the Refrain', links Varèse's '*sound machine*' to 'the age of the cosmic' practices that go beyond the Simondonian schema of matter-form modulation grounded in the earth, and instead elaborate a molecularised and deterritorialised material (ibid. 342–3). Such practices are a 'technique' of consolidation, of developing a consistent material capable of harnessing cosmic forces, 'a cosmic energy' (ibid. 343); 'it is now a [question of the] direct relation *material-forces*' (342).

Unlike *sound machines*, the phylum appears grounded in the earth;

Nomadology conceives it as a 'subterranean thread' (ibid. 407) extracted and brought to the earth's surface by mining and metallurgy. The phylum's metallurgical formulation makes it a robust avatar of Holocene media, in the sense that this geological epoch was marked by human expansion, anthropogenic megafauna extinction, technological revolution and diffusion of weapons. However, in diagnosing the Holocene, and therefore implicitly also its current extractivist 'Anthropocene' acceleration, Deleuze and Guattari draw attention to the *potential* of the deterritorialised matter-flows that select assemblages, with mines as sites that engender lines of flight and catalyse social resistance (ibid. 412–13).[6] Furthermore, since the phylum is also conceived by Deleuze and Guattari as 'matter-energy' (ibid. 407) it cannot be solely grounded as geo-media linked to metals, mining and metallurgy but also engages the cosmos.[7]

On this reading, the phylum is therefore *geo-cosmic*. This is already intimated by Simondon, who views a living individual, such as a plant, as a mediation, or internal resonance, between the cosmic and the infra-molecular orders of magnitude; this mediation 'distribut[es] the chemical species contained in the soil and in the atmosphere by means of light energy received in photosynthesis' (Simondon 1964: 22, n. 1; see also 10, n. 1; my translation). As I see it, grounded in and diagnosing the damaged earth, phylum nonetheless harbours non-extractivist potential to invent unforeseen modes of individuation that engage the ungrounded – the cosmic, furnishing speculative scenarios for a sustainable future. In fact, I wish to stretch the concept of the phylum in the direction of what philosopher Yuk Hui calls *cosmotechnics*, that is, 'the unification of the cosmic order and moral order through technical activities' (2017: 4),[8] echoing his gesture of extending Simondon's notion of the associated *techno-geographic milieu* of a technical object, exemplified by the Guimbal turbine and the river that makes its operation possible, by suggesting it has a '*cosmo-geographic* a priori' (11–19).

The phylum's c(ha)osmotechnical character is affirmed not only by Varèse's *sound machines* extracting timbral textures from a grouping of metallic instruments that electrically charge the air and the sonic material it propagates (Deleuze 1979; Deleuze and Guattari 2005: 343), but also by a minor avatar of the phylum, particularly resonant with Think Crazy. Drawing on Charrière (1979: 177–85) and Grousset (1970: 11–17), Deleuze and Guattari direct our attention to decorative plaques or fibulas – framed as 'Scythian art', 'jewellery', 'minor' and 'nomad art' – made of precious metals (gold or silver) (*motif*) attached to 'small movable objects' (*support*) such as 'the horse's harness, the sheath of the sword, the warrior's garments' or arrowheads (2005: 401) (Fig. 7.1). Such technical elements of the human-horse assemblage were associated with the Scythians – the Early Iron Age pastoral horse-riding warrior nomads of the Eurasian steppes.

Abundant evidence suggests that in the first millennium BCE early nomadic cattle-breeding groups inhabiting vast grasslands – the steppe (and forest-steppe) belt extending from northern China to the Danube – belonged to a shared cultural horizon distinguished by the Scytho-Siberian so-called *animal style* which fused abstract ornamentation with animal motifs, as well as a three-winged arrow head and horse riding. The Scythians originated in southern Siberia in the ninth

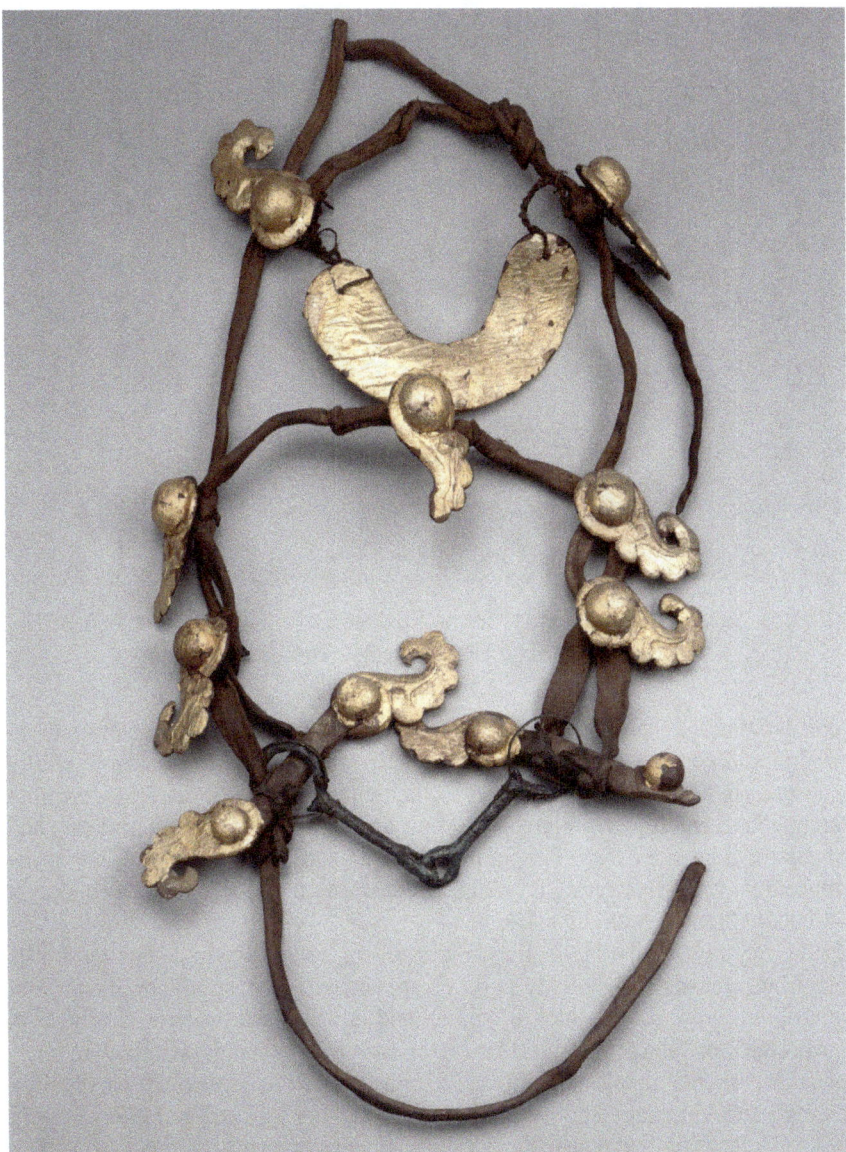

Figure 7.1 Horse's bridle decorated with stylised griffins' heads. Pazyryk
Culture, third century BCE.
Courtesy of The State Hermitage Museum, St Petersburg.

century BCE and gradually made their way westward to the territories north of
the Black Sea (the Pontic steppe), to be replaced in the third century BCE by
the Sarmatians – the Scythians' eastern neighbours who shared a comparable
culture. Some scholars (van Geel et al. 2004: 1735) link the development and

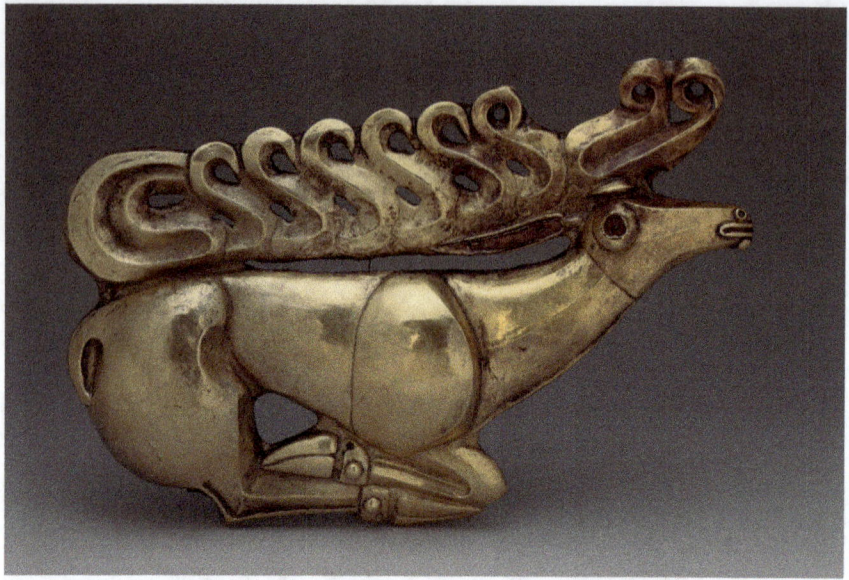

Figure 7.2 Shield plaque in the form of a deer. Scythian Culture, c. 600 BCE.
Courtesy of The State Hermitage Museum, St Petersburg.

expansion of the Scythian culture to a Late-Holocene climate change in southern Siberia and central Asia: 'an abrupt climatic shift towards increased humidity caused by a decline of solar activity' which changed 'hostile semi-deserts' into 'steppe landscapes with a high biomass production' attractive for herbivores and hence for nomadic tribes. The Sarmatians were assimilated by the Huns in the 4th century CE, disappearing into Eastern European forest-steppes (see Bunker et al. 2002; Chochorowski 2004).

The Scytho-Siberian animal style was distinguished by single animal motifs featuring animals whose body parts or appendages (horns, antlers, manes and tails) pass into a proliferation of spirals and curls, which at times terminate in bird-shapes or foliage (Fig. 7.2).[9] Animal style also encompasses coupled compositions where animals are entwined together in a death struggle, typically prey animals attacking ungulates (see Grousset 1970: 11–17; Charrière 1979: 177–85).

For Deleuze and Guattari, the jewellery plaques belong to 'nomad art' (2005: 401), the latter defined in the preceding chapter as 'a dynamic connection between support and ornament [which] replaces the matter-form dialectic' (369). The plaques 'constitute traits of expression of pure speed, carried on objects that are themselves mobile and moving' (ibid. 401), and hence go beyond the figure-ground opposition. Their constitutive motif-support relation should therefore be understood in kinetic and dynamic terms. Furthermore, gold or silver plaques are inseparable from the metalworking technologies that have given rise to them (ibid.). As such, these specimens of nomad art are indissociable from 'nomad science' defined as 'an art as much as a technique' (ibid. 369).

The plaques are distinguished by their iridescent affect: the capacity to 'lend colors the speed of light, making gold glow red [*faisant rougeoyer l'or*] and making silver a white light [*faisant de l'argent une lumière blanche*]' (ibid. 401, modified translation). The metallic-plate-in-motion forces attention to silver's bright white glow or gold's red-yellow gleam. Relativistic quantum chemistry sees the particular quality of lustre as marking energetic changes in the electronic structure of precious metals (see Hussong et al. 2015: 10,331). The plaque's extensive displacement thus envelops a more fundamental intensive movement bound up with qualitative change. Scythian artefacts are a metallic material become expressive, whereby the plaque's material support does not pass into sensation without metallicising it.

Deleuze and Guattari are, however, not simply content with drawing the plaques' ontogenesis. They (2005: 495–9) also draw a phylogenetic line of nomad art which links together (1) Scythian, Sarmatian and Hunnic 'art of the steppes' (Deleuze and Guattari 2005: 574, n. 30), analysed by Grousset (1970: 11–25); and (2) the 'abstract' 'Northern line' (Deleuze and Guattari 2005: 496) of Gothic art broadly conceived by Worringer (see 1997: 106–21, 1920: 43–63) as including the art of 'the Germanic and Celtic migrations of the North' (Deleuze and Guattari 2005: 495).[10] For Deleuze and Guattari, such a conceptual operation aims to decouple nomad art from its capture by sedentary empires (such as Egyptian, Assyrian, Persian or Chinese) and affirm its intermediary status between the East and the North (2005: 495–6; see also 2005: 574, n. 30).[11]

Nomad art is distinguished by close vision, haptic space and the Worringerian abstract line (Deleuze and Guattari 2005: 492–9) which differs from the *concrete line* subordinate to outlining prior form and contour. The concrete line is striated as a form of expression (figuration, imitation, representation) of organic life and its natural laws, a logic at work in classical organic ornamentation (ibid. 497–8; 574, n. 34). The classical ornament enshrines the primacy of the human organism with its symmetry and the inside/outside divide, unlike the abstract 'mutant line . . . without outside or inside, form or background, . . . alive as a continuous variation' (ibid. 498). The liberated abstract line carries material traits of expression of the inorganic life of forces (ibid.). This is the line that Worringer understands, as Deleuze and Guattari aptly summarise, as 'mechanical, but in free action and swirling' (ibid.).

Deleuze and Guattari seem to suggest that the abstract line is an affect of animal style shared by both Scythian art and the types of art that Worringer (1920: 43) discusses under the rubric of 'early northern ornament', i.e. Migration Period (that is, 4–8 CE Celtic and Germanic art) and Romanesque art, shot through the implicit undercurrent of 'the latent Gothic' or 'Gothic form will' (ibid.). *A Thousand Plateaus* illustrates the concept of the abstract line via an image of body parts turning into ribbons and spirals (Deleuze and Guattari 2005: 498–9) without identifying its context or provenance. In fact, such an image is characteristic of animal-style motifs, both Scythian and (proto-)Gothic (see Grousset 1970: 12–14; Worringer 1920: 56).

In turn, coupled motifs depicting animal combat, seen by Grousset (1970:

14) as death struggles whose 'slowness' is usually removed through ornamental stylisation entwining the animal figures together, serve to theorise the plaques' constituent support-motif relation in terms of 'the ornamental abstract line and animal motifs, . . . the speed with which the line integrates and carries expressive traits, and the slowness or fixity of the animal matter traversed, . . . a line of flight . . . and an almost immobile swirling' (Deleuze and Guattari 2005: 499). The two aspects compose 'a single becoming' (ibid.). The animal motif is 'pure animality experienced as inorganic, or supraorganic' (ibid.). The motif envelops the functioning of an inorganic force that traverses animal material; it is a becoming-animal understood as a material trait of expression of force. The ornament-animal motif relation inscribed on the plaque is inseparable from the plaque's constituent relation to its own moving material support, the latter relation made visible through the plaque's metallic lustre.

To sum up, the logic of the motif-support constituent of the Eurasian nomad animal-style metal plaques as it is conceived in Nomadology can be understood in terms of (1) the phenomena of single and coupled motifs and their relation to the abstract line of forces; (2) a technical mediation of both the earth and the cosmos producing metallic affects (colour, lustre); as well as (3) the phylum's ontogenetic and phylogenetic operation. I shall designate such operative motif-support modality as *steppe c(ha)osmotechnics*.[12]

Deleuze (2003: 160–1) reprises the motif-support relation at work in Scythian plaques in his case study of Francis Bacon's paintings through the notion of 'mannerism'. The concept refers both to the works of Bacon and to Michelangelo's 1504–6 *The Holy Family* whose entwined human figures compose 'a single continuous flow' (ibid. 160), 'an acrid and strident polychromy, striated with flashes, like a metal plate' (ibid. 161). Strained by invisible forces, the figure undergoes deformation revealing 'the body beneath the organism' (ibid. 160). Deleuze described this change also as a relation between the Figure and vast monochrome fields (ibid. 12), the latter termed 'the armature or material structure' (ibid. 30) in a possible nod to the armature of reinforced concrete.

In following the motif-support logic of Eurasian Early Iron Age nomad artefacts, Deleuze's case study of Bacon makes steppe metallurgy resonate with contemporary art. Such reading deterritorialises Eurocentric art history, just as the Deleuzoguattarian (2005: 414) 'metallurgical peoples . . . bor[e] holes in European space'. Building on Deleuze and Guattari, I approach the *steppe c(ha) osmotechnics* as an inorganic mode of liaison whose lineage subsists in certain contemporary artistic practices including Think Crazy, allowing us to rethink the notion of media and attend to its aesthetic potential for social change.

Marek Konieczny: Periods and Styles in Unilinear Art History

Konieczny studied at the Industrial and Civil Engineering faculty at the Silesian University of Technology in Gliwice. Silesia has been home to large-scale coal mining (part fuelling Bełchatów, Europe's largest coal-fired power plantt and its massive carbon dioxide emissions), heavy industry and metallurgy whose

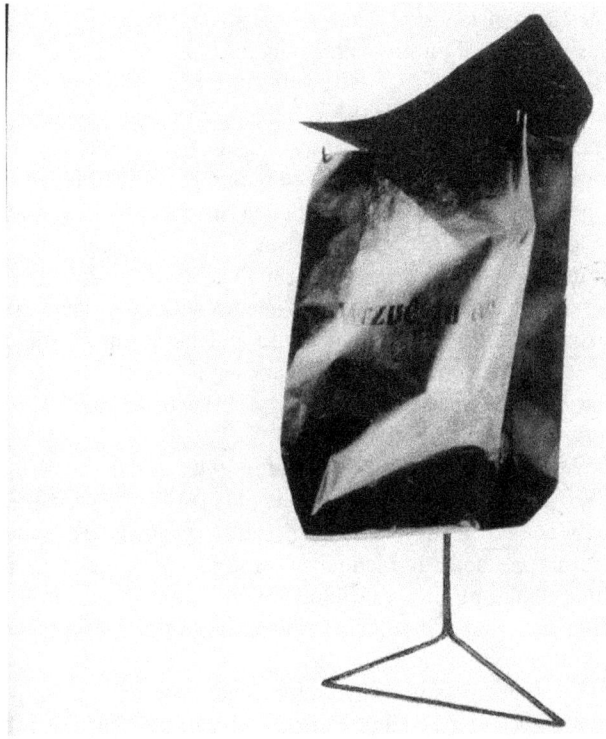

Figure 7.3 Marek Konieczny, *Drop Something in Here*. Installation in public
space, silver aluminium bag on metal stand, 1968/1986.
Courtesy of Marek Konieczny, Klaus Groh and Forschungsstelle
Osteuropa, Bremen.

tradition goes back to the Ages of Metal. The artist obtained his Master's degree
in 1961 as a structural engineer specialising in construction materials and building
components technologies. During his studies, Konieczny developed an interest in
topology and curved spaces. Between 1961 and 1966, he studied interior design at
the Warsaw Academy of Fine Art (ASP) while also participating as a constructor in
several architectural teams responsible for designing major modernist landmarks.
Konieczny worked – in a team led by the eminent architect Oskar Hansen – on the
Osiedle Słowackiego housing estate in Lublin, where he constructed a hyperbolic
paraboloid (*hypar*) (saddle-shaped) thin-shell roof in reinforced concrete. During
his ASP years, Konieczny set off his artistic trajectory with geometric abstractions, eventually abandoning construction design upon graduation.

Across the years Konieczny embarked on Fluxus-type instruction-based, algorithmic intersubjective actions in public space (1968–70) such as *Drop Something
in Here* (1968) (Fig. 7.3); aleatory-stochastic situations (1969–73) at the threshold of conscious thought, including those provoked with bursts and dissipations
of light generated with photographic flash and recorded on photographic film

(1969–71), the manual gestures of randomly etching transparent foils (1972–3), mail art (1972–) and transmissions of purely mental signals (1971–3); as well as performance art (1971–).

In 1974, Konieczny launched Think Crazy: intermedia performance including body art (1974–) and experimental film (1974–6) as well as installations (1974–). Think Crazy also comprises metal reliefs and textured paintings, over time rearranged, divided or compounded as diptychs or triptychs in the artist's studio (1976–), the latter since 1975 called 'Moonarium'. Since 1981 Konieczny has engaged with traditional decorative woodworking technologies. In the 2000s he produced framed reliefs typically incorporating ready-mades such as toy animal figurines derived from contemporary consumer culture and its cheap plastics. In 2012, a major retrospective of Konieczny's work took place at the Zachęta National Gallery of Art in Warsaw, facilitated by his erstwhile student and presently acclaimed New York-based artist Piotr Uklański.

Konieczny was part of the Polish neo-avant-garde of the 1970s that designated, as aptly summarised by Wojciech Cesarski (Kępińska et al. 1981: 2), 'a veritable eruption' of various practices such as Conceptualism, mail art, media art (photography, film), and performance, body and land art. These practices broke with the previous understanding of the plastic arts (ibid.), in terms of the modernist paradigm of a pure, self-critical and self-sufficient object, but at the same time were, for the most part, not explicitly political.

The neo-avant-garde developed its own institutional network of the semi-independent so-called 'author's galleries', and engendered a panoply of critical responses. For the aesthetician Stefan Morawski (2007), it is 'the diverse, sheer extra-artistic matter [that] becomes the substance of the creative endeavours and achievements of the neo-avant-garde. . . . Choices are now made beyond art, and this is something which some researchers convincingly designate as the end of the *sensu stricto* avant-garde' (all translations of Polish texts are mine).[13] The curator Łukasz Ronduda (2009) classifies Think Crazy as belonging to the 'conceptual-sensuous' strand of 'existential post-essentialist' conceptual practices which opened up to reality by posing questions about the essence both of art and of existence.

As I see it, launched in 1974, Think Crazy is a radical affirmation of the mystery of change,[14] something already implicit in Konieczny's earlier experimentation engaging the disparate levels that Katherine Hayles (2014) sees as the triad of conscious thought, 'cognitive nonconscious' as well as purely material processes. Think Crazy entailed Konieczny's new-found preoccupation with specific aggregates of the phylum, chiefly metallic, called 'Special Equipment'. These materials – quintessentially gold, but also aluminium and schlagmetal, as well as non-metallic matters such as fabric – erupt in folds or engender rectilinear, polygonal, curved, conical or spiral shapes. Simply put, Konieczny covered different body parts and objects with gold, documenting their mutual contacts.

The inventory of Special Equipment includes black velvet cloaks, thick cord tassels, gilded spiral horns, golden sickles and miniature pyramids, but also unspecified biomatter arranged into orifices, foldings, mucous membranes

Figure 7.4 Marek Konieczny, *Epitaph*. Metal relief, artist's studio, 1976. Courtesy of Marek Konieczny, Klaus Groh and Forschungsstelle Osteuropa, Bremen.

(mouth, labia); genitalia (vagina, penis) and body parts such as breasts, buttocks, head and thighs. All those become disorganised as molecular technical elements that install an elaborate system of complex mediations, spatio-temporal couplings and resonances. They are brought into experimental contact with one another via performance, photography and analogue film. Importantly, these contingent Think Crazy intermedia operations attach themselves to molar aggregates of the early modern Western and Old Polish art and culture, something diagrammed by such titles as *1672–1974* (1974), *Still Life with a Little Bird* (1974), *Santa Conversatione* (1975), *Epitaph* (1976) (Fig. 7.4) and *Think Crazy for the Sistine Chapel* (1976–80), and function as their vector of deterritorialisation or cosmicisation (the latter alluded to by the eponymous neighbouring constellations of *Orion's Sickle*, 1974, and *Monoceros*, 1980).

1974: 'He gilds his head and it is him' – Think Crazy's Ontogenetic Line(age)

Following the logic of machinic phylum, I am going to discuss Konieczny's practices in terms of its ontogenetic and phylogenetic line(age)s.

Seen from the perspective of its ontogenetic line(age), its process of individuation, Think Crazy is inseparable from a serialisation, launching as it does between 1974 and 1983 several line(age)s of Special Equipment apparatuses for effecting change across physical, biological, psychic and social matter. In this respect, I am going to develop a c(ha)osmotechnical reading of Szwajewska's 1980 dialogical interview with Konieczny. This important dialogical intervention, contemporary with *A Thousand Plateaus*, includes insights on Think Crazy, the relation between Think Crazy and Special Equipment, as well as a catalogue of the singular modalities of Special Equipment: what the artist designates as *martwe natury* ('still lifes', lit. 'dead natures'), *żywe obrazy* ('living images') and *miniatury* ('miniatures'), as well as metal reliefs.

For Konieczny (qtd in Szwajewska 1980: 109), what matters in Special Equipment, as epitomised in the still lifes and their deployment of miniature golden pyramids, is 'artificiality, and by the same token, the emergence of a new artistic reality'. Its precursor might be found in Konieczny's 1970 *Generator of Stochastic Processes*. Marking the artist's interest in cybernetics and stochastics, both Markovian and non-Markovian,[15] the generator was a small cuboid device fitted with casters and motors whose autonomous movement was driven by cosmic rays measured with Geiger counters. According to Konieczny (qtd in Szwajewska 1980: 110), Think Crazy affirms the 'constructive' aspect of madness through 'activities directly impact[ing] not so much the associations of the imagination as [its] "hard structure" stemming from experiences, our habits [which] ought to be relaxed and changed'. Think Crazy's artificiality works to loosen and ultimately break the sensory-motor schema organically linking sensory perception (reaction) to motor response (action), which Deleuze saw at play in the classical cine-image.

Think Crazy installs a mannerist point of view that destratifies the human by virtue of the inhuman forces it follows. As Konieczny (ibid. 109) points out, 'one can also look at a very concrete activity, *Drop Something in Here*, . . . as a manner. This syntheticity, this derealisation, . . . is a call for an individualisation, a de-standardisation of the human. This de-standardisation . . . is particularly resonant [the word *nośny* is also an engineering term signifying 'load-bearing'] and constructive, especially vis-à-vis the extremely robust and rigid external structures surrounding us.' *Drop Something in Here* is a 1968 action in public space which saw Konieczny install golden and silver aluminium bags with the eponymous call for action on metal stands throughout Warsaw, including the notorious Różycki Bazaar, running a black market of goods in defiance of centrally planned economy. The action prompted by-standers to drop various objects into the bags. Think Crazy's mannerist machine liberates the abstract line drawn by the bag's creased material and the iridescent haptic zone of its metallic relief from their role as mere facilitators of intersubjective sensorimotor actions in extensive space and linear time.

I understand Special Equipment in terms of the Deleuzoguattarian (2005: 141–3, 510–12) conceptualisation of the generative potential (*abstract machine*)[16] of a concrete assemblage as a coupling of 'unformed matters' bearing singularities (*phyla*) and 'nonformal', 'diagrammatic functions' (*tensors*) that stretch assemblages to their limit point (ibid. 99). Phyla designate material variation of Special Equipment. In turn, tensors refer to Special Equipment's provisional functioning as self-portraits, still lifes, living images, miniatures and metal reliefs – in other words, to their different powers of deterritorialisation and deformation, of *thinking crazy*. The diverse series of Special Equipment tensors are shot through with a metallic phylum. Konieczny deems gold his preferred material because of its 'absolute artifice' (Szwajewska 1986: 11). The artist (conversation between Konieczny et al. 2015) explained that when natural light is split through a prism into the spectrum of its constituent colours, 'there is no gold in the analysis of the spectrum . . . The golden colour is a mere reflection of natural light off the mineral that is gold . . . an artificial colour, one which does not exist; . . . It is not a gift of the sun.' This preference for gold is, however, more like a tendency or desire. While Konieczny strove to acquire gold, he often employed both gold and a range of other alloyed metals. His operations harnessed such metallic affects as lustre, from silver's white glow through gold's red-yellow to copper's red, as well as gold's supreme malleability and softness which allowed him to bespeckle various surfaces with metal leaf.

The metallic line erupts in 1974 as a series of self-portraits. *Orion's Sickle* (Fig. 7.5) sees the nude artist posing for a full-length profile portrait with a golden sickle slid between his thighs. This 'body art' (Szwajewska 1986: 14) is documented in two photographs. One, black-and-white, barely shows Konieczny's face while overexposure renders invisible the front contour of his body beneath the nipples. The other, in colour, captures his body in a headless profile, only from the chest down, with one hand clutching the shaft of the sickle, the genitalia seemingly tucked inside the thighs. Metallic intensities of the traditional silver halide chemical process and its chromogenic version at work in film photography co-create these new provisional organs. The work's metallic synthesis dismantles the hierarchical stratification of the human body which prioritises the (male) face while sexualising the genitalia. This deterritorialisation corresponds to a becoming-cosmic of the work's eponymous mythological hunter.[17]

Seen by Konieczny as 'installation' (ibid.), the *1672–1974* collage manipulates a reproduction of a seventeenth-century portrait of a Polish-Lithuanian nobleman. Konieczny's preoccupation with rendering texture of the figure's attendant textiles, insignia and armour turns the likeness into a planar and haptic surface akin to a metallic bas-relief. Finally, *Still Life with a Little Bird* captures Konieczny's body *en face*, from the waist down, with a miniature gaudy-coloured plastic bird installed atop his genitalia.

Konieczny's still lifes are aggregates of Special Equipment materials for potential use in his performances. Variously including a golden horn, sickle or pyramid,

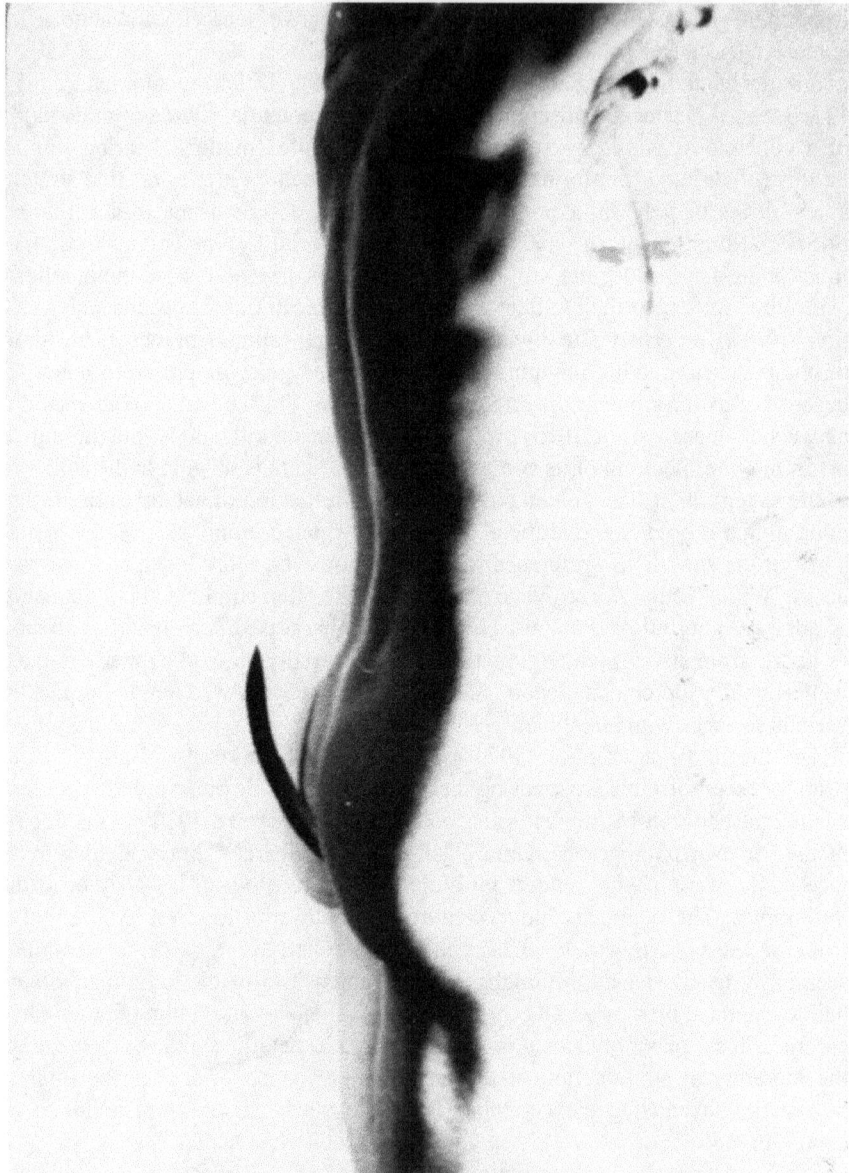

Figure 7.5 Marek Konieczny, *Orion's Sickle*. Body art, artist's studio, 1974.
Courtesy of Marek

and a black velvet cloth, still lifes are characteristically laid out on a flat surface
– at once a small table and the frame of a photograph. What interests Konieczny
in his still life is 'the fact of [its] installation', 'the artificiality of the generated
situation' and 'the emergence of a new artistic reality', whereas its relation to a

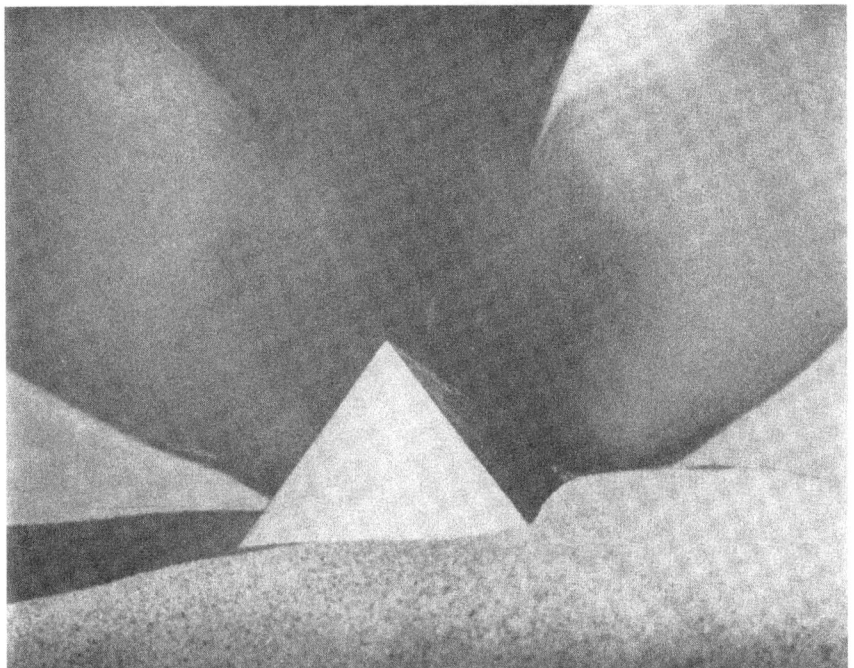

Figure 7.6 Marek Konieczny, *Dialogue with a Pyramid*. Still frame,
16 mm film, 3 min, 1975.
Courtesy of Marek Konieczny, Klaus Groh and Forschungsstelle
Osteuropa, Bremen.

'painterly situation' comes only as an afterthought (Konieczny qtd in Szwajewska 1980: 109). Konieczny (in conversation with the author in September 2019) extends this logic to a seventeenth-century Dutch still life with asparagus that he saw in the Rijksmuseum in 1974, viewing painting as merely a 'technology' of 'installation'. Self-portraits resulting from pairings of Special Equipment materials with the artist's body can be considered a subset of still lifes.

His living images are mostly three-minute, looped 16 mm films from 1975 whose captured frames engender miniatures (see Szwajewska 1980: 110). The films document and relaunch couplings of disparate Special Equipment realities. Here, aggregates of metallic phylum intervene in human bodies, transferring the spasm of the encounter to a projector fitted with a looping apparatus and/or to the film's own surface. For example, traversed by rhythmic flickers, *At Sea – Seven Evenings – Seven Mornings* documents a co-modulation of labia and a miniature golden ship. In turn, *Dialogue with a Pyramid* (Fig. 7.6) features an encounter between labia and the eponymous golden pyramid, while *Santa Conversatione*, aphoristically described by Hungarian art historian László Beke (qtd in Konieczny 1982) as 'he gilds his head and it is him', stages a dialogue between a bald human head and breasts, all covered in gold leaf.

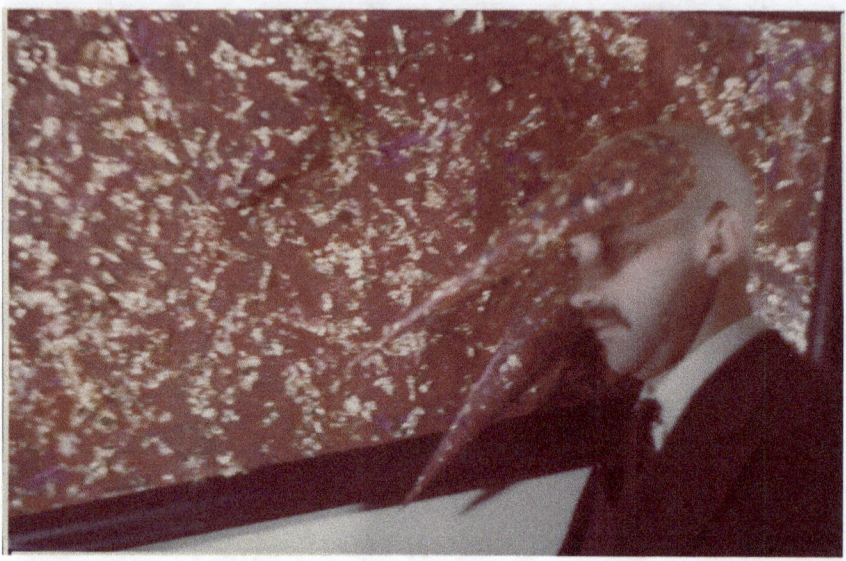

Figure 7.7 Marek Konieczny, *Unfeeling Rocks with Self-Portrait*. Performance
with metal relief, artist's studio, 1979.
Courtesy of Marek Konieczny, Klaus Groh and Forschungsstelle
Osteuropa, Bremen.

Between 1976 and 1983, Think Crazy occupied the traditional fine arts genres
of painting and sculpture, opening Moonarium to processes of (dis)assembling
textured paintings, sculptures and metal reliefs for variable spans of time, either
years or minutes. As part of this installation, the works were also brought into
contact with other Special Equipment apparatuses such as the artist's body. This
specific strain of serialisation that harnesses various speeds of temporal modulation began in 1976 with *Epitaph*, a metal relief composed of varied pieces
of thin aluminium bounded by an irregular hexagonal wooden frame, in 1979
compounded with a gilded wooden plank. In the same year, *Unfeeling Rocks*, a
textured aluminium relief in right-angled trapezoid frames featuring a protrud-
ing gilded horn, was briefly coupled with an analogous golden horn affixed to
Konieczny's temple, thus giving rise to *Unfeeling Rocks with Self-Portrait* (Fig.
7.7). *Unfeeling Rocks* was also coupled (1979–83) with a two-panel textured
painting featuring a trophy roe deer head. The emergent ensemble was called
Think Crazy Forest Inspectorate, Formerly a Diptych, Now a Triptych (Fig. 7.8).
The work's name encapsulates its path of mutation, thematising the problem of
change in itself.

Konieczny's metal reliefs, including *Epitaph* and *Unfeeling Rocks*, were first
exhibited outside his studio at the BWA gallery in Bielsko-Biała only for a
brief period of time (23 January to 4 February 1982). As the gallery's erstwhile
director, the art historian, curator and critic Helena Dobranowicz, recalls (2019),

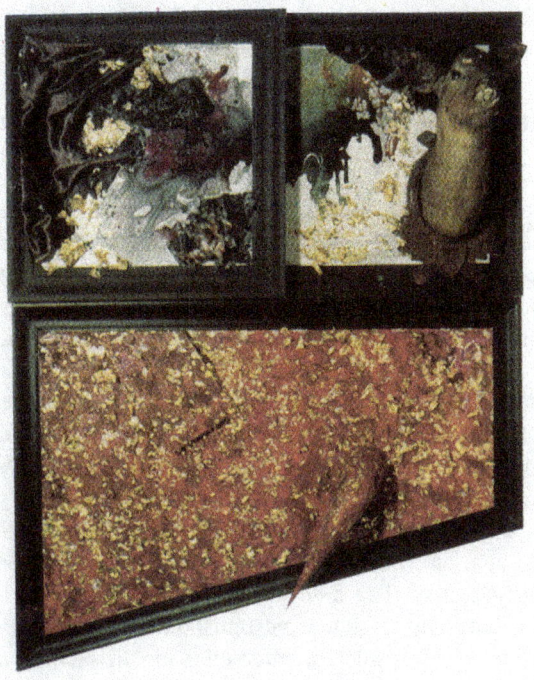

Figure 7.8 Marek Konieczny, *Think Crazy Forest Inspectorate, Formerly a Diptych, Now a Triptych*. Three-panelled ensemble of textured paintings and metal relief, artist's studio, 1979–83.
Courtesy of Marek Konieczny, Klaus Groh and Forschungsstelle Osteuropa, Bremen.

the exhibition, called *Unfeeling Rocks*, was scheduled to open in December 1981. However, in the wake of the introduction of martial law by the state authorities, imposed to suppress Solidarity, and the ensuing massacre of the workers of the Wujek coal mine who opposed the state's crackdown, as well as the country-wide boycott of state-run galleries by the artists, Konieczny chose to arrange the artworks amidst the gallery space covered with black theatrical curtains, blocking light in such a way that the works were illuminated only by a reflector spotlight. As Dobranowicz (ibid.) recalls, one entered the *Unfeeling Rocks* exhibition as if into a tomb. There was no *vernissage* nor other accompanying events.

The *Unfeeling Rocks* as an exhibition that was-not-to-be, and hence forming a crack in the eponymous rocks, resonates with the Solidarity movement whose edge of deterritorialisation lodged itself in 1981 in a Silesian coal mine. Its modest catalogue significantly brought together short quotes from Konieczny's friends, fellow artists, critics and art historians, recording their divergent encounters with Think Crazy.[18] In this way, the *Unfeeling Rocks* exhibition stages molecular revolution defined as '*a process that brings about mutations in the unconscious social field, at a level beyond discourse*' (Guattari and Rolnik 2007: 259), which Guattari saw at work also in Solidarity.

1672: Sarmato-Baroque as Think Crazy's Phylogenetic Line(age)

Think Crazy's ontogenetic line of variation, its internal differentiation as outlined above, is indissoluble from its transhistorical, phylogenetic operation rippling across technological cultures. Such logic decouples the radical future of Think Crazy from its subordination to periods and styles in a linear art history. Instead, Think Crazy enters resonance with the cultural formation of the multi-ethnic landed nobility (*szlachta*) of the Polish-Lithuanian Commonwealth called 'Sarmatism', which reached its peak of intensity in the seventeenth century.[19] Such formulation echoes Guattari and Rolnik's (2007: 219) understanding of Solidarity as a molecular revolution whereby 'desire on a collective scale invests in traditional formations'.

My departure point for approaching the phylogenetic operation of Think Crazy is the Deleuzoguattarian (2000: 84–105) schizoid world-historical delirium developed in *Anti-Oedipus*. The delirium conjoins historical and geographical designations with crossings of intensive thresholds traced on a body without organs. This vision is encapsulated, inter alia, in Nietzsche's assertion 'I'm Polish' (ibid. 86) as an example of his schizoid 'names of history' (ibid. 21). In *Ecce Homo* Nietzsche (2007: 10) declares: 'I am a Polish nobleman pur sang ... But even as a Pole I am a tremendous atavism.' Such schizoid designation at once marks a change of intensity and diagnoses Nietzsche's socius and its specific loci of otherness. Think Crazy's production of intensities invests the social. Symptomatically, while for Szwajewska (1986: 12) Think Crazy 'resides in a crevice fleeing control where madness runs wild', for Stefan Morawski (qtd in Konieczny 1982) 'madness proposed by Marek Konieczny makes sense inasmuch as it is in fact deeply related to today's civilizational and cultural changes'.[20]

In what follows, I am going to outline the fundamental characteristics of Sarmatism and demonstrate how these are creatively reworked, or rather arise as something else, in Think Crazy. One cannot assess the nuance of Konieczny's deterritorialisations without a robust understanding of the functioning of the seventeenth-century artefacts operating within Sarmatism taken as at once a socio-political, cultural and aesthetic assemblage. By focusing on insights from cultural history as well as the variation in materials – their singularities, operations and affects – I seek to draw attention to the non-ideological nomadic potentialities of the seventeenth-century Commonwealth art.

Sarmatism conjoined (Polish) *szlachta*'s claim to descent from the Sarmatians (the designation 'Sarmatia' appeared in presentist Renaissance histories reworking classical sources, whose spatial scope strategically included the territories of the Commonwealth), with a composition of entangled Ottoman Turkish, Crimean Tatar and Safavid Persian elements found in lifestyle, textiles, armour, weaponry, jewellery and attire, as well as vernacular and Western components (Gothic, Mannerist, Baroque) associated with fine art (painting, architecture and sculpture) (see Mańkowski 1946, 1935: 108–16; Ostrowski 1999a).[21] As Mańkowski (1946: 97–8) points out, Islamic art, deemed Sarmatian, was not considered exotic, but intrinsic to Old Polish culture. The phenomenon took root in the Polish-Lithuanian Commonwealth (1569–1795). As a consequence of the formal union between the Kingdom of Poland and the Grand Duchy of Lithuania in 1569, the latter since the fourteenth century home to Lipka Tatar settlers, the Commonwealth art and culture became open to Turkic cultures, especially as Poland-Lithuania was neighbouring with a Crimean Khanate allied with the Ottoman sultan (see Zamoyski 1999). The union transferred to the Kingdom the Duchy's Ruthenian palatinates corresponding to the present-day Ukraine. The incorporated territories, which retained many of their rights, became home to a manorial economy, fuelled by mostly Ruthenian serf labour, growing grain for western European markets. There has been an ongoing discussion whether the Commonwealth can be considered as a colonial periphery and whether the situation of its peasants can be seen in terms of colonial and class oppression (see Sowa 2011). Poland-Lithuania was a republic of nobles (gradually taken over by their upper strata), who constituted nine percent of the population. Its monarch was elected directly by the mounted assembly of all (male) nobility. A consequence of the principle of unanimity was the practice of *liberum veto* whereby an objection made by a single noble could effectively nullify the legislation of the whole legislative assembly. The *liberum veto* (admired by Nietzsche (2007: 100) and vital to his becoming-Polish-nobleman) played a major role in producing the political impasse that opened the way to the country's eighteenth-century partitions.

The period of Sarmatism corresponds to what art historian Aleksandra Koutny-Jones (2015: 11) terms the 'long Baroque' between 1580 and 1772, variously framed as a harmonious symbiosis of Western Baroque fine art characterised by 'a cult of splendour' and decorative artistic craft inspired by Islamic art, the two united in a shared sensualism (Mańkowski 1935: 112), or as 'a confrontation between an emerging Eurocentric modernity . . . and the nomadic values of Crimean Tartars and Ottoman Turks' (Murawska-Muthesius 2004: 158). One can also understand Sarmatism as a drawing out of nomadic multiplicities and multiple entanglements working beneath the sedentary Ottoman and Safavid empires, carried out by Armenian and Greek itinerant merchants and artisans (on the role of the latter, see Mańkowski 1959). Art historian Thomas DaCosta Kaufmann (1999: 18) argues that Sarmatism 'received little expression in art' beside gentry portraits in the 'Sarmatian' (i.e. Ottomanising) garb, seen as 'distinctively iconographic motifs'. Such formulation, however, only considers fine art to the exclusion of decorative technologies. As I see it, the notion of Sarmatism[22] can be extended to artisanal production. I shall term this aesthetic-cultural aggregate 'Sarmato-Baroque'.

Sarmatism rises in 1974 in Think Crazy but already as something else. Think Crazy is a past-future technics of emergence simultaneously working its way through the early modern art and culture of the Commonwealth, the 1970s and a yet-unspecified future. This at once transhistorical and world-historical functioning of Think Crazy is emblematised in Konieczny's 1974 collage *1672–1974* (also known as *Self-Portrait 1683–1973*) taken together with his 1975 short looped film *24012008 Think Crazy*. The two works are expressly linked by the artist (conversation between Konieczny et al. in 2015).

The *1672–1974* self-portrait entails a manipulation of a reproduction of a seventeenth-century portrait of a Commonwealth nobleman. The portrait uncannily resembles the artist, not in the sense of any specific facial features but by dint of his bald head and a Tatar moustache. In turn, the film features a humanoid figure with a gilded head, enveloped in a black velvet cloak flapping in the wind. The figure is captured with its back facing the viewer against a deep blue sky. The faceless figure continues to swerve and flap in the wind infinitely in the radical future of becoming. The two self-portraits compose a diptych which constitutes the impersonal, non-human time of Think Crazy as the Deleuzian (1994: 89) caesura of eternal return. This event perpetually eludes the present, drawing the past and the future together as its two intrinsic, fixed aspects: the before and the after of a new temporal series. The coupled artworks draw a diagram of Think Crazy as an impersonal pure potentiality that effaces chrono-empirical time and stages the death of the figure of the artist as a constituted subject, effectuating a becoming-imperceptible. This depersonalisation harnesses black velvet's affect of extreme light absorption, blotting out the sun and its human-centred universe. Think Crazy was thus launched with a series of artworks whereby the artist's personal death corresponds to a topological opening to intensive multiplicities.[23]

A becoming-imperceptible is also at work in Konieczny's 1976 *Epitaph*. Described by Szwajewska (1986: 12) as 'a black, creeping, all-embracing texture – aware of the secret of the other side of life', this hexagonal metal relief is a deterritorialisation or cosmicisation of Sarmato-Baroque coffin portraits and their attendant epitaphs. The metallic *Epitaph* has been frequently accompanied since 1981 by a short poetic, or conceptual, epitaph which intersperses designations of the artist's spatio-temporal and earth-bound status (such as 'lives in Europe / . . . a graduate of two universities) with an exposition of the affective powers afforded by his relation to the forces of cosmos and harboured by an emerald gemstone ('Born under the sign of Cancer / son of the Moon / an emerald will bring him luck') (see Konieczny 1982).

How can we conceptualise the transhistorical operation of Think Crazy? It is not a recollection of the past in the present because such formulation does not account for qualitative change. Rather, in 1974 Konieczny succumbs to the Deleuzian (1994: 89–90) synthesis of the eternal return corresponding to a radical future in which the self is 'carried away and dispersed in the shock of multiplicity to which it gives birth: what the self has become equal to is the unequal in itself'. Think Crazy is untimely in the Nietzschean sense of a functioning 'counter to time, . . . on our time and, let us hope, for the benefit of a time to come' (Nietzsche qtd in Deleuze and Guattari 1994: 112). It aligns itself with the Nietzschean 'unhistorical' (Nietzsche qtd in ibid. 296) becoming which, as Deleuze and Guattari (ibid.) remind us, is opposed to history. Think Crazy's Sarmato-Baroque intensities also epitomise what cultural analyst Mieke Bal designates as 'preposterous art history'

(1999: 7) whereby chronologically prior periods, genres and artworks serve to theorise, and thus become alive 'as an aftereffect' in, chronologically posterior works. The long Baroque becomes decoupled from a sedentary, essentialist and linear art history and arises as a non-ideological power, untimely and preposterous, of joining together of heterogeneous dimensions. Its hybrid character now designates the pure mobility of Scytho-Sarmatian affective weapons harbouring the potential for change – a steppe c(ha)osmotechnics.

Sarmato-Baroque includes a panoply of bastard artefacts which fall outside the domain of the fine arts (architecture, sculpture, painting) or otherwise swarm at its limits. They are either categorised as the decorative ('minor') arts, or else are construed as occasional installations or provincial mutations of the established forms. All converging in the funeral ceremony, the artefacts are not constituted objects but arise as modulatory operations harnessing singularities – as Think Crazy's Special Equipment. This operative inventory includes decorative elements of horse harness including a pair of feathered wooden wings fastened either to the cantle or to the backplate of the hussar armour; tomb banners in purple damask; *buńczuk*s – Turkic standards consisting of a wooden pole crowned with a tassel-like arrangement of horsetail hair; metal plates bearing coats of arms which the archaeologist Tadeusz Sulimirski (1970) linked to the Eurasian nomadic *tamga* clan signs; jewellery-encrusted curved weapons such as the Ottoman-inflected sabre with a hilt resembling a bird's head in profile (*karabela*), making possible lateral movement with the cutting edge of the blade; and war maces, of Turkic or Persian lineage, with a bulbous (*buława*) or flanged head (*buzdygan*) that served as military command batons and insignia of rank (see Mańkowski 1959).

In turn, the so-called 'Sarmatian' portraits were full-length likenesses conjoining an extreme veristic likeness of the sitter's face with an abandonment of the pictorial illusion of volume through linear perspective and chiaroscuro. Distinguished by flat patches of vivid colour and a 'planar, ornamental and conventional treatment of the whole figure and the scenery' (Chrzanowski 1988: 122), the two-dimensional portraits also feature a disproportional elongation of the body in relation to the head coupled with a meticulous rendition of jewellery, armour, weaponry and textile folds. Moreover, the portraits feature set elements such as an armoured arm bent at the elbow and holding a weapon, as well as a small kilim-covered table aggregating and isolating material attributes of heraldic clan and social status: 'a small table for arranging a still life of the attributes [of kin and social status]' (Chrzanowski 1995: 29).

Finally, the coffin portrait (*portret trumienny*) (Fig. 7.9) is a singular artefact of unclear origins (Ostrowski 1999b: 48) entailing a veristic bust-length facial likeness of the deceased depicted as alive, in a ¾ profile and against a monochrome background, the latter at times gilded or silver-plated. The portraits were oil-painted on a polygonal – mostly hexagonal but also octagonal, trapezoidal or rectangular – partly curved or, rarely, oval metal plate. Rendered in copper, lead, tin or silver, the plate was made to fit a shorter side of the coffin (see Ostrowski 1999b: 47–8; Chrościcki 1974: 67–70; Koutny-Jones 2015: 146–54; Chrzanowski 1995: 109–20). For Chrzanowski (1988: 232), the coffin effigies bring the 'veristic

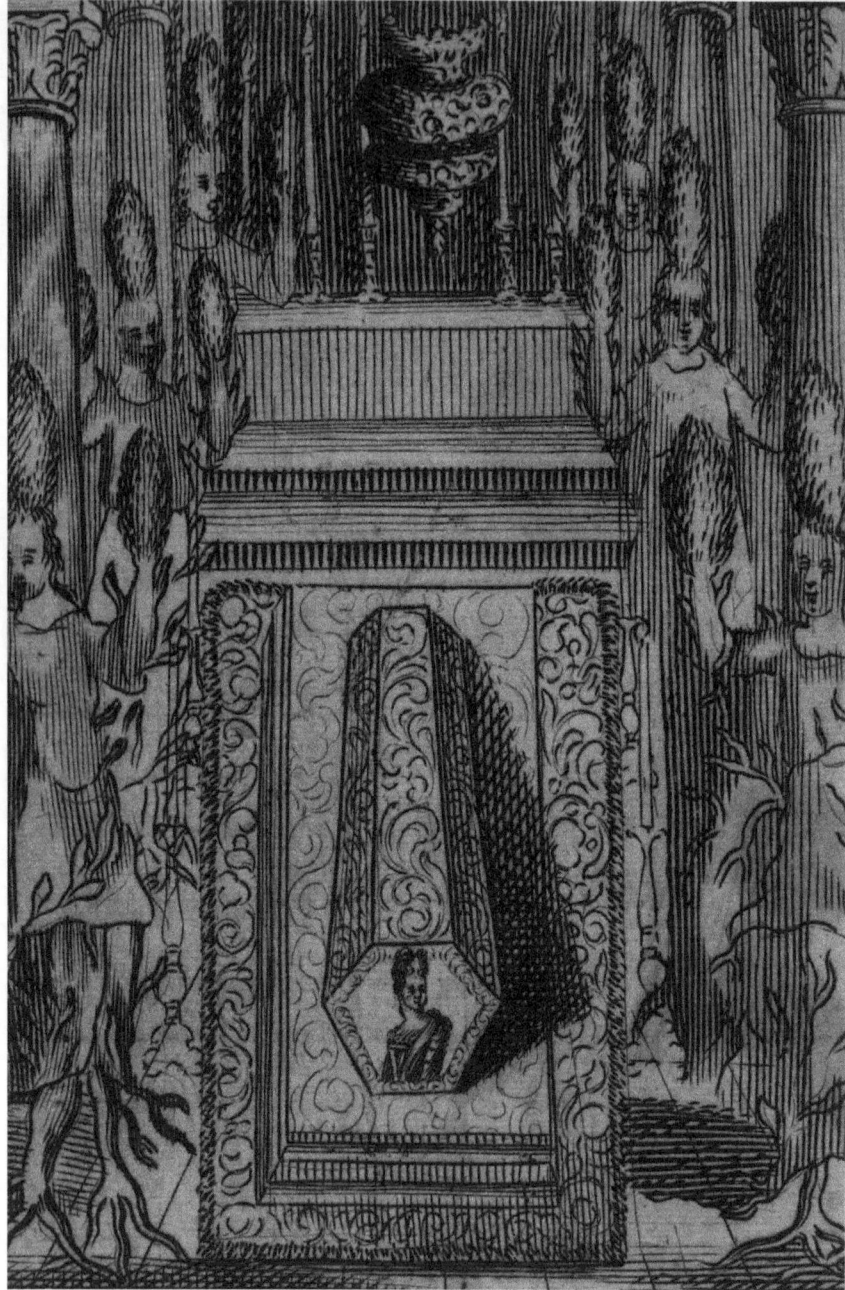

Figure 7.9 Coffin with a coffin portrait mounted at its front end, resting atop a catafalque, decoration of the funeral of Teresa Antonina Łącka, Jesuit church, Poznań, 1700, fragment of copperplate engraving.
From the collection of Warsaw University Library.

bluntness, naïve detailing, pictorial concreteness' of the Sarmatian portrait to bear on death and eternity. For Koutny-Jones (2015: 154, 207), 'largely indigenous' to Poland-Lithuania, the coffin portrait was an 'esoteric art-form' expressing 'the often eccentric nuances of the Commonwealth's commemorative culture'.

The portrait is indissoluble from its associated assemblage. It was part of the funerary installation composed of a canopied catafalque designed to house the coffin (*castrum doloris*). A castrum doloris was built inside a church and adorned with candles for the duration of an elaborate funeral replete with panegyric addresses and elements of theatrical spectacle (*pompa funebris*). Rendered in silver, gold, copper or lead, heraldic plates – bearing the initials and date of death as well as the maternal and paternal lineage of the deceased – were attached to the longer sides of the coffin, whereas a metal plate bearing an epitaphic inscription was affixed to its shorter side.

As Koutny-Jones (2015: 126) explains, the coffin portrait was transported in a funereal carriage and taken to the church whereas the coffin itself was transported separately. For the duration of the ceremony the effigy was placed at a shorter side of the coffin facing the congregation. After the funeral, the portrait was detached and affixed, alongside the heraldic plates and the textual cartouche, to a wooden panel, thus forming an epitaphic ensemble subsequently hung on a church wall (Ostrowski 1999a: 285, 1999b: 47; Koutny-Jones 2015: 126, 147–8). Sometimes, as Chrościcki points out (1974: 70), it was melted down into an ingot for subsequent re-use.

The funeral and the coffin portrait itself were designed to convey the living presence of the deceased and draw attention to their elite social status. Drawing on Kantorowicz's concept of 'the king's two bodies' whereby the office of the medieval king unites his timeless spiritual 'Body politic' with his mortal 'Body natural', Koutny-Jones (2015: 151) frames coffin portraits as visual allusions to the deceased ' "spiritual" body that was to rise at . . . the Last Judgement, as opposed to the "natural" body which was to be buried in the coffin'. Viewed in this way, the coffin portrait enacts the Deleuzoguattarian (2005: 115–17) understanding of signifiance as bound up with *faciality*.

Under the signifying regime, a signifier's 'pure formal redundancy' is necessarily grounded in a material, or rather corporeal, support encapsulated in the despotic face which constitutes its central, formal 'substance of expression' – 'the face crystallizes all redundancies, it emits and receives, releases and recaptures signifying signs' (ibid. 115). Faciality, alongside its segregative racialisation, is opposed to 'an affective semiotic' Deleuze and Guattari detect in nomad jewellery plaques (ibid. 401), which constitute an asignifying trait of expression of forces. The signifying sign is 'written upon an immobile, objective matter' (ibid.), and thus indexed to a semiotically formed (corporealised, organised) material support affirming the hylomorphic dualism of form and matter. Conversely, the nomadic sign 'operates only upon the mobile body itself' (ibid. 397) and is therefore indexed to a fundamentally mobile material support (ibid. 401) and the wider milieu of relations of forces it taps into. The metal plaque affirms the model of a mobile sign (*motif*) inscribed on a mobile support subject to forces, and thus already in the process of ungrounding itself. The signifying sign, on the other hand, always falls back on objective matter that grounds it.[24]

Konieczny's world-historical delirium encounters conceptual and aesthetic technologies of the seventeenth-century Commonwealth, extracting the perverse potential for change harboured by the fabulation of the Sarmatian nomadic lineage. What Konieczny's practice draws out in particular from Sarmatism is precisely a nomadic, asignifying sign. Think Crazy is a transversal becoming that reinvents the nomadic sign it finds in the seventeenth century as a neo-avant-garde practice. It reveals Sarmato-Baroque as an artisanal operation that captures the powers of metals and extends their nonorganic life, even and especially in portraits. *Pompa funebris* rises in Think Crazy as an assemblage of metallic phylum crystallising around the expressive traits of the coffin portrait whose polygonal shape corresponded to a shorter side of the coffin, and whose metallic surface was designed to reflect the light of candles.

Special Equipment, as encapsulated in *Unfeeling Rocks with Self-Portrait* and *Epitaph*, deterritorialises the molar understanding of the coffin portrait as obeying the duality of the natural and the spiritual body. Think Crazy draws out the portrait's nomadic intensities, its metallic steppe technics whereby intensive movement is bound up with qualitative change. Rather than a ritual centred on the human spiritual face which emanates meaning and confers timeless legitimacy upon the nobility's class lineage, coffin portraits undergo change upon encounter with Think Crazy, becoming a metallic conductor that carries operations of dismantling the face and disorganising the body. *Pompa funebris* no longer designates a hylomorphic spectacle in which transcendental, splendorous form resuscitates inert matter. Instead, it now affirms the operative nomadic sign Deleuze and Guattari saw at work in Early Iron Age steppe metallurgy.

Think Crazy self-portraits, still lifes and living images reinvent *pompa funebris* and its associated coffin effigies as an acentred death metal composition that exchanges forces. The Sarmato-Baroque funerary pomp becomes an event which sweeps away the attendant attributes of noble humanity – corporeal organisation, subjectivity and meaning – in a becoming-imperceptible. No longer an anthropocentric status-conferring procedure, *pompa funebris* explodes into an endless series of operations; it is a media technology of the cosmos. The operations include thermal and mechanical deformations of metals as well as (dis) assembling the resulting aggregates, the latter encapsulated in the performative and technical nature of the Commonwealth-era epitaphic compositions hung in a church. Think Crazy relief series unleash the powers of polygonal variation harboured by coffin portraits, akin to allotropic crystalline forms. Sarmato-Baroque epitaphs, which inscribe into a flat surface various elements previously distributed in space and time, can now be approached not as the present record of a past performance, but as a creative diagram for the future, a Special Equipment. In the same way, (Polish-Lithuanian) Commonwealth-era still lifes aggregating insignia of social privilege incorporated into the Sarmatian portraits become something else in Think Crazy still lifes. Liberated from their subordination to communicating social rank, Sarmato-Baroque still lifes appear in Think Crazy's future of eternal return as non-ideological diagrams of pure potentialities, something that at once has already happened and is about to happen.

Konieczny's constant recycling of the reliefs and his preoccupation with gold's lustre corresponds to the metallic synthesis of the funerary art machine. Mobile arrangements of light, as well as sculptural, architectural and pictorial elements at work in Sarmato-Baroque funerary pomp, return as the disruptive intermedial event of the crossing of a threshold. At this threshold, a metal-mediated decomposition of the body of the deceased and its conversion into minerals simultaneously gestures towards the purely speculative modes of individuation. As such, it echoes Konieczny's living images understood by Szwajewska (1980: 110) as 'an intimation of a future world, yet unknown to us'.

Sarmato-Baroque, and Think Crazy, does not launch the totality of a Baroque allegory sounding metaphysical harmony[25] but an open ecology of the real whereby art functions, to use philosopher Monika Bakke's framework, as a 'metabolic force [acting] in deep time environments' (2017: 41). For Bakke, '[metabolic] pathways of matter ... flow through organic and nonorganic formations undergoing biological and mineral evolutions' (ibid. 42). Metabolism is decoupled from its traditional bio-centric formulation and instead refers to 'inorganic activity [which] includes self-assembly processes as well as dynamic forces' enabling biological and mineral individuation (ibid.). Interfacing biomatter, metals and thought, *pompa funebris* affirms metabolism viewed by Bakke (ibid. 50) as a force of entangling that affects biological, mineral, technological and artistic domains.

As we have seen, the phylogenetic line of Think Crazy connects to the seventeenth-century art and culture of the Polish-Lithuanian Commonwealth whence it derives its nomadic asignifying sign which is also a technology of harnessing of forces. The nomadic features of seventeenth-century 'Sarmatian' artworks make them resonate with Eurasian Iron Age Scytho-Sarmatian artefacts in the animal style, exploding the linear art-historical time into a shared past-future of serialised becomings. Think Crazy de-sedentarises the Long Baroque, emphasising its constellations of itinerant media. Such gesture dovetails with a cartography of 'travels of the abstract line' developed by Laura U. Marks in *Enfoldment and Infinity* (2010) in relation to Islamicate art, foregrounding the role of 'nomadic art, the product of itinerant artisans dismissed as merely decorative, when in fact it infectiously transmits the performative qualities of non-figurative art between cultures' (in email to author, 4 July 2020). Think Crazy becomes an impulse for a transversal media archaeology of the period's marginalised aspects such as provincial church art; folk artisanry; travelling Hasidic tunes (*nigunim*); multi-tiered wooden synagogue roofs whose angular folds erupted in Frank Stella's *Polish Village* relief series (1970–74); Tatar manuscripts (*tefsir, kitab, chamaił*) and talismanic artefacts (*muhir, dałavar, hramotka, duajka*). All those dimensions stretch the Sarmato-Baroque farther and bring about another multiplicity.

1979: *Unfeeling Rocks with Self-Portrait* as a Steppe C(ha)osmotechnics for the Future

Unfeeling Rocks with Self-Portrait provides a rich material for thinking crazy, interfacing together the three threads of Think Crazy outlined in the introduction. The work instigates a speculative geology that goes beyond the human scale, and in this sense is *inhuman*, but does so traversing the human as a biological and historical category, which makes it *ahuman*. The eponymous rocks are a heterogeneous material aggregating pigments (paint), Styrofoam (horn) and wood (frame), all briefly coupled with human biomatter. The coupling is made possible and supported by metals, distributed as a single surface of the relief and as a sea of randomly dispersed particles that bespeckle both the relief and the artist's prosthetic horn. The metallic line thus sets up an intermediary zone of indiscernibility between the biological and the physical. This corresponds to a coupling of two horned appendages that occupies the space between the relief and the artist. One is a projection affixed to Konieczny's temple, while the other is a sculptural protrusion of the metal relief. The curved outgrowths entwine the pair in a shared field of turbulence. Locking horns, the couple passes through a becoming-animal. The animal motif does not signify an essence but ushers in an in-betweenness already intimated by the deep time lineage of the animal horn, which is an externalised mineralisation, or calcification, internal to the biological individuation.[26]

Unfeeling Rocks with Self-Portrait sets off a change that sweeps both the human and the relief's eponymous rocks. It is a scene of animal combat, resonating with the Scytho-Siberian plaques, where the biological and the physical domains become different entanglements of metabolic forces selected by the stochastics of cosmic contingency. What changes here is the *self* as an embodied human subjectivity constructed via specular reflection and investing objects with emotion (*feeling*), alongside its accompanying history of cultural and artistic production grounded in the auto-reflection, as encapsulated in the fine arts genre of portraiture. Self-portraiture as an avatar of anthropocentricism is deformed upon contact with the inhuman geological scale. Rather than a model of spatio-temporal extension and transhumanist augmentation of human transcendent thought, Konieczny's horn is a deterritorialising technical apparatus, a selfie stick for deformation of the human figure, and at once the actualisation of an atavistic human trait cutting across linear species development.

The eponymous unfeeling rocks of the metal relief undergo change, too. What changes is the layering, striating habit at work in sedimentary geo-matter identified by Deleuze and Guattari (2005: 40–1; Bogue 2018: 49), whereby substances extracted from matter-flow are statistically formed into strata, such sediments subsequently stabilised via further structuration into compact aggregates that make up sedimentary rocks. The rocks' encounter with the human precipitates the growth of a horn, transversal in relation to their successively accumulated strata and their underlying double articulation of content, composed of formed matter, and expression, composed of molar, overcoded content. The work's coupled horns are also transversal in relation to time, becoming a far-future fossil of an alternative, crazy rock formation. This transversality corresponds to Szwajewska's (1986: 12) geological understanding of Think Crazy as 'resid[ing] in a crevice fleeing control where madness runs wild, in an abyss of uncertainty and undecidability where one makes discoveries and acts of creation'.[27] The relation between the artist's body and the metal relief can also be speculatively approached as what mineralogist Robert M. Hazen (see Bakke 2017: 42–3) terms *mineral evolution*, a multifaceted process of diversification of mineral species in a deep-time perspective precipitated to a considerable degree by biomatter.

Concluding Remarks

Unfeeling Rocks with Self-Portrait affirms art as a technical installation of metallic apparatuses for sensing, amplifying and converting forces. As such, the work encapsulates the whole ontogenetic line(age) of Think Crazy, drawing out the implicit metallic potentialities of Konieczny's earlier work as an engineer, and in particular his 1962–3 construction of a reinforced concrete hypar shell. Informally designated as *Birds* by the artist, Konieczny's roof deterritorialises its concrete through the tensile powers of steel, harnessing the bird-affect of its composite material. In turn, the inhuman figure composed of an aluminium bag on a triangular metal stand liberates a germinal mannerism harboured by *Drop Something in Here*.

At the same time, Think Crazy extracts its affective weapons from a wider phylogenetic line(age) of metallic affects and operations it shares with Scytho-Siberian animal-style metal plaques and Sarmatian (coffin) portraits or other Sarmato-Baroque artefacts. And in doing so, it effects a becoming-steppe of Eastern European art and culture. Think Crazy installs the surface of an intensive steppe populated with metallic species, phyla and tensors.

Self-portraits are no longer grounds for specular identification but resonant frames through which the self ungrounds itself. Still lifes unfold an artificial and inhuman world, even though they incorporate elements traditionally construed as alive such as various organs and membranes of the human body. Living images are technological mediation become cosmic. These looped films capture a conversation across the biological and the inorganic. By dint of their looping technique and accidental material flickers and scratches of their film surface, living images eternalise the action of forces they share with their 16 mm film camera and projector. In this way, both living images and still lifes are ultimately different modes of installation of forces that deterritorialise the clichéd opposition between, on the one hand, the organic individuation conflated with biomatter and construed as somehow alive, and the inorganic formation associated with geological matter and considered somehow inert, on the other, as well as between the natural and the artificial.

To conclude, Konieczny's practices reconfigure neo-avant-garde art as a steppe c(ha)osmotechnics through (1) their logic of coupling, resonance and qualitative changes between distinct modes of Think Crazy functioning, such as living images or still lifes, harnessing the power of metals; (2) their transhistorical phylogenetic connection with the Sarmato-Baroque; as well as (3) their fundamental operation as a media technology engaging the cosmos.

Think Crazy's individuation of crazy thought arises out of the variation and technical manipulation of materials, and constitutes a material (motif) in itself. Think Crazy is the metallurgical thought of Special Equipment, and it is crazy since it is supported by the stochastic forces of the cosmos. Think Crazy launches a materialist conceptualism reducible to neither a materialised idea nor a dematerialised object. Already implicit in Konieczny's stochastic generator cube and explicitly at work in Moonarium, housing for almost forty-five years a variable arrangement of artworks, Think Crazy reveals art as an intensive engineering of forces and the technical process of installation of the cosmos itself – in solidarity with its inhuman and ahuman materials.

In turn, the coupling of Deleuze and Guattari with Konieczny and Szwajewska produces a new reading of the machinic phylum and thus draws a new phylum. This rereading harnesses the power of Think Crazy, which had effectuated Szwajewska's mutual contamination of art history and affect, and Konieczny's resonance between engineering and art. On the one hand, in following Simondon's idea of 'evolution of technical objects', the concept of the machinic phylum makes rudimentary processes of biological life, ontogeny and phylogeny, to bear on the non-human, something that is echoed today in Hazen's notion of 'mineral evolution'. On the other hand, what Deleuze and Guattari extract from Early Iron Age Eurasian nomadic technological cultures, Monod's 'molecular engineering' as well as structural engineering, is the machinic phylum as a multiplicity – as an engineering of forces.

Notes

1. The 1974–80 period of Think Crazy was scrutinised in a seminal article by art historian Monika Szwajewska written in 1980 for the Wrocław-based *Odra* monthly. The article is a dialogue between Konieczny and Szwajewska. This encounter is framed by Szwajewska's brief art-historical and critical overview of Konieczny's practices. With her 1980 article Szwajewska launches a speculative art history whereby a chronological mapping of facts coexists with an affective unmapping and speculation. The Konieczny-Szwajewska dialogue is my point of departure because it provides unique insights into Konieczny's conceptualisations of his practices. As I shall argue, in Think Crazy thinking and making are two inseparable aspects which jointly compose the artist's signature material conceptualism. In a recent article on Konieczny, I employed Foucault's conception of the event in terms of 'an incorporeal materialism' to approach the theory of art's ontogenesis put forward by Jerzy Ludwiński (1930–2000), an art historian, critic and curator associated with the Polish neo-avant-garde. Foucault's notion also aptly describes Konieczny's mutation of conceptualism (see Przedpełski 2019: 78, 81 n. 38).

2. Solidarity was declared illegal in 1981 but nonetheless endured as an underground movement throughout the 1980s.

3. As Guattari and Rolnik (2007: 261) asserted in 1982, 'revolutionary transformation' is also bound up with 'a cultural revolution, a kind of mutation among people, without

which we lapse into the reproduction of an earlier society. It is the whole range of possibilities of specific practices of change in the way of life, with their creative potential, that constitutes what I call molecular revolution, which is a condition for any social transformation.' This revolution is '*a process that brings about mutations in the unconscious social field, at a level beyond discourse.* We could call it a process of existential singularization' (ibid. 259).

4. This line of deterritorialisation includes the current resurrection of Russian Cosmist philosophy preoccupied with the idea of immortality, encapsulated in Anton Vidokle's artistic repurposing of a metallic ioniser dish developed by Soviet biophysicist Alexander Chizhevsky. The device, believed by Chizhevsky to have a rejuvenating effect on the body, emits an electric field which negatively charges ion particles of the air. For his 2015 film *The Communist Revolution Was Caused by the Sun*, Vidokle installed a locally commissioned version of Chizhevsky's apparatus at a Muslim village cemetery on the Kazakh steppe (see Zhilyaev 2016). The infinite line of deterritorialisation also passes through Slavs and Tatars' interest in 'an area east of the former Berlin Wall and west of the Great Wall of China' (2019); Metahaven's Kiev-Beirut amalgamation; Chto Delat's revision of the October Revolution and Lenin's thought as a zombie communism which exhausts hope for a better (capitalist) life and instead sides with the zombie 'who . . . does not have any hope, but still has a desire' (Timofeeva 2015); Almagul Menlibayeva's coalescence of Soviet futurism and a 'personal atavism' afforded by a 'thought-form' specific to the steppes (2019); Almaty's Astral Nomads initiative; Mongolian fusion metal group the HU; and Bojana Piškur's curatorial reactivation of the Non-Aligned Movement (NAM).

5. The cybernetic notion of the 'machinic' and the machine is taken over from *Anti-Oedipus* where it accounts for the functioning of desire as a play of non-signifying productive unconscious syntheses. The concept of the machinic in *Anti-Oedipus* is extracted from the work of molecular biologist Jacques Monod, who described the operative logic of the so-called 'allosteric proteins' as one of 'at the molecular level, a veritable machine—a machine in its functional properties, but not, we now see, in its fundamental structure, where nothing but the play of blind combinations can be discerned. Randomness . . . converted into order' (Monod qtd in Deleuze and Guattari 2000: 289n). According to Monod (qtd in ibid. 288), 'an allosteric protein should be seen as a specialized product of molecular "engineering," enabling an interaction, positive or negative, to come about between compounds without chemical affinity, and thereby eventually subordinating any reaction to the intervention of compounds that are chemically foreign and indifferent to this reaction.' Deleuze and Guttari (ibid. 289) understand allosteric interactions in terms of 'Markov's chains', i.e. 'aleatory phenomena that are partially dependent'. In turn, the notion of the 'phylum' seems to be a deterritorialisation, the term coined by controversial Darwinian naturalist Ernst Haeckel (1834–1919), for whom (Haeckel qtd in Richards 2008: 134, n. 60) 'the stem or phylum is the collection of all organic species that have arisen from one and the same spontaneously generated monadic form'. As Richards (ibid. 134) summarises, the phylum 'consists of the series of genealogically related species that sprang from an original parent in the deep evolutionary past'. For Haeckel (qtd in ibid.), 'every phylum is a plurality of blood-related species and each species is a plurality of the same or rather highly similar reproductive cycles'.

6. The role of metallurgy and mining as loci of resistance can be seen in Solidarity, whose origins in 1980 are associated with a shipyard electrician, Lech Wałęsa, and a welder-turned-crane operator, Anna Walentynowicz, just as the 1981 strike at the

Wujek coal mine in Silesia was launched to sustain the resistance. As of 10 July 2020, Upper Silesia has recorded the highest number of COVID-19 cases in Poland, its coal mines becoming the epicentre of the pandemic.

7. Symptomatically, Deleuze and Guattari (2005: 165) understand BwO as 'pure matter, a phenomenon of physical, biological, psychic, social, or cosmic matter', opening the Simondonian understanding of physical, biological, psychic and collective individuation to the forces of the cosmos.

8. I am employing Yuk Hui's concept of *cosmotechnics* with a number of qualifications, which make it undergo a change in the process. First of all, I understand cosmos after Deleuze, i.e. not in terms of an ordered transcendent cosmos defined in opposition to chaos, but as an infinite cosmos suffused with chaos. What is at stake here is a 'chaosmos' diagrammed by the immanent formula of 'chaos = cosmos' that Deleuze saw at play in works of Borges and Gombrowicz (Deleuze 1994: 123), as well as in the Nietzschean eternal return he viewed as 'the internal identity of the world and of chaos' (ibid. 299). This idea is taken up in *What Is Philosophy?*, where art is designated in terms of 'a composition of chaos that yields the vision, or sensation, so that it constitutes a chaosmos, a composed chaos' (Deleuze and Guattari 1994: 204). Furthermore, I would like to replace the notion of the moral taken as a unifying grounding principle with Spinozian immanent ethics. On this reading cosmotechnics becomes a *c(ha)osmotechnics*.

9. Scythian art is epitomised by a sixth-century BCE golden plaque from the Kostromskaya barrow in the Kuban area (Fig. 7.2). The plaque bears the motif of a recumbent stag whose antlers proliferate into nine intertwined spirals. This lineage culminates with the fourth-century BCE Sarmatian art from the Filippovka kurgan in the southern Urals. The kurgan contained a number of golden plaques and standing gilded figurines made of birch, all bearing the motif of a deer whose multiplying antlers equal or exceed the size of its body. Filippovka deer are highly geometricised composites of features of different animals (see Jacobson 2006). It is impossible to do justice within the limited space of this chapter to the complex phenomenon of nomadic art and its interplay of cultural continuity and difference. As art historian Esther Jacobson-Tepfer (in email to author, 20 April 2020), an expert in the field, points out, 'there is a big difference there [between the Scythians of the Black Sea region and the whole nomadic world, from Mongolian Altai to the Black Sea], since the Scythians came under the influence of the Hellenistic world and the Altai nomads (the original Scytho-Siberians) were affected more by the Chinese empire. Grousset, Gryaznov, and Charrière were very important sources, but they are now rather dated'. On the other hand, Antiquity historian Anca Dan (2017), whom I would like to thank for important comments on the chapter, argues that the persistent historiographical identification of Sarmatians with the Iranian *ethnos* is a Graeco-Roman etic construct occluding the heterogeneity of the Eurasian steppe nomads.

10. In this project, Deleuze and Guattari seem to have been drawing on Grousset. In a footnote (2005: 574, n. 30), they point out that '"the art of the steppes" had a specificity that was communicated to the migrating Germans', referring the reader to Grousset (1970: 11–25). The mentioned passages from Grousset contain his analysis of Scythian, Sarmatian and Hunnic art, which concludes with a remark on the continuity between Sarmatian art and Germanic art. As Grousset (1970: 16) points out, 'This is the first appearance in Europe of premedieval art, an art which the Sarmatians were to hand on to the Goths and the Goths to all the Germanic tribes of the *Völkerwanderung*, or great migration of peoples.' This passage provides a link to Worringer's expanded

understanding of Gothic art as also encompassing *Völkerwanderung* art. It is important to clarify here that the Deleuzoguattarian gesture of drawing a line of nomad art which links Grousset's (1970: 19) 'art of the steppes' with Worringer's (1920: 48) 'northern line' is not tantamount to a gesture of finding a chronologically anterior, noble foundational and mythical narrative which legitimises and animates a posterior work, or – to use Simondonian framework – an abstract principle of individuation posited before the operation of individuation itself. Rather than a *lineage*, in the sense of a striated chronological line going from the origin A to the destination B, the Deleuzoguattarian operation is a case of drawing a transversal *line* cutting across A and B, and thus coupling them in shared resonance. What is at stake here is a transformative connection made on the basis of the phylum's singularities, operations and affects – *how does it work?* – and not a classification of essences – *what is it?* The phylogenetic lineage can be therefore understood in terms of the Simondonian 'allagmatics'. As Audronė Žukauskaitė explains in her chapter in this volume (p. 37), 'multiplicities can be compared not on the basis of what they are but on the analogy of their operations. . . . Following Simondon, Deleuze creates a theory of analogical differentiations, allowing a comparison between different kinds of multiplicities.' I would like to thank James Elkins for his generous comments and for pointing out the complexities of the Deleuzoguattarian gesture of connecting Worringer and Scythian art.

11. The Deleuzoguattarian project of decoupling nomad art from its capture by sedentary empires is an unfinished project because in *A Thousand Plateaus* the insights from Grousset and Charrière and their analysis of Scythian art are relegated to mere footnotes, whereas it is Worringer who becomes the spokesman for nomad art in the body of the text and across the whole Deleuzoguattarian oeuvre. The barely acknowledged legacy of Grousset and Charrière, as well as of Scythian art, is encapsulated by an uncredited drawing of a nomadic chariot (dated between the fifth and the fourth centuries BCE) from Altai that prefaces Nomadology (Deleuze and Guattari 2005: 351). The drawing, a diagram of nomadic mobility, is a rendition of a photograph of a reconstructed nomad chariot found in the Pazyryk kurgan in Altai which appears in Charrière (1979: unpaginated plate, fig. 330). This exceptionally well-preserved chariot was excavated by S. I. Rudenko in 1949 and is presently exhibited at the Hermitage under the inventory number 1687-404.

12. Many scholars identify a link between Scytho-Siberian artefacts and the cosmos. For example, the archaeologist Bokovenko (2000: 305) argues that the way metal plaques are distributed within the ancient nomad horse harness corresponds to the types of animal motifs they are bearing. Specific animal motifs correspond to the bridle, others to the saddle, prompting Bokovenko to suggest a possible shamanistic function of the harness linking the animal parts to various locations within ancient nomadic mythologies. Accordingly, bird motifs placed on the horse's neck and head correspond to the 'Upper Word'; animal struggle motifs associated with the chest, saddle pillow and pommel are linked to the 'Regular World', whereas motifs of defeated animals and fish hanging down from the saddle correspond to the 'Lower World'. As I see it, the cosmic horse is a machine by which different body parts embark on animal becoming, ultimately tapping into cosmic forces.

13. See Przedpełski 2019 for an overview of the critical reception of Konieczny and his relation to the Polish neo-avant-garde of the 1970s. Contemporary critics subordinate Think Crazy to periods, styles and aesthetic categories in a linear and canonical art history, such as Surrealism, Oskar Hansen's theory of modernist architecture and Fluxus (see Guzek 2017: 252–4). In his article for the *Piktogram* art magazine, Łukasz

Ronduda (2007: 31–3) develops the theme of Think Crazy as a 'romantic' reactivation of the category of beauty as well as 'sensual and purely aesthetical experience' under the conditions of the cold analytical conceptualism linked to the technoscientific rationalism of People's Poland in the 1970s. As I see it, this masculinist theme of liberation through a binarily gendered display of hot eroticism and sexualised desire, emblematised by stills from Konieczny's *Santa Conservatione* featuring gilded breasts selected for the *Piktogram* cover, does not attend to Think Crazy's disruptive ungenderings and its molecular engineering of desexualised desire. I would like to thank Bojana Pejić for her insightful comments on this matter.

14. For Szwajewska, Think Crazy is a paradoxical object of inquiry, and encounter, which engenders at times contradictory accounts. She identifies Think Crazy (1986: 7–9) with a transition, which occurred in 1975, from a dematerialisation of the art object in favour of ideas and experiences, whereby the ideas were recorded in many different, incidental ways. She argues that 'the works are subordinated to this very idea of "crazy", "unbounded" thinking' (ibid. 9). At the same time, Szwajewska identifies a germinal moment in Think Crazy where 'the idea begins to be materialised in the . . . shape of the material object [understood] as a work of art' (ibid. 9–11). However, such a hylomorphic account is further complicated because even though 'the works are a materialised idea', they are also 'a new, different way of transmission' whereby 'their use by the artist lends them another dimension, changes their character; they become a part of THINK CRAZY' (ibid. 11). What is interesting in this account is its technical ('use') and cybernetic ('transmission') imagery bound up with the notion of change. As I hope to demonstrate, Think Crazy is not so much a case of the artist's *use* of objects, but a metallurgical thought which arises out of the material.

15. Konieczny (1970a) subscribed to the Markovian understanding of stochastics whereby 'we get information concerning the interval of time on the basis of information from the given moment' and thus not on the basis of 'the additional information about earlier moments'. Therefore, as Konieczny (ibid.) further explains, the information drawn from the present state of affairs, 'the knowledge of realization in one given moment of time' – independently of its past displacements – allows us 'to calculate the probability connections of [a] certain realization in the future moments'. He also perceived stochastics in a non-Markovian way in terms of randomness generated through a technical device, initially expressed in terms of sets. For Konieczny (1970b), 'the stochasticism of human nature is the driving engine of emotions and actions. A set composed of people, complemented by a given element or a set of elements, produces in itself stochastic processes; the role of such a complement is a generation and creation of that process.' Konieczny's artistic trajectory can be seen as a tension between the two modes of approaching stochasticism.

16. According to Deleuze and Guattari (2005: 510), 'abstract machines operate within concrete assemblages' and hence are 'dated and named' (511), which corresponds to the formulation of the schizoid delirium in *Anti-Oedipus* as world-historical (2000: 88–9).

17. In Greco-Roman mythology, Orion was a giant hunter who threatened to kill all the earth's animals. After he was killed by a giant scorpion sent by the angered earth goddess Gaia, Orion was immortalised as a celestial constellation (see March 2014).

18. Those affective testimonies symptomatically included an intervention by Zbigniew Thielle. According to this pioneering psychologist and therapist specialising in drug addiction in Poland, Think Crazy affords 'a stimulus which . . . will allow the human to expand consciousness, or even create consciousness' (Konieczny 1982).

19. In this sense, Think Crazy aligns itself with Ludwiński's (in Kępińska et al. 1981: 3) understanding of the 1970s neo-avant-garde as exploding a linear evolution of art grounded upon a chronological succession of sharply delineated (as if cut with a razor) discrete layers he saw at play in the previous avant-gardes, and instead defined by a trans-temporal functioning across distances that re-visions radical breakthrough as an act of connecting or gluing together of disparate dimensions. Ludwiński (ibid.) remarks that 'what interests us the most are kinds of art most removed in time and space, barely comprehensible to us', noting that 'the 1970s initiated a recuperation of tendencies that were not so long ago considered traditional'.

20. Think Crazy's radical contingency is also concrete in the sense that it diagnoses the social field of the Polish People's Republic under the First Secretary, Edward Gierek (1970–80). Gierek, originally a miner from Sosnowiec, launched a hybrid socialism combining central planning with Western consumerism encapsulated in selected luxury items made available in specially designated stores and the production of cheap ersatz goods. The luxuriousness of Special Equipment diagnosed production of desire under the specific conditions of the Gierek era. The so-called 'Real Socialism' of Gierek's decade abandoned a revolutionary pursuit of communism (see Negri 2006) through outward terror in favour of a technocratic populist regime committed to scientific-technological progress and exerting control through mass media, bureaucracy and panoptical surveillance. By the mid-1970s, the effects of this 'progress' became manifest in pollution and environmental degradation, just as the deepening economic crisis galvanised a wave of strikes and creation of the first organised opposition in 1976. The period was distinguished not only by the consumption of the Baudrillardian simulacra but also, as literary scholar Przemysław Czapliński (2011: 87–98) points out, by the production of history as a simulacrum, a process he sees at work in *Sir Wołodyjowski* (1968) and *The Deluge* (1974) – cinematic blockbuster adaptations of Henryk Sienkiewicz's historical epic trilogy set in seventeenth-century Poland-Lithuania. If Think Crazy is therefore coextensive with the social field, it is nonetheless irreducible to it.

21. I do not subscribe to the hylomorphic reading of Sarmatism as a founding historical myth, or theory of origins, subsequently incarnated into socio-political practice and material culture put forward by historian Tadeusz Ulewicz (see 2006: 173, 197). The nobility's professed link to the Sarmatians was not uniform across the country; it chiefly applied to Polish gentry and coexisted, or competed, as a certain horizon with alternative legendary pedigrees such as Roman aristocracy (Lithuanians), the Ruriks (Belarussians) or the Roxolanian Sarmatians (Ukrainians). Art historian Tomasz Grusiecki (in email to author, 4 July 2020) remarks that early modern chroniclers wrote 'a historical chorography of an ancient place described as European Sarmatia by classical geographers; [not] the genealogy of a people, but rather the geographic study of a place. It's a presentist narrative because it's written from the perspective of an early modern polity that laid claim to the historical lands of the European Sarmatia, but it's not a self-orientalising narrative'. I see Sarmatism as an affective presentism, oscillating between segregative geo-politics and nomadic geo-poetics. I would also like to thank historians Robert Frost, Dariusz Kołodziejczyk, Tomasz Kamusella and Kristina Sabaliauskaitė for incisive comments on the Commonwealth sections.

22. 'Sarmatism' was in itself a deprecatory designation coined by the Enlightenment-era intellectuals of the Commonwealth, viewing from the 1760s onwards the previous cultural paradigm as an epitome of backwardness. For Sowa, the Commonwealth was the imperial project of colonisation of non-Polish others linked to the class hegemony

of the nobility, whereas Sarmatism was only ever a colonial myth (2011: 197) and ideology which can be viewed in terms of Lacanian psychoanalysis as a 'complex of Symbolic and Imaginary structures' (ibid. 259), a fundamental falsity covering up the void of the Real, i.e. the lack of a proper, sovereign state apparatus embodied in the figure of the king and constituting 'the [Kantorowiczian] king's body politic' (ibid.). For Czapliński (2011: 19), while Sarmatism constituted the '"foundational enemy"' of Polish modernity, its potential was nonetheless harnessed by Solidarity as a way of empowering the whole society (98). It is impossible to discuss this complex problem in more detail here. I see the Commonwealth as a molar assemblage *grounded* in what Timothy Morton (see 2016: 42–5) calls *agrilogistics*, a now widespread 'agricultural program' which originated 12,000 years ago during the Axial Age. Unlike Sowa (2011: 387–410) I do not regard Sarmatism as a schizophrenic-paranoiac psychotic phantasy foreclosing the Real, but in terms of the Deleuzoguattarian (2000: 105) world-historical delirium with its 'two poles, racist and racial, paranoiac-segrega-tive and schizonomadic', flush with the real, akin to the oscillations of Nietzsche's becoming-Polish and Worringer's becoming-Northern. The decolonial delirium of Think Crazy draws (out) a cutting edge of deterritorialisation of the molar agrilogistic assemblage, and populates it with queer cosmicisations and metallicisations. As we shall see, these schizonomadic deterritorialisations are encapsulated in the perverse asignifying potentialities of the coffin portrait, whose logic Koutny-Jones relates to Kantorowicz's theory of the two bodies of the king.

23. Think Crazy can be understood in terms of what art critic Jan Verwoert (2014) identi-fies in works of some Eastern European neo-avant-garde artists such as Július Koller and Stano Filko working under the communist regime as launching a certain non-rep-resentational, non-ideological 'practice [which] invents its own beginnings. . . . a new virtual reality . . . out of which tumbles a new body of work'. This type of radical practice is linked to the artist undergoing a 'death experience, . . . giving birth to a new virtual reality'. Verwoert shows how through linguistic or chromatic modulation Koller and Filko recover an unpredictable cosmos from its ideological takeover by the state and its monopoly over interpretation of the past and imagining the future.

24. The distinction between the signifying sign bound up with faciality as a logic of rep-resentation and the asignifying sign bound up with a logic of affect (the latter corre-sponding to the mobile motif-support relation at work in nomad art such as Scythian plaques) has fundamental implications for art history. The facialised and hylomorphic logic of representation can be detected in Panofsky's (1972: 3) *iconography* defined as 'that branch of the history of art which concerns itself with the subject matter or meaning of works of art, as opposed to their form'. Panofsky identifies, hierarchically organised, '*three strata of subject matter or meaning*' (ibid. 16), each of those demanding a dif-ferent interpretative operation. Accordingly, '*pre-iconographical description*' engages the domain of *motifs* and consists of recognising 'pure *forms*' (line, colour, volume) as 'representations', or 'carriers of *primary* or *natural meanings*', i.e. as determinate subjects, objects, events and expressions; such correctly recognised forms constitute *motifs* and *compositions* of *motifs* (ibid. 5). '*Iconographical analysis in the narrower sense*' engages the domain of *images* and consists of recognising *motifs* as 'carriers of a *secondary* or *conventional* meaning', i.e. as concepts and themes; such correctly recognised motifs constitute *images*, *stories* and *allegories* (ibid. 6–7). Finally, '*iconog-raphy in a deeper sense*', synthetic *iconology* as the proper goal of analysis, consists of recognising *images* as carriers of '*intrinsic meaning* or *content*', i.e. 'a symptom of something else' – '*symbolical*' *values*. The Deleuzoguattarian (2005: 401) analysis of

(Scythian) nomad plaques – not in terms of 'the relation between . . . form-matter but of motif-support, where the earth is no longer anything more than ground (*sol*), where there is no longer even any ground at all because the support is as mobile as the motif' – explodes Panofsky's understanding of the *motif* as a form grounded in transcendent meaning and ushers in a new, immanent speculative art history.

25. See Deleuze 2006: 144 on Baroque allegory as encapsulated in the emblem drawing together images, inscriptions and personal signatures of owners, the three elements corresponding to acts of 'seeing, reading, dedicating', something which is clearly at play in the castrum doloris. The allusive titles of Konieczny's works, e.g. *Orion's Sickle*, do not contribute to a harmonious totality but can be considered disruptive inscriptions, or incisions, which further amplify the inner tension of the heterogeneous elements that make up the crazy emblematic material of the Think Crazy practice.

26. Bakke (2017: 52) sees mineralisation (calcification) which produces 'bones, egg shells, but also . . . kidney and gall stones' as 'a trace of the affinity between biological and mineral species'. In turn, for the palaeontologist Leroi-Gourhan, as Daniel Smith (2019: 259) aptly summarises, while 'technical artefacts are biological phenomena because they are extensions or "externalisations" of the motor skills and organs of the body', 'one can find a "proto-technicity" throughout the plant and animal kingdoms'. Such proto-technicity is at work in the bird's egg, which is an externalisation of the ovum.

27. *Unfeeling Rocks* decouples rocks from their stratifying operation and unleashes their potential for functioning in a transversal, contingent manner. This vision of intensive rocks resonates with Ludwiński's conception of art of the 1970s not as the (neo-)avant-garde gesture of seeking to annex reality framed as distinct from it and diagrammed as a set of progressively accumulated geological strata or rings of a tree, but as *implosive art* launching an internal genesis that immanently and non-violently affirms the world in the sense of seeking to 'preserve [and] protect' it, in contradistinction to the (historical) avant-garde which 'seek[s] to transform the world and improve the human as operating within it' (see Ludwiński 2009a: 141). Symptomatically, Ludwiński does not refer to implosive art, also called *third art*, as (neo-)avant-garde but as an 'underground art' (2009b: 158). Implosive art is diagrammed in terms of an alternative geology. 'Art is the opposite case when compared to geology,' writes Ludwiński (ibid.). 'In the latter case, that which is older is lodged more deeply; with art, it is – at least on the surface – the same case; however, one difference here is that the most creative phenomena, those most visionary and penetrating, tend to descend underground. Indeed, one no longer speaks of the "avant-garde", but the "underground". . . . The mountain of art accretes into its depth and towards its middle. That's why archaeology of art is completely different.'

References

Bakke, Monika (2017), 'Art and Metabolic Force in Deep Time Environments', *Environmental Philosophy*, 14(1): 41–59.

Bal, Mieke (1999), *Quoting Caravaggio: Contemporary Art, Preposterous History*, Chicago: University of Chicago Press.

Baxandall, Michael (1985), 'Excursus Against Influence', in *Patterns of Intention: On the Historical Explanations of Pictures*, New Haven and London: Yale University Press, pp. 58–62.

Bogue, Ronald (2018), 'Who the Earth Thinks It Is', in Henry Somers-Hall, Jeffrey A. Bell and James Williams (eds), *A Thousand Plateaus and Philosophy*, Edinburgh: Edinburgh University Press, pp. 46–63.

Bokovenko, N. A. (2000), 'The Origins of Horse Riding and the Development of Ancient Central Asian Nomadic Riding Harnesses', in *Kurgans, Ritual Sites, and Settlements: Eurasian Bronze and Iron Age*, BAR International Series 890, pp. 304–10.

Brown, Katherine Reynolds (1995), *Migration Art, A.D. 300–800*, New York: Metropolitan Museum of Art.

Bunker, Emma C., James C. Y. Watt and Zhixin Sun (2002), *Nomadic Art of the Eastern Eurasian Steppes: The Eugene V. Thaw and Other New York Collections*, New York: Metropolitan Museum of Art; New Haven: Yale University Press.

Charrière, Georges (1979), *Scythian Art: Crafts of Early Eurasian Nomads*, New York: Alpine Fine Arts Collection Ltd.

Chochorowski, Jan (2004), 'Scythians', in Peter I. Bogucki and Pam J. Crabtree (eds), *Ancient Europe 8000 B.C. – A.D. 1000: Encyclopaedia of the Barbarian World, Vol. 2: Bronze Age to Early Middle Ages (c. 3000 B.C. – A.D. 1000)*, New York: Charles Scribner's Sons, pp. 411–13.

Chrościcki, Juliusz A. (1974), *Pompa funebris. Z dziejów kultury staropolskiej* [Pompa funebris. From the History of Old Polish Culture], Warsaw: Państwowe Wydawnictwo Naukowe.

Chrzanowski, Tadeusz (1988), *Wędrówki po sarmacji europejskiej. Eseje o sztuce i kulturze* staropolskiej [Peregrinations across European Sarmatia. Essays on Old Polish Art and Culture], Kraków: ZNAK.

Chrzanowski, Tadeusz (1995), *Portret staropolski* [Old Polish Portrait], Warsaw: Wydawnictwo Interpress.

Czapliński, Przemysław (2011), *Resztki nowoczesności: dwa studia o literaturze i życiu* [Remnants of Modernity: Two Essays on Literature and Life], Kraków: Wydawnictwo Literackie.

Dan, Anca (2017), 'The Sarmatians: Some Thoughts on the Historiographical Invention of a West Iranian Migration', in Felix Wiedemann, Kerstin P. Hofmann and Hans-Joachim Gehrke (eds), *Vom Wandern der Völker. Migrationserzählungen in den Altertumswissenschaften*, Berlin: Edition Topoi, pp. 97–134.

Deleuze, Gilles (1979), 'Cours Vincennes, 27 February 1979', trans. Timothy S. Murphy, <https://www.webdeleuze.com/textes/186> (last accessed 6 March 2020).

Deleuze, Gilles (1994), *Difference and Repetition*, trans. Paul Patton, New York: Columbia University Press.

Deleuze, Gilles (2002), *Bergsonism*, trans. Barbara Habberjam and Hugh Tomlinson, New York: Zone Books.

Deleuze, Gilles (2003), *Francis Bacon: The Logic of Sensation*, trans. Daniel W. Smith, London and New York: Continuum.

Deleuze, Gilles (2006), *The Fold: Leibniz and the Baroque*, trans. Tom Conley, London and New York: Continuum.

Deleuze, Gilles and Félix Guattari (1994), *What Is Philosophy?*, trans. Graham Burchell and Hugh Tomlinson, New York: Columbia University Press.

Deleuze, Gilles and Félix Guattari (2000), *Anti-Oedipus: Capitalism and Schizophrenia*, trans. Robert Hurley, Mark Seem and Helen R. Lane, Minneapolis: University of Minnesota Press.

Deleuze, Gilles and Félix Guattari (2005), *A Thousand Plateaus: Capitalism and Schizophrenia*, trans. Brian Massumi, London and Minneapolis: University of Minnesota Press.

Dobranowicz, Helena (2019), email to the author, 4 December 2019.

Grousset, René (1970), *The Empire of the Steppes: A History of Central Asia*, trans. Naomi Walford, New Brunswick, NJ: Rutgers University Press.

Guattari, Félix and Suely Rolnik (2007), *Molecular Revolution in Brazil*, trans. Karel Clapshow and Brian Holmes, Los Angeles: Semiotext(e).

Guzek, Łukasz (2017), *Rekonstrukcja sztuki akcji w Polsce* [Reconstruction of Action Art in Poland], Warsaw and Toruń: Polski Instytut Studiów nad Sztuką Świata.

Hayles, N. Katherine (2014), 'Cognition Everywhere: The Rise of the Cognitive Nonconscious and the Costs of Consciousness', *New Literary History*, 45: 199–220.

Hui, Yuk (2017), 'On Cosmotechnics: For a Renewed Relation between Technology and Nature in the Anthropocene', *Techné: Research in Philosophy and Technology*, 21(2–3): 1–23.

Hussong, Matthias W., Wilhelm T. Hoffmeister, Frank Rominger and Bernd F. Straub (2015), 'Copper and Silver Carbene Complexes without Heteroatom-Stabilization: Structure, Spectroscopy, and Relativistic Effects', *Angewandte Chemie International Edition*, Wiley Online Library, 54: 10,331–5.

Jacobson, Esther (2006), 'The Filippovka Deer: Inquiry into their North Asian Sources and Symbolic Significance', in Joan Aruz, Ann Farkas and Elizabetta Valsz Fino (eds), *The Golden Deer of Eurasia: Perspectives on Steppe Nomads of the Ancient World*, New York: Metropolitan Museum of Art; New Haven: Yale University Press, pp. 182–95.

Kaufmann, Thomas DaCosta (1999), 'Definition and Self-Definition in Polish Culture and Art', in Jan K. Ostrowski (ed.), *Land of the Winged Horsemen: Art in Poland 1572–1764*, trans. Krystyna Malcharek, Alexandria: Art Services International, pp. 15–25.

Kaufmann, Thomas DaCosta (2010), 'Periodization and its Discontents', *Journal of Art Historiography*, 2: 1–6.

Kępińska, Alicja, Jerzy Ludwiński, Stefan Morawski and Jan Świdziński (1981), 'Czy mamy awangardę neo czy pseudo' [Do We Have a Neo or Pseudo Avant-Garde?], discussion moderated by Wojciech Cesarski, *Sztuka*, 8(4): 2–6; English overview 69–70.

Kobiak, Jerzy and Wiesław Stachurski (1991), *Konstrukcje żelbetowe* [Reinforced Concrete Structures], vol. 4, Warsaw: Arkady.

Konieczny, Marek (1970a), *Pokaz Numer 1* [Show Number 1] (exhibition catalogue), Warsaw: Studio Audiowizualne Galeria.

Konieczny, Marek (1970b), 'A Pronouncement at the Symposium in Galeria 10 – 150770', in *Violet* (exhibition catalogue), Warsaw: Galeria Współczesna.

Konieczny, Marek [1981] (1982), *Marek Konieczny – Nieczułe Skały – wystawa* [Marek Konieczny – Unfeeling Rocks – An Exhibition] (exhibition catalogue), Bielsko-Biała: BWA.

Konieczny, Marek and Radek Przedpełski, conversation about Marek Konieczny's artistic strategies, Warsaw, 28 September 2019.

Konieczny, Marek, Monika Szwajewska and Radek Przedpełski, conversation about Marek Konieczny's artistic strategies, Warsaw, 1 April 2015.

Koutny-Jones, Aleksandra (2015), *Visual Cultures of Death in Central Europe: Contemplation and Commemoration in Early Modern Poland-Lithuania*, Leiden and Boston: Brill.

Ludwiński, Jerzy [1979] (2009a), 'Epoka outsiderów' [The Epoch of Outsiders], in Jarosław Kozłowski (ed.), *Sztuka w epoce postartystycznej i inne teksty* [Art in the Post-Art Epoch and Other Texts], Poznań: Akademia Sztuk Pięknych; Wrocław: Biuro Wystaw Artystycznych, pp. 140–2.

Ludwiński, Jerzy [1982] (2009b), 'Góra' [The Mountain], in Jarosław Kozłowski (ed.), *Sztuka w epoce postartystycznej i inne teksty* [Art in the Post-Art Epoch and Other Texts], Poznań: Akademia Sztuk Pięknych; Wrocław: Biuro Wystaw Artystycznych, pp. 157–8.

Mańkowski, Tadeusz (1935), *Sztuka islamu w Polsce w XVII i XVIII wieku* [Art of Islam in Poland in the 17th and 18th Centuries], Kraków: Gebethner i Wolff.

Mańkowski, Tadeusz (1946), *Genealogia sarmatyzmu* [A Genealogy of Sarmatism], Warsaw: Łuk.

Mańkowski, Tadeusz (1959), *Orient w polskiej kulturze artystycznej* [The Orient in Polish Artistic Culture], Wrocław: Zakład Narodowy im. Ossolińskich.

March, Jenny (2014), 'Orion', in *Dictionary of Classical Mythology*, Oxford and Philadelpha: Oxbow Books, pp. 1,127–9.

Menlibayeva, Almagul (2019), 'Artist Statement', <http://www.almagulmenlibayeva. com/artist-statement-1.html> (last accessed 12 March 2020).

Morawski, Stefan [1985] (2007), 'Awangarda artystyczna (o dwu formacjach XX wieku)' [The Artistic Avant-Garde (on Two 20th-Century Formations)], in Piotr J. Przybysz and Anna Zeidler-Janiszewska (eds), *Stefan Morawski. Wybór pism estetycznych* [Stefan Morawski. Selected Writings on Aesthetics], Kraków: Universitas, p. 213.

Morton, Timothy (2016), *Dark Ecology: For a Logic of Future Coexistence*, New York: Columbia University Press.

Murawska-Muthesius, Katarzyna (2004), 'Poland and Lithuania 1500–1800', in John Onians (ed.), *Atlas of World Art*, London: Laurence King, pp. 158–9.

Negri, Antonio (2006), *Goodbye Mr. Socialism*, New York and London: Seven Stories Press.

Nietzsche, Friedrich (2007), *Ecce Homo: How to Become What You Are*, trans. Duncan Large, Oxford and New York: Oxford University Press.

Onians, John (ed.) (2004), *Atlas of World Art*, London: Laurence King.

Ostrowski, Jan K. (ed.) (1999a), *Land of the Winged Horsemen: Art in Poland 1572–1764*, trans. Krystyna Malcharek, Alexandria: Art Services International.

Ostrowski, Jan K. (1999b), 'Polish Baroque Art in its Social and Religious Context', in Jan K. Ostrowski (ed.), *Land of the Winged Horsemen: Art in Poland 1572–1764*, trans. Krystyna Malcharek, Alexandria: Art Services International, pp. 38–53.

Panofsky, Erwin (1972), *Studies in Iconology: Humanistic Themes in the Art of the Renaissance*, New York: Icon Editions.

Parikka, Jussi (2012), *What is Media Archaeology?*, Cambridge: Polity Press.

Parikka, Jussi (2015), *A Geology of Media*, Cambridge, London and Minneapolis: University of Minnesota Press.

Przedpełski, Radek (2019), 'Elements of Think Crazy Topology: Encountering Neo-Avant-Garde Practices of Marek Konieczny through Ludwiński and Deleuze', in Marika Kuźmicz (ed.), *Revisiting Heritage: Material from the Conference Revisiting Heritage 7th–8th of June 2018, National Museum, Warsaw*, Warsaw: Arton Foundation and Warsaw Academy of Fine Arts.

Richards, Robert J. (2008), *The Tragic Sense of Life: Ernst Haeckel and the Struggle over Evolutionary Thought*, Chicago and London: University of Chicago Press.

Ronduda, Łukasz (2007), 'Think Crazy: The Artistic Strategies of Marek Konieczny', *Piktogram*, 8: 26–37.

Ronduda, Łukasz (2009), 'Polska sztuka lat 70. Między postesencjalizmem a pragmatyzmem' [Polish Art of the 1970s. Between Post-Essentialism and Pragmatism], in Łukasz Ronduda, *Sztuka polska lat 70. Awangarda* [Polish Art of the 1970s. The Avant-Garde], Jelenia Góra: Polski Western, pp. 8–15.

Simondon, Gilbert (1964), *L'individu et sa genèse physico-biologique*, Paris: Presses Universitaires de France.

Simondon, Gilbert (2017), *On the Mode of Existence of Technical Objects*, trans. Cecile Malaspina and John Rogove, Minneapolis: Univocal.

Slavs and Tatars (2019), 'About', *Slavs and Tatars*, <https://slavsandtatars.com/about> (last accessed 7 October 2019).

Smith, Daniel W. (2019), 'André Leroi-Gourhan', in Graham Jones and Jon Roffe (eds), *Deleuze's Philosophical Lineage II*, Edinburgh: Edinburgh University Press, pp. 255–74.

Sowa, Jan (2011), *Fantomowe ciało króla. Peryferyjne zmagania z nowoczesną formą* [The King's Phantom Body. A Peripheral Struggle with Modern Form], Kraków: Universitas.

Sulimirski, Tadeusz (1970), *The Sarmatians*, London: Thames & Hudson.

Szwajewska, Monika (1980), 'Think Crazy', *Odra*, 5: 109–10.

Szwajewska, Monika (1986), *Marek Konieczny. Elementy Topologii Think Crazy* [Marek Konieczny. Elements of Think Crazy Topology] (exhibition catalogue), Lublin: BWA.

Timofeeva, Oxana (2015), 'Manifesto for Zombie-Communism', *Mute*, 12 January, <http://www.metamute.org/community/your-posts/manifesto-zombie-communism> (last accessed 12 March 2020).

Ulewicz, Tadeusz [1950] (2006), *Sarmacja. Zagadnienie sarmatyzmu* [Sarmatia. The Problem of Sarmatism], Kraków: Collegium Collumbinum.

van Geel, B., V. G. Dirksen, G. I. Zaitseva, N. A. Bokovenko, N. D. Burova, M. Kulkova, H. Parzinger, A. Nagler, K. V. Chugunov, V. A. Dergachev, S. S. Vasiliev and J. van der Plicht (2004), 'Climate Change and the Expansion of the Scythian Culture after 850 BC: A Hypothesis', *Journal of Archaeological Science*, 31(12): 1735–42; <https://doi.org/10.1016/j.jas.2004.05.004>.

Verwoert, Jan (2014), 'A Pun and a Plunge: UFO Rides into the Deep Blue', in Joanna Kordjak-Piotrowska and Stanislaw Welbel (eds), *Cosmos Calling! Art and Science in the Long Sixties*, Warsaw: Zacheta Narodowa Galeria Sztuki, pp. 123–5.

Worringer, Wilhelm (1920), *Form Problems of the Gothic*, New York: G. E. Stechert & Co.

Worringer, Wilhelm (1997), *Abstraction and Empathy: A Contribution to the Psychology of Style*, trans. Michael Bullock, Chicago: Ivan R. Dee.

Zamoyski, Adam (1999), 'History of Poland in the 16th–18th Centuries', in Jan K. Ostrowski (ed.), *Land of the Winged Horsemen: Art in Poland 1572–1764*, trans. Krystyna Malcharek, Alexandria: Art Services International, pp. 27–37.

Zhilyaev, Arseny (2016), 'Factories of Resurrection: Interview with Anton Vidokle', *E-flux*, 71, <https://www.e-flux.com/journal/71/60539/factories-of-resurrection-interview-with-anton-vidokle/> (last accessed 12 March 2020).

8

Body without Organs as Pure Potentiality in Patricia Piccinini's Sculptural Installations

Burcu Baykan

The essence of a thing never appears at the outset, but in the middle, in the course of its development.

(Deleuze 2013: 3)

This chapter stages an encounter between Deleuze and Guattari's concept of 'body without organs' and the bodily mutations at play in the Australian visual artist Patricia Piccinini's two sculptural installations: *Still Life with Stem Cells* (2002) (Fig. 8.1) and *The Atlas* (2012) (Fig. 8.2). Working within the range of sculpture, photography, drawing and video installation, Piccinini investigates humanity's intervention into nature and engages with various contentious issues related to contemporary biotechnologies, including stem cell research, genetic modification, tissue engineering, cloning and cross-species breeding. The idea that recent biotechnological innovations have furthered the transgression of the fixed limits of the human body, as well as traditional species barriers, is not new. According to bio-artist Ionat Zurr, for example, 'the combination of stem cell and tissue engineering technologies opens up a gateway to the treatment of a living body as a malleable entity' (2002). As a consequence, Zurr says, 'the traditional view of a body as one autonomous unchangeable self will go through a radical change' (ibid.). Responding to the concerns regarding these debates around the genetic manipulations in an increasingly technologised world, Piccinini constructs imagery that depicts the profound transfigurations of the human body and other life forms. This imagery, in turn, highlights their potential for corporeal plasticity via the imaginary potentials of biotechnology. In her study of Piccinini's art, technoculture theorist Donna Haraway suggests that much of the artist's works are 'premised on bioscientific practices of manipulation and alteration of living beings, of creating "new worlds" if "only" in art' (2007). In addition to Haraway, curator Juliana Engberg argues that the essence of her projects is 'to give form to some of the concepts with which we currently grapple' (2002: 3). Indeed, Piccinini's fabrications are timely; they refer to numerous contemporary discussions about manipulating nature, as well as the potential implications, challenges and contradictions of biogenetic engineering. The artist's large-scale wax sculptures allude to living beings composed of both human and non-human

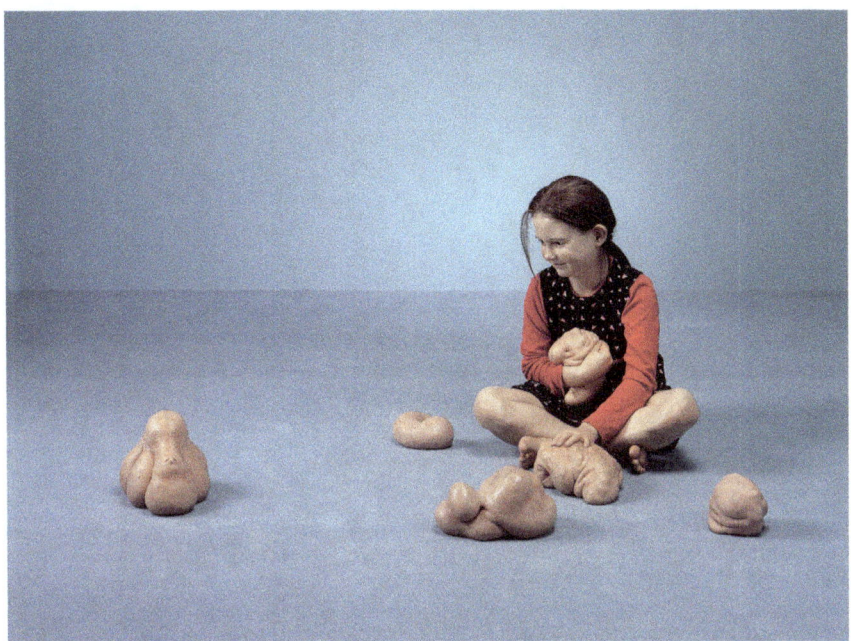

Figure 8.1 Patricia Piccinini, *Still Life with Stem Cells*, 2002. Silicone, polyurethane, human hair, variable.
Courtesy the artist, Tolarno Galleries and Roslyn Oxley9 Gallery.

animals through trans-species reproduction. The two focus works of this chapter, in turn, point towards the nebulous boundaries between techno-human-animal worlds, as well as between nature and artifice.

Still Life with Stem Cells[1] focuses on a little girl who sits on the floor playing with an array of weird and ambiguous lumps of flesh, the imagined creations of stem cell research, as the title suggests. These fleshy forms allude to various indistinct body parts. Their skin tone, soft folds, creases and blood vessels all hint at living tissue. Adorned with blemishes, orifices, hair and pores, their all-too-realistic rendition is arresting. Neither quite formed animals nor fully grown humans, they have an unresolved ontological status that contradicts all recognisable taxonomy. For Engberg, they share 'qualities and attributes with hairless rats, cats, dogs, baby mice and piglets' yet they still have 'a close affinity to humans' (2002: 40). Haraway also points to this dimension of the piece, arguing that they 'do not yield to clean judgments or bottom lines—especially not about what is living or non-living, organic or technological, promising or threatening' (2007). Yet, despite their tremendously strange physiognomy, the girl does not appear to be threatened by their companionship, gently cradling one of them. The scene in *Still Life with Stem Cells* is oddly contradictory; the tender and peaceful relationship between the category-defying figures and the little girl looks simultaneously cute and troubling, attractive and repulsive. *The Atlas*[2]

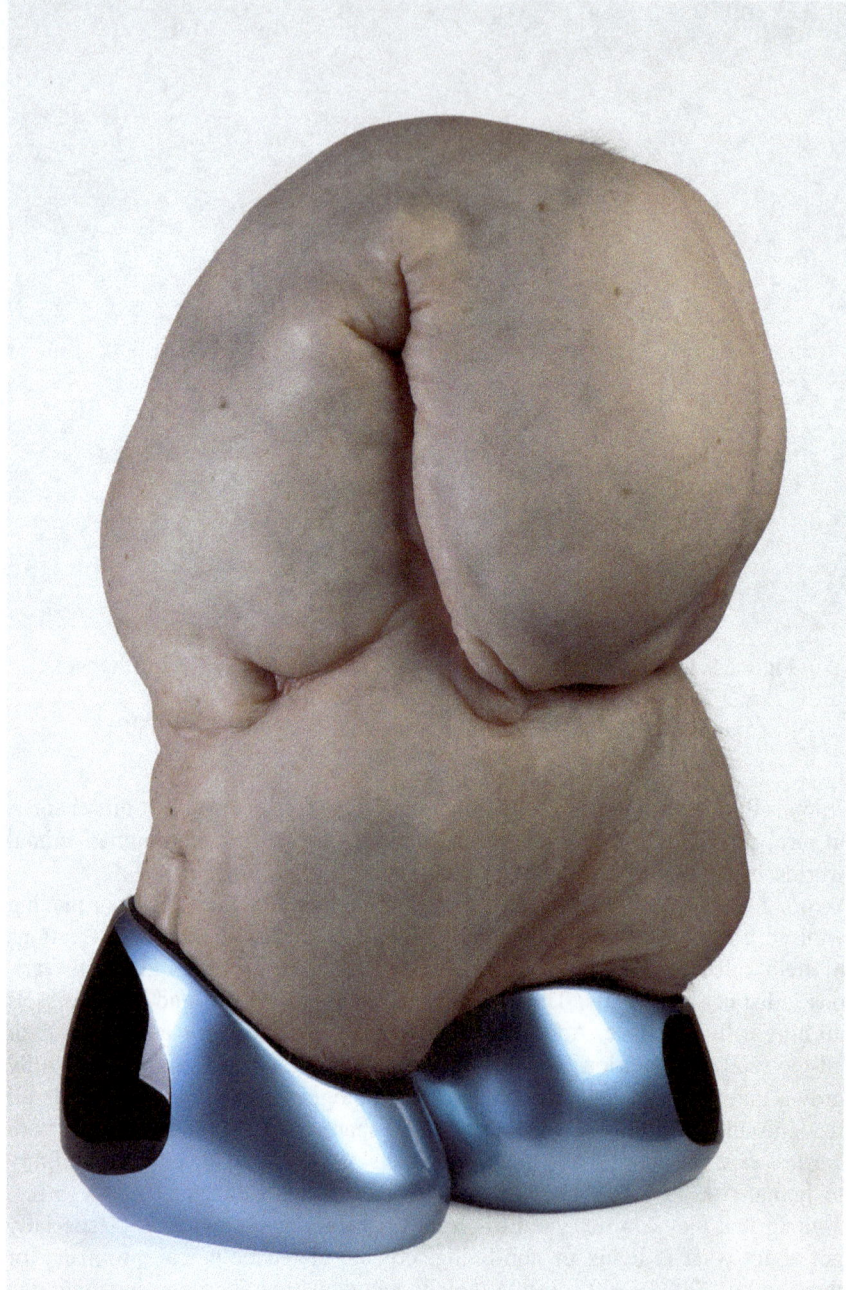

Figure 8.2 Patricia Piccinini, *Atlas*, 2012. Silicone, fibreglass, human hair, auto paint. 84 x 54 x 50 cm.
Courtesy the artist, Tolarno Galleries and Roslyn Oxley9 Gallery.
Photo by Drome Studio.

displays another biotechnologically transfiguring body, yet with a more futuristic look. It is a contorted, vague, grotesque corporeal creation that sits on top of a shiny fibreglass structure: an unusual juxtaposition of hard surfaces with soft folds of the silicone sculpture. The figure, unable to be a complete body with its own boundaries, fails to conform to any given orderly structures. The uncannily convincing details, pink flesh, freckles, body hair and veins enable the audience to relate to it in a direct visceral manner. At once shocking and alluring, alien and familiar, *The Atlas* continues to explore the ambiguity of genetic transition and the morphing of human and non-human animal.

The notion of mutation is a far-reaching theme in both the scholarly and mainstream reception of Piccinini's work, but the range of questions asked about the topic has been limited in scope. Taking the representational and identitarian frameworks of change as the entry point to the discussion, the secondary literature on Piccinini mainly interprets the bioengineered organisms from the outset as an inventory of empirical givens, relegating the creative force of change to a fixed and reified content. As soon as the scholarship considers the biogenetically modified body in its givenness, it tends to objectify, classify and frame it via other ontological presuppositions and fixed articulations, predominantly via such lenses as cyborgian and posthuman approaches. In her book *Cyborgs and Barbie Dolls: Feminism, Popular Culture and the Posthuman Body*, Kim Toffoletti characterises the composite figures conjoined from different species in Piccinini's practice as 'by-products of scientific research' (2007: 152) and 'posthuman forms' that 'render the potential effects of biotechnology on the body' (134). Echoing this perspective, Anitra Goriss-Hunter defines her practice as concerned with 'hyper-real mutants and cyborgean blendings of animal/machine/human bodies' (2004: 542). Other liminal figures such as monsters, chimeras, hybrids and their various combinations are also widely used to tackle the sculptural embodiments in Piccinini's work.[3] Brian Massumi, however, presents a different angle towards posthumanism, one that is closer to the current account developed here. According to Massumi, for the 'posthuman approaches . . . as part of their cultural studies inheritance, "the subject"' still remains 'a privileged analytical category' (2014: 117). While most of the scholarly treatments of posthumanism, as Massumi details, 'assert that the animal and the human, nature and culture, are on a continuum', they are nevertheless 'insufficiently supernormal, and too seriously inoculated against subjectivities-without-a-subject' (ibid.). In addition to Massumi, John Appleby contends that a 'movement towards a supposedly post-human condition (even if that position is one of diversification)' is still 'strongly teleological' (2002: 110) and 'reifies the human as a fixed point that can be passed or overtaken' (107). Kate McGowan makes a similar point concerning the inadequacy of cyborg theories for conceptualising the in-itself of change and the non-teleological modes of subjectivity: 'That the "cyborg is our ontology", merely replaces one form of ontology for another. It replaces the human with another form of the human, and in so doing does nothing whatever to challenge the ontological status of the human as such' (2007: 138).[4] Hence, examining the biotechnologically inspired mutations in Piccinini's body sculptures persistently through the filter of such pre-constituted parameters, the existing literature hardly ever moves beyond the limits of the *changed* or *transformed* subject. This line of interpretation does no more than creating a quantitative leap; it implicitly reduces the body to snapshots of change – from humanist accounts of subjectivity to cyborgian, hybridised and posthuman ones via a techno-intervention – seamlessly filtering out the 'transindividual immediacy' of its creation (Massumi 2014: 77). While all of these criteria make an important contribution to the theorisation of the engineered fusions of biological-technological systems in Piccinini's sculptures, as well as the unsettled boundaries between various dichotomies, in such commentaries no space is provided for the ontogenetic dynamics and emergent processes at work in their creation.

Thus, while the majority of secondary literature prioritises the extensive, quantified, techno-scientifically transformed outcomes in Piccinini's practice – categorising them as pre-set image types which can be analysed with respect to various social concerns – this chapter insists on an accentuated attention to the intensive, qualitative, ontogenetic processes at play in her corporeal figures, as that which engender such transformative possibilities. In arguing for such an engagement with Piccinini's work, this chapter does not dismiss the value of the mentioned accounts that rely upon representational and empirical knowability of bodies. Rather than rejecting the models of representation and subjectivity, it argues that they offer only a partial reading of the logic of transformation at stake in her sculptural settings. As such, these representational and outcome-based paradigms can never be fully disengaged or grasped separately from the specific conditions of emergence that bring them about. As Elizabeth Grosz sums up, in order to appreciate any formed thing or given entity, it is essential to 'acknowledge the in-between of things, the plural interconnections that cannot be utilized or contained within and by things but which makes them possible' (2005: 141). In a similar vein, Erin Manning aptly notes that it is never enough to 'seek to assess only the form-as-such (the object, the body)' and one also needs to get 'invested in the milieu through which it comes into emergence' (2009: 103). That said, this chapter aims to complement these existing methodologies by attending to the ontogenetic dimension of Piccinini's corporeal forms beyond their given ontologies, and create a theoretical path that regards the theme of bodily mutation as a process worthy of attention in its own right. It does so by setting up an encounter with the Deleuzoguattarian concept of the body without organs and its attendant vocabularies of 'provisional organs' and 'eggs'. Rather than the subject-oriented and outcome-driven perspectives, I argue in favour of approaching the sculptural bodies in *Still Life with Stem Cells* and *The Atlas* through this notion and its related ideas, which reorient the focus towards the ontogenetic potentials, threshold states, transitions and liminalities. In this fashion, I seek to theorise the uncanny mutating dimension that is often overlooked in the principal receptions and critiques on Piccinini.

Body Without Organs, Provisional Organs and Eggs

The correlation between the body without organs and these two sculptural pieces by Piccinini might seem evident at first glance, because of their violation of the proper boundaries of natural organisms. Yet, in what follows, I delve deeper into the notion and take a close look at its various subtleties. It is through this extended elaboration of the body without organs that one can go beyond what is obvious at first sight. Following the lead of Antonin Artaud, who declares the organism as a constraint imposed on the body, or an oppressive 'judgment of God' (1976: 553), Deleuze and Guattari question the traditional biological construction of the body through their notion of the body without organs. The body without organs, or 'BwO' as the authors abbreviate, does not oppose or reject the organs, but rather the hierarchical and systematic organisation of the organs: the organism as an organic, ordered, integrated whole. For such a body, 'the organs are not its enemies. The enemy is the organism' (Deleuze and Guattari 1987: 158). As such, the organism is considered by Deleuze and Guattari in *A Thousand Plateaus* as a 'phenomenon of accumulation, coagulation and sedimentation' that imposes on us 'forms, functions, bonds, dominant and hierarchised organisations, organised transcendences' (1987: 159). These coagulating and sedimenting processes lead to reified, organised and hierarchised beings by concealing their affective capacities. In short, they create a molar organism whose forms, meanings and functions are fixed. The BwO, therefore, emerges as Deleuze and Guattari's attempt to resist all such reifying tendencies, to reject hierarchisation, coagulation, stabilisation and biological organisation. It designates the dis-organisation and dis-articulation of the three grand strata – 'the surface of the organism', 'the angle of significance' and 'the point of subjectification' – that bind humans in fixed articulations and congeal multiplicities into unified totalities (ibid.). It is in this sense that con-structing a BwO is a matter of looking for a point to 'dismantle the organisation of the organs we call organism' to reach the unformed, unstructured and destratified body (1987: 161). In dismantling the traditional biological construction of the self and disarticulating the strata that constitute humans, the organic, static and closed unity of the body is ruptured, which is, in turn, connected with the world. With this opening outwards to new affective connections, the body passes into a BwO – a state of continual transition, passage and becoming. In this fashion, the BwO can also be understood as the becoming-body that allows for the creation of new 'circuits, conjunctions, levels and thresholds, passages and distributions of intensity' (1987: 160).

    Developing this line of thought further, Deleuze and Guattari define BwO as 'what remains when you take everything away' (1987: 151), when the organic wholeness of the organism is stripped away. This process of stripping the organ-ism away causes 'asignifying particles or pure intensities to pass or circulate' (1987: 4), in that it refutes all attempts to create a coherent significatory system related to the human subject. Hence, the body as BwO is not a domain of rep-resentation, identity or meaning, rather of the 'anorganic', the 'asignifying' and the 'asubjective' (1987: 279). In this non-representational, non-identitarian and non-signifying state, instead of having fixed, static and well-defined organs, the body has only unspecified or temporary organs with varying functions. In his exposition of Francis Bacon's painterly rendition of human figures, Deleuze further relates BwO to the provisional organs that are defined by a certain malleability and mutability of the torso. According to Deleuze, 'the body without organs is not defined by the absence of organs' but rather 'by *the temporary and provisional presence* of determinate organs', which is 'one way of introducing time into the painting' (2003: 48, original emphasis). Indeed, for him, 'time itself is being painted' in Bacon's work, since 'the variation of texture and color on a body, a head or a back . . . is actually a temporal variation regulated down to the tenth of a second' (ibid.). In this manner, Deleuze expounds on the figures in Bacon's paintings as BwOs, in which the indeterminate organs or the contortions of the torso lead to transitory, provisional and temporal corporeal states.

Of even greater importance for the current investigation is how Deleuze and Guattari characterise this asignifying and asubjective BwO not as an outright chaos, but by focusing on the idea of potentiality. The BwO is conceptualised as an experimentation with the new potentialities and capabilities that are formerly unrealised by the unified organism. In theorising this state of potentiality, the authors draw a parallel between the BwO and the egg, an unformed, unstructured and pre-actualised ontological system: 'We treat the BwO as the full egg before the extension of the organism and the organisation of the organs, before the formation of the strata' (1987: 153). They write again: 'The BwO is an enormous undifferentiated object' (1983: 7). In this fashion, the embryonic egg becomes a curious metaphor for the BwO that exists before an organism takes shape. Like the egg, the BwO corresponds to a productive zero degree intensity before it sediments or congeals into an organised body, a coherent subject, a fixed signification: 'The BwO is nonstratified, unformed, intense matter, the matrix of intensity, intensity=0; but there is nothing negative about that zero, there are no negative or opposite intensities. Matter equals energy' (1987: 153). At this ontological degree of zero intensity or egg-like state, the body becomes pure potential: an open, formless, virtual matter prior to its stratification or coagulation into a developed form with fully differentiated organs. Drawing on Deleuze and Guattari's comparison, Manuel DeLanda also likens the egg to 'a topological space' that progressively undergoes a 'qualitative differentiation to become the metric space represented by a fully formed organism' (2002: 51–2). The BwO, then, is an ontogenetic field as the potential source of qualitative transformations, continual metamorphoses and processual becomings, rather than an actualised, quantified and finalised state. Hence, it is rightly characterised by Audronė Žukauskaitė as 'a platform or an intensive spatium which engenders a qualitative change' (2014: 80). An accentuated attention to these subtleties, in turn, generates a more complex and nuanced understanding of the capacities and functions that the concept of the BwO could have.

Ontogenetic Potential of the Formless Mass

It is in the preceding analysis of the BwO that one finds an evocative lens for theorising the mutational potential of the grotesque body on display in Piccinini's *The Atlas*. The figure is characterised by the artist herself as an 'amorphous, fleshy and abstractly corporeal form' (2012). Indeed, this is an overwhelmingly obscure, misshapen figure that does not follow the organic order and well-defined contours of the organism. With this work, Piccinini has removed all fixed significations and representations that bind the body. There is no indication of gender, species or any other identity markers. It is not assigned with specific organs with pre-arranged functions either. This is a disturbingly liminal, pliable and indeterminate flesh that does not signify. It exists before meaning, articulation and organisation, I suggest, primarily as a BwO, as that which remains 'when you take everything away' (Deleuze and Guattari 1987: 151). In this experience of the BwO, the body of *The Atlas* is taken back to a state of 'unorganised mass', which is controversially described by Deleuze and Guattari as having 'No mouth. No tongue. No teeth. No larynx. No esophagus. No belly. No anus', drawing from Artaud (Deleuze and Guattari 1983: 8). Remaining as an open-ended formation whose final form and functions are yet to be determined, it powerfully enacts the non-subjective and non-signifying potential of the BwO.

While the notion of a provisional or transient organ forms a significant part of Deleuze's theorisation of the BwO in painting, its use in his conceptualisation of sculpture has remained uncharted. In this context, I also want to argue for this notion's relevance for mapping out the dynamic potentiality inherent within *The Atlas*, as well as to explore how it might be creatively deployed within the medium of sculpture. As an unorganised mass with no definitive articulations, the contorted and twisted flesh here evokes a torso in-process that never fully coheres. It suggests a restless corporeality that continually strives to become a body. In a further statement, Piccinini reflects on her own piece as such: 'I'm not quite sure this figure could be called a creature or being . . . It reflects this idea of protean corporeality' (2012). It is through her comments on this protean quality of her sculpture that the artist begins to suggest specific issues regarding how a form continually comes into being, which is of particular significance to the current discussion. I wish to extend this argument by suggesting that the protean aspects of *The Atlas* spotted by Piccinini demonstrate how the provisional embodiment introduced by Deleuze may be understood to function in contemporary body-based sculpture. Indeed, this is a flesh that exists provisionally, as a 'polyvalent and transitory' torso in a temporal variation or qualitative differentiation (Deleuze 2003: 52). As Massumi would say, it is 'always provisional because always in becoming' (2002: 205). While perpetually morphing and striving to become a body, at the same time, it plays out the immanent potentialities prior to its representation as a finished product or a fully differentiated organism. This, I further claim, refers to a biogenetically induced state of ontogenetic potential associated with the BwO, during which no distinction can yet be made between male and female, human and animal. This reading of *The Atlas*, in turn, begins to highlight mutation and change in their specificity, as a transindividual and transformative force that passes among categorical orders.

The formulation of the BwO as an egg is also relevant for the analysis of Piccinini's *Still Life with Stem Cells*. The stem cell family of the sculptural setting, which is depicted in a tactile connection with the girl, appears genetically ambiguous. Glaringly unusual, the members of this family oscillate between human and animal body parts, overriding all known species categories. Within the context of the uncanny blobs of flesh, it is no longer possible to discern any signs of individuality or any meaningful anatomical point of reference. Although Piccinini provides no clear explanations, the matching skin tone, texture, curves of flesh and wrinkles of the girl and the amorphous fleshy lumps implicitly suggest that they are created from the girl's own stem cells. They are described by Engberg as 'things' that 'recall the indistinct characters' (2010: 24). Engberg further delineates these formations as 'perpetually infant progenies of science and biology' (2002: 43). For curator Linda Michael, as well, these are 'unidentifiable' (2003: 10) lumps that have a 'nascent sensitivity' (13). While these figures' utter formlessness and their failure to conform to any taxonomic schemes have been recognised by other scholars, I would like to stretch their observations and think of the nascent and perpetually infant qualities of these ambiguous lumps of flesh as the pure potentiality that characterises the BwO. According to art theorist Suzanne Anker, stem cells are 'pluripotent', that is, they are 'raw cellular material with the capacity to morph into numerous other types of cells, such as muscle, nerve, and skin cells' (2012: 39). In a similar vein, Zurr states that 'embryonic stem cells are cells before differentiation. Hence, these cells have the ability to become any type of tissue, when they are given the right conditions and appropriate growth factors' (2002). Like the embryological egg, then, which is directly affiliated with the BwO, these stem cell figurations actively refer to a virtual state, to a 'nonstratified, unformed, intense matter' pertaining to the metamorphic phase of tissue cultivating (Deleuze and Guattari 1987: 153). Retaining all the potential of growing into different organisms, they remain as shapes in-formation or ontogenetic expressions prior to their coagulation into fully specified and actualised beings. The new flesh, in a manner resonant with the Deleuzoguattarian egg, exists at the 'zero degree' (ibid.) that carries any thought of the negative to a productive difference – a difference in its pure state. This is where one begins to conceive change on its own account beyond any empirical condition and where the significance of the current exposition lies: beyond the formed matter lurks the BwO in its full aliveness, an unadulterated mutational potential waiting to be actualised through techno-scientific means. Hence, 'the life in question' here, in Deleuze and Guattari's words, is 'inorganic, germinal, and intensive, a powerful life without organs, a body that is all the more alive for having no organs' (1987: 499).

Yet, understanding difference in its pure or unadulterated state does not necessarily imply that these new forms of existence are equally capable of positive effects, or that these BwOs in the sculptural context are intrinsically desirable in real life. In relation to the sculptural setting of *Still Life with Stem Cells*, Michael, for instance, raises these questions: 'Is this the destruction of life implied in this scene? Do the forms result from or anticipate a failed experiment? Or are they its desired outcome?' (2003: 13). There is no doubt that such questions on Piccinini's work are valid. Crossing into the limits of the unnatural and the unknown, the strange corporeal forms that constitute her sculptural portrayals bring to the surface certain anxieties about the potential implications of manipulating nature through stem cell and cloning technologies.[5] According to curator Robin Held, these technologies are 'widely expected to revolutionize medicine, providing knowledge that will enhance control over specific human diseases', yet at the same time 'the potential dangers of misuse . . . cannot be underestimated' (2003: 267). For this reason, a thorough consideration of this technologised flesh requires focusing on Deleuze and Guattari's further analysis of the notion of the BwO, especially in terms of the different types of BwOs they develop. That said, the rest of the chapter considers Piccinini's sculptural scenarios as examples of how these various types of BwOs can be animated in the field of biotechnologically inspired artistic praxis.

Full Body Without Organs or its Dangerous Doubles?

In plateau 6 of *A Thousand Plateaus*, 'How Do You Make Yourself a Body without Organs?', Deleuze and Guattari provide distinctions between the diverse kinds of BwOs that we can construct once we have 'sufficiently dismantled our self' (1987: 151). It is clear from this section that certain elements of risk are inherent in this destratification, and there are no guarantees that there will be positive consequences. The authors write: 'This is not reassuring, because you can botch it' (1987: 149). On the one hand, there is the 'full BwO' through which many intensities and energies can pass and circulate (1987: 165). Yet, on the other, there are its dangerous 'doubles' (ibid.), the unsustainable or unsatisfactory outcomes of botched or 'too violent' attempts (1987: 161), such as the empty, suicidal, cancerous or fascistic BwOs. Deleuze and Guattari provide such examples as the '*hypochondriac*', the '*paranoid*', the '*schizo*', the '*drugged*' and the '*masochist*' bodies (1987: 150, original emphasis) that have all unproductively '*emptied themselves of their organs* instead of looking for the point at which they could patiently and momentarily dismantle the organisation of the organs we call the organism' (1987: 161, original emphasis). For the sake of the argument here, I would like to concentrate on the cancerous BwOs that materialise out of too much stratification. These types of BwOs, which construct themselves dementedly, can also be understood in terms of the proliferating tumour cells that run amok:

A cell becomes cancerous, mad, proliferates and loses its configuration, takes over everything; the organism must resubmit it to its rule or restratify it, not only for its own survival, but also to make possible an escape from the organism, the fabrication of the 'other' BwO on the plane of consistency. (Deleuze and Guattari 1983: 163)

Therefore, the BwO, instead of a single acceptable one, has several potential effects: full, empty or cancerous.

Looking at Piccinini's stem cell creations as an experience of the BwO, it is not easy to tell whether it is full or botched, favourable or unfavourable. In the world of biotechnology that encapsulates Piccinini's artistic praxis, stem cells can be manipulated for harmful as much as for beneficial ends. Despite their broad medical promise, there is also a fear that they will be 'exploited for commercial gain and narcissistic purposes—whether by pharmaceutical companies through prohibitively expensive medical treatments or the "design" of genetically modified progeny' as stated by Jane Messenger (2011: 136). A prevalent metaphor for the potential harms or misuse of genetic research is a malignant growth, with its uncontrollably multiplying cells. As such, with their dazzlingly irregular and irrational shapes, the embryonic forms of *Still Life with Stem Cells* seem threatening for the normative order of things. In a view consonant with this perspective, Christine and Margaret Wertheim remark that they 'resemble nothing so much as cancerous wads leapt free from their hosts' (2003: 25). In a similar vein, Engberg claims that with their 'tumorous and perplexing' appearance, these creations suggest 'an out-of-control growth: a troubling malignancy that has unsettling portent' (2010: 39). On this reading, experimenting with stem cell technologies can lead to failures or catastrophic outcomes – cancerous BwOs – through the demented and paranoid proliferation of pathological cells.

But if one looks at Piccinini's creations from the viewpoint of the positive uses of genetic technologies, the perspective changes drastically. Due to their pliable capacity to morph into any type of organ or tissue, stem cells promise to extend lifespan through the replacement of failed organs. The calm and serene setting of the sculpture also contributes to the optimism regarding the possibilities of cure through tissue regeneration. The apparent comfort and the natural attire of Piccinini's child suggest that these strange-looking creatures are, in fact, simply benign. In relation to this, Engberg also suggests that her 'obvious lack of concern is reassuring, counterbalancing the potential menace of the unsettling form' (2010: 49–50). Seen from this point of view, Piccinini's strategy might allow one to perceive the positive potentials of these stem cell lumps.

One can speculate on the various uses of biotechnology and attempt to judge these lumps as promising or perilous, desired or unwelcome BwOs depending on these results, yet, I argue, one can never know in advance. Any speculation of how this new flesh will eventuate or where it might lead to, in Deleuze's words, 'always refers existence to transcendent values' and functions as a 'system of judgement' (1988: 23), risking a pre-constituted knowledge of what it is. The bodies at stake here, by contrast, have no predefined coordinates; instead of formed entities one can posit conclusively, they remain as shapes in-progress, in continuous development and change. As discussed earlier, these amorphous stem cell creations hover in a pluripotent state, in an open and active field of potentiality that holds back all actualised and individualised possibilities. In this pluripotent state, they are suspended in a moment of change, or in 'a transformation-in-place' whose outcome for Massumi is 'yet unknowable, and consequently inexpressible' (2014: 32). This yet-unknowable aspect has to do with the fact that becoming seeks or represents nothing other than itself. It is not about producing something in particular, apart from the pure potential of change, be this change for good or bad. As Deleuze has shown in *Negotiations*: 'Processes are becomings, and aren't to be judged by some final result but by the way they proceed and their power to continue' (1995: 146). Following from these descriptions, Manning also argues that such processes 'only propel: they promise nothing. They create openings, intervals, fluxes of potential relation. They propose. They risk. And they move' (2013: 52). Based on these criteria, there are no certain end-states or predetermined expectations that drive these transformations.

In the context of Piccinini's *Still Life with Stem Cells* and *The Atlas*, this would mean that the body's tendency to become-other on the way to a BwO comes with a certain unpredictability and risk. In this mutating activity, unknown possibilities are unleashed by biogenetics. Within this framework, whether these becomings are promising or menacing, good or not, or safe or not cannot be known from the outset, for the simple reason that these are continual transformations that operate in themselves, as autonomous forces of change beyond any identitarian ends. Defying any attempts to postulate them strictly on the side of promise or peril, the technologised flesh of *Still Life with Stem Cells* and *The Atlas* can at best be characterised as BwOs, in which positive potentials associated with the full ones join and blend with the disturbing potentials of their dangerous doubles. These are pre-personal bodies full of ontogenetic potentials and unknown capacities. They are in perpetual emergence, thus never affirming a good or bad result. Hence, my theorisation of Piccinini's sculptural settings in this chapter not only allows for an exploration of the fluid and liminal states of transformation, but also allows for an evaluation of both the hopeful and dreadful potentials of that very change. It becomes reflective of 'the ambiguities that are inherent in science and technology—activities that can cure or kill, create or destroy, provide benefits or cause harm' (Anker and Nelkin 2004: 76), as well as the equally complex and ambiguous approach towards genetic technologies in Piccinini's work.[6]

Conclusion

This chapter argues that in order to engage critically with the biotechnologically mutated bodies in Piccinini's sculptural practice and their various socio-cultural implications, one needs to consider first mutation in its own right. This cannot be solely addressed via a pre-given set of discursive categories that convey static and quantified images of representation (the image of cyborg, posthuman or monster, for instance), but rather by an attention paid to the specific modes of emergence of these sculptural corporealities: the elusive in-betweens, ontogenetic dynamics, qualitative changes and active potentials that compose these beings. The strategy of the BwO and its related set of terminologies provide a means to account for these qualitative processes and ontogenetic dimensions. By reconceptualis-ing Piccinini's speculative bodily scenarios according to this method – which does not exclude the transitional, liminal and temporal states among categorical orders – this chapter reveals a complexity and significance in them previously not acknowledged by critics. Within this approach, biotechnologically altering flesh encountered in *Still Life with Stem Cells* and *The Atlas* does not merely correspond to newly fixed subject-positions or prefigured identity categories, but remains as processual figures always in the midst of becoming and filled with potential. Complementing the existing scholarship that adheres to the empirical givens and end results of transformational processes, this chapter demonstrates that it is not merely the biogenetically modified outcome that matters, but also how it comes into being within complex negotiations between human and non-human bodies. In this manner, it proposes a new way to think about the body on the level of creation and emergence, thus releasing the generative potential of change from the containment of finalised and reified images. Consequently, this close juxtaposition of Piccinini and Deleuze not only discloses the breadth of the philosophical thrust behind her bizarre creations, but also demonstrates how the notion of the BwO can be creatively reworked, developed and mobilised in biotechnologically mediated contemporary artistic praxis.

Notes

1. *Still Life with Stem Cells* was first exhibited at the Sydney Biennale, 2002. For an image of the sculpture see <https://www.patriciapiccinini.net/127/77> (last accessed 17 March 2020).
2. *The Atlas* was displayed as a part of Piccinini's exhibition *I have spread my dreams under your feet*, at Roslyn Oxley9 Gallery, Australia, 2013. For an image of the sculpture see <https://www.patriciapiccinini.net/33/16> (last accessed 17 March 2020).
3. An overview of the whole scope of such newly defined subject-positions would go far beyond the scope of this chapter, as countless other derivatives of such definitions have been advanced. Yet, the most readily available interpretations include framings such as 'chimeras and transgenic beings' by Jane Messenger (2011: 16); 'the human/animal DNA chimeras' by Tarsh Bates (2010: 97); 'monstrous hybrids' by Jessica Ullrich (2009); and 'fleshy hybrid animal-human' by Nato Thompson (2005: 98). Annemarie Jonson and Alessio Cavallaro also describe Piccinini's figures in terms of 'monstrous chimeras' whose identities are 'permanently partial' (2002: 184).
4. One can add other derivatives to Massumi's and McGowan's arguments. See, for instance, Barbara M. Kennedy (2002: 20): 'Even Donna Haraway's claim for a cyborg heteroglossia, whilst it has been substantially liberatory for rethinking feminist politics, has a notion of subjectivity, albeit cyborgian.'
5. For bioethical debates surrounding cloning and genetic engineering in contemporary culture and visual art, see for instance Joanna Zylinska (2005, 2009), Eduardo Kac (2007), and Suzanne Anker and Dorothy Nelkin (2004), among others.
6. Piccinini refuses to take sides with respect to genetic engineering, cloning and stem cell research. She evades a deterministic approach towards such technologies, neither affirming nor critiquing them. See Piccinini (1999): 'I begin with a very ambivalent attitude towards both technology and nature. They are both forces, and both are too massive and too complex to be easily defined as good or bad.'

References

Anker, Suzanne (2012), 'The Extant Vamp (or the) Ire of It All: Fairy Tales and Genetic Engineering', in Mark W. Scala (ed.), *Fairy Tales, Monsters, and the Genetic Imagination*, Nashville: Vanderbilt University Press, pp. 37–49.

Anker, Suzanne and Dorothy Nelkin (2004), *The Molecular Gaze: Art in the Genetic Age*, New York: Cold Spring Harbor Laboratory Press.

Appleby, John (2002), 'Planned Obsolescence: Flying into the Future with Stelarc', in Joanna Zylinska (ed.), *The Cyborg Experiments: The Extensions of the Body in the Media Age*, London and New York: Continuum, pp. 101–13.

Artaud, Antonin (1976), 'To Have Done with the Judgment of God (1947)', in *Selected Writings*, ed. Susan Sontag, trans. Helen Weaver, New York: Farrar, Straus and Giroux, pp. 553–71.

Bates, Tarsh (2010), 'InterUterine: Exploring the Reprotech Body through an Interspecies Aesthetic of Care', *Hecate*, 36(1/2): 92–100.

DeLanda, Manuel (2002), *Intensive Science and Virtual Philosophy*, London and New York: Continuum.

Deleuze, Gilles (1988), *Spinoza: Practical Philosophy*, trans. Robert Hurley, San Francisco: City Lights Books.

Deleuze, Gilles (1995), *Negotiations 1972–1990*, trans. Martin Joughin, New York: Columbia University Press.

Deleuze, Gilles (2003), *Francis Bacon: The Logic of Sensation*, London: Continuum.

Deleuze, Gilles (2013), *Cinema 1: The Movement-Image*, trans. Hugh Tomlinson and Barbara Habberjam, London: Bloomsbury Academic.

Deleuze, Gilles and Félix Guattari (1983), *Anti-Oedipus: Capitalism and Schizophrenia*, trans. Robert Hurley, Mark Seem and Helen R. Lane, Minneapolis: University of Minnesota Press.

Deleuze, Gilles and Félix Guattari (1987), *A Thousand Plateaus: Capitalism and Schizophrenia*, trans. Brian Massumi, Minneapolis: University of Minnesota Press.

Engberg, Juliana (2002), *Retrospectology: The World According to Patricia Piccinini*, Melbourne: Australian Centre for Contemporary Art.

Engberg, Juliana (2010), *Patricia Piccinini: Relativity*, Adelaide: Art Gallery of Western Australia.

Goriss-Hunter, Anitra (2004), 'Slippery Mutants Perform and Wink at Maternal Insurrections: Patricia Piccinini's Monstrous Cute', *Continuum: Journal of Media & Cultural Studies*, 18(4): 541–53.

Grosz, Elizabeth (2005), *Time Travels: Feminism, Nature, Power*, Durham, NC: Duke University Press.

Haraway, Donna (2007), 'Speculative Fabulations for Technoculture's Generations: Taking Care of Unexpected Country', <https://patriciapiccinini.net/printessay.php?id=30> (last accessed 16 April 2020).

Held, Robin (2003), 'Gene(sis): Contemporary Art Explores Human Genomics', in Robert Mitchell and Phillip Thurtle (eds), *Data Made Flesh: Embodying Information*, New York: Routledge, pp. 263–78.

Jonson, Annemarie and Alessio Cavallaro (2002), 'Visible Unrealities: Artists' Statements', in Darren Tofts (ed.), *Prefiguring Cyberculture: An Intellectual History*, Cambridge, MA: MIT Press, pp. 181–208.

Kac, Eduardo (ed.) (2007), *Signs of Life: Bio Art and Beyond*, Cambridge, MA: MIT Press.

168 BURCU BAYKAN

Kennedy, Barbara M. (2002), *Deleuze and Cinema: The Aesthetics of Sensation*, Edinburgh: Edinburgh University Press.

McGowan, Kate (2007), *Key Issues in Critical and Cultural Theory*, London: McGraw-Hill Education.

Manning, Erin (2009), *Relationscapes: Movement, Art, Philosophy*, Cambridge, MA: MIT Press.

Manning, Erin (2013), *Always More Than One: Individuation's Dance*, Durham, NC: Duke University Press.

Massumi, Brian (2002), *Parables for the Virtual: Movement, Affect, Sensation*, Durham, NC: Duke University Press.

Massumi, Brian (2014), *What Animals Teach Us about Politics*, Durham, NC: Duke University Press.

Messenger, Jane (2011), *Patricia Piccinini: Once Upon a Time*, Adelaide: Art Gallery of South Australia.

Michael, Linda (2003), 'We Are Family', in Margaret Wertheim, Christine Wertheim and Linda Michael (eds), *Patricia Piccinini: We Are Family*, Surry Hills: Australia Council, pp. 9–20.

Piccinini, Patricia (1999), 'Artist Statement', <http://www.patriciapiccinini.net/writing/1/304/63> (last accessed 17 March 2020).

Piccinini, Patricia (2012), 'Those Who Dream by Night', <https://www.patriciapiccinini.net/printessay.php?id=38> (last accessed 16 April 2020).

Thompson, Nato (2005), 'Patricia Piccinini', in Nato Thompson, Joseph Thompson and Christoph Cox (eds), *Becoming Animal: Contemporary Art in the Animal Kingdom*, North Adams: Mass MoCA Publications, pp. 98–105.

Toffoletti, Kim (2007), *Cyborgs and Barbie Dolls: Feminism, Popular Culture and the Posthuman Body*, London: I. B. Tauris.

Ullrich, Jessica (2009), 'Patricia Piccinini', <http://becoming-animal-becoming-human.animal-studies.org/html/piccinini.html> (last accessed 17 March 2020).

Wertheim, Christine and Margaret Wertheim (2003), 'Teratology', in Margaret Wertheim, Christine Wertheim and Linda Michael (eds), *Patricia Piccinini: We Are Family*, Surry Hills: Australia Council, pp. 25–9.

Žukauskaitė, Audronė (2014), 'Intensive Multiplicities in *A Thousand Plateaus*', in Paul Ardoin, S. E. Gontarski and Laci Mattison (eds), *Understanding Deleuze, Understanding Modernism*, New York and London: Bloomsbury Academic, pp. 75–89.

Zurr, Ionat (2002), 'On Humans and Other Animals "Becoming" Each Other', *Artlink*, 22(1), <https://www.artlink.com.au/articles/2520/on-humans-and-other-animals-becoming-each-other/> (last accessed 16 April 2020).

Zylinska, Joanna (2005), *The Ethics of Cultural Studies*, London and New York: Continuum.

Zylinska, Joanna (2009), *Bioethics in the Age of New Media*, Cambridge, MA: MIT Press.

9

Refugees as Multiplicities

S. E. Wilmer

Although Deleuze and Guattari do not offer an explicit political response to refugees, they venture into the same arena with many of their concepts, such as becoming-minor, nomadism, smooth space, lines of flight, deterritorialisation, and 'a people to come'.[1] In asserting the political nature of their work, Paul Patton (2012: 206) argues that such Deleuzoguattarian concepts 'are not meant as substitutes for existing concepts of freedom, equality, or justice but they are intended to assist the emergence of another justice, new kinds of equality and freedom, as well as new kinds of political differentiation and constraint'. While not addressing the problem of refugees as explicitly as, for example, Hannah Arendt (1943) or Giorgio Agamben (1995, 1998: 126–80), Deleuze and Guattari hint at possibilities for social reform, and their work can be applied to some of the social conditions that have prompted the increasing number of refugees throughout the world.

In this chapter I want to argue that Ariane Mnouchkine's production of *Le Dernier Caravansérail (Odyssées)* exemplifies the proposition that refugees can be regarded as both quantitative and qualitative multiplicities. In differentiating between the two, Deleuze and Guattari indicate that quantitative multiplicities are essentially numerical and can be counted, whereas qualitative multiplicities cannot be counted in that they differ in kind from one another.[2] On the one hand, we can readily agree that refugees are countable. For example, the newspapers are filled with the numbers of refugees in camps, or on the move in processions from one country to another, or who have died crossing the Mediterranean. Likewise national governments seem to consider refugees in terms of quantity: the number of refugees to be allowed in to the country, the number to be housed or detained, the number to be deported. On the other hand, one can also argue that refugees are not of a single kind. Politicians, for example, often try to distinguish between economic migrants and political refugees, despite these being very broad and overlapping categories. Likewise, the United Nations has specified conditions (which can be difficult to prove) for refugees to achieve asylum: 'A refugee, according to the Convention, is someone who is unable or unwilling to return to their country of origin owing to a well-founded fear of being persecuted for reasons of race, religion, nationality, membership of a particular social group, or political opinion' (UNHCR 2010: 3).[3]

The reasons for becoming a refugee differ significantly from one individual or family to another, and their circumstances are not only diverse but often in constant flux. Refugees can be differentiated, for instance, by their ethnicity, gender, age, mobility, health, language, sexual orientation, nationality, skills, employability, and size and age of family members.[4] The reasons for refugees leaving home can include religious persecution, sexual violence, ethnic violence or ethnic cleansing, poverty, hunger, war, climate change, loss of home or habitat, intimidation, threats of violence, fear, dispossession, loss of legal rights, loss of employment, death, disappearance or debilitation of a family member, alteration of national boundaries, or imposition of hostile or punitive laws. Likewise, reasons for moving to another place can include the success of friends and family elsewhere, job opportunities, higher wages, better housing, social support, a more favourable climate, a more welcoming environment to practise religion, sexual orientation, more equitable laws, more possibilities for integration, naturalisation and citizenship, an opportunity to reunite with family, friends, religious or ethnic group, or simply to escape danger. Thus, at the risk of stretching Deleuze and Guattari's notion of qualitative multiplicity, we could say that refugees are qualitative multiplicities in the sense that they are not identical but highly differentiated.

Moreover, descriptive categories such as nomad, migrant, displaced person, asylum seeker and refugee are often misleading. In a 'Treatise on Nomadology' from *A Thousand Plateaus*, Deleuze and Guattari (1987: 420–1) try to differentiate between nomads and migrants:

> The nomad distributes himself in a smooth space; he occupies, inhabits, holds that space; that is his territorial principle. It is therefore false to define the nomad by movement. Toynbee is profoundly right to suggest that the nomad is on the contrary *he who does not move*. Whereas the migrant leaves behind a milieu that has become amorphous or hostile, the nomad is one who does not depart, does not want to depart, who clings to the smooth space left by the receding forest, where the steppe or the desert advances, and who invents nomadism as a response to this challenge . . . If the nomad can be called the Deterritorialized par excellence, it is precisely because there is no reterritorialization *afterward* as with the migrant.

However, contrary to what Deleuze and Guattari argue, migrants do not always succeed in reterritorialising and nor do refugees. The refugee sometimes succeeds only in deterritorialising because the process of reterritorialisation may be too long and arduous or too difficult to achieve, and possibly endless. More often than not, the refugee is stopped at national borders, or dies en route, or is held in refugee camps or detention centres, awaiting asylum or deportation. Moreover, nomads can also reterritorialise by evolving into today's settled citizens as their conditions for survival and employment become more sedentary or governments impose restrictions on their movement or force them to migrate to the cities or to other places. Likewise, forcibly displaced persons (who are more numerous today than ever, reaching more than seventy million in 2018)[5] can behave more like nomads in certain circumstances, wanting to return home (when the current danger has passed) rather than settling in another location (such as those escaping the Syrian civil war). Thus, Deleuze and Guattari's distinction between the migrant and the nomad does not necessarily hold true because the lives of such individuals (including refugees and displaced persons) are in flux and evolving, rather than static.

Refugees often strive to break free of striated space into the smooth space of nomads. But as Deleuze and Guattari warn in *A Thousand Plateaus* (1987: 551):

> smooth spaces are not in themselves liberatory. But the struggle is changed or displaced in them, and life reconstitutes its stakes, confronts new obstacles, invents new paces, switches adversaries. Never believe that a smooth space will suffice to save us.

Also refugees sometimes move with others for self-protection as heterogeneous groups of different nationalities and languages, as in the processions of refugees from Greece towards Western Europe in 2015 or from Latin America towards the United States in 2019. Such processions form and reform. Individuals and families drop out, while others continue. They move at different paces, some trying to keep up, others falling away or taking different routes, similar to the packs of nomads in smooth space that Deleuze and Guattari (1987: 534) describe as resembling their nomadic terrain: 'Not only is that which peoples a smooth space a multiplicity that changes in nature when it divides – such as tribes in the desert: constantly modified distances, packs that are always undergoing metamorphosis – but smooth space itself, desert, steppe, sea, or ice, is a multiplicity of this type.'

In their discussion of packs, Deleuze and Guattari indicate the influence of Elias Canetti on their approach:

> Canetti distinguishes between two types of multiplicity that are sometimes opposed but at other times interpenetrate: mass ('crowd') multiplicities and pack multiplicities. Among the characteristics of a mass, in Canetti's sense, we should note large quantity, divisibility and equality of the members, concentration, sociability of the aggregate as a whole, one-way hierarchy, organization of territoriality or territorialization, and emission of signs. Among the characteristics of a pack are small or restricted numbers, dispersion, nondecomposable variable distances, qualitative metamorphoses, inequalities as remainders or crossings, impossibility of a fixed totalization or hierarchization . . . there is no more equality or any less hierarchy in packs than in masses, but they are of a different kind. . . . Canetti notes that in a pack each member is alone even in the company of others . . . each takes care of himself at the same time as participating in the band. (1987: 37)

Thus, arguably, rather than being distinct, the conditions of the migrant, the refugee and the nomad bleed into one another. In a sense they are all minority-becomings, transforming cultural roles and social norms, and can evolve into each other. Deleuze and Guattari indicate something along these lines in *A Thousand Plateaus* (1987: 274–5), where they claim that 'packs, or multiplicities, continually transform themselves into each other, cross over into each other . . . This is not surprising, since becoming and multiplicity are the same thing. A multiplicity is defined not by its elements, nor by a centre of unification or comprehension. It is defined by the number of dimensions it has.'

Théâtre du Soleil: Nomadic Artists

In this section I will discuss some of the Théâtre du Soleil's unusually nomadic features and then, in the following section, go on to examine their production of *Le Dernier Caravansérail (Odyssées)*, which depicted a multiplicity of refugees in various parts of the world seeking a better life. I will argue that, while the state and media tend to reduce refugees to numerical multiplicities, the theatre and the arts can transform them into qualitative multiplicities by indicating their singularities and individualities.

Le Dernier Caravansérail (Odyssées) (The Last Caravan Stop (Odysseys)) conjures up a panorama of human movement from all over the globe to convey the so-called 'migration crisis' at the beginning of the twenty-first century. In their production, the Théâtre du Soleil creates multiple subjectivities and potentialities, dismantling national and linguistic boundaries in a highly evocative performance that traverses the world with boat people and other migrants, leaving behind their national identities in search of a better life.[6] In its six-hour performance, *Le Dernier Caravansérail* touches on a variety of reasons and circumstances that cause migration, and it distinguishes their qualitative differences as the refugees struggle against government representatives, border guards, police, smugglers and traffickers, as well as difficulties with weather, climate and terrain. Such situations for refugees resemble what Deleuze and Guattari attribute to the position of the nomad: 'the depersonalisation of subjectivity such that the subject identifies with the multiplicity of the smooth spaces they traverse or inhabit, which places them in a hostile relation to the State, as well as to sedentary existence (i.e. existence with controlled, relative movement) and to striated space (actualized in a war-machine)' (Young 2013: 222).

While Deleuze and Guattari praised the work of nomadic artists from different periods of history, they did not mention the Théâtre du Soleil. However, it is clear that members of the theatre company were strongly influenced by some of the same impulses that inspired the philosophers.[7] Both Hélène Cixous, the writer in residence of the company, and Ariane Mnouchkine, its director, have referred to themselves as 'exiles', 'non belonging' or 'nomads'.[8] Cixous said about her background, 'I was lucky to have strangeness and exile as my time and place of birth' (in McEvoy 2006: 217).[9] According to Adrian Kiernander (1993: 125), Cixous is 'half-French, half-German, but also Jewish, brought up in Algeria and identifying with the eastern end of the Mediterranean'.[10] Ariane Mnouchkine also came from an immigrant family. Her father, a Russian Jew, fled to France following the Russian revolution.[11] In 1962–3, Mnouchkine took a year off from university to tour the Middle East and Asia, where she developed a passion for non-Western (such as Indian, Balinese, Chinese and Japanese) theatre forms. This experience would influence her interest in applying non-Western theatre techniques to Western classics (such as Asian theatrical styles for productions of Shakespearean and ancient Greek tragedy) and developing an intercultural or transcultural repertoire.

The Théâtre du Soleil was created in 1964 out of a student theatre group that Ariane Mnouchkine had founded while studying at the Sorbonne in Paris. Already expressing a leftist outlook, she and her fledgling theatre company were deeply affected by the experience of May 1968. During the insurrection in the streets and the shutdown of the theatres, the Théâtre du Soleil took their work to non-theatrical venues such as factories to entertain the striking workers. Eventually they squatted in an old, disused armaments factory (the Cartoucherie), which became their home base in Paris from 1970 onwards.

The Théâtre du Soleil's involvement in revolutionary politics, reflecting the student and worker concerns of May 1968, led to productions in the 1970s about the French revolution and questions of social justice (*1789* and *1793*). From an alternative, highly politicised theatre group, the company evolved into a widely appreciated force in French theatre, particularly noted for its innovative aesthetics. As a result of the election of the socialist government of Mitterand at the beginning of the 1980s, it achieved greater self-sufficiency when the newly appointed Minister of Culture, Jack Lang, doubled the size of its state subsidy. Not only did this make it possible for the actors to become employed full-time, but it also enabled larger productions, more frequent workshops by outside practitioners, and considerable foreign touring. The Théâtre du Soleil quickly grew into France's most highly state-subsidised private theatre, touring throughout the world with more than fifty people in the company. Today, it is considered to be one of the most innovative theatre companies in the world.

In the early 1980s Mnouchkine asked Cixous to write a play for the company, and this would lead to a close collaboration for the next thirty years. With Cixous on board, the productions became more transnational in theme and more intercultural in form, with plays about Cambodia in *L'Histoire terrible mais inachevée de Norodom Sihanouk, roi du Cambodge* (The Terrible but Unsuccessful History of Norodom Sihanouk, King of Cambodia) in 1985, India and Pakistan in *L'Indiade, ou L'inde de leur rêves* (The Indiad, or the India of their Dreams) in 1987, China in *Tambours sur la digue* (Drums on the Dam) in 1999, Australasia and Europe in *Le Dernier Caravansérail (Odyssées)* (The Last Caravan Stop (Odysseys)) in 2003, and South America in *Les Naufragés du fol espoir (Aurores)* (The Castaways of Mad Hope (Sunrises)) in 2010.

The Théâtre du Soleil has worked together as a closely knit company for five decades, expanding and contracting as individual artists come and go. It prefers non-conventional spaces to perform, regularly travelling through Europe and to North America, Asia, Australia and New Zealand. Although it maintains a permanent base at the Cartoucherie in the Bois de Vincennes in Paris, the theatre sometimes leaves Paris for considerable lengths of time. In 2001–2, for example, it spent almost an entire year touring in Asia, Australia and New Zealand. As well as identifying as a French company, its members represent a cross-section of the world. According to Judith Miller (2007: 14), 'As of 2005, there were seventy-five members from thirty-five countries, speaking twenty-two different languages.' Their productions frequently incorporate a transnational approach in both form and content, using, for example, East Asian and South Asian theatre techniques of movement, music, costume and acting style, and addressing trans-formative political situations in various parts of the world.

The Théâtre du Soleil projects an anti-capitalist ethic. Anticipating in some ways its ethos and its way of working, Deleuze wrote in *Difference and Repetition* (2004b: 45–6) that in contrast to the norms of private property

> there is a completely other distribution which must be called nomadic, a nomad *nomos*, without property, enclosure or measure. Here, there is no longer a division of that which is distributed but rather a division among those who distribute themselves in an open space – a space which is unlimited, or at least without precise limits . . . Even when it concerns the serious business of life, it is more like a space of play, or a rule of play, by contrast with sedentary space and *nomos*.

The actors in the Théâtre du Soleil, as members of a workers' cooperative receiving the same salary, promote a collective spirit of working together on all aspects of the enterprise, including cooking and cleaning.[12] For example, during some of their performances, the actors in full costume serve food during the inter-mission. While Hélène Cixous has been their writer in residence, the play texts are often devised collectively from improvisations by the actors and edited into more coherent form by Cixous. Furthermore, unlike most theatre companies, their emphasis has been as much on process as on product, with long rehearsal periods, elaborate workshops to develop new techniques, and opening nights being delayed for many days until the show is considered ready.

The Théâtre du Soleil do not like commodifying their art as capitalist products. According to Judith Miller (2007: 10–11), 'Mnouchkine does not see her pro-ductions as "packages", but rather as encounters between two creative groups in a process of exchange.' Mnouchkine (in Dickson 2012) says, 'We're not a shop. It's unfortunate we need people's money, but we're not selling something. That's why I hate the word "production": it's not produced, it's a ceremony, it's a ritual, it is something which is very important for your mental strength.'

Some of their productions have manifested a distinctly anti-capitalist and polit-ical intent. They have engaged in direct political actions, such as entertaining striking workers for free in 1968; squatting in the Cartoucherie until the city allowed them to stay there in 1970; producing a sketch for Foucault's prison reform campaign in 1973; organising a hunger-strike against the inaction of the French government during the ethnic cleansing in Bosnia in 1995 (in which Mnouchkine participated for thirty days); and housing more than 300 refugees from Mali who had been evicted from a Paris church where they had taken sanctuary in 1996. As Ariane Mnouchkine (in Miller 2007: 25) has said about the communal ethos of the theatre, it is a place where you can 'have your friends and your lovers in the same place and you can still be a nomad'.

In productions by the Théâtre du Soleil, the actors are often masked or anonymous or playing a variety of roles, often against gender and ethnicity, and sometimes as puppets. Compared to more conventional British and American theatre, the actors work as an ensemble, developing new techniques by combining non-Western and Western aesthetics. Depending on the particular play (unless it is based on a classic text by Shakespeare or Aeschylus), the actors tend to be less recognisable or identifiable as specific characters, trying out different roles in rehearsal, and often playing 'universal' (Miller 2007: 19) rather than individualised characters. According to David Finkle (2005), 'actors as personalities is not Mnouchkine's interest, and her players humbly and admirably comply with her wishes.' Moreover, the sheer expansion of the company (from an initial nine members in 1964 to seventy-five by 2012) inhibits a concentration on star performers, and the number of foreign artists decentres its French identity.[13]

Similar to Julian Beck and Judith Malina's Living Theatre, the Théâtre du Soleil has acquired some of its members en route as the company has travelled the globe, and the Cartoucherie itself has become a refuge at times for migrants. William McEvoy (2006: 212) asserts that, 'From the mid-seventies onwards, the Cartoucherie acted as a shelter and rallying point for immigrants and *sans-papiers* in Paris, promoting the idea of theatre as a site of hospitality and reinforcing the company's emerging practice of intercultural performance.' Likewise, Brian Singleton (2007: 26) argues that

> the company has now become known as a hub for migrating theatre artists. However, because of the economic demands on theatrical production and the necessity to change the repertoire and tour extensively, the theatre can only serve as a hub temporarily. But during this limited time the theatre can act as a workplace, sanctuary and staging post for stateless actors in flight to apply for legalised status as citizens.

Because of the dominance of Mnouchkine and Cixous amongst the artistic personnel, the theatre has also tended to present increasingly feminist and non-hierarchical subject matter, especially since the mid-1990s with productions such as *La Ville Parjure* (about the scandal concerning the National Blood Transfusion Centre that was using blood contaminated with HIV), *Tambours sur la digue* (about ecological issues) and *Les Naufragés du fol espoir (Aurores)* (recalling the early days of silent films).

The Théâtre du Soleil is perhaps unique in its transcultural approach of performing across a variety of aesthetic forms, and mixing up the cultural codes.[14] Using and combining Kathakali, Noh, Bunraku, Kabuki and other Asian techniques with the conventions of the Western canon as well as creating new theatrical forms, Mnouchkine has forged a nomadic style of work that she keeps developing with each production. According to Kiernander, writing in 1993 (1–2), 'Mnouchkine is

best known for the innovative nature of her productions, and the Théâtre du Soleil
has at various periods in its roughly thirty-year history created performances
which were unlike anything else which had been seen at the time. . . . Mnouchkine
above all is an extremist, a quality which has characterised all her best work.' Not
only does the company cross borders geographically, culturally, ethnically and
aesthetically, they also cross genre borders in reinterpreting classics and devising
new dramatic material. Likewise, by accepting exiles into their company, housing
refugees and touring extensively, they convey the impression of a constantly
changing enterprise, open to new ideas, and welcoming, interpreting and representing the dispossessed in society.[15]

Mnouchkine (in Miller 2007: 27) takes pride in the transformative power
of her work: 'Theatre is still a place where one learns, where one tries to
understand, where one is moved, where one encounters the Other and where one
becomes other.' Similarly, Cixous (2004: 28) refers to their theatre as a place of
education:

> I myself am always an apprentice there. Ariane too, for the Théâtre du Soleil
> is a world which reflects on itself, sounds itself out, reworks itself from play
> to play. It is a school and its laboratory, and the workshop of all the despairs
> which accompany theatrical creation . . . Once the 'right' subject . . . the Fable
> has been glimpsed in the distance – and we see first of all only the coastline – I
> set off on my way, and Ariane on hers. While I write, she constructs: the entire
> Theatre is pulled down and rebuilt as the receptacle of the new arrival.[16]

Le Dernier Caravansérail (Odyssées)

Le Dernier Caravansérail (Odyssées), which premiered in 2003 and continued in
repertoire until 2005, and was then released as a film in 2006, provides a prime
example of the Théâtre du Soleil's transnational theatricality. Concerned with
the European Union closing its borders to migration as well as with the plight
of refugees throughout the world following the collapse of the Soviet Union and
various civil wars and regime changes, the play addressed what was becoming a
major geopolitical concern.[17]

Le Dernier Caravansérail takes its name 'caravansérail' from the roadside
shelters and inns in Arab, Middle Eastern and Asian countries where nomadic
caravans would traditionally stop to rest or engage in commerce. The title emphasises the theme of nomadic mobility and the need for refuge that is expressed
throughout the play, bearing 'witness to the blighted new nomads who wander
the world, looking for a landfall to call home' (Lahr 2005). During an extensive
foreign tour of Tambours sur la digue (Drums on the Dam) at the beginning of the
twenty-first century, Mnouchkine and other members of the troupe visited refugee
camps in Australia, New Zealand, Indonesia and France and interviewed many
of the inhabitants, especially those at the inadequate Sangatte centre near Calais
(that was later closed by the government, leading to the inhospitable conditions of
the Calais 'jungle').[18] Mnouchkine, Cixous and the company devised an episodic

play from verbatim testimony that they had collected from migrants, and from which the actors improvised scenes along approximately eight different lines of narrative.

The six-hour performance, whose authorship is credited to the actors and members of the production team, is divided into two acts entitled 'The Cruel River' and 'Origins and Destinies'. At the beginning of each act, the characters attempt thrilling journeys in dangerous conditions over turbulent rivers and seas represented by billowing silk fabric. In the second of these episodes, which portrays the harrowing sea journey from Asia to Australia of a small crowded boat, the Australian military arrive by helicopter, in what seems like a last-minute rescue, only to announce: 'Go back where you came from! Australia will not accept you' (TdS 2006). Despite its inordinate length, the pace of the performance is fast-moving, with short scenes in chaotic order emphasising the tumultuous lives of refugees in different countries enduring oppressive conditions and striving to escape and reach new destinations. As Singleton (2007: 26) points out, 'it depicts in broad and sweeping performative brush strokes the causes and more specifically the effects of conflict migration and the human trafficking, dislocation, and suffering that ensues from that migration.'

Le Dernier Caravansérail portrays refugees fleeing from many different countries in Europe, the Middle East, Asia and Africa, including Afghanistan, Iran, Iraq, Kyrgyzstan, Russia, Bulgaria, Bosnia and Nigeria, making their way to Western Europe as well as to Australia and New Zealand. Numerous escape scenes take place in which the characters try to cross bridges, climb fences, invade tunnels or otherwise transgress borders. Their migration originates from a variety of causes, with scenes portraying economic migrants, people fleeing war zones, Eastern European women trafficked for sexual exploitation, and members of the Taliban passing themselves off as refugees.

The play displays a wide variety of transport, from bicycles and motorcycles to boats, trains, aeroplanes, helicopters, and people on foot. To convey their constant mobility and vulnerability, actors are wheeled on and off stage on mobile platforms by others in the cast. This novel feature elicited numerous comments from critics trying to interpret their use metaphorically. John Lahr (2005) describes the production in New York as

a dramatic inquiry into desolation, a way of making the audience imagine an unmoored life. To this end dollies, skillfully manipulated by the crew, transport the characters into view and out of sight. Like surreal figments in a dream, the refugees constantly scuttle across the vast expanse of the empty stage, propelled as if their feet never touched the ground. Glide replaces drift. The swift movement takes naturalism out of the narrative and gives the people and their stories a sort of mythic metabolism.

Michael Kustow (2003), seeing the performance in Paris, also commented on the effect of this fluid movement of actors and stagehands:

No one makes a normal theatrical entrance or exit. Each actor is rolled on and off stage standing on skateboard-like platforms, then pushed and twirled into place by stagehands or other actors. The locations themselves – a house in Kabul, railway sidings in Teheran – are also wheeled on in little trucks. This fluid staging becomes a metaphor for an existence in endless transit: the frozen figures on rolling platforms are in limbo.

Le Dernier Caravansérail addresses the barriers that prevent migration, such as the measures taken to prevent refugees from entering particular countries or to relocate them in detention centres or prisons, and it reveals the caged lives that many of these refugees experience. Sympathising with the refugees who try to break through barriers and enter countries illegally, the play demonstrates how nation states prohibit the free movement of peoples and undermine the human rights of individuals to settle where they want. In one particular scene, when the refugees are struggling to climb a border fence and are intercepted by German border guards, the 'Ode to Joy' from Beethoven's Ninth Symphony accompanies their desperate attempts to flee the guards and escape imprisonment, making clear that the positive sentiments of the European anthem, which professes the unity of mankind, hide the fact that European society is controlled by violent means, and that Europeans watching the show are implicated in the EU's 'fortress Europe' policies.

The play also reveals the conditions at Sangatte near Calais, which was run by the Red Cross and became not much better than a detention centre (until it was torn down and later transformed into 'the jungle'), and from which the refugees tried to obtain illegal passage to England by container, lorry, boat or the Eurotunnel.[19] The theatre troupe's interviews with the residents of Sangatte and other refugee centres are used as testimony, both on screen in Powerpoint and through voiceover by actors, to convey the conditions as well as the hardships that the refugees have endured. As an educational piece, the production emphasises the lack of common space in the divisible, capitalist world of Western Europe, condemning the inhumane treatment of refugees by the French and Australian governments as well as by traffickers demanding huge fees or sex and the many others who take advantage of them. In his review of the New York production, Jeremy McCarter (2005) writes that Mnouchkine 'gives us humanity at its most despicable. The show is awash in thieves, pimps, thugs, murderers, and every kind of opportunist.' According to Lara Stevens (2016: 110):

[T]heatre, in particular a work such as *Le Dernier Caravansérail*, can potentially redefine how we think about hosting asylum seekers and the legal and political practices that limit our capacity to enact a compassionate response. By revealing the contradictions in the principles of liberty, equality, and fraternity upon which Western nation states are constructed in their national mythologies, *Le Dernier Caravansérail* strives to offer a praxis for realizing hospitality on a national scale.

In *Le Dernier Caravansérail* the material in the scenes is based on verbatim interviews, giving specificity to the locations, characters and situations. As the narratives relate to the verbatim accounts of refugees, William McEvoy (2006: 213–14) argues that 'the production was able to challenge the violent ahistoricity and disembodiment that tend to accompany media representations of clandestine immigration'. For example, in one scene, a man expresses concern for his father in Kurdistan whose eyesight is failing and who has to keep moving to remain safe from military attack. However, there is little character development in the play. Many of the characters are briefly sketched to indicate their torn and tortuous lives, and tend to be archetypal or universal rather than psychologically individualised.

Thus the production focuses more on situations than characters, and the situations are not static but constantly fluid, conveying multiple features and facets of migration. The actors change characters from one scene to the next, often regardless of ethnicity and background, and it is frequently difficult to follow the various storylines and to know which actors are on stage because of their variety of costumes, make-up and beards. Christopher Isherwood (2005), in his review for the *New York Times*, records:

> As it sweeps across nearly a dozen countries and weaves together the experiences of too many people to count, 'Caravansérail' disdains the niceties of theatrical convention that allow us to identify who is who and what is going on at any given moment. Some characters come and go too quickly to be identified properly, and some scenes are performed in foreign languages with no subtitling at all.

The actors in the production come from all over the world and in at least one case had been 'saved' (Miller 2007: 14) from a refugee camp. Although physical movement predominates, the actors speak a variety of languages in the performance. The soundscape provided by the composer, Jean-Jacques Lemêtre, and technicians evokes the various cultures and locations where the play is set and sometimes overwhelms the actors' voices in sound effects. In conveying the 'horror of refugee life' (Miller 2007: 30), the production emphasises the rights of all peoples throughout the world rather than privileging certain ethnicities, genders, classes or nationalities. It proposes a cosmopolitan approach to society, supporting diversity and difference rather than ethnocentrism and assimilation, in its 'depiction of the migration of the refugees/asylum-seekers as transnational subjects caught up in a maelstrom of migrancy in which identities are bartered, sold, prostituted, falsified, or simply not known' (Singleton 2007: 29). The final curtain call illustrates the utopian theme of the piece with actors divided into two long lines, facing each other. At first they glare at each other and then run across to hug each other, a gesture of solidarity and overcoming difference which is repeated as long as the applause continues.

In addition to the desubjectivation of the characters in the play, Lara Stevens (2016: 110–11) argues that the audience experiences a similar affect:

Rather than trying to remake the other in the image of the self or self-same, Cixous challenges artists and spectators alike to remake themselves *as* the stranger, to assert the right to be an other. . . . *Le Dernier Caravansérail*'s representation of the other in a new and strange light enables spectators to avoid collapsing that other into the self or turning it into the self-same, thereby dissolving that other's singularity. Instead it challenges spectators to remake the self with greater compassion, hospitality and openness to the possibility of the other within the self and recognize the self within the other.

Le Dernier Caravansérail is eclectic in its portrayal of humankind across the world, depicting many different kinds of scenes, lifestyles and dilemmas. The play was, at the time, also a strident attack on European and Australian immigration policies and reveals the appalling conditions for refugees throughout the world. As a performance it is unusual in terms of its length, its variety of locations, its use of actors from so many countries speaking different languages, and its multiple manifestations of migration. Similar to Deleuze's article on 'The Exhausted' (1997), one might say that the company exhausts the possibilities of migration and the multiplicity of attempts to find a new home. The production also displayed breathtaking originality in some of its scenes, such as the bridge crossing and sea voyage scenes at the beginning of each act and some of the other attempts to escape, as well as in the novel use of trolleys to move the actors on and off stage. William McEvoy (2006: 222), another critic who interpreted the dolly effect metaphorically, wrote:

> It portrayed immigrants and refugees as an 'archipelago of individuals', standing on a small piece of land that symbolized the ground beneath their feet, the part of home that never left them and which they cannot leave behind, marking them out as perpetually displaced. The gliding of the rollers led to silent entrances and exits that evoked the dynamics of clandestinity. Visually, the appearance of gliding made the characters look eerie and uncanny, somewhat inhuman without the distinctive physical rhythms of walking and running, thereby cannily capturing external projections of strangeness and differences onto migrants.

One particular issue with which the production team obviously struggled was how to tell the stories of the individual refugees they interviewed in a way that portrayed them fairly. The company abandoned early efforts by Cixous to write a coherent narrative and instead improvised episodic scenes around the individual stories told by the refugees that they had interviewed, with the sounds of their recorded voices occurring in voiceovers in their various languages and with translations appearing alongside their original languages in surtitles. In her self-critical programme notes for the production, Cixous raised questions about how best to approach the individual and singular accounts of refugees. She indicated (in McEvoy 2006: 219) their effort to produce a novel method of delivery in order to adequately depict those who normally would have no voice in society:

How do we avoid replacing the word from your lips with the sound of good intentions? How do we avoid replacing your foreign language with our French language? How do we keep your foreign language without being impolite or inhospitable to the public, our host in the theatre? . . . How do we avoid appropriating other people's anguish when we use it to make theatre?

In addition to Cixous's comments, the programme notes included many different artefacts relating to the production such as 'poems in various languages (usually with translations), lists (of immigrants interviewed, heavily annotated), newspaper cuttings, critical or theoretical texts, email, graffiti (in original languages and translated), scraps of notepaper, manual typewriter texts, a sketched map of global routes of migration' (McEvoy 2006: 221). McEvoy (2006: 121) indicates that this potpourri demonstrates a self-conscious attempt to show the difficulties that the representation of the other entailed:

Unlike typical programmes, this one drew attention to its own representational processes, to its deficits, gaps, and omissions, its messy inability to organize heterogeneous stories and lives into linear and closed narratives. The texts in the programme . . . also visually and physically embody the difficulties of reading, understanding, interacting with, and representing the migrant other.

Conclusion

Although the Théâtre du Soleil is a tightly organised group that stresses its professionalism as a French theatre company, it exhibits many transnational and nomadic features. Rather than advocating nationalist discourses, it has promoted an outward-looking cosmopolitanism by welcoming people of different ethnicities and cultures from many parts of the world into its activities. Similarly, its events and performances, which have taken it to many countries in Europe, North America and Australasia, have challenged capitalist values, favouring the migratory over the sedentary, the smooth over the striated. Its artists have experimented with new forms and styles of work that have been iconoclastic and transformative in the Deleuzian sense of becoming other.

Le Dernier Caravansérail bears witness to the variety and individuality of refugee lifestyles and circumstances, transforming refugees from quantitative to qualitative multiplicities and emphasising their singularity and their becoming-minor. Jonathan Roffe (2005: 182), in defining Deleuzian terminology, argues that 'we live among actual multiplicities (and are ourselves multiplicities)'. Each refugee comprises a multiplicity, with the complexities of their lives and intersections forming a patchwork rather than a clearly defined pattern or pathway.

Le Dernier Caravansérail represents a variety of individual circumstances and a multiplicity of attempts by refugees to find new homes. It opens up ways of seeing and thinking differently about refugees and nomads, awakening audiences to the possibility of change: for hospitality, for sharing space, for dismantling borders, for inclusiveness, transnationalism and becoming other. By portraying the diversity of humankind in migration, its work has helped to address the limitations of identity politics, ethnocentrism, sexism, religious fundamentalism and nationalism.

Notes

1. Deleuze and Guattari argue in *What Is Philosophy?* (1994: 109), 'Becoming is always double, and it is this double becoming that constitutes the people to come and the new earth.'
2. Deleuze and Guattari's notion of multiplicity varies considerably in different iterations. In one of these in *A Thousand Plateaus* (1987: 36–7), they discuss their concept in relation to the various formulations by Riemann, Meinong and Russell, and Bergson: 'Thus we find in the work of the mathematician and physicist Riemann a distinction between discreet multiplicities and continuous multiplicities ... And in Bergson there is a distinction between numerical or extended multiplicities and qualitative or durational multiplicities. We are doing approximately the same thing [as them] when we distinguish between aborescent multiplicities and rhizomatic multiplicities.'
3. Following World War II and the establishment of the United Nations, the UN published the 'Universal Declaration of Human Rights', which proclaimed, 'Everyone has the right to seek and to enjoy in other countries asylum from persecution' (UN 1948: Article 14). In 1951 the UN passed a new resolution, clarifying in its preamble that 'A refugee, according to the Convention, is someone who is unable or unwilling to return to their country of origin owing to a well-founded fear of being persecuted for reasons of race, religion, nationality, membership of a particular social group, or political opinion' (UNHCR 2010: 3). This UN resolution also clarified certain important rights for refugees. Article 33 prohibited host nations from the *refoulement* of refugees: 'No Contracting State shall expel or return ('refouler') a refugee in any manner whatsoever to the frontiers of territories where his life or freedom would be threatened on account of his race, religion, nationality, membership of a particular social group or political opinion' (UNHCR 2010: 30). Also Article 31 proclaimed that refugees should not be punished for arriving illegally in the host country: 'The Contracting States shall not impose penalties, on account of their illegal entry or presence, on refugees who, coming directly from a territory where their life or freedom was threatened in the sense of article 1, enter or are present in their territory without authorization, provided they present themselves without delay to the authorities and show good cause for their illegal entry or presence' (UNHCR 2010: 29).
4. European governments tend to reserve a special status for unaccompanied minors, who are often given temporary permission to stay until their eighteenth birthday, at which time they have to apply for permission to remain in the host nation.
5. UNHCR, <https://www.unhcr.org/en-us/news/stories/2019/6/5d08b6614/global-for ced-displacement-tops-70-million.html> (last accessed 18 March 2020).
6. This section is developed from an earlier essay, 'Two Approaches to Nomadism: Fluxus and Théâtre du Soleil', in *Performing Statelessness in Europe* (Wilmer 2018).
7. When Hélène Cixous was finishing her doctorate on *L'Exil de James Joyce ou l'Art du remplacement* (*The Exile of James Joyce, or the Art of Displacement*), which Deleuze (2004a: 230) called 'a beautiful book', she also participated in the events of 1968. At this time, according to Eric Prenowitz (2004: vii), 'Cixous's friends and

collaborators included such scholars and artists as Michel Foucault, Gilles Deleuze, Jacques Derrida, Jean Genet and Jacques Lacan, some of whom she recruited to join Paris VIII.' Cixous became a leading critic, fiction writer, poet, playwright, professor and philosopher, helping to found the experimental Université de Paris VIII and creating the first doctoral programme in feminist studies at a European university.

8. Cixous (in Prenowitz 2004: 10), who has characterised herself as 'non belonging', has spoken of a recurring figure of the border-crosser in her theatrical work: 'These are characters who do not belong to any house, who precisely do not belong, who are not identified with houses and who are the messengers the envoys the border-crossers of theatre, of the spirit of the theatre, of the spirit of humanity, from one place to another.'

9. Cixous first encountered Mnouchkine in the context of Michel Foucault's advocacy for prison reform. Cixous (2004: 27) recalls, 'I met Ariane in 1972 in overdetermining and prophetic circumstances. I went to see her and took along my friend Michel Foucault to get her involved in the work of the Group Information Prison which Michel Foucault had founded.' Ariane Mnouchkine decided to stage a short sketch to support Foucault's action, about which Cixous (2004: 27–8) recalls,

> The first 'play' which brought us together lasted four minutes and was supposed to be performed outside prisons. But I never saw it: no sooner had we unloaded the boards than the police were at us with their truncheons. Between 1972 and 1981 we called each other and went to all the political demonstrations in which we put body and soul: I called her towards women, she towards artists and the outcasts and the prisoners of the universe, and we each moved towards the other's side until the day she opened up the doors of her 'Globe' to me. It was a real *coup de théâtre*.

10. Writing of Cixous and Mnouchkine, Kiernander (1993: 125) observes, 'Both have names which sound strange to a French ear.' Moreover, according to Eric Prenowitz (2004: vii), 'Her citizenship was revoked by the anti-Jewish laws of the Vichy regime. Her profound mistrust of nationalism and the concept of nationality can be dated to this decisive experience.'

11. During the Nazi occupation of France, he and his wife hid with Ariane in Bordeaux, while his own parents, who were betrayed by their concierge, were deported and died in a concentration camp. Later he became a famous film director (making films such as *The Man from Rio*), influencing Ariane's theatre sensibilities with his eclectic choice of subjects and aesthetic approaches.

12. According to Andrew Dickson (2012), 'salaries are still more or less equal across the company, and far from generous: €1,400 a month for new arrivals, €1,800 for long-term members, including Mnouchkine herself.'

13. Needless to say, this has caused problems for Cixous, who has to write for all these actors of diverse backgrounds. She comments (2004: 27), 'The Théâtre du Soleil is not only enormous in everything, in art, in ambition, in ethical commitment, but first and foremost in scale and number. There is an economy of the Soleil, a company made up of sixty permanent staff that imposes obligations on the author; I have to give play to my pen for twenty or thirty fervent and famished actors, and therefore ensure the existence of fifty characters.'

14. Similarly, Deleuze (2004a: 253) discussed the nomadic practice in Nietzsche's work of mixing cultural codes: 'For Nietzsche, it is about getting something through in every past, present, and future code, something which does not and will not let itself be recoded.' He added (2004a: 254), 'Nietzsche's enterprise is an attempt at uncoding,

... to get something through which is not encodable, to mix up all the codes.' And (2004a: 260): 'the nomadic adventure begins . . . by escaping the codes.'

15. Their approach to their audiences is perhaps unique among major theatres. According to Andrew Dickson (2012):

> People who buy a ticket to the Théâtre du Soleil don't simply get a show: they are absorbed into a dramatic experience whose every detail, from the *navette* that picks them up from the Métro to the meal they eat beforehand, has been carefully, almost ritualistically planned. Members of the company cook and serve; visitors are invited to peer through windows into dressing rooms to observe the cast putting on their makeup. This is one of the few theatre companies where audiences are required to put in nearly as much mental preparation as the actors; one of the earliest, too, to explore the concept of theatre as immersion, decades before Punchdrunk and other such companies.

16. With regard to the act of writing, Cixous (in McEvoy 2006: 217) noted her need as a playwright to get out of herself, becoming other: 'To write for the theatre, I have to move far from myself, to set out and travel for a long time in darkness until I no longer know where or who I am, which is very difficult, until I feel the space becoming a totally foreign country, until I end up lost in a region I don't recognize.' She also spoke of the 'long and fabulous suspension of the I which is no longer I and not yet You' (Cixous in McEvoy 2006: 218). Likewise, Eric Prenowitz (2004: viii) points out that Cixous uses French in a minoritarian manner: 'She herself has often spoken and written about her intense, complex, "foreign" relationship to the French language. Even in the original, her texts call for a certain intralingual translation, a careful reading capable of interpreting subtle *displacements* of the French language within the French language.'

17. It was not the theatre company's first play on this topic. *L'Âge d'or* (The Golden Age) in 1975 addressed the issue of migrant workers from former French colonies in North Africa. Moreover, after providing sanctuary for 382 Malian refugees in 1996, the company devised *Et Soudain des nuits d'éveil* (And Suddenly Wakeful Nights), based on this event. Premiered in 1997, the play, according to Judith Miller (2007: 12), 'mirrors this experience by confronting the characters of theater-makers with the characters of illegal immigrants who invade the formers' theater, only to eventually return home'.

18. Emine Fisek (2008: 206) describes the Sangatte Refugee Centre as

> founded in August 1999 through the joint efforts of the Red Cross and the French government. Housed in a giant warehouse, the centre functioned as a 'transit camp', providing accommodation for immigrants (mostly Iraqi Kurds, Afghans and Iranians) on their way to Britain. Originally designed to hold 500, by 2001 the centre housed around 1500 refugees. . . . many crossed the channel on foot, in containers and otherwise and arrived, illegally, in Britain. When the British government tightened control of Chunnel territory at its end, Sangatte's identity, composition and future changed. The visibility of the camp mafia (smugglers who allowed refugees entrance into the tunnel in return for several hundred dollars) increased, as did the casualties of this voyage.

19. Citing an anthropological study by Didier Fassin in 2005, Fisek (2008: 206) reports

that when Britain tightened its border controls around the Eurotunnel, violence increased in Sangatte, caused by the existence of a smugglers' mafia, which led to a proliferation of security guards to the extent that it resembled an internment camp. In December 2002, the French government closed the camp, leading to the creation of the 'jungle' in Calais:

> In December [2002], then Minister of the Interior, Nicolas Sarkozy, bolted shut the doors of Sangatte. He argued first that the centre had become a magnet for illegal immigration and second, that the uneasy image of a confinement camp did not befit a modern democratic nation ... While some asylum seekers were able to secure safe voyages as well as entry documents to the UK, many others for whom Sangatte had become home (along with those who continued to arrive) were emptied on to the streets of Calais.

References

Agamben, Giorgio (1995), 'We Refugees', *Symposium*, 49(2): 114–19, trans. Michael Rocke, <http://www.faculty.umb.edu/gary_zabel/Courses/Phil%20108-08/We%20Refugees%20-%20Giorgio%20Agamben%20-%201994.htm> (last accessed 17 March 2020).

Agamben, Giorgio (1998), *Homo Sacer: Sovereign Power and Bare Life*, trans. Daniel Heller-Roazen, Stanford: Stanford University Press.

Arendt, Hannah (1943), 'We Refugees', *The Menorah Journal*, 31(1): 69–77; reprinted in Hannah Arendt (2007), *The Jewish Writings*, New York: Schocken Books.

Braidotti, Rosi (2011), *Nomadic Subjects: Embodiment and Sexual Difference in Contemporary Feminist Theory*, 2nd edn, New York: Columbia University Press.

Cixous, Hélène (2004), 'Enter the Theatre', trans. Brian Mallet, in *Selected Plays of Hélène Cixous*, ed. Eric Prenowitz, London: Routledge, pp. 25–34.

Cixous, Hélène (2010), 'The Laugh of the Medusa', in *The Portable Cixous*, ed. Marta Segarra, New York: Columbia University Press, pp. 27–39.

Deleuze, Gilles (1997), 'The Exhausted', trans. Anthony Uhlmann, in *Essays Critical and Clinical*, Minneapolis: University of Minnesota Press, pp. 152–74.

Deleuze, Gilles (2004a), *Desert Islands and Other Texts, 1953–1974*, ed. David Lapoujade, trans. Michael Taormina, Los Angeles: Semiotext(e).

Deleuze, Gilles (2004b), *Difference and Repetition*, trans. Paul Patton, London: Continuum.

Deleuze, Gilles and Félix Guattari (1987), *A Thousand Plateaus: Capitalism and Schizophrenia*, trans. Brian Massumi, Minneapolis: Minnesota University Press.

Deleuze, Gilles and Félix Guattari (1994), *What Is Philosophy?*, trans. Hugh Tomlinson and Graham Burchell, New York: Columbia University Press.

Dickson, Andrew (2012), 'Ariane Mnouchkine and the Théâtre du Soleil: A Life in Theatre', *The Guardian*, 10 August, <https://www.theguardian.com/culture/2012/aug/10/ariane-mnouchkine-life-in-theatre> (last accessed 17 March 2020).

Finkle, David (2005), 'Le Dernier Caravansérail (Odyssées)', *Theatremania*, 21 July, <http://www.theatermania.com/new-york-city-theater/reviews/07-2005/le-dernier-caravanserail-odyssees_6368.html> (last accessed 17 March 2020).

Fisek, Emine (2008), 'Le Dernier Cartoucherie: Refuge and the Performance of Care', *Research in Drama Education: The Journal of Applied Theatre and Performance*, 13(2): 205–10.

Isherwood, Christopher (2005), 'Never Touching the Ground in a Constant Search for Refuge', *New York Times*, 19 July, <http://www.nytimes.com/2005/07/19/theater/reviews/never-touching-the-ground-in-a-constant-search-for-refuge.html?_r=0> (last accessed 17 March 2020).

Kiernander, Adrian (1993), *Ariane Mnouchkine and the Théâtre du Soleil*, Cambridge: Cambridge University Press.

Kustow, Michael (2003), 'Wondrous Strangers', *The Guardian*, 18 June, <https://www.theguardian.com/stage/2003/jun/18/theatre.artsfeatures> (last accessed 17 March 2020).

Lahr, John (2005), 'The New Nomads: Ariane Mnouchkine Turns Asylum Seekers into Voyagers', *The New Yorker*, 1 August, <http://www.newyorker.com/magazine/2005/08/01/the-new-nomads> (last accessed 17 March 2020).

McCarter, Jeremy (2005), 'Lost', *New York Magazine*, 20 July, <http://nymag.com/nymetro/arts/theater/reviews/12292/> (last accessed 17 March 2020).

McEvoy, William (2006), 'Finding the Balance: Writing and Performing Ethics in Théâtre du Soleil's *Le Dernier Caravansérail* (2003)', *New Theatre Quarterly*, 22(3): 211–26.

Miller, Judith G. (2007), *Ariane Mnouchkine*, London: Routledge.

Patton, Paul (2012), 'Deleuze's Political Philosophy', in Daniel W. Smith and Henry Somers-Hall (eds), *The Cambridge Companion to Deleuze*, Cambridge: Cambridge University Press, pp. 198–219.

Prenowitz, Eric (ed.) (2004), *Selected Plays of Hélène Cixous*, London: Routledge.

Roffe, Jonathan (2005), 'Multiplicity', in Adrian Parr (ed.), *The Deleuze Dictionary*, New York: Columbia University Press, pp. 181–2.

Singleton, Brian (2007), 'Performing Conflict Migration and Testimony', in Karen Fricker and Ronit Lentin (eds), *Performing Global Networks*, Newcastle: Cambridge Scholars, pp. 25–37.

Stevens, Lara (2016), *Anti-War Theatre after Brecht: Dialectical Aesthetics in the Twenty-First Century*, London: Palgrave Macmillan.

TdS (2006), *Le Dernier Caravansérail (Odyssées)*, film, directed by Ariane Mnouchkine, Paris: Bel Air Classiques, ARTE France Développement, CNDP.

UN (1948), 'Universal Declaration of Human Rights', <http://www.un.org/en/universal-declaration-human-rights/> (last accessed 17 March 2020).

UNHCR (2010), *Convention and Protocol Relating to the Status of Refugees*, <http://www.unhcr.org/protect/PROTECTION/3b66c2aa10.pdf> (last accessed 17 March 2020).

Wilmer, S. E. (2018), *Performing Statelessness in Europe*, London: Palgrave Macmillan.

Young, Eugene B. with Gary Genosko and Janell Watson (2013), *The Deleuze and Guattari Dictionary*, London: Bloomsbury.

10

Guattari's Ecosophy and Multiple Becomings in Ritual

Barbara Glowczewski

A few weeks before his death on 29 August 1992, in his last text advocating a new foundation for social practices, Guattari (1996: 271) affirms the necessity of 'ecosophical cartographies' that could produce 'an assumption of responsibility for future generations', an aesthetic paradigm that is also ethical. As he had explained during a filmed conference in a Los Angeles art school, this aesthetic paradigm is not an aestheticisation of the social and the political but the invitation to pay attention 'to a production of the self that can only be conceived as an open and indeterminate process, in the manner of a performance'.[1] Such an approach does not oppose nature to culture. On the contrary, the Guattarian ecology of the environment includes both nature and all its technological transformations as bound up with social ecology and mental ecology. Guattari's ecosophical project is different from the concept of 'ecosophy' forged in Oslo in 1960 by Arne Naess (1993), who defined man as a part of the ecosphere but promoted a form of transcendental vision of the relation between man and nature, a 'deep ecology' as wilderness. Guattari defines ecosophy as a praxis of immanence in order to change through art, politics, (psycho)analysis and new uses of technology the way we relate to all the living, in a manner transversal in relation to the earth, and more specifically in micropolitical reterritorialisations. Such a vision has taken on renewed relevance with current experiences of communal usage of land and urban buildings, or projects of common land restoration inspired by historical commons.[2] The transversality of social, artistic and ecological practices called for by Guattari also confronts the debates involving the recent notion of the 'Anthropocene', which points to a double arrogance:

Arrogance of the history of modernity because, by extending his idea of nature to all that was foreign to him, the *homo occidentalis* of Enlightenment rejected in an exploitable environment animals, plants and soils, as well as all of the other human existences . . . Arrogance of the word Anthropocene, which in the Anthropos forgets all existences that so far have not or very little participated in the forcing of the climate . . . 'It's Not the Anthropocene, It's the White Supremacy Scene; or, The Geological Color Line' is the title of Nicholas Mirzoeff's paper,[3] who reminds us that it is a Western minority enriched by colonisation that is responsible for the state of the current world, even if the 'Capitalocene' seduces today other regions of the world where transnational companies accelerate the destruction of the earth and all that lives. (Glowczewski and Laurens 2018: 141–2; my translation)[4]

Despite many critical redefinitions of the term 'Anthropocene' in order to politicise the sciences (Saldanha and Stark 2016), the common understanding of this proposed new geological era often ignores the fact that past and present economic processes responsible for impacting the whole globe are the result of a colonial system that continues to reject other human choices – those advocating old or new alliances with the non-humans. Anthropocentrism does not fit with the necessity to respond to the environmental and climate change alert by learning again how to desubjectify humans so as to apprehend our existential territories as creative and restorative assemblages of human and non-human agents, a multiplicity advocated by Guattari and Deleuze, together and in their respective works, which was advocating thinking through the *milieu*. As the French theoretician Frédéric Neyrat (2014) pointed out in an interview:

> From its beginnings, environmental thought has contested human exceptionalism, this dangerous transcendence that enabled Descartes to argue that we can become 'masters and possessors of nature'. And thanks to the concept of immanence – say, from Spinoza to Deleuze – it was possible to contest the fictions of transcendence. . . . thanks to the concept of the Anthropocene, contemporary theory should be compelled, first, to recognize the ongoing extent of human colonization and, second, to understand that to contest human exceptionalism does not *only* mean to criticize anthropocentrism or to propose a flat (*plate*) ontology where humans and non-humans are put on the same footing. Contrasting to this flatness (*platitude*), I argue that to contest exceptionalism is to give rise to powerful differences, to generate outsides, and to assign a status of exception to every existential arising.

We will see here how Guattari's ecosophical cartography combines four domains (*actual* versus *virtual, real* versus *possible*) into four dynamic polarities (existential territories, flows, incorporeal universes of value or refrains, and machinic phyla; see Fig. 10.1). Such cartography helps us think powerful differences which emerge from Indigenous resistance to colonisation as well as other struggles against both the colonial past and the present forms of activity that destroy the planet. I will show how the processes of actualisation and virtualisation are at the heart of Australian ritual totemism, which was the base for Indigenous Australians to claim back the land that had been taken from them through British colonisation. Guattari was drawing on my research among the Warlpiri of Central Australia when he defined the relation between existential territories and incorporeal universes of value as the 'asignifying' key to understand the possibility of emergence of collective assemblages of enunciation which through desire can transform the real. I have called Indigenous Australian assemblages that entangle

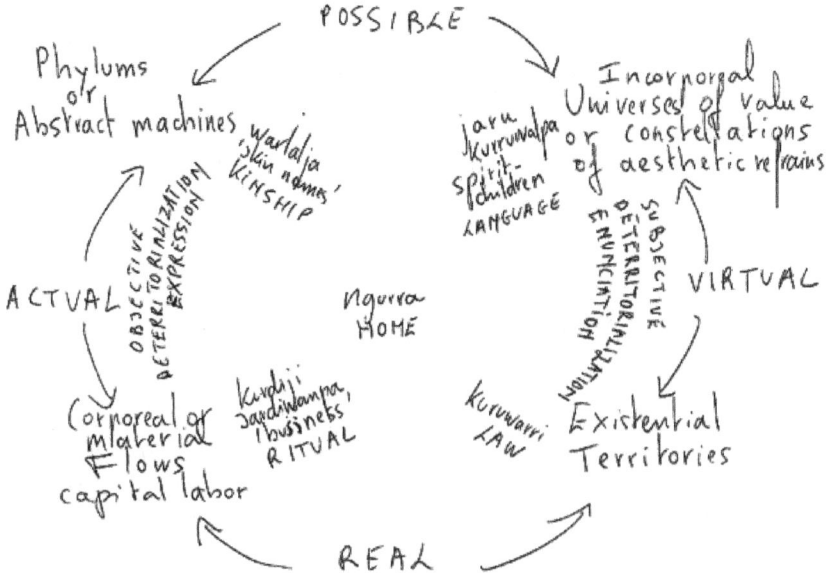

Figure 10.1 Mapping Guattari's ecosophical chaosmosis and Warlpiri
Dreaming (*Jukurrpa*) concepts.
Courtesy of Barbara Glowczewski and n-1 edições.

them materially and spiritually with non-human 'totemic becomings' in order
to highlight this process of de-essentialisation. The non-human entails not only
animals and plants but also specific rivers, rocks and stars. There are many other
political forms of differentiation experienced by different collectives around the
world seeking to find alternatives to extractivist globalisation and monotheist religions. The politics of Aboriginal art and its use of magic, Afro-Brazilian rituals
of incorporation, as well as the problem of reparation, recognition and affirmation
will all be discussed in the second half of the chapter.

Actualisation and Virtualisation of Australian Totemic Becomings

> It was a grave error on the part of the structuralist school to try to put everything
> connected with the psyche under the control of the linguistic signifier! . . . In
> archaic societies, it is through rhythms, chants, dances, masks, marks on the
> body, ground and totems, on ritual occasions and with mythical references, that
> other kinds of collective existential Territories are circumscribed. (Guattari
> 1995: 5, 15)[5]

Guattari was especially sensitive to the way the Warlpiri and other desert
people in Central Australia produce and reassemble – through dreams or ritual

interpretations – networks of totemic stories embodied in the landscape as the traces of nomadic mythical ancestors: Kangaroo, Plum or Rain People who turned part of their bodies into sacred rocks, waterholes or trees. All named things have their mythical ancestral traveller(s) who are called *Jukurrpa*, Dreamings, and continue to live and dream in the *Jukurrpa* Dreaming space-time. Men and women can see or hear them during their sleep and receive sometimes new designs to paint on the body or sacred boards, new songs and dances for specific places and the rituals that celebrate the particular Dreaming that groups and individuals identify with.

The dream-inspired production of relations with the land was for Guattari (2012) an ideal example of Existential Territories (*virtual and real*) which are constantly re-enacted in an asignifying cartography where images are self-referential and immanent to a collective. He called this Indigenous form of transindividual subjectivation an example of 'Universes of value' or 'incorporeal constellations of aesthetic refrains' (*virtual and possible*).[6] Such constellations are indeed expressed in the traditional cosmovision of Aboriginal people (in the desert, but also on the coasts) through totemic rituals: songs, designs or dances related to Dreaming geographical networks. It is such networks of totemic and oneiric mythscapes that Aboriginal people from the desert started to transpose to acrylics on canvas for the art market in the 1970s. The success was such that it changed the Aboriginal paradigm from 'primitive' art to contemporary art, demonstrating the minoritarian impact of their creations on the major art market.

Aboriginal existential territories (*virtual and real*) are constantly deterritorialised and reterritorialised in a subjective manner with multiple layers of value or constellations of aesthetic refrains (*virtual and possible*) which involve here not only new ritual totemic songs, designs and dances, but also the redefinition of Dreamings through art and negotiations for rights and protection of land or mining, Christianity and digital images adopted since the 1990s. For Guattari (1995, 2012), the two functors of virtualisation (existential territories and constellations of refrains) have different relations, folds and unfolds, with two functors of actualisation: Flows or Fluxes (*actual and real*), which include money, water, petrol and other energies from the land as well as body fluids like blood, and Machinic Phyla (*actual and possible*). According to Manuel DeLanda (1997: 51), 'The concept of the "machinic phylum" was created in an effort to conceive the genesis of form (in geological, biological and cultural structures) as related exclusively to immanent capabilities of the flows of matter-energy-information and not to any transcendent factor, whether platonic or divine.' Elsewhere DeLanda comments on the following quote from *A Thousand Plateaus* (Deleuze and Guattari 1997: 329) – 'The machinic phylum is metallurgical, or at least has a metallic head, as its itinerant probe-head or guidance device' – by extending the notion of the metallic in such a way that, despite the lack of metal use by Indigenous Australians, it could resonate with their perceptions of the earth and the multiplication of life forms:

We can imagine our planet, before living creatures appeared on its surface, as populated by metallic particles which catalyzed reactions as they flowed through the Earth, in a sense allowing the planet to 'explore' a space of possible chemical combinations, that is, allowing the planet to blindly grope its way around this space, eventually stumbling upon proto-living creatures, which as many scientists now agree, were probably autocatalytic loops of materials, that is, proto-metabolisms. (DeLanda 1998: 43)

For Guattari, machinic phyla can include mathematics and computer systems, but also other generative principles, natural or artificial; for me this includes kinship systems in Australia that operate in a classificatory way, mixing humans with totemic Dreamings and mineral places on earth and in the galactic space, a system of social organisation intertwined with a cosmopolitics that explains a resistance to hierarchical models such as chiefdoms or states (see Glowczewski 2020). As Guattari understands it, the objective deterritorialisation between flows and machinic phyla stimulates a movement of virtualisation whose thresholds of intensity are the condition for the emergence of multiple becomings through existential territories and universes of value (as aesthetic constellations). In the Australian case the tension between flows (traditional trade routes but also the importance of totemic body fluids as markers of land as well as healing tools) and phyla (kinship distribution of social roles, duties and obligations towards the land and others, as well as catalysts of healing) demonstrates a particular affirmation of a reticular way of organising society which clashes with the colonial and postcolonial imposition of new flows (money, roads, etc.) and phyla (mining, genealogical data to reclaim land, and so on).

For Brian Massumi (2002a: 43), 'It is the edge of the virtual, where it leaks into actual, that counts. For that seeping edge is where potential, actually, is found.' For me, it is the other side of that threshold, where and when the actualised leaks back to the virtual, that counts in order for us to understand the mystery of multiple becomings stimulated through rituals of Australian totemic Dreamings. It is also the case in Afro-Brazilian cults of incorporation by Orixás and dead spirits, which I am going to discuss later on in the chapter. The crossing of the threshold *from the actual back to the virtual* is what Deleuze (2010: 122) calls 'crystallisation', while acknowledging Guattari for being right to define in his *Machinic Unconscious* the 'crystal of time' (or the 'crystal of the unconscious') as a *ritournelle* ('refrain') *par excellence*. As Guattari (2007: 116) explains,

What counts in these 'crystallizations' of behaviors seems to be less the intrinsic nature of each one of their components – hormonal, perceptive, ecological, social . . . – than the spatial and rhythmic devices that they generate and from which diagrammatic strategies and tactics of stratification make it possible to create 'interchanges' launching semiotic bridges between parallel universes which seemed to never have to communicate together.

Translated as 'refrain', the French *ritournelle*, like the Italian *ritornelo* in music, refers to a sort of tune that tends to wrap up inward, digging into affective memory. The refrain for Deleuze and Guattari does not necessarily refer to music or the sound of birds but also to colours and gestures. In that sense human rituals, like those of all other animals, are mainly territorialised through aesthetic expression. As Deleuze and Guattari (1997: 322–3) framed it in *A Thousand Plateaus*:

> The territory arises in a free margin of the code, one that is not indeterminate but rather is determined differently. Each milieu has its own code, and there is perpetual transcoding between milieus; the territory, on the other hand, seems to form at the level of a certain *decoding*. . . . we call a refrain any aggregate of matters of expression that draws a territory and develops into territorial motifs and landscapes (there are optical, gestural, motor, etc., refrains).

Warlpiri men and women from the Central Australian desert inherit songlines and storylines in the landscape that you can only see if you read geographical, topographical and geological traces as imprints of ancestral events whose tracks were left in the land to be read. It was a time when animals did not look like the animals or plants of today, nor did the humans, who call themselves Kangaroo or Yam. Emu Dreaming, for instance, was a giant bird whose traces – engraved as arrows in rocks uncovered by big tides of the Indian Ocean – are identified today with dinosaurs. Emu, Kangaroo or Yam Dreamings were totemic becomings, individual or collective morphing agents *who*, after walking, dancing, singing and painting, turned into places on the earth but also in the sky. Emu's footprints can be seen in rocks on the north-west seashore and his whole body in the black outline inside the Milky Way (Fuller et al. 2014). All the agents of those events as well as their stories and songlines are called *kuruwarri*, the Warlpiri word for any image. In relation to the Dreamings, *kuruwarri* are life-forces or, as I prefer to say, force-images – that is, images of concepts epitomised by words like 'kangaroo', 'wind', 'sky', 'two women', 'two men' or 'invincible'. As force-images, those mythical agents were sowing particles as they were travelling in an infinity of lines of flight that the Warlpiri call *Jukurrpa*, Dreamings. All words are thus concepts in motion – unfolded in various mythical stories – that left imprints, Force-images, in the land when the corresponding Dreamings were travelling on the earth.

All Dreamings are said to be alive in their respective places and reactualise themselves generation after generation as animals, plants or other things they bear the name of. Men or women who are born or initiated with one or the other of the totemic becomings are said to be 'brothers and sisters' of the relevant animal, plant or phenomena like rain, or fire. They have the duty of singing, painting and dancing the rituals that aim at looking after the relevant places. If Kangaroo is your brother and the brother of Mulga seeds, then these seeds are also your brothers and sisters, but other animals and plants or phenomena, like water or wind, become your mothers, fathers or potential spouses or in-laws. Basically, all Warlpiri Dreamings are dispatched into eight sets of 'skin' brothers and sisters bearing the same *skin-name*.[7] These eight *skin-names* define many different relations of classificatory filiation and alliance that together define what mathematicians call a dihedral group, the properties of a cube. This figure is an artefact that

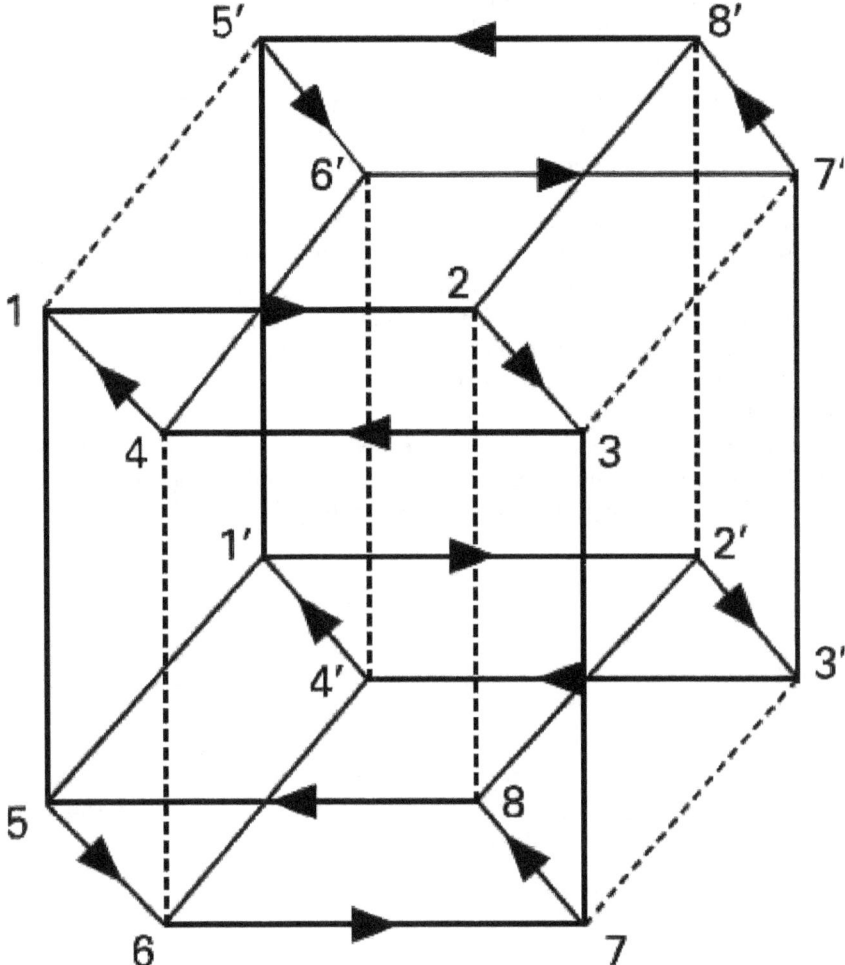

Figure 10.2 Hypercube with eight skin-names split in two.
Courtesy of Barbara Glowczewski and n-1 edições.

in the Warlpiri case seems to organise relations between all the named elements of the whole cosmos but can be complexified, into a topological hypercube, a figure of the fourth dimension, where we shift from reciprocal exchange to generalised asymmetric exchange (requiring chains of at least four local groups, instead of two) extended to non-human agents in a way where Euclidean oppositions between the inside and the outside, as well as the basic perspective, do not apply any more (Fig. 10.2).

It is interesting to note that when computer engineers generalised the hyper-cubic model for the internet, Polish art historian and critic Mieczysław Porębski (1921–2012), in his 1978 article 'Styl epoki' [Style of an Epoch], reprinted in the volume *Sztuka a informacja*, which can be translated as 'art versus information', used a hypercube to provide a model for transformations of artistic styles based on a first cubic combination of four factors: 'history' [*historia*] (H), 'myth' [*mit*] (M), 'metaphor' [*metafora*] (F) and 'metonymy' [*metonimia*] (N); producing 'mannerism' [*manieryzm*] (HFN), 'eclectism' [*eklektyzm*] (HNN), 'idealism' [*idealizm*] (HFF), 'realism' [*realism*] (HNF), 'syntheticism' [*syntetyzm*] (MNN), 'constructivism' [*konstruktywizm*] (MFN), 'naturalism' [*naturalizm*] (MNF) and 'expressionism' [*ekspresjonizm*] (MFF) (Porębski 1986, Figs 10.3 to 10.5).[8] As art historian Wojciech Bałus (2012: 445) explains, 'Beginning with his article "Art and Information" (1962), Porębski developed an approach on the basis of French structuralism, cultural anthropology and information theory. . . . [he] tried to formulate a general theory of art and a conception of its development.' I would add that his work was first and foremost topological and, in that sense, less structuralist than it might initially look.

I have shown that hypercubic properties were embodied in the way Warlpiri people interchanged ritual roles of custody (*kirda*) and management (*kurdungurlu*) when celebrating Dreamings whose custody is dispatched between the

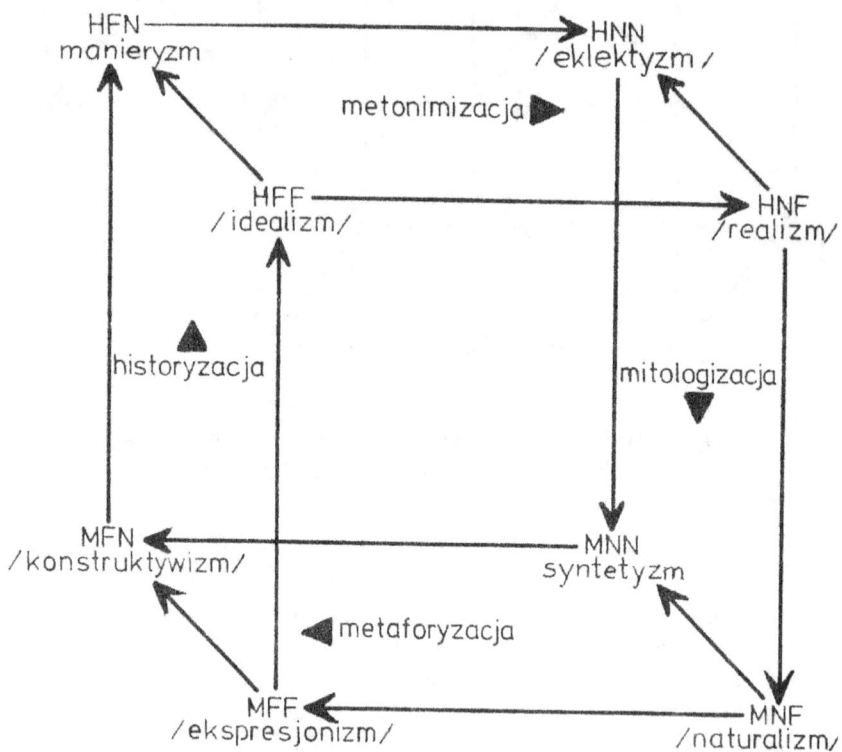

Figure 10.3 Hypercubic designs by Polish art historian Porębski.
Courtesy of the estate of Mieczysław Porębski.

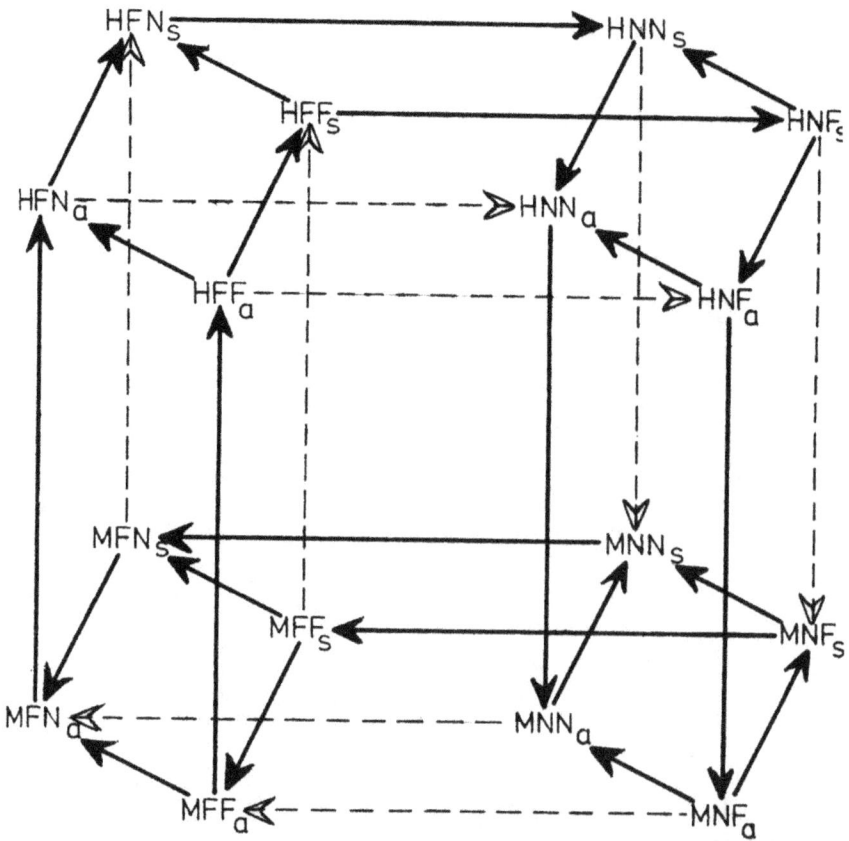

Figure 10.4 Hypercubic designs by Polish art historian Porębski.
Courtesy of the estate of Mieczysław Porębski.

skin-names according to a classificatory kinship of the cosmic and totemic elements connected with places and songlines that connect them. Their Warlpiri *cosmokin* topological network is like a diagram, a *machinic phylum*, a role game for all the living, allowing the constant dreamlike work of a dynamic rhizome of totemic becomings. For the desert Aboriginal people the rhizome is *not* a metaphor; while yams spread underground as rhizomes of roots, the Yam Dreaming is an embodied concept that connects with other Dreamings in a rhizomatic way (Glowczewski 2011, 2020). As Deleuze and Guattari (1997: 11) put it,

The wisdom of the plants: even when they have roots, there is always an outside where they form a rhizome with something else – with the wind, an animal, human beings (and there is also an aspect under which animals themselves form rhizomes, as do people, etc.)

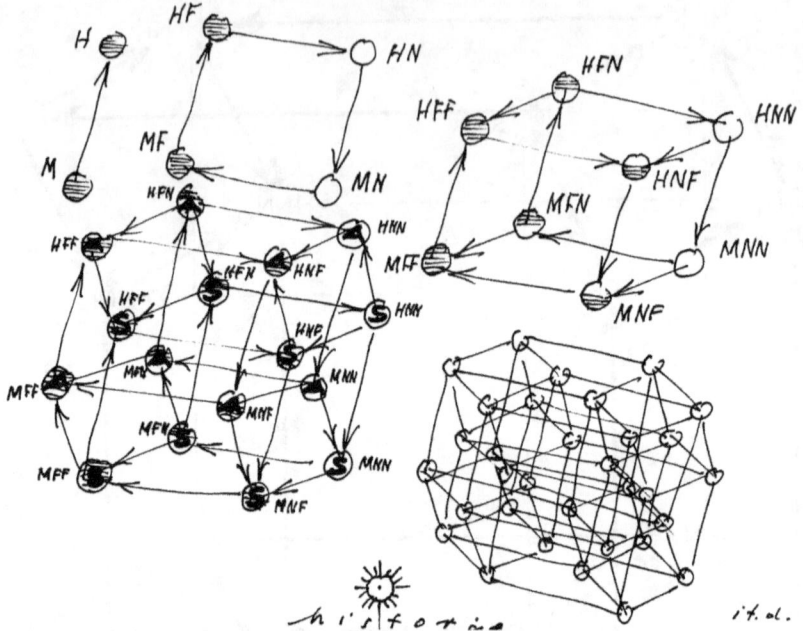

Figure 10.5 Hypercubic designs by Polish art historian Porębski.
Courtesy of the estate of Mieczysław Porębski

For Warlpiri Lawmen and Lawwomen, rituals involve transformations between *kanunju* ('inside', 'underneath') and *kankarlu* ('outside', 'on top'), the two cosmological realms that I translated in the 1980s as *virtual* (for 'underneath'/ 'secret') and *actual* (for 'on top'/'public'). The *virtual* does not only designate 'underground' but also the faraway, distant cosmos beyond the Milky Way, as well as the virtual space where one travels in dreams. In every ceremony, for the most part held on ritual grounds restricted to men or to women, each gender performs the ritual by *actualising* and *revirtualising* the force-images (*kuruwarri*) that are 'underneath', that is, virtual with regard to the cosmos, in a different way. These force-images, or virtual becomings, were once sown by the totemic ancestors as particles that looked like bird down or wild cotton, and actualise themselves in each generation in people and other things that their names designate. Force-images also actualise themselves in all places connected to their stories through imprints or externalisation and metamorphosis of some flows like blood into red ochre, tears or urine into a spring, as well as dismantled organs or body parts turned into various rocks or trees. The Dreaming heroes are said to still dream there the life on earth and their traces have become living waters or stones.

The mapping of the connections between all the *kuruwarri*, force-images (as totemic songlines and stories) of anything that is named in Warlpiri culture and nature, needs to be regularly dreamt. Men and women dream the place of actualisation of the image/song/name of the babies to be born, and some also dream new ritual songs, dances and images to paint on the body or sacred boards. Traces of dreams are indices, prints and proofs of real actions before their interpretations. As Deleuze (1991: 218) points out in the glossary at the end of *Cinema 1: The Movement-Image*, 'ACTION-IMAGE (the force or act)' declines in four different ways. One of these is

> *Index*: used by Peirce in order to designate a sign which refers to its object by a material link. Used here in order to designate the link of an action (or of an effect of action) to a situation which is not given, but merely inferred, or which remains equivocal and reversible. We distinguish in this sense *indices of lack* and *indices of equivocity*: the two senses of the French word *ellipse* (ellipse and ellipsis).

Deleuze (1991: 217–18) translates Peirce's other two concepts as follows: he proposes the notion of 'MENTAL IMAGE' (designating '*abstract relations*') for the notion of '*Symbol*', 'used by Peirce to designate a sign which refers to its object by virtue of a law', and 'AFFECTION-IMAGE (quality or power)' for Peirce's '*Icon*', that is, 'a sign which refers to its object by internal characters'. Painting on canvas for sale is a new *iconic* way to actualise the content of myths and previous rituals through the reinterpretation of traces (indices as action-images) in the space-time of the Dreaming that is experienced both in the geography and in sleep. Paintings on canvas also virtualise the possible by providing new patterns/ designs (*motifs*) of connections between totemic heroes and the stories which are anchored in places. The proliferation of colours made possible by the acrylics and many new styles are also traces of past in becoming. Because acrylic paintings are said to be 'inhabited' by force-images (*kuruwarri*), they become taboo at the death of the artist.

All Warlpiri rituals unfold force-images to spread them between all participants, with some people being painted upon and dancing, while others are assigned the role of painting them and doing the choreography; it depends on the 'Dreaming' that is enacted in the ritual. But at the end of the ritual, Warlpiri say that all these force-images that were spread 'on top' need to be sent back 'underneath' (they must be virtualised). Sending back to the virtual is expressed through ritual gestures, for instance the pulsation of hands over the painted sacred boards which the women put on the ground at the end of a ritual and the erasing of the remaining design before each new ritual. Each Image-force painted on their breasts is also virtualised: time erases the ochre, or rather, as Warlpiri women say, the ochre enters the body to nourish it. As I see it, Aboriginal ochre images become crystals of time in the sense explained in *Cinema 2: The Time-Image* (Deleuze 2010: 82–3):

> In Resnais' film [*Je t'aime je t'aime*] the opaque hyper-sphere is one of the most beautiful crystal-images, while what we see in the crystal is time itself, the gushing forth of time. Subjectivity is never ours, it is time, that is the soul or the spirit, the virtual. The actual is always objective, but the virtual is

subjective: it was initially the affect, that which we experience in time; then time itself, pure virtuality which divides in two as affector and affected, 'the affection of self by self' as definition of time.

Force-images, Death and Payback

For the opening of a major art exhibition held in Darwin in 2011 called *Yulyurlu*, from the Warlpiri name of the deceased artist Lorna Napurrurla Fencer, whose paintings were bought by museums and art collectors all around the world, a group of Warlpiri women were invited. With painted chests, they first walked in a line carrying special leaves to brush all the paintings in order to clean them from the imprints of the artist's spirit; they were thus performing a ritual to send back to the virtual the force-images (*kuruwarri*) of the painted Yam, to 'virtualise' them for a new becoming. Such is their role at any death: women have to brush all places and things that were used by the deceased person, which include the art centre, collective buildings and private houses, ritual camps, mattresses, and so on. During the exhibition opening, after the women had performed the first stage of a ritual dance of the Yam Dreaming in front of a big canvas, a Warlpiri teacher who became a cultural activist, Wanta Steve Patrick Jampijinpa, quickly put his hand on the painting to capture the forces so they would nurture him. In other terms, Wanta 'reactualised' the force-images for himself. The touching point between his hand and the canvas was exactly the threshold where the virtual leaks to the actual, from the force-images released by the designs to his body and spirit. He acted as in a death ritual where men are invited to the women's ceremonial ground – normally restricted to women – in order to touch a sacred pole that is imbued with the force-images of the Dreaming heroes and heroines that the women painted on it, and danced with before erecting it in the ground. A line of men is invited to come to touch the painted top of the pole so as to share the painted Dreaming force-images through them. The action of this male touch of a painting has the reverse effect to the women's brushing.

The man's actualisation (*kankarlu*) of the force-images of the canvas maintains the power in the canvas so that it remains inalienable (even if the painting is sold, the power of the artist's Yam force-images will stay active for the relevant Warlpiri people). On the contrary, when women use their leaves to brush the canvas they are redirecting the force-images back to the virtual (*kanunju*) in order to empty the designs – here of the Yam Dreaming – of the living imprint of the artist who painted it; this 'cleansing' of dead people's traces is the condition for sending them back underneath to the virtual to allow for the force-images to be 'virtualised' so that the dead person's spirit finds its way in the virtual and does not haunt the living. It is a way to care for the dead spirit, the mourners in pain, and all the living, including the land which might also be affected. Interestingly, from the point of view of a curator, both gestures of contact with the painting would appear as a lack of care, with a risk of spoiling the 'value' of the art. From the Warlpiri point of view, the value is not fixed in an object but constantly refabricated. This is why paintings are ephemeral (erased from the body, the sacred boards or the ground) even if virtually present in the memory of the Dreaming to be re-enacted for each ritual. It is the condition for the power of re-emergence of force-images to be ritually 'revirtualised', that is, erased from vision.

This is precisely the reason why when twelve Warlpiri men from Lajamanu came to Paris in 1983 to execute a ten-metre-long ground painting on sand at the Museum of Modern Art, they wanted to erase it before their departure back to Australia in their own ritual way – that is, by dancing on it. They finally accepted not to do so on the condition that the painting would be destroyed at the end of the exhibition in a specific way. It has to be noted that during their stay in Paris the Warlpiri men danced at the theatre of Peter Brook a ceremony dreamt by a woman, Janjiya Nakamarra, for the same sacred place, Jurntu, that was mapped on their sand painting.[9] The performance in the Théâtre des Bouffes du Nord was thus part of the art installation at the Museum.

As Deleuze (1997: 62–3) explains in *Essays Critical and Clinical*:

The libido does not undergo metamorphoses, but follows world historical trajectories. From this point of view, it does not seem that the real and the imaginary form a pertinent distinction. A real voyage, by itself, lacks the force necessary to be reflected in the imagination; the imaginary voyage, by itself, does not have the force, as Proust says, to be verified in the real. This is why the imaginary and the real must be, rather, like two juxtaposable or superimposable parts of a single trajectory, two faces that ceaselessly interchange with one another, a mobile mirror. Thus the Australian Aborigines link nomadic itineraries to dream voyages, which together compose 'an interstitching of routes,' 'in an immense cut-out of space and time that must be read like a map.'[10] At the limit, the imaginary is a virtual image that is interfused with the real object, and vice versa, thereby constituting a crystal of the unconscious. It is not enough for the real object or the real landscape to evoke similar or related images; it must disengage its *own* virtual image at the same time that the latter, as an imaginary landscape, makes its entry into the real, following a circuit where each of the two terms pursues the other, is interchanged with the other. 'Vision' is the product of this doubling or splitting in two . . . , this coalescence. It is in such crystals of the unconscious that the trajectories of the libido are made visible.

And the chapter ends: '*Trajectories* and *becomings*: art makes each of them present in the other, it renders their mutual presence perceptible' (ibid. 67). This 'process of interchange of images' corresponds to what Deleuze calls 'disjunctive synthesis' at work in the crystal image, a way to understand shamanism as proposed by Viveiros de Castro (2007) for the Yanomami of Brazil. In Australia, shamans of some regions are supposed to change their skin by turning inside out like a glove; this magical reversal 'actualises' and 'realises' a virtual ('inside', *kanunju* in Warlpiri) by creating a new actual ('on top', *kankarlu*) of the surface. But this actualisation must allow a revirtualisation, the emergence of a new power of action: the possibility of healing for the shaman. Interestingly, this power of healing is crystallised in quartz. These 'strong' stones which shine like crystals are said to be harboured by Warlpiri and other desert shamans inside their bodies to help some cures by 'crystallising' the disease out of their patients and being then spit out by the healer – again a topological inside out.[11]

In 1988, a Warlpiri artist from Papunya, Michael Nelson Jakamarra, was commissioned to provide a painting for a vast memorial ground mosaic located in front of the new parliament building in Canberra erected in celebration of the Australian bicentenary. Some media called the mosaic a 'curse' after an Aboriginal writer and activist, Kevin Gilbert, talked about cursing the federal building. In a later interview, the activist writer denied the painting was a 'curse' but talked about a spiritual creative energy that transformed the mosaic into a 'stone of judgement', the expression of law and *payback*, after a ritual was performed on the mosaic by a group of women from Papunya. The Warlpiri artist said that his mosaic was a gift, a blessing for all, a promise of a 'gathering place'. But four years later he came back to Canberra and gave the following speech:

> White people. You don't seem to understand. They look at my work, all they see is a pretty painting. You, the white people, took this country from us ... White people must understand. ... The Government of Australia has not recognised our people and our culture, it is abusing my painting and insulting my people. I want to take my painting back to my people. (*The Australian*, 28 September 1993, p. 3, qtd in Smith 2001)

The artist, Michael Nelson Jakamarra, then bent to touch the centre of the painting with a hammer and a chisel, but he did not physically take a piece of the mosaic as expected, but simply said he was taking it back. This event, which enflamed the media, is analysed by Brian Massumi (2002b) in an article published in French as an example of Deleuze's notion of stuttering deployed in *Essays Critical and Clinical* and usefully explained in a dialogue between François Roche and Natanel Elfassy (2010):

> Stuttering is conflictual, it appears as a disruption of continuity between emotion and language – where they simultaneously corrupt each other, creating a synaesthetic rapprochement where the degree or level of confusion reveals the impossible negotiation between something that tries to articulate knowledge in the public sphere and the protest of the body against being reduced to its simple appearance. It could appear as a field of battle, where the forces present produce noise and chaos, beauty and barbarism, Eros and Thanatos, impulses of life and death. But more to the point, it is the contradictory aesthetic generated from this field of battle that matters.

I would like to add here that the way desert Aboriginal people use the word *payback* is also an example of crystallisation: a compensation crystallising a virtual debt. The literal Aboriginal English expression *paying back* is used for a counter-gift which acts as a blessing in renewing an alliance or forging a new one, but it's also used for the punishment of a transgression that takes the form of a payment, like a fine, or a distant spell or a revenge expedition to make the culprit fall sick, sometimes to death. Therefore, *taking back* the painting was a form of *payback* as an exercise of the Warlpiri Law, a form of justice which can be viewed as a diplomatic response to what Nelson and other Aboriginal people might have experienced as a break of an alliance by the government who did not respect its promise. This promise was expressed by the Prime Minister upon receiving, during the celebrations of the bicentenary in Barunga in 1988, another painting. The painting was rendered by Warlpiri and Yolngu artists on a small bark with a typed statement pasted in the middle, asking for four things: a Treaty; an autonomous political body to represent Indigenous Australians; social justice, especially in relation to deaths in custody; and the recognition of the UN Declaration on the Rights of Indigenous Peoples.[12] As these issues were not addressed properly, the gesture of *taking back* the mosaic crystallised its potential to become again a stage for negotiation, to call for a future action from the government. Even today some Aboriginal people still take turns squatting in a camp composed of huts, a tent, Aboriginal flags and a fire burning day and night. They do so to reactivate continuously the first fire lit when activists came to Canberra in 1972 to sit under a beach umbrella they called the 'Aboriginal Embassy', with a flag designed to stand for an Aboriginal nation that brings together over 200 languages (Foley et al. 2013). Since then, the activists have been constantly reactualising the fact that they are being treated as foreigners in their own country, as what I called 'refugees from the inside'.[13] Maintaining the fire in front of the Parliament crystallises the affirmation of a virtual sovereignty: Australia as their original home before colonisation by the British. Such Indigenous performances are deeply ecosophical in Guattari's sense: at the same time political, artistic, social, ecological and mental. As Zourabichvili (2012: 157) points out, the concept of the crystal,

> one of Deleuze's last, presents the difficulty of condensing just about all of his philosophy. The crystal is the ultimate state of the problematic of 'real' experience, and is presented as a deepening of the concept of becoming. First, it confirms that in any becoming (becoming-animal, becoming-woman, etc.) it is not the terminus that is sought-after (the animal or the woman that one becomes) but the becoming itself, which is to say the conditions for the continuation[14] of desiring production or experimentation.

This is exactly what could be said about totemic rituals but an experiment in becoming and desiring also implies the valued production of heterogeneity among the different people of any collective assemblage. In other terms, as I have shown with reference to desert Aboriginal rituals, becoming-men for women, or becoming-women for men, is not the same according to the totem or Dreaming involved: for a man or a woman becoming-bird-woman is different from becoming-wallaby-people, becoming-digging-stick-woman or becoming-whirlwind-two-men. These multiple becomings necessitate constant reterritorialisation in various forms of performed stories and embodied force-images, bodies being human or not.[15]

Incorporations, Affirmation and Compensation

Actualising a ritual heterogeneity in order to make virtual becomings possible can be observed also in Afro-Brazilian rituals, although the way to achieve it is different from Aboriginal Australian rituals (Glowczewski 2020). In 2013, I was invited to stay in Brazil for six months to give a series of lectures and conferences. Based in Florianopolis, I filmed every week for five months an Afro-Brazilian Umbanda cult (Tenda Spirita Vo Cirina) whose followers say that they incorporate African entities called Orixás and spirits of the dead organised in 'families' such as Beijada Children, Caboclo Indians, Preto Velho (old black slaves) and Exus, that is, outlaws, street people, including prostitutes dressed like gypsies.[16] In their *Assemblages* film installation developed, in homage to Guattari, for the touring *Animism* exhibition (2010–12), Maurizio Lazzarato and Angela Melitopoulos (2012: 51) wrote that Afro-Brazilian rituals express 'trans-individual polysemic animist subjectivity' which does not constitute a 'vestige' or even a simple 'renaissance' of ancestral ritual practices in capitalist societies but 'uncovers the possibility of producing and enriching itself in societies such as that of Brazil (and, according to Guattari, in another way in Japan) by means of updated "animist" rituals. This fascinated Guattari.' Lazzarato and Melitopoulos (ibid.) interviewed Rosangela Araujo, a master of Capoeira (the latter designates a combat training through dance invented by slaves), who explained that this subjectivity 'is activated as both micro and macropolitical forces that nourish resistance and creativity of the "dominated"'.

For Brazilian psychoanalyst Suely Rolnik (co-author, with Guattari, of *The Molecular Revolution in Brazil*), 'these practices contain a "popular knowledge of the unconscious which is very strong and very effective". If they play a major role in the elaboration of the trauma of slavery in a "beyond post-colonial" situation, they can and should play a major political role' (qtd in Lazzarato and Melitopoulos 2012: 55).[17] Indeed, thousands of Afro-Brazilian *terreiros* (a name given to houses where Candomblé or Umbanda rituals take place) have battled for the recognition of their social role to care for and heal the body, the spirit and the collectivity. After being persecuted for decades, they gained a form of religious status but are now confronted with constant attacks from fundamentalist Evangelists, including murders of some of their religious leaders, the *babalorixas* in charge of the *terreiros* (Oliveira Santos 2019). Guattari was a pioneer for grasping what is at stake in anthropological debates: a politically ethical and aesthetic paradigm which requires not only to question the dualisms of old categories at the foundations of social sciences, but also to redefine the position of anthropology and other social sciences in what Brazilian Deleuzian anthropologist Viveiros de Castro (2014) calls the 'decolonization of thought' for an anti-narcissistic science.

As an anthropologist, I am constantly confronted with identity debates where culture is framed in terms of filiation and supposed authenticity, instead of recognising that a culture can only be alive if it is recreated, not just for museums and art stages, but in order to reactivate the whole society through affinities and new alliances. During the Deleuze studies conference in Istanbul which took place in July 2014, I proposed to consider that the three forms of culture that Guattari had differentiated in his essay 'Is Culture a Reactionary Concept?' (Guattari and Rolnik 2007: 21–34) correspond to three of his functors: *culture as merchandise*, which operates like flows; *culture as value* (of an exclusive elite, the supposed 'civilisation'), which operates like the universes of value (and constellations of refrains); while *culture as soul* (common to any ethnic, religious or local group) operates like existential territories. I then asked if a fourth non-reactionary concept of culture could be imagined for the fourth functor, that is the machinic phylum. The proposed hypothesis was to define different forms of culture of resistance as machinic phylum.

During the Deleuze Studies conference in Manipal, India, in 2015 I proposed further to consider this culture of resistance through some works of art, for instance films produced by Indigenous peoples, which could even be analysed as a form of *war machines*, that is, assemblages which for Deleuze and Guattari are not just military formations used by or against the state, but can be observed in various expressions of existential affirmation. I took as an example the film *Samson and Delilah*, which stages an Aboriginal young man who sniffs petrol and a young woman who helps her grandmother to paint the world-renowned desert dot paintings but suffers violence from both a traditional punishment and a racist rape; all through the film the two kids are in love and try to help each other and seem to fail at every new obstacle. But at the end, Aboriginal filmmaker Warwick Thornton stages a line of flight which is based on a recreated reterritorialisation on the land of the girl. Indeed, reoccupying the land has been a form of affirmative resistance for Indigenous Australians. A Tamil student, Deepak Prince, suggested, then, that instead of a general culture of resistance, for him it is the digital culture that operates like a machinic phylum. Indeed, the digital can be used for resistance, although its expanding algorithms remain predominantly in the service of science, capitalism and surveillance.

In *The Three Ecologies*, Guattari (2000: 137–8) defines the founding mechanisms of integrated world capitalism as four main semiotic regimes, which are in tension in his cartography:

1. techno-scientific semiotics (plans, diagrams, programmes, studies, research) operate like machinic phyla (*actual and possible*);
2. economic semiotics (monetary, financial and accountancy mechanisms) operate like flows (*actual and real*);
3. juridical semiotics (property deeds, various legislative measures and regulations) operate like incorporeal universes of value (*virtual and possible*);
4. semiotics of subjectivation (including architecture, town planning, public amenities, and so on) operate like existential territories (*virtual and real*).

The violent British invasion of Australia, massacres, forced sedentarisation, imposed lifestyle and Christian values, removal of children, constant bureaucratic confrontation with the state, and negotiations with mining companies, alongside pressures from the art market or tourism, have affected all Aboriginal semiotics by 'striating' the Australian desert, as well as bodies and minds. In this respect, I proposed to consider that the rhizomatic cut-out of Dreaming tracks in the land (and later painted on canvas) is probably more of a *holey space* than a *smooth space*,[18] especially since colonisation started two and a half centuries ago: even without metal, Aboriginal people had a virtual form of warrior-becoming which was actualised through colonial resistance and became a *war machine* with their struggle for land rights in the 1960s.

When I published *Desert Dreamers* in 1989 (Glowczewski 2016), many readers were surprised to see the various forms of resistance and incredible creativity that Warlpiri men and women demonstrated from within their inherited traditions. All across the continent, Aboriginal groups and activists have been affirming their singularity, responding over the decades to all the levels of the four semiotic regimes defined by Guattari, as per above:

1. Economically, they accepted royalties for some mining exploration on the land they had won back and started to paint in the mid-1980s for the global art market. But they continue to fight for sovereignty against uranium mining and fracking.
2. Techno-scientifically, they used the internet immediately and participated in various programmes to promote their traditional knowledge in conjunction with new technologies, like micro fire burning with macro scale mapping through GPS and drones.
3. At the juridical level, Aboriginal people from the desert, the rivers, the forest and the coasts fight constantly to ask for social or environmental justice, such as the Royal Commissions into Death in Custody, the Stolen Generation and the Stolen Wages cases, as well as reparation for traditional land destroyed by pollution and development. They challenged in court the notion of *terra nullius* that was finally abolished by the federal government in 1992, which allowed many successful claims under the Native Title Act 1993. They won a National Apology from the Government in 2008 and continue to struggle for the recognition of rivers as living waters to protect.
4. Finally, at the level of subjectivation that includes town planning, they changed their traditional political system of governance without rulers by adopting the Western mode of elected councils. But they immediately invented a mode of dissent to constantly question the way those councils were operating with other political, administrative powers, that is through constant consultations and negotiations.

Despite this Aboriginal adaptability to intertwine a dynamic ancestral vision and practice of the Australian continent with the violence of a constantly changing neo-liberal world (Lea 2017; Povinelli 2016), some scholars still do not accept this creativity as proof of a social, cultural and political *affirmation*. They see this creative process as a non-authentic 'invention' influenced by non-Indigenous people. Such sceptical scholars also fear ethnic essentialism in any Indigenous claims for recognition, not understanding the possibility of an Indigenous *philosophy of rela-*

tion. Such a philosophy was advocated by a friend of Guattari, Édouard Glissant (2008), the famous writer from Martinica (French Caribbean island), who opposed essentialism with what he called the 'relation-identity' of archipelagic networks. During the last Biennale in Marrakech, Glissant's friend, New York-based Malian artist Manthia Diawara (2016), wrote that his 'concept of relation ... moves beyond the oppositional discourse of the same and the other, operating instead with a new vision of difference as an "assembler of the dissimilars"'.

Interestingly, a similar accusation of non-authenticity has provoked debates in relation to Afro-Brazilian rituals. When members of such cults claim a relation both to Africa and to the history of colonial Brazil, and sometimes use anthropological writings of anthropologists such as Pierre Verger or Roger Bastide, they are accused of inventing their history. Against such allegations, Marcio Goldman (2015) has shown that what counts is the way in which a people affirm their becomings and create their own process of reappropriation of what was written about themselves.[19] Affirmation indeed can be essentialist, including the worst form of nationalism, the one with 'walls going up everywhere to stop the free movement of people, nations withdrawing into themselves and people returning to identities predetermined by absolutistic genealogies' (Noudelman qtd in Diawara 2016).[20] But various academics have demonstrated that 'affirmation' is not necessarily based on an essentialising exclusion but advocates multiple transformations in an ethical (and political) framework. Rosi Braidotti and Patricia Pisters (2012: 2) defined affirmative values in relation to nomadic normativity:

The key notions in this vitalist philosophy that aims at the actualization of virtual modes of becoming are: immanence, rather than the transcendence of universal norms; differential social assemblages, instead of either the assurance of *dogma* or the cynicism of *doxa* and the emphasis on the genesis of emerging, transversal collective affirmative values, rather than the implementation of canonical laws.

In her article 'Affirmation versus Vulnerability', Braidotti (2006: 248) argues that 'Edouard Glissant (1991) provides a perfect example of this productive ethics in his work on race and racism. An ethical relation cannot be based on resentment or resignation, but rather on the affirmation of positivity', which she defined earlier as 'the practice of transforming negative into positive passions', as 'a gesture of affirmation of hope in the sense of affirming the possibility of moving beyond the stultifying effects of the pain, the injury, the injustice. This is a gesture of displacement of the hurt, which fully contradicts the twin logic of claims and compensation' (ibid.).

I follow Braidotti's point on the 'affirmation of positivity' as hope, as it resonates with some of my work (see Genosko 2015), but I am not sure about her rejection of the 'twin logic of claims and compensation' which is at the heart of the current movement for various historical reparations, from slavery to Indigenous dispossession. I witnessed over forty years the ambiguous process of Aboriginal land claims striving for the recognition of their traditional rights on the land that had been taken away from them through the colonisation process, which has persisted even until today with the threat of 'closing' Aboriginal communities in order for them to move to towns. Despite the way the state constantly reframes the legal possibilities to reduce their scope, claiming sovereignty over Aboriginal land is at the heart of all Indigenous struggles (in Australia or elsewhere) to affirm their own way of valuing multiple becomings despite the violent impact of settler-colonialism. Similarly, I would not reject as just a negative emotion the claims for compensation in Australia, the US, Canada or France for the long-term transgenerational harm caused to displaced children. Such cases include Indigenous children taken away from their mixed families to be sent to institutions and trained to work for white settlers. On the French island of Réunion French children descending from enslaved Africans and from indentured labour from India were forcibly taken to France to work on farms. In Europe and North America deaf children were abused in institutions. Irish, Scottish or English children who lost a parent during the Second World War were sent from Liverpool to Australia, where they were abused in Christian institutions, especially by Catholic priests. Many survivors of such a traumatic history have over the past thirty years called for reparation, attempting to heal their pain through various forms of recognition: self-affirming their sovereignty, teaching history and memory of colonisation and deportation, designing policies against discrimination, and engaging in Royal Commissions and UN Forums and Declarations. Claims for financial compensation, land and new protocols (Dussart and Poirier 2017; Langton 2018) are other tools in the decolonisation process, which is always under the threat of being disempowered by state assimilation policies and capitalistic cannibalism (Coulthard 2014; Ferdinand 2019). This tension is ecosophical.

There are also strong debates around the claims for compensation of the descendants of the slave traffic from African countries to the Americas and other European colonies. Singer Tiken Jah Fakoly,[21] born in Ivory Coast, sings that Africa has already paid its supposed current debt through slavery and massive benefits from stolen resources by France and other countries. Following this logic, one form of 'slavery compensation' could consist in a salutary lifting of those unjust 'debts' imposed on Africa by internationally integrated capitalism. Similarly, the compensation for harm against Indigenous people in Australia and elsewhere could consist in stopping the ongoing process of the destruction of the earth and biodiversity through extractive industries and fossil energies which are concentrated on their lands. The world is multiplying victims of history but the responsibility to respond to claims for compensation could be a way of inventing new forms of planetary exchange in an ethical redress of justice.

When Guattari was invited to Brazil in the 1980s, he was fascinated by the possibility opened by the end of the dictatorship to involve micromovements – mobilised around gender, race and ecology – to literally transform macropolitics (Guattari and Rolnik 2007). The current corruption and crisis in Brazil changed the parameters in which Guattari and many Brazilians had invested their hopes and actions, but the ecosophical project is now more than ever needed to be experimented with everywhere:

It is to be hoped that the development of the three types of eco-logical praxis outlined here will lead to a reframing and a recomposition of the goals of the emancipatory struggles. And let us hope that, in the context of the new 'deal' of the relation between capital and human activity, ecologists, feminists, antiracists, etc., will make it an immediate major objective to target the modes of production of subjectivity, that is, of knowledge, culture, sensibility and sociability that come under an incorporeal value system at the root of the new productive assemblages. (Guattari 2000: 49)

'The virtual necessitates the gesture,' wrote Gilles Châtelet (1993; qtd in Alliez 2013: 39); the gesture 'is not a simple spatial movement: it decides, liberates and proposes a new modality of "the moving" (*le mouvoir*)'. The experience of 'the moving' is the key to be moved (affectively and so incited to an effective action) by Indigenous or Afro-Brazilian rituals and movements of affirmation. Through ritual dance and specific gestures Brazilian Orixá becomings are like Australian totemic becomings, emerging image crystals playing with time, proofs of the real and possible in their desiring tensions from actual to virtual. 'Speculative gesture' for Isabelle Stengers (Stengers and Debaise 2015: 14) is a 'response to the insistence of a possible' that could be the characteristic of our time today; when 'all the landscape of our practices is ravaged', she calls for the 'arts of discernment', that is, an art to learn, to cultivate and to experiment. I follow Stengers here. Guattari was calling for 'creating the condition of emergence of an existential nomadism as intense as the one of Indigenous people of Pre-Columbian America or of Australia', which is different from what he called 'the false nomadism that leaves us stuck in one place'.[22] One can say that many people today, especially refugees, do invent, day after day, an existential nomadism with the right to move homes, which is so intense that states respond by destructive violence so as not to let such movements be contagious. At stake in this multiplicity of attempts to survive is the affirmation of forces of life that underlie a necessary transformation of the world. If the violence of the conflicts and flows of refugees is actualised, the crystallisation of all the threats virtualises other *possible(s)*: new assemblages of humans and non-humans with the earth.

Notes

1. Introduction by French artists who transcribed the conference for the website of the *intermittents du spectacle* (performance artists, filmmakers, and so on, in precarious employment). See Guattari 1991 (my translation).
2. See the current experience of Notre-Dame-des-Landes in France: <https://encommun. eco/>; see also projects of ecological restoration: <https://www.commonland.com/> (both last accessed 19 March 2020).
3. Mirzoeff 2018; this paper was published online in 2015.
4. Written for a conference in 2015.
5. See Guattari 1995: 32, n. 11: 'See the role of dreams in the mythical cartographies of Australian Aborigines. Barbara Glocewski [*sic*], *Les Rêveurs du désert*, Plon, Paris,

1989.' When Guattari was elaborating his fourfold schizoanalytic cartography as a practice to experiment with his ecosophical project in the early 1980s, he used some elements of my ethnographic work with Aboriginal people from Central Australia. Two of our joint seminar discussions from 1983 and 1985 published in the first issue of *Chimères* in 1987 were translated into an American edition (see Glowczewski 2015, chapter 1) and republished in a British edition (see Glowczewski 2020, chapter 2).

6. See Guattari (2012: 67) expanding on 'a dream logic' and 'a logic of archaic intensities' in a footnote: 'That of Australian aboriginals, for example, who on the basis of a collective labour on their dreams and from a very pragmatic point of view which isn't in the slightest mystical, endeavour to localize the potentials for the transformation of their real and/or incorporeal Universe: "the dream, as law, is not a divine synchronic model frozen in an image, but almost a diachronic, but non-causal, method. What counts is the principle of adaptation as a transformational potential represented by the mythical metamorphoses of totemic species." Barbara Glowczewski *Le rêve et la terre*. Thèse de 3e cycle en ethnologie, Paris, Université de Paris VII, p.44' (Guattari 2012: 271, n. 22).

7. Uncles and aunts on the father's side are differentiated from the ones on the mother's side: they are called by different terms and skin-names in Warlpiri. See Glowczewski 2016 and 2020.

8. Special thanks to Radek Przedpełski for showing me Porębski's hypercubes.

9. See 'The Warlpiri in Paris', chapter from Glowczewski 2016, reprinted in Geel and Gaillard 2019.

10. In this chapter of *Essays Critical and Clinical*, titled 'What Children Say', discussing the experimental pedagogical work of the 'wander lines' of autistic children under the care of Fernand Deligny, Deleuze quotes from my book; see Glowczewski 1991, chapter 1.

11. I have described this magical operation as illustrated by the bottle of Klein, a topological figure with a reversed entry used by Lévi-Strauss in *The Jealous Potter* to describe an American mythical itinerary (Glowczewski 2019); see the testimony of the Australian healer Lance Sullivan at <https://vimeo.com/233652286> (last accessed 19 March 2020; commented on and transcribed in the last chapter of Glowczewski 2020).

12. The Declaration was being drafted in the 1980s, when an Aboriginal activist from the Kimberley, Peter Yu, travelled to Geneva with Maori and Native Americans. Australia signed the treaty in 2008, when Kevin Rudd was elected, but had refused to sign (with the USA, Canada and New Zealand) when the Declaration was adopted by the UN in 2007; see Glowczewski's introduction in Glowczewski and Henry 2011.

13. See <http://spheres-journal.org/resisting-the-disaster-between-exhaustion-and-crea tion/> (last accessed 19 March 2020; republished as chapter 11 in Glowczewski 2020).

14. The French word *relance* means 'reactivation' more than 'continuation'.

15. 'To paint a Dreaming is at once to regenerate one's forces and to connect the object or the person to the earth and to the space-time of the hero who "dreams" the life of people and their environment' (Glowczewski 2016, qtd in Manning 2009); see also Grosz 2008 on the paintings of Petyarre and a 'becoming-lizard'.

16. See film presented during the *Cosmocolors* performance at the BAC, Geneva, 2015: <https://www.utopiana.art/fr/cosmocouleurs>; <https://vimeo.com/173509321#t=Na Ns> (both last accessed 20 March 2020).

17. Interviewed in 2009.

18. Deleuze and Guattari in *A Thousand Plateaus* (see 1997: 416 on holey space, as well

as chapter 14, 'The Smooth and the Striated') show how such spaces 'transverse' each other and communicate with free holey spaces, whether in a desert, steppe or ice, a sea, a sky or a city. I commented on this at the first camp and conference of the Deleuze and Guattari Studies Collective in India, University of Manipal, 2015: <http://www.deleuzeindia.com/> (last accessed 20 March 2020). See also the introduction in Glowczewski 2020.

19. See also the exchange of letters between Verger and Bastide analysed by Fernanda Arêas Peixoto (2015).

20. François Noudelman convening a 2008 Paris conference, *The Politics of the One-World* (*Tout-Monde*, The One-World in relation, is another of Glissant's concepts). 'One-World' does not really translate the concept of 'Tout-Monde' of Glissant, who insists on the multiplicity of the whole rather than its unity.

21. 'L'Afrique doit du fric' [Africa owes dough], song by Tiken Jah Fakoly, © 2006 Barclay, available at <https://www.youtube.com/watch?v=z_alflRRwXY> (last accessed 20 March 2020).

22. My own translation of Guattari, 'Pratiques écosophiques et restauration de la cité subjective', in Eduardo Portella (ed.) (1993), *Un autre partage, homme, ville, nature*, Paris: Erès, pp. 103–18 (conference in Rio de Janeiro, 25–27 May 1992, held at the Fundação Casa de Rui Barbosa, accompanying a UN Conference on environment and development, 3–4 June 1992); republished in Guattari 2013: 31–57.

References

Alliez, Éric (2013), *Défaire l'image: de l'art contemporain*, Paris: Presses du Réel.

Bałus, Wojciech (2012), 'A Marginalised Tradition? Polish Art History', in Matthew Rampley, Thierry Lenain, Hubert Locher, Andrea Pinotti, Charlotte Schoell-Glass and C. J. M. Zilmans (eds), *Art History and Visual Studies in Europe: Transnational Discourses and National Frameworks*, Leiden and Boston: Brill, pp. 439–49.

Braidotti, Rosi (2006), 'Affirmation versus Vulnerability: On Contemporary Ethical Debates', *Symposium: Canadian Journal of Continental Philosophy*, 10(1): 235–54.

Braidotti, Rosi and Patricia Pisters (eds) (2012), *Revisiting Normativity with Deleuze*, London: Bloomsbury.

Châtelet, Gilles (1993), *Les enjeux du mobile: Mathématique, physique, philosophie*, Paris: Seuil.

Coulthard, Glen Sean (2014), *Red Skin White Masks: Rejecting the Colonial Politics of Recognition*, Minneapolis: Minnesota University Press.

DeLanda, Manuel (1997), 'The Machinic Phylum', in Joke Brouwer and Carla Hoekendijk (eds), *TechnoMorphica*, Rotterdam: V2_Organisation, pp. 34–59, available at <https://v2.nl/archive/articles/the-machinic-phylum> (last accessed 19 March 2020).

DeLanda, Manuel (1998), 'Deleuze and the Open-Ended Becoming of the World', presented at Chaos/Control: Complexity Conference, University of Bielefeld, Germany, 27 June 1998, available at <http://www.cddc.vt.edu/host/delanda/pages/becoming.htm> (last accessed 19 March 2020).

Deleuze, Gilles [1983] (1991), *Cinema 1: The Movement-Image*, trans. Hugh Tomlinson and Barbara Habberjam, Minneapolis: University of Minnesota Press.

Deleuze, Gilles [1993] (1997), *Essays Critical and Clinical*, trans. Daniel W. Smith and Michael A. Greco, Minneapolis: University of Minnesota Press.

Deleuze, Gilles [1985] (2010), *Cinema 2: The Time-Image*, trans. Hugh Tomlinson and Robert Galeta, Minneapolis: University of Minnesota Press.

Deleuze, Gilles and Félix Guattari [1980] (1997), *A Thousand Plateaus: Capitalism and Schizophrenia*, trans. Brian Massumi, Minneapolis: University of Minnesota Press.

Diawara, Manthia (2016), 'Édouard Glissant's Worldmentality: An Introduction to *One World in Relation*', leaflet published by the Marrakech Biennale contextualising the video *NEGRITUDE: A Dialogue between Senghor and Soyinka* (2015), available at <https://www.documenta14.de/en/south/34_edouard_glissant_s_worldmentality_an_ introduction_to_one_world_in_relation> (last accessed 19 March 2020).

Dussart, Françoise and Sylvie Poirier (eds) (2017), *Entangled Territorialities: Negotiating Indigenous Lands in Australia and Canada*, Toronto: University of Toronto Press.

Ferdinand, Malcolm (2019), *Une écologie décoloniale*, Paris: Seuil/Anthropocène.

Foley, Gary, Andrew Shaap and Edwina Howell (2013), *The Aboriginal Tent Embassy: Sovereignty, Black Power, Land Rights and the State*, London: Routledge.

Fuller, Robert S., Michael Anderson, Ray P. Norris and Michelle Trudgett (2014), 'The Emu Sky Knowledge of the Kamilaroi and Euahlayi Peoples', *Journal of Astronomical History and Heritage*, 17(2): 171–9.

Geel, Catherine and Clément Gaillard (eds) (2019), *Extended French Theory and the Design Field. . . On Nature and Ecology: A Reader*, Paris: T&P Publishing.

Genosko, Gary (2015), 'Micropolitics of Hope – A Reply to Barbara Glowczewski', *Spheres: Journal for Digital Cultures, #2 Ecologies of Change*, <http://spheres-journal. org/micropolitics-of-hope/> (last accessed 19 March 2020).

Glissant, Édouard [1990] (1997), *Poetics of Relation*, trans. Betsy Wing, Ann Arbor: University of Michigan Press.

Glissant, Édouard (2009), *Philosophie de la Relation*, Paris: Gallimard.

Glowczewski, Barbara (1991), *Du rêve à la loi chez les Aborigènes*, Paris: Presses Universitaires de France.

Glowczewski, Barbara (2011), 'Guattari and Anthropology: Existential Territories among Indigenous Australians', in *The Guattari Effect*, New York: Continuum, pp. 99–111.

Glowczewski, Barbara (2015), *Totemic Becomings: Cosmopolitics of the Dreaming/ Devires totemicos. Cosmopolitica do Sonho*, Sao Paulo: n-1 edições (bilingual).

Glowczewski, Barbara [1989] (2016), *Desert Dreamers*, Minneapolis: University of Minnesota Press.

Glowczewski, Barbara (2019), 'Entre totémisme aborigène et umbanda brésilienne – Empreintes, lignes de fuite et cristallisation des hétérogénéités', in Anne Querrien, Anne Sauvagnargues and Arnaud Villani (eds), *Agencer les multiplicités avec Deleuze*, Paris: Hermann, pp. 119–29 (*Deleuze: virtuel, machines et lignes de fuites*, Deleuze decade, Cerisy, August 2015).

Glowczewski, Barbara (2020), *Indigenising Anthropology with Guattari and Deleuze*, Edinburgh: Edinburgh University Press.

Glowczewski, Barbara and Rosita Henry (eds) (2011), *The Indigenous Challenge: Between Spectacle and Politics*, Oxford: The Bardwell Press.

Glowczewski, Barbara and Christophe Laurens (2018), 'Le conflit des existences à l'épreuve du climat, ou l'anthropocène revu par ceux qu'on préfère mettre à la rue et au musée', in Catherine Larrère and Rémi Beau (eds), *Penser l'anthropocène*, Paris: Sciences Po Presses, pp. 141–56 (filmed conference 'How to think the anthropocene?', November 2015, available at <http://www.fondationecolo.org/l-anthropocene/video> (last accessed 19 March 2020).

Goldman, Marcio (2015), 'Reading Roger Bastide: Deutero-Learning the African Religions in Brazil', *Etudes Rurales*, *Multiplicités anthropologiques au Brésil*, 196:

9–24, available at <https://journals.openedition.org/etudesrurales/10347> (last accessed 19 March 2020).

Grosz, Elizabeth (2008), *Chaos, Territory, Art: Deleuze and the Framing of the Earth*, New York: Columbia University Press.

Guattari, Félix (1991), 'Produire une culture du dissensus: hétérogenèse et paradigme esthétique' [To Produce a Culture of Dissent: Heterogenesis and Aesthetic Paradigm], *CIP-IdF Coordination des Intermittents et précaires d'Île-de-France*, available at <http://www.cip-idf.org/article.php3?id_article=5613> (last accessed 19 March 2020).

Guattari, Félix [1992] (1995), *Chaosmosis: An Ethico-Aesthetic Paradigm*, trans. Paul Bains and Julian Pefanis, Bloomington and Indianapolis: Indiana University Press.

Guattari, Félix [1992] (1996), 'Remaking Social Practices', in Gary Genosko (ed.), *The Guattari Reader*, trans. Sophie Thomas, Oxford: Blackwell, pp. 262–72.

Guattari, Félix [1989] (2000), *The Three Ecologies*, trans. Ian Pindar and Paul Sutton, London: Athlone Press.

Guattari, Félix [1979] (2007), *The Machinic Unconscious*, trans. Taylor Adkins, Los Angeles: Semiotext(e).

Guattari, Félix [1989] (2012), *Schizoanalytical Cartographies*, trans. Andrew Goffey, London: Bloomsbury Academic.

Guattari, Félix (2013), *Qu'est-ce que l'écosophie?*, ed. Stéphane Nadaud, Abbaye d'Ardenne: Éditions Lignes/IMEC.

Guattari, Félix and Suely Rolnik [1986] (2007), *The Molecular Revolution in Brazil*, trans. Karel Clapshow and Brian Holmes, expanded version of *Micropolitica: Cartografias do desejo*, Los Angeles: Semiotext(e).

Langton, Marcia (2018), *Welcome to Country: A Travel Guide to Indigenous Australia*, Melbourne: Hardie Grant.

Lazzarato, Maurizio and Angela Melitopoulos (2012), 'Machinic Animism', in Sabine Folie and Anselm Franke (eds), *Animism: Modernity through the Looking Glass*, Cologne: Walther König, pp. 45–56.

Lea, Tess (2017), 'Infrastructure Reform in Indigenous Australia: From Mud to Mining to Military Empires', in Penny Harvey, Casper Bruun Jensen and Atsuro Morita (eds), *Infrastructures and Social Complexity: A Companion*, Abingdon: Routledge, pp. 64–75.

Manning, Erin (2009), *Relationscapes: Movement, Art, Philosophy*, Cambridge, MA: MIT Press.

Massumi, Brian (2002a), *Parables for the Virtual: Movement, Affect, Sensation*, London: Duke University Press.

Massumi, Brian (2002b), 'Sur le droit à la non-communication des différences', *Ethnopsy. Les mondes contemporains de la guérison*, 4, *Sur le Droit à la Non-Communication de la Différence*, Special Issue, ed. Isabelle Stengers and Tobie Nathan, 'Propositions de paix', 93–131.

Mirzoeff, Nicholas (2018), 'It's Not the Anthropocene, It's the White Supremacy Scene; or, The Geological Color Line', in Richard Grusin (ed.), *After Extinction*, Minneapolis: University of Minnesota Press, pp. 123–49.

Naess, Arne (1993), *Ecology, Community, and Lifestyle: Outline of an Ecosophy*, trans. David Rothenberg, New York: Cambridge University Press.

Neyrat, Frédéric (2014), 'On the Political Unconscious of the Anthropocene', interviewed by Elizabeth Johnson and David Johnson, *Society + Space*, available at <https://www.societyandspace.org/articles/on-the-political-unconscious-of-the-anthropocene> (last accessed 19 March 2020).

Oliveira Santos, Abrahão de (2019), 'Agencement-Condomblé et lignes de fuite brésiliennes', in Anne Querrien, Anne Sauvagnargues and Arnaud Villani (eds), *Agencer les multiplicités avec Deleuze*, Paris: Hermann, pp. 131–42 (*Deleuze: virtuel, machines et lignes de fuites*, Deleuze decade, Cerisy, August 2015).

Peixoto, Fernanda Arêas (2015), *A viagem como vocação: Itinerários, parcerias e formas de conhecimento*, São Paulo: Editora da Universidade de São Paulo.

Porębski, Mieczysław [1978] (1986), 'Styl epoki' [Style of an Epoch], in *Sztuka a informacja* [Art versus Information], Kraków: Wydawnictwo Literackie, pp. 185–214; the article originally appeared in *Biuletyn Historii Sztuki* [Art History Bulletin], 40 (1978): 41–54.

Povinelli, Elizabeth A. (2016), *Geontologies: A Requiem for Late Liberalism*, Durham, NC: Duke University Press.

Roche, François with Natanel Elfassy (2010), 'Stuttering', LOG, available at <http://www.new-territories.com/blog/?p=457> (last accessed 19 March 2020).

Saldanha, Arun and Hannah Stark (2016), 'A New Earth: Deleuze and Guattari in the Anthropocene', *Deleuze Studies*, 10(4): 427–39.

Smith, Terry (2001), 'Public Art between Cultures: The Aboriginal Memorial, Aboriginality, and Nationality in Australia', *Critical Inquiry*, 27(4): 629–61.

Stengers, Isabelle and Didier Debaise (eds) (2015), *Gestes spéculatifs* (Colloque Cerisy), Paris: Presses du Réel.

Viveiros de Castro, Eduardo (2007), 'The Crystal Forest: Notes on the Ontology of Amazonian Spirits', *Inner Asia*, 9: 13–33.

Viveiros de Castro, Eduardo [2009] (2014), *Cannibal Metaphysics: For a Post-Structural Anthropology*, ed. and trans. Peter Skafish, Minneapolis: University of Minnesota Press.

Zourabichvili, François [2003] (2012), *Deleuze: A Philosophy of Event, together with The Vocabulary of Deleuze*, trans. Kieran Aarons, Edinburgh: Edinburgh University Press.

11

Ripples of Serialism:
Boulez, Deleuze and the San Francisco Bay Area

Adi Louria Hayon

In February 1978, IRCAM – the Institute for Research and Coordination of Music in Paris – convened a group of musicians and philosophers in order to discuss the theme of 'Musical Time'. Participants included Gilles Deleuze, Pierre Boulez, Roland Barthes, Gerald Bennett, Michel Foucault, Michel Decoust, Jean-Claude Risset and Luciano Berio. And yet, mythic as this summit might seem, the movements around 'Musical Time' were hardly new. The participants outlined strands of thought more than a decade prior to this gathering. In his commentary, Deleuze focused on the heterogeneous nature of musical tempo tying the multiple temporalities generated in the process of becoming with the free play of serial networks offered by Boulez's compositions. For him, art offered a privileged domain for philosophical explorations of the transcendental domain of sensibility. One of the problems raised within this discussion was the longstanding question of transcendental empiricism, which for Deleuze centred on the paradox of individuation conditioned on the differential temporal fault line (or the cut) pervading actual and virtual formations (Williams 2011: 80). Individuation is conceptualised as a dynamic complex of actual and virtual relations between differentials. It is a temporal complex composed of multiple differential processes perpetually changing their constitution without reference to prior unity. Such differentials are the elements of relational intervals which form the movement of identity thought as a substantive multiplicity amid multiplicities (Roffe 2012: 52–6). When Deleuze describes the structure of such complexes, he refers to their 'internal multiplicity – in other words, a system of multiple, non-localizable connections between differential elements which is incarnated in real relations and actual terms' (1994: 183). He ties these indeterminate formations to the problem of time and the logic of multiplicities found in serial musical compositions, perception, and his ongoing conversations with his friend Boulez, regarding polyphonic combinations and the creation of serial sonorous blocks, heterologies of impulses and bundles of time. Martin Scherzinger asserted that Boulez's orchestral technique may figure as a metaphor for the becoming of what he terms the Dividual: a multi-directional split necessary for the process of becoming (2008: 135, 156).[1] The temporal nature of music is key to understanding the Deleuzian-Boulezian relations, especially those pertinent to the work of internal difference and heterogeneous multiplicities (see

Bogue 2003; Buchanan and Swiboda 2004; Nesbitt 2004; Hemmet 2004; Bidima 2004; Scherzinger 2008; Hulse and Nesbitt 2010; Campbell 2015; Criton and Chouvel 2015). For Deleuze, creating compositions was related to producing concepts. 'Music', he wrote in 'Boulez, Proust and Time', 'has always had this object: individuations without identity, which constitute "musical entities." ... the system of blocks and bubbles implies a generalized refusal of every identity principle in the variations and distributions which define it' (1998: 71–2).

From Arnold Schoenberg's atonal revolution to Boulez's integral serialism, blocks, or intervals, which posit differential relations, became the principle constituents of serial note rows characterised not as successive lines but as proliferating aggregates (Nesbitt 2004: 67–8; Scherzinger 2008: 141–5; Scherzinger 2010: 123; Campbell 2013: 25, 38). In strict serialism such intervals mark differences in pitch between two sounds or notes. They are distributed without hierarchy while altered through three methods: (1) inversion, that is, where particular notes are reversed; (2) retrograde, where a note row is reversed; and (3) retrograde inversion, when the inversion is set backwards. Serial rows became building blocks that were substantially invariant and yet repeated in various relational juxtapositions (Witkin 1998: 101). In later developments Webern fragmented and composed rows in complex inter-relations that expanded texture, and Stravinsky emancipated rhythmic metre from continuity. Since the 1940s 'total' or 'integral' serialism expanded the technique to encode parameters such as duration and dynamics by Messiaen and later Babbit, Stockhausen and Boulez. Integral serialism also distributes multiple serial processes in an unequal manner, alluding to coincidence and dispersion, noted in Deleuze's blocks and bubbles. Integral serialism, unlike Schoenberg's twelve-tone series, discards the ruling mechanisms of a patterning authority. What remains is a playing out of a concrete structure, or collection, of shapes which abandon their articulative generative-construal through their own repeated presence. The plural repetitive movements of intervals and successional rows are the shared mechanisms of distinct kinds of serialism. However, intervallic blocks and distributed bubbles are constants reverberating in Deleuze's musical entities and they specifically allude to Boulez's serial transformations in relation to the creative process of individuation without identity. In this chapter I will elucidate two trajectories. The first will show how the differential interval proposed by Kant and Boulez influenced Deleuze's thought. The second trajectory will trace the historical route carving the translation and importation of Deleuze and Boulez's *sound-figures* to the artistic practice of the American West Coast, in particular to the work of composer Steve Reich and artist Bruce Nauman, working in the San Francisco Bay Area.

A Discordant Accord

The aesthetic experience of musical temporality forming the process of individuation is already sketched in Deleuze's early book *Kant's Critical Philosophy* (1963). Deleuze listened to Kant's aesthetic philosophy. This sonic reading shows how Deleuze crystallised Kant's concept of the discordant accord in order to consolidate the paradox of individuation contingent upon a temporal dissonant flow reverberating amidst the faculties. This trajectory expands present comparative analysis of musical difference and self-division (Scherzinger 2008; Nesbitt 2004; Campbell 2013). The aesthetic experience of the discordant accord maintains the repetition of internal splits generating multiple temporalities. James Williams describes Deleuzian repetition as follows: 'The most important definition of repetition . . . for itself is that the "for itself" of repetition is difference – there is no repetition of the same thing for any other thing, only an open variation that occurs with an individual' (2003: 92). Replacing repetition with variation means giving primacy to the non-continuous relations of intervals that no longer function in stable serial structures but multiply in various directions. Boulez named these partitionings 'sound-blocks', and they were to influence Deleuze's concept of the 'cut' and the generation of multiplicities. Differential partitionings are principal operators of pure differentiation occurring within the serial synthesis of time.

In several writings Deleuze signifies the great Kantian shift from time as a measured movement to time that conditions movement, or what he terms 'time out of joint' (see Deleuze 1984, 1990, 1994, 1997; Deleuze and Guattari 1987).[2] His return to Kant draws on the distinction between possible and real experience of reason; the first is found in transcendental aesthetic and the second in empirical synthesis. Deleuze will connect the two, replacing their distinction by a differential force of production which activates perception as the condition of creation. Reason's purposiveness will no longer strive for knowledge by dint of representation, but actualise virtual differentiation as genesis of real experience, that is, of the undecidable experience of the subject formation which fractures and folds in time. Deleuze exposes the drama of time in the transcendental aesthetic of the sublime and the genius in the *Critique of Judgment*. He describes the Kantian ongoing struggle between the imagination and reason, between understanding and inner sense, as 'a tempest in the depths of a chasm opened up in the subject' (1984: xii). The *Critique of Judgment* exhibits the aggregated faculties, 'no longer determined by any one of them, and which [the accord] is all the deeper because it no longer has any rule, and because it demonstrates a spontaneous accord of the Ego and the *I*' (ibid., original emphasis). The free play of the faculties in the aesthetic experience of the sublime exhibits the nature of the mind as an aggregate and deep *discordant accord* played at the limits of the unregulated faculties within time (ibid. 51).[3] The discordant *I* is unhinged more than twice: the first, a multiplicity of fissures cracking the natural harmony of the faculties, the second, an interval between the Ego and *I*. This is why Deleuze distinguished between the aesthetic feeling of the discordant accord and the harmony legislated by the faculty of knowledge, which he terms a '*final* accord' (ibid. 14, original emphasis). His critical reading of Kant's philosophy will resonate across his writings, suggesting that Kant did not pursue his transcendental deduction to its full end, since the split cutting through the subject cannot be resolved by time's self-determination, nor by God, nor by pure passive receptivity (Deleuze 1994: 58; Williams 2011: 82–3; Smith 2012: 63). The emancipation of dissonance, argues Deleuze, or the discordant accord, is the great discovery of the *Critique of Judgment*, the final Kantian reversal. 'It is the discord', he writes, 'that produces an accord. . . . A new music as discord, and as discordant accord, the source of time' (Deleuze 1997: 35).

By 1968 Deleuze's paradox of inner sense discussed in *Difference and Repetition* has forged his critique of the Kantian determination of the transcendental subject into his own philosophy of time. James Williams shows how this critique was to unhinge 'the subject as philosophical foundation of any kind (logical, intuitive, phenomenological)' and maintain the transcendental deduction in order to 'deduce the conditions for a difference across inseparable ontological realms as they connect to and determine one another, where the form of a difference in one realm is conditional on a difference in another' (Williams 2011: 80). The transcendental deduction became a method for Deleuze, who displaces the pure *I* contingent on *a priori* time with a split *I* composed by a temporal difference interiorised in the fracture dividing the subject and self. This is the temporal paradox of inner sense and it marks the fundamental difference between Kant and Deleuze: while the Kantian subject is a receptive being which can only represent its own representation in passivity according to external time, the Deleuzian subject distinguishes the time of the receptive passive self from the time internalised as a rupture (or what he would call 'wound' in *The Logic of Sense*) in the *I*. Hence, we are offered two temporal movements which are both external and internal: one transcendental, the other empirical/perceptual. Between them, Deleuze finds a traversed fissure, a cut. A fault line that signifies time:

> It is as if the 'I' is traversed by a fault line: it is fractured by the pure and empty form of time. In this form it is the correlate of the passive self appearing in time. This is what time signifies: a fault or fracture in the 'I', passivity in the self; and the correlation of the passive self and the fractured 'I' constitutes the transcendental discovery or the element of the Copernican revolution. (Deleuze qtd in Williams 2011: 82)[4]

The correlation of the passive self and the differing activity of *I* now multiply in doubling: Ego and *I*, thought and being, determinable and undeterminable, mutually contingent on their relation and on their separation. The passivity of the self presupposes a form of determinability, and yet it is this very form of determinability which necessitates the split in the consciousness of the subject. Deleuze defines this fissure as the differential pure and empty time infinitely producing synthesis in the present. On each of its sides we find the asymmetrical relations of past and future. In *The Logic of Sense*, they double into multiple processes, the vertical infinite stretching out limitlessly, that is the pure and empty time of Aion, and the horizontal actions of bodies expressed by blockages and disconnections. Time is multiplied in a series of repetitions by each side of the fracture and by the pure time of the fracture, yielding the Deleuzian transcendental empirical subject which is contingent on the virtual and actual dimensions of Aion and Chronos.[5] *Difference and Repetition* outlines the three syntheses of time as manners of repetition. Both repetition as difference and difference as repetition are processes of actual series and pure becoming.

Music

The temporal fault line calls for a tuned ear which will detect that Deleuze turns to Kant's discordant accord in order to release its differential forces. For him, the discordant accord is a sonorous differential force drawing on the virtual lines of musical intervals. This tendency will culminate in *A Thousand Plateaus* and *The Fold*, turning to nomadic polyphonies. The question raised within this style, within this musical *poeisis*, is what musical currents dwell in the paradox of individuation and the temporal fissure. Music – from the Viennese School to Wagner, Messiaen, Ligeti, Cage, Reich, Xenakis and Boulez – allowed Deleuze to raise abstract concepts of time while turning to musical technique in order to carve out the process of becoming in the creation of concepts while expanding perception to the sonorous. Daniel Smith demonstrated how the critique of the identity of the self has its exact parallel in the critique of identity concepts. Both are multiplicities as they are self-differential processes that are continuous and discrete. If self-reflection is the manner of a never attained identity, then concepts are reflected by their own means, however indiscernible. To this Deleuze adds that, since both are creative acts that correspond to sensible aggregates, they also have an affinity to art. This creative act aligns the philosopher with the artist (Smith 2012: 62–9). Once creation is contingent upon the differential principle, we should ask: If music and philosophy touch upon the difference of the pure and empty form of time, that is, of the unthinkable and the inaudible, how are we to perceive temporal formations determined within these senses? Deleuze suggests sound as the medium which renders the mute force of time sensible. In this respect, it was the Boulezian interval of serial music that cut through the heart of Deleuze's sonorous subject, and it is the Boulezian series of transformations that reverberate in the multiplicity of the synthesis of time. In what comes ahead I will concentrate on Boulez's techniques of serial encoding to show how they influenced Deleuze's serial repetitions. Although the documented discourse between the two is dated to the 1970s, the various similarities between the early writings of *Difference and Repetition* and *The Logic of Sense* dated to the 1960s and the early writings of Boulez's spanning the 1950s–1960s call for examination that may shed light on the cross-pollination seen in the later writing. But it may also allude to Deleuze's early exposure to the intellectual passages of the composer.

Series

If Deleuze critiqued the Kantian accord regulating the harmonious correspondence between subject and object (the self and the 'I think'; the faculties; and the theological principle)[6] to replace it with the differential fault line distributing inequality and creating the possibility for multiple temporal series, Boulez redefined the concepts of chord, counterpoint and series in light of developing his technique of serial encoding after the novelties of the Viennese School. Whereas Deleuze was to unground the univocal guarantor, Boulez stripped the harmonic function of the chord:

> A chord is a generalizable entity . . . More recently, having gradually lost its structural functions, the chord has come to be simply an aggregate of sounds, chosen for itself, for its possibilities of internal tension and release, according to the registers it inhabits and the intervals it brings into play . . . which would seem to prove that the genuinely harmonic period of Western European music is over. (Boulez 1991b: 223)

The abolition of the chord and its transformation into a sound aggregate was later developed to sound-blocks: 'I think of them as aggregates of frequencies, as it were sound-blocks,' Boulez wrote in *Possibly*. . . . These new units allowed him to produce irrational series that did not adhere to rational additive progress. 'What happens', he later wrote, 'is that we multiply the components of each block by one another. Thus if you transpose (multiply) an aggregate of three notes by one of four [4x3], you get in theory an aggregate of twelve notes . . . but with common notes . . . the new sound block will only have ten notes' (Boulez 1991d: 128–9). His guiding conception was to create work that generated a moving expanding universe, where form becomes autonomous and expressive, and yet still unknown. Struggling with the concept of discontinuous time in *Le Marteau sans maître* (1952–5), he wrote to Stockhausen of the premises for undetermined composition devoid of *a priori* delineation while perceptible in the continuity of its disclosure:

> I believe that one must accept increasingly that not everything is determined and it would be more satisfying for the mind . . . not to create a hierarchy before commencing, but to discover this hierarchy as we go along with the work. . . . Thus one would be led to compose without sketches, which would be very pleasant!! The sketches would be made in the course of the work and not before. I intend to integrate that into the variation *principles* (generative *principles*) which would themselves be submitted to a vertical and horizontal serial universe. Consequently this would . . . be . . . part of a construction where the materials are renewed, reappear and always combine in different ways. The form would no longer be envisaged in time such as an organising, globally perceptible hierarchy, but the form would only be perceptible in the continuity of its unfolding. . . . It would in any case be a plausible synthesis and very fascinating for the language as such with the very structure of this language deferred to a superior level. (Boulez qtd in Piencikowski 2016: 99, original emphasis)[7]

What Boulez is trying to construct is a method of composition that would please the mind, such that it will be devoid of *a priori* plans or a hovering external guarantor but would adhere to an immanent generative principle of becoming contingent on a present synthetic selection. In 'Current Investigations' he asks, 'What is a series?'

> I wish only to propose for now a musical work in which this division into homogeneous movements would be abandoned in favour of a non-homogeneous distribution of developments. . . . a concept of discontinuous time made up of structures which interlock instead of remaining in airtight compartments. . . . Let us try to think of it as a domain in which, in some sense, one can choose one's own direction. (Boulez 1991c: 19)[8]

Aggregates marked the birth of Boulezian serialism with networks of possibilities which deviate from the traditional opposition of vertical simultaneity and horizontal succession. For him, intervals of a theme become absolute intervals able to pass from the horizontal succession to the vertical aggregate. A year prior, Boulez explained the grounds of serialism in terms of polyphony as counterpart, or what he called 'an unequal polyphony' (Boulez 1986b: 134). The aggregates of sound, that is different sounds, had two relations: (1) to a constant, and (2) to the scale of sonorities. The constant is a stable element whereas the scale of sonorities constantly changes and therefore moves the whole aggregate. Therefore, aggregates of sounds were linked to a constant but movable according to the scale of sonorities. These systems yielded the generation of n series contingent on constantly changing complexes. His series did not adhere to successive calculation, but to the relations between smooth and striated spatio-temporalities. Boulez proposed a formal time striving for more abstract and more extensive elements yielding his dialectical notation system, which he called neumatic and proportional. The first marked a regression from symbolic notation, smooth (*lisse*) or amorphous time; the second, the proportional, represented a pulsating system, or striated time. However dialectical, the two systems symbiotically interact as Boulez regarded these 'two categories as capable of reciprocal interaction' (Boulez 1986c: 87).[9] Morphing potential interactions of dynamic couplings, he offered the diagonal, or the *sound-figure*: an in-between formation predicated on the contingent relations between the smooth and the striated (Boulez 1991d: 117).[10]

For Boulez, who did not separate material from creation, the diagonal was produced between two poles of continuity. Each one was a series: the neumatic and proportional each held a different temporality, a different rhythm, and the diagonal produced a third dimension of time. Musical time is therefore simultaneously the time generated from an initial cell, that is a sound-aggregate, that elapses and proliferates while perpetually traversing the striated pulse and smooth heterologies.[11] It has been shown that Deleuze and Gauttari build upon these Boulezian categories most clearly in the closing chapter of *A Thousand Plateaus*, '1440: The Smooth and the Striated', to develop the concept of occupying without counting. This productive activity is opposed to regulated space-time where one counts in order to occupy (Bogue 2003: 34, 38; Sauvagnargues 2015: 93). The diagonal already appears in the third synthesis of time as a differential fault line of aesthetic creation disturbing, dispersing and uniting the sedimentation of the mind:

in depth the proximity and simmering of the third synthesis make themselves
felt, announcing the universal 'ungrounding'. Depth is like the famous geological line from NE to SW, the line which comes diagonally from the heart of things
and distributes volcanoes: it unites a bubbling sensibility and a thought which
'rumbles in its crater'. . . . depth . . . remains buried, like the sublime principle of
the *differend* which creates them. (Deleuze 1994: 230, original emphasis)

Deleuze's diagonal reverberates with the principle of the differend, imbued with a
crowded interval contingent upon the virtual and the actual. 'Limitation and opposition', he wrote in *Difference and Repetition*, 'are first- and second-dimension
surface effects, whereas the living depths, the diagonal, is populated by differences without negation' (1994: 266–7). He refers to the intensive difference of
sensibility, alluding to the deeply hidden principle of the Kantian transcendental
operation. Nevertheless, Deleuze does not follow Kant's delimited faculties in
their unified harmony, but transposes their juridical synthetic activity toward
the dispersion of the disjointed faculties. If for Kant the possibility of empirical
cognition is contingent upon the potential of the synthetic unity of the faculties,
Deleuze concentrates on the Kantian aesthetic experience to transpose synthesis
to 'a serial connection between the faculties and an order in that series. . . .
[That is] a properly paradoxical operation, . . . a *discordant harmony*, since each
communicates to the other only the violence which confronts it with its own
difference and its divergence from the others' (1994: 145–6, original emphasis).
This will be the operation of the sublime and the disjointed faculties and it will
be discussed again in relation to *disjunctive synthesis* of the heterogeneous series,
where disjunction means both pure difference and transformation of the structure
and genesis of sense (Deleuze 1990: 67–9, 229).

Sonorous Aesthetic

Whereas Deleuze's early understanding of cognitive experience and Boulez's
musical creation developed separately, the proposition of the sonorous is regarded
by both as a relative formal virtuality. Or perhaps we should follow the opposite
direction, suggesting first that the musical serialism from the 1950s marked empirical explorations of possible serial structuring. In Boulez's *Alea* (1957) and *Form*
(1960), we find the paradox of individuation in a serial potential contingent on
the cyclic motion of self-renewing that resists, even contradicts, its own identity:

> First, as regards the structure of the work, the rejection of a pre-established
> structure, the legitimate wish to construct a kind of labyrinth with a number
> of paths; on the other hand, the desire to create a self-renewing kind of mobile
> complexity. . . . an evolving form which rebels against its own repetition: in
> short, a relative formal virtuality. (1991a: 29)

> The universe of serial thought being essentially a *relative* universe, there can
> be no question of fixed, non-relative forms. We have seen that the generation

of networks of possibilities, which are the raw material for *l'opérateur* – to use a significant term of Mallarmé's – has from the outset tended increasingly to produce a material that is constantly evolving. (1986a: 90)

In *The Logic of Sense*, Deleuze develops these trajectories to replace the *a priori* time of the transcendental subject with the virtual event belonging to the generative time of Aion:

> It is this new world of incorporeal effects or surface effects . . . which draws the sounds from their simple state of corporeal actions and passions. It is this new world which distinguishes language, prevents it from being confused with the sound-effects of bodies, and abstracts it from their oral-anal determinations . . . Sense and event are the same thing – except that now sense is related to propositions. It is related to propositions as what is expressible or expressed by them, which is entirely different from what they signify, manifest, or denote. It is also entirely different from their sonorous qualities, even though the independence of sonorous qualities from things and bodies may be exclusively guaranteed by the entire organization of the sense-event. (1990: 166–7)

For Deleuze, sonorous qualities are characterised by a double nature. On the one hand, their potential effect is detached from signification. On the other, as such, their sonorous qualities maintain their relational autonomy. In his 1986 essay dedicated to Boulez and Proust, Deleuze articulated the connections between sonorous materiality and the sensibility of time, alluding to the relation between the musical composer and the philosopher: 'It is by developing functions of temporalization that are exerted on sonorous material that the musician captures and renders sensible the forces of time' (1998: 73). The following sentence connects the two, that is, the function of sonorous material and sensible forces, to produce a third time. He phrases his thought by inversion of the previous sentence: 'The forces of time and the functions of temporalization unite to constitute the Aspects of *implicated time*. In Boulez as in Proust, these aspects are multiple, and cannot simply be reduced to the opposition "lost-regained"' (ibid., original emphasis). Implicated time here refers to the living present occupying time. Metric multiplicities, directional spaces and musical productions correspond to sonorous, non-metric dimensional temporalities (Deleuze and Guattari 1987: 477). To explain the nature of this correspondence, Deleuze turns to Boulez's *sound-figure* and the condition of the non-metric which are contingent, he asserts, on interruption and proximity. Interruption carries more than one function: it allows the heterogeneous system to keep its discrete, and therefore multiple, nature; it functions in blocking pre-given streams of 'regulated' instruments/ organs; and finally it dictates new polyphonies by the nature and contingency of blockage. For Deleuze, Boulez's *sound-figure* exhibits the different formations of the cut, the diagonal, the sound-block and the time bubbles. In *Anti-Oedipus* we find the same concept: 'Far from being the opposite of continuity, the break or interruption conditions this continuity' (Deleuze and Guattari 1983: 36). And in the opening sentences of his 1986 text on Boulez, Proust and time, Deleuze (1998: 70) remarks that 'the same gesture constructs the continuity of the literary text and the musical text, and makes the cuts pass between them'. Thus, it is the cut, the interrupting machine, that makes sense. It collapses the pyramid into labyrinths, intermezzos devoid of *telos*.

Sonorous-Blocks

It is therefore not surprising that during 1963, the year Deleuze published his work on Kant, Boulez published *Penser la musique aujourd'hui*, where he proposed a sonic model for an immediate, non-representational immanent sound plane (Boulez 1963: 35–6; Nesbitt 2004: 65). In *Possibly. . .* Boulez defines the sound-block as a sound-complex, a rhythmic cell or a parent-cell of serial encoding: 'I think of them rather as aggregates of frequencies' (1991d: 128). Describing the nature of his techniques of serial transformations, this cell is a generative force. It is empty of harmonic function and has the potential of transposing (multiplying) aggregated networks through regular and irregular augmentation, irrational alteration, silence substitution, syncopation, self-reproduction, decomposition, and replacement of a pivot-note or symmetrical note. When the sound-block acts like a force-block cutting through the striated and the indeterminable of the smooth, it is detached from its origin and is called a 'time bubble'. Deleuze differentiates the sound-bubble from the sound-block since it does not divide by numbers but distributes the elements in the bubble in dispersion, relatively similar to the third synthesis of time. In the later writing of *A Thousand Plateaus* Deleuze and Guattari describe the unequal distribution of Boulez's smooth time as a series of transcoding *sound-blocks* 'that no longer has a point of origin' (Deleuze and Guattari 1987: 296), 'which is always given along with that to which it gives rise' (ibid. 267). The sound-bubble is pure becoming, an intermezzo (milieu), and a block of sound that passes amid (*au milieu des*) sounds and propels itself by its own non-localisable middle. It prevents, yet predicates, and permeates organization (ibid. 297).[12] The polyrhythmical pulsations of such sonorous intervals transcode formations amidst multiple series. 'There is rhythm', write Deleuze and Guattari, 'whenever there is a transcoded passage from one milieu to another, a communication of milieus, coordination between heterogeneous space-times' (ibid. 313). Thus, rhythm may be considered as transgression, as effacement, and as chaotic formation.

Serial Transduction

The potentials of serial processes and techniques offered by Boulez were actualised by other composers and artists passing transnationally. They injected a new creative vitalism by way of disrupting the making of music and art. By 1960, Boulez's ideas were widespread, especially after his lecture series at Darmstadt, and they were soon to be imported to the American West Coast by Boulez's colleague and friend Luciano Berio.[13] The Italian-born composer engaged in serialisation of discrete dynamic succession from 1952 and together with Bruno Maderna co-founded the Studio di Fonologia Musicale in Milan in 1955. Fonologia connected serialism with phonetic and acousmatic sound. During the late 1950s, alongside Boulez, Stockhausen and Nono, he developed the system of smooth shifting between fixed points and dynamic continuum.[14] In 1962 Darius Milhaud invited Berio to teach at Mills College, California, where he was to teach irregularly up to 1967. His work with voice, recording and experimental electroacoustics soon attracted Steve Reich to enrol to Mills College for his graduate studies. Although Reich announced that from Berio he learned what not to do, he developed his 'gradual processes' from repetition of isolated incidental materials and phase shifts (Cole 2012: 318). Departing from the concept of series, his writings deliberate a shift into indeterminate real-time processes. From 1968, *Pendulum Music* is a ten-minute piece where '2, 3, 4, or more microphones are suspended from the ceiling by their cables ... free to swing with a pendular motion. Each microphone's cable is plugged into an amplifier which is connected to a speaker. Each microphone hangs a few inches directly above or next to its speaker' (Reich 2002: 32, example 1.5: reproduced handwritten score for *Pendulum Music*). When it was performed at the *Anti-Illusion: Procedures/ Materials* exhibition at the Whitney Museum in 1969, Reich collaborated with artists Richard Serra, Michael Snow, James Tenney and Bruce Nauman to release the microphones, that is, to initiate a first push. Reich described this musical theatre as 'audible sculpture' scrutinising the variable and discontinuous temporal dimensions of the physical generative forces stipulated by the movement of the microphones, amplifying their presence through the sonic effect of swing, gravity and proximity with the speakers. Each cabled speaker carries out its own distribution in serial repetition; the repeater repeats and is repeated every time in different limitation. Reich's performance of discordant processes sought to free them from the first conditional sway by disjointed movements. The question raised here, and also in Deleuze, is whether such release is possible.

However problematic, Reich did succeed in posing the question of multiplicity generated within serial processes of moving bodies and perception. The dialogue between sound and image was central to the work of several of his contemporaries including Nauman. In 1968 Nauman completed his *Study for First Poem Piece*, which was sold that year and immediately fabricated by the Belgian collectors Martin and Mia Visser. The work comprised a 500-pound, two-centimetre-thick steel plate laid on the floor and featuring the incised words aggregated in columns that read from left to right: 'YOU', 'MAY', 'NOT', 'WANT', 'TO', 'BE', and, in the last column, both 'HERE' and 'HEAR'. To remind us of the Greek aesthetic proportions, the seven words were engraved and repeated at the intersections of eighteen horizontal and eight vertical lines of a grid. Some of the words were emphasised while others were rubbed out, leaving only traces or blanked intervals. Each horizontal line is at once a self-ruling propositional process, that is, a premise, a postulation, a plan, an image and a potential, and a semiotic sentence posed in relation to its others. As a proposition, its proper structure featured in the first full sentence has two sides comprising three words on each, differentiated in the middle by the verb 'want' (You May Not | Want | To Be Here). And yet Nauman dislocates the affirmation of difference by will. He shifts the cuts back and forth to create variations: 'You May Not Want To Be Here' / 'You Want To Be' / 'You May Not Want To Be' / 'You May Not Want To Hear', etc. (Simon et al. 1994: 222). It is these shifting intervals that distort stable centres and in turn propel indeterminate processes of individuation.

Through the interplay of words 'here', marking place, and 'hear', activating sonic perception through vision, Nauman marks the move from *a priori* space, *here*, to making space in the sense of a sonorous activity, *hearing*. The word 'hear' replaces 'here' at the lower portion of the compositions. Being here, being in the world, in the multiplicity of subjective perception requires the transformation of attention from the mute grounds of ocular unconscious to the sonorous body. Multiplicity is predicated on sonic hearing, on the multiple pulsations of the repeated rows, on the distribution of pulse touching the subjective voice reading in silence, skipping and connecting rhythmic patterns with the eyes. The assembling eyes choosing routes on the repetitive plane (repeating words, repeating the grid's squares), surfing across language, unhinge the grip of the underlying grid. These trains of thought heed chance operations; however, they are tuned in to muteness, to eyesight alone. They forget hearing – can you hear the movement?

The nominal 'here', marking space, marking place, is replaced by active hearing. 'Here' appears three times in the first three rows, then is syncopated for seven, and reappears as 'hear' eight times, providing a visual representation of the transformation taking place within the geometric division. This is no mere chance, or is it? It's a mode of operation rooted in the musical matrices of Arnold Schoenberg and Boulez. In 1908 Schoenberg commenced developing atonal music. By 1923 he had fully developed the twelve-tone system of pitch organisation, in which all unique pitches are arranged in ordered rows, very similar to Nauman's sentences. When considered visually, the twelve-tone rows are placed one after another on gridded surfaces, providing the ground for particular inversions, retrogrades and transpositions (Forte 1973: ix). The matrices also determine whether the set inverts itself, that is, folds back to the same pitches of the original set, creating shifts in repetition. Nauman had a particular interest in Schoenberg's atonal technique during his undergraduate studies at the University of Wisconsin (Morgan 2002: 101). He does not hold to the twelve-tone chart; however, he does adapt the gridded system, as well as Schoenberg's atonal composition methods.

As a mathematician and a student of music theory, Nauman's disciplinary practice became an interplay with formal systems that lends to the slippage of different topographies into one another. In the genealogy of Schoenberg's systematically arranged atonal matrices we find Boulez's structures. For Boulez, Schoenberg's matrices created templates for material seriality, which he further developed through detached rhythms from the horizontal and vertical planes. Serial technique, explained Boulez, is rooted in Schoenberg Op. 23, where intervals of a theme become absolute intervals, that is to say, detached, released from rhythm, 'able to pass from the horizontal succession to the vertical aggregate' (1991d: 113). While Webern, according to Boulez, abolished the horizontal-vertical opposition, the second Viennese School in general did not relate rhythm to serial technique. They mark a 'destructive' generation, which brought tonality and regular metre to an end. It was Stravinsky who developed rhythm on the entirely new structural elements of dissymmetry, independence and development of rhythmic cells, but remained trapped in the law of equilibrium, thus staying within a dialectical system. Boulez's task was 'to link rhythmic to serial structures through a common organization . . . and then to expand this morphology . . . into serial encoding' (ibid. 115). For this aim, Boulez used Schoenberg's matrices, which, as discussed earlier, he perceived as networks of possibilities. The under-lying horizontality of these permutation tables generates irrational rhythms that, in turn, introduce untampered sound spaces (ibid. 117). Boulez explained that the tables represent transpositions as replacements, and they generate multiple series within a given frequency. The innovative move marked by Boulez makes seriality an in-between movement. It is the play of mobile and immobile topographies in which repetition expressed in series is contingent on interference. At this crucial junction, Boulez exposes a *modus operandi* which will arise later in Nauman. Boulez wrote: 'There are many kinds of interference to be set up between the series itself and the register, on the basis that either of these two elements can be mobile or immobile in relation to the other' (ibid. 119–20).

The instability arising between mobile and immobile sets is seen in Nauman's body and on the geometrical ground, the divided ground, and between seeing and hearing. Nauman's turn to the sonorous, to the sounding body permeating confined structures, marks a vital move into the minimalist foundations at its peak by the mid-1960s. If the geometrical surface pattern haunting the optical unconscious, and even the modern unconscious, is epitomised in the concrete geometrical underpinning of Carl Andre, Sol Lewitt, Dan Flavin, Eva Hesse and others, Nauman fosters presentness by introducing the sonorous body into the geometrical surface. Nauman's movements above the patterned surfaces and in the topographies governed by optical illusion have a direct relation to musical composition innovations rooted in Schoenberg's atonal charts fathering Boulez scores. Played out within hexagrams, Boulez's serial compositions derived from diagonal movements performed within the grid: a generative block that forgets *ground* while *becoming* in time.

Notes

*   I thank Radek Przedpełski and Steve Wilmer for their illuminating responses and generous comments. This research was supported by The Israel Science Foundation (Grant No. 1730/18).

1.   At present there seems to be a dispute amidst Deleuzian scholars regarding the tight relations between the philosophical concepts and musical techniques. On the one hand, Brian Hulse and Edward Campbell noted that it is not possible to think of iden-tity in musical becoming (Hulse 2016: 282; Campbell 2015: 147); on the other, we find a rich discourse encompassing major and minor Deleuzian concepts of becoming in regard to music and sound in general and Boulez's work in particular (Stoïanova 1974, 1978; Murphy 1998; Bogue 2003; Buchanan and Swiboda 2004; Nesbitt 2004,

2010; Bidima 2004, 2010; Scherzinger 2008, 2010; Hasty 2010; Campbell 2013). Boulez best described his intellectual friendship with Deleuze as a point of departure for philosophical reflections. In a conversation with Pierre-Michel Menger, Boulez described their relationship as follows: 'I myself am not educated in philosophy, but I have forced myself to reflect on compositional practice, and I have tried to arrive at a formulation of my own ideas that is general enough to be accessible to others . . . in this way my reflections could serve as a point of departure for a philosophical reflection' (Murphy 1998: 69). A year after Deleuze's death, he wrote of the 1978 symposia at IRCAM: 'In a brilliant presentation he showed the acute perspicacious manner in which he grasped the problems of musical composition and perception' (ibid.).

2. Deleuze cites Shakespeare's *Hamlet* (1609) and Rimbaud's *Letter to George Izambard* (1871). On the temporality of the split in Rimbaud see Voss 2013: 195–6, 213.

3. When examining the relations between mathematical concepts and pure intuition, Simon Duffy notes that the faculties are aptly associated with a temporal schema, since time as a form of inner intuition is the form of every sensible intuition whatsoever. Here, time retreats from the modes of succession, permanence and simultaneity to an immutable manner which governs the temporal determination of the subject's undetermined existence (Duffy 2013: 65).

4. I refer here to Williams's translation of Deleuze's description of the self split by *une fêlure* as 'fault line' (Deleuze qtd in Williams 2011: 82; the original passage in Deleuze 1968: 117). Paul Patton translates the French wording as 'fracture' (Deleuze 1994: 86).

5. Voss stresses how the empirical self experiences the virtual effects of thought as a temporal form of interiority (2013: 196).

6. 'In dogmatic rationalism the theory of knowledge was founded on the idea of a correspondence between subject and object, of an accord between the order of ideas and the order of things. This accord had two aspects: in itself it implied a finality; and it demanded a theological principle as source and guarantee of this harmony, this finality' (Deleuze 1984: 13).

7. Letter to Stockhausen (no. 23; c. 26 April 1953), Paul Sacher Stiftung, Sammlung Karlheinz Stockhausen.

8. In 'Alea', Boulez will write: 'To offset such compositional renunciation, one must have recourse to a new concept of development which would be essentially discontinuous . . . hence the need for "formants" of a work, and for that "phrasing" which is so indispensable to the relating of heterogeneous structures' (1991a: 33).

9. Boulez developed these ideas into a lecture series given in 1960 at Darmstadt. The series is transcribed in *Penser la musique aujourd'hui*. However, the lecture 'Time, Notation and Coding' (Boulez 1986c) was not included in the publication.

10. Mary Roriche expands on the origin of the serial diagonal in radical structuring and morphological potential by Webern and its influence on Foucault's and Deleuze's late writings (2006: 300–8).

11. On transitions and time-flotation that Boulez detects in Wagner, Debussy and Varese, see Nattiez 1986; Feneyrou 2015.

12. Deleuze repeats the idea of interference as a generating device: 'If it is true that the cut [*coupure*] is not the opposite of continuity, if the continuous is defined by the cut, one could say that the same gesture constructs the continuity of the literary text and the musical text, and makes the cuts run between them' (1998: 70). The two systems show a relationship to Edmund Husserl's phenomenological critique of the pre-given 'pure idealities' of science – adequate to pure geometry, pure mathematics and spa-

tio-temporal shapes – and the practical application of sense-experience. 'So familiar to us is the shift between a-priori theory and empirical inquiry in everyday life', writes Husserl, 'that we usually tend not to separate the space and the spatial shapes . . . of experienced actuality, as if they were one and the same' (1970: 24).

13. The Darmstadt lecture series was transcribed in *Penser la musique aujourd'hui* (1963).

14. By 1977 he was co-directing IRCAM together with Boulez, advancing electroacoustic compositions with voice (Born 1995: 103, 172). In an undated letter, Deleuze wrote, 'Dear Berio . . . You are perhaps the only musician who has found a means to maintain joy' (Quaglia 2010: 228).

References

Bidima, Jean-Godefroy (2004), 'Music and the Socio-Historical Real: Rhythm, Series and Critique in Deleuze and O. Revault d'Allonnes', in Ian Buchanan and Marcel Swiboda (eds), *Deleuze and Music*, Edinburgh: Edinburgh University Press, pp. 176–95.

Bidima, Jean-Godefroy (2010), 'Intensity, Music, and Heterogenesis in Deleuze', in Brian Hulse and Nick Nesbitt (eds), *Sounding the Virtual: Gilles Deleuze and the Theory and Philosophy of Music*, Farnham: Ashgate, pp. 145–58.

Bogue, Ronald (2003), *Deleuze on Music, Painting and the Arts*, New York and London: Routledge.

Bogue, Ronald (2004), 'Violence in Three Shades of Metal: Death, Doom and Black', in Ian Buchanan and Marcel Swiboda (eds), *Deleuze and Music*, Edinburgh: Edinburgh University Press, pp. 95–117.

Born, Georgina (1995), *Rationalizing Culture: IRCAM, Boulez, and the Institutionalization of the Musical Avant-Garde*, Berkeley: University of California Press.

Boulez, Pierre (1963), *Penser la musique aujourd'hui* [To Think Music Today], Paris and Geneva: Éditions Gonthier/Denoël.

Boulez, Pierre [1960] (1986a), 'Form', in *Orientations: Collected Writings*, ed. Jean-Jacques Nattiez, trans. Martin Cooper, Cambridge, MA: Harvard University Press, pp. 90–6.

Boulez, Pierre [1951] (1986b), 'The System Exposed', in *Orientations: Collected Writings*, ed. Jean-Jacques Nattiez, trans. Martin Cooper, Cambridge, MA: Harvard University Press, pp. 129–42.

Boulez, Pierre [1960] (1986c), 'Time, Notation, and Coding', in *Orientations: Collected Writings*, ed. Jean-Jacques Nattiez, trans. Martin Cooper, Cambridge, MA: Harvard University Press, pp. 84–9.

Boulez, Pierre [1957] (1991a), 'Alea', in *Stocktakings from an Apprenticeship*, ed. Paule Thévenin, trans. Stephen Walsh, Oxford: Clarendon Press, pp. 26–38.

Boulez, Pierre [1958] (1991b), 'Chord', in *Stocktakings from an Apprenticeship*, ed. Paule Thévenin, trans. Stephen Walsh, Oxford: Clarendon Press, p. 223.

Boulez, Pierre [1954] (1991c), 'Current Investigations', in *Stocktakings from an Apprenticeship*, ed. Paule Thévenin, trans. Stephen Walsh, Oxford: Clarendon Press, pp. 15–19.

Boulez, Pierre [1952] (1991d), 'Possibly. . .', in *Stocktakings from an Apprenticeship*, ed. Paule Thévenin, trans. Stephen Walsh, Oxford: Clarendon Press, pp. 111–40.

Buchanan, Ian and Marcel Swiboda (eds) (2004), *Deleuze and Music*, Edinburgh: Edinburgh University Press.

Campbell, Edward (2013), *Music after Deleuze*, London: Bloomsbury.

Campbell, Edward (2015), 'Musicology after Deleuze: Response to Brian Hulse's Review of *Music after Deleuze* – All Music is "Deleuzian"', *Deleuze and Guattari Studies*, 9(1): 145–52.

Cole, Ross (2012), '"Fun, Yes, but Music?" Steve Reich and the San Francisco Bay Area's Cultural Nexus, 1962–1965', *Journal of the Society for American Music*, 6(3): 315–48.

Criton, Pascal and Jean-March Chouvel (eds) (2015), *Gilles Deleuze: la pensée-musique*, Paris: Centre de documentation de la musique contemporaine.

Deleuze, Gilles (1968), *Différence et répétition*, Paris: Presses Universitaires de France.

Deleuze, Gilles [1963] (1984), *Kant's Critical Philosophy: The Doctrine of the Faculties*, trans. Hugh Tomlinson and Barbara Habberjam, London: Athlone Press.

Deleuze, Gilles [1969] (1990), *The Logic of Sense*, trans. Mark Lester and Charles Stivale, New York: Columbia University Press.

Deleuze, Gilles [1968] (1994), *Difference and Repetition*, trans. Paul Patton, New York: Columbia University Press.

Deleuze, Gilles [1984] (1997), 'On Four Poetic Formulas that Might Summarize the Kantian Philosophy', in *Essays: Critical and Clinical*, trans. Daniel W. Smith and Michael A. Greco, Minneapolis: University of Minnesota Press, pp. 27–35.

Deleuze, Gilles [1986] (1998), 'Boulez, Proust and Time: "Occupying Without Counting"', trans. Timothy S. Murphy, *Angelaki: Journal of the Theoretical Humanities*, 3(2): 69–74.

Deleuze, Gilles [1981] (2002), *Francis Bacon: The Logic of Sensation*, trans. Daniel W. Smith, Minneapolis: University of Minnesota Press.

Deleuze, Gilles and Félix Guattari [1972] (1983), *Anti-Oedipus: Capitalism and Schizophrenia*, trans. Robert Hurley, Mark Seem and Helen R. Lane, Minneapolis: University of Minnesota Press.

Deleuze, Gilles and Félix Guattari [1980] (1987), *A Thousand Plateaus: Capitalism and Schizophrenia*, trans. Brian Massumi, Minneapolis: University of Minnesota Press.

Deleuze, Gilles and Félix Guattari [1991] (1994), *What Is Philosophy?*, trans. Hugh Tomlinson and Graham Burchell, New York: Columbia University Press.

Duffy, Simon B. (2013), *Deleuze and the History of Mathematics: In Defense of the 'New'*, New York: Bloomsbury Publishing.

Feneyrou, Laurent (2015), 'Séries en série: Jean Barraqué, à l'aune de Gilles Deleuze et de Michel Foucault (et Pierre Boulez non loin de là)', in Pascal Criton and Jean-March Chouvel (eds), *Gilles Deleuze: la pensée-musique*, Paris: Centre de documentation de la musique contemporaine, pp. 15–28.

Forte, Allen (1973), *The Structure of Atonal Music*, New Haven and London: Yale University Press.

Hasty, Christopher (2010), 'The Image of Thought and Ideas of Music', in Brian Hulse and Nick Nesbitt (eds), *Sounding the Virtual: Gilles Deleuze and the Theory and Philosophy of Music*, Farnham: Ashgate, pp. 1–22.

Hemmet, Drew (2004), 'Affect and Individuation in Popular Electronic Music', in Ian Buchanan and Marcel Swiboda (eds), *Deleuze and Music*, Edinburgh: Edinburgh University Press, pp. 76–94.

Hulse, Brian (2016), 'Off the Grid: Hasty and Musical Novelty in Smooth Time', in Suzannah Clark and Alexander Rehding (eds), *Music in Time: Phenomenology, Perception, Performance*, Cambridge, MA: Harvard University Press, pp. 281–92.

Hulse, Brian and Nick Nesbitt (eds) (2010), *Sounding the Virtual: Gilles Deleuze and the Theory and Philosophy of Music*, Farnham: Ashgate.

Husserl, Edmund [1936] (1970), *The Crisis of European Sciences and Transcendental Phenomenology: An Introduction to Phenomenological Philosophy*, trans. David Carr, Evanston: Northwestern University Press.

Jones, Caroline A. (2005), *Eyesight Alone: Clement Greenberg's Modernism and the Bureaucratization of the Senses*, Chicago: University of Chicago Press.

Morgan, Robert C. (2002), *Bruce Nauman*, Baltimore: Johns Hopkins University Press.

Murphy, Timothy S. (1998), 'Boulez/Deleuze: A Relay of Music and Philosophy', in Gilles Deleuze, 'Boulez, Proust and Time: "Occupying Without Counting"', trans. Timothy S. Murphy, *Angelaki: Journal of the Theoretical Humanities*, 3(2): 69–74.

Nattiez, Jean-Jacques (1986), 'On Reading Boulez', in Pierre Boulez, *Orientations: Collected Writings*, ed. Jean-Jacques Nattiez, trans. Martin Cooper, Cambridge, MA: Harvard University Press, pp. 11–30.

Nesbitt, Nick (2004), 'Deleuze, Adorno, and the Composition of Musical Multiplicity', in Ian Buchanan and Marcel Swiboda (eds), *Deleuze and Music*, Edinburgh: Edinburgh University Press, pp. 54–75.

Nesbitt, Nick (2010), 'Critique and Clinique: From Sounding Bodies to the Musical Event', in Brian Hulse and Nick Nesbitt (eds), *Sounding the Virtual: Gilles Deleuze and the Theory and Philosophy of Music*, Farnham: Ashgate, pp. 159–79.

Piencikowski, Robert (2016), '"A score neither begins nor ends; at most it pretends to": Fragmentary Reflections on the Boulezian "*non finito*"', in Edward Campbell and Peter O'Hagan (eds), *Pierre Boulez Studies*, Cambridge: Cambridge University Press, pp. 93–107.

Quaglia, Bruce (2010), 'Transformation and Becoming Other in the Music and Poetics of Luciano Berio', in Brian Hulse and Nick Nesbitt (eds), *Sounding the Virtual: Gilles Deleuze and the Theory and Philosophy of Music*, Farnham: Ashgate, pp. 227–48.

Reich, Steve (2002), *Steve Reich: Writings on Music, 1965–2000*, Oxford: Oxford University Press.

Roffe, Jon (2012), *Badiou's Deleuze*, Montreal and Kingston: McGill-Queen's University Press.

Roriche, Mary (2006), 'Passing through the Screen: Pierre Boulez and Michel Foucault', *Journal of Literary Studies*, 22(3–4): 294–321.

Sauvagnargues, Anne (2015), 'Occuper sans compter', in Pascal Criton and Jean-March Chouvel (eds), *Gilles Deleuze: la pensée-musique*, Paris: Centre de documentation de la musique contemporaine, pp. 93–100.

Scherzinger, Martin (2008), 'Musical Modernism in the Thought of "Mille Plateaux", and its Twofold Politics', *Perspectives on New Music*, 46(2): 130–58.

Scherzinger, Martin (2010), '*Enforced* Deterritorialization, or the Trouble with Musical Politics', in Brian Hulse and Nick Nesbitt (eds), *Sounding the Virtual: Gilles Deleuze and the Theory and Philosophy of Music*, Farnham: Ashgate, pp. 103–28.

Simon, Joan, Janet Jenkins and Toby Kemps (eds) (1994), *Bruce Nauman: Exhibition Catalogue and Catalogue Raisonné*, Minneapolis: Walker Art Center.

Smith, Daniel W. (2012), 'On the Nature of Concepts', *Parallax*, 18(1): 62–73.

Stoïanova, Ivanka (1974), 'La troisième sonate de Boulez et le projet mallarméen du Livre', *Musique en jeu*, no. 16, Paris: Seuil, pp. 9–28.

Stoïanova, Ivanka (1978), *Geste – texte – musique*, Paris: Union Générale d'Éditions.

Strauss, Erwin (1963), *The Primary World of Senses: A Vindication of Sensory Experience*, trans. Jacob Needleman, New York: Free Press Glencoe.

Voss, Daniela (2013), 'Deleuze's Third Synthesis of Time', *Deleuze Studies*, 7(2): 194–216.

Williams, James (2003), *Gilles Deleuze's Difference and Repetition: A Critical Introduction and Guide*, Edinburgh: Edinburgh University Press.

Williams, James (2011), *Gilles Deleuze's Philosophy of Time: A Critical Introduction and Guide*, Edinburgh: Edinburgh University Press.

Witkin, Robert W. (1998), *Adorno on Music*, London and New York: Routledge.

12

Talisman-Images: From the Cosmos to Your Body

Laura U. Marks

This chapter identifies a kind of image, the *talisman-image*, that intervenes in the order of the cosmos in order to effect specific changes here on Earth. In the hands of a competent magician, talismans compel the universe to bend according to forces of *contact, correspondence, sympathy* and *passion*. As the thirteenth-century Latin *Picatrix*, a translation of the tenth-century Arabic magic text the *Ghayāt al-ḥakīm* (Goal of the Sage), puts it, 'The talisman is nothing other than the force of celestial bodies that influence bodies' (*Picatrix* 2003: 120). As I will argue, talismanic practice gives us a deep history of the theory of affect as a culti-vated contact and mimetic sympathy among human practitioners, the things they wish to affect, heavenly bodies, and a series of linked intermediaries. The *Picatrix* defines magic as the exertion of action at a distance by means of an intervening image (Bakhouche et al. 2003: 19): the talisman is one such image.

Another definition of magic from medieval times is 'the awareness of the interrelatedness of all things in the world by means of a simple but refined sense perception' (Glucklich 1997: 12). Muslim and medieval European magi-cians cultivated this awareness of the inter-relatedness of things by refining their perceptions and making themselves microcosms of the universe: creating, as I will explain, a ceremonial body. They fashioned talismans to also represent the cosmos in miniature. Deploying a model of the universe as a manifold, I will ask whether, in our seemingly disenchanted times, it is still possible to re-fold the universe, grasping the points of disparate histories and places and drawing them together: to do modern magic.

Talismans Now

A media archaeology[1] of digital apps will find their origins in small devices, fash-ioned of particular stones and metals at particular calendrical moments, inscribed with mysterious diagrams, prayed over using powerful invocations, and worn or buried to begin their work. Talismans constitute the deep source of contemporary media technologies that exert action at a distance. Penelope Gouk draws attention to the parallel between these Renaissance technologies for action at a distance and technologies of our time for rapid secret communication and remote surveillance

(1997: 230). Talismans are the precedent for technologies that rely on the inter-connectedness of seemingly separate things, and for images that don't represent but carry out operations. They deepen the genealogy of 'devices of wonder', at once visible and legible, that Barbara Maria Stafford and Frances Terpak (2001) trace from small-screen media to cabinets of curiosities. You could value the contemporary technology over the early one and say not that apps are modern tal-ismans, but that talismans were medieval apps. Indeed, our smartphones do some of the things that talismans were supposed to do, like attract a lover or destroy an enemy. However, we will see that talismans pose demanding criteria for efficacy that few media works of our time are able to meet.

Like talismans, digital applications carry out algorithmic operations on the physical world, folding together distant points. Also like talismans, most of them are small, fitting easily into the hand or a pocket. They use their powers to affect things at a distance to send messages instantly, invest your money, protect you from maleficent intruders, and perhaps locate and attack the distant home of your enemy.[2] They use their powers of divination to predict the weather, magically draw music and movies down from the clouds, predict when you will be fertile, and of course read what your stars are doing today. And like talismans, they aim to present the cosmos in miniature.

Magic requires a cosmology. Digital applications and networked media corpo-rations require a cosmos interconnected partly by physical infrastructure, partly by rhetoric. These technologies, developed to serve shareholder capitalism and the military, rely on physical connections between the human-computer interface, wireless networks, remote servers, energy sources and the internet, as well as on the labourers who produce digital devices and mine the rare earths that go into them.[3] They mystify these material connections with an aura of intimacy and serendipity. Given the *Picatrix*'s definition of magic as the exertion of action at a distance by means of an intervening image, our most talisman-like contemporary images are operational images. Operational images 'do not represent an object, but rather are part of an operation', mystifying the human agency involved (Farocki 2004). Examples include images generated by facial-recognition technology and images that smart bombs produce of their targets. While, as we will see, human physicality and intention were crucial to the operation of medieval talismans, the human-computer interface of digital apps is often a rather insulting cover for operational images that only need humans as data.

To compare the cosmoi of contemporary apps and medieval talismans, you can imagine our planet Earth surrounded by spherical or elliptical orbits of influence. High Earth orbit satellites, such as weather and communication satellites, look down upon the globe from about 36,000 kilometres. GPS satellites orbit the planet at an altitude of 20,200 kilometres. Imaging satellites graze Earth's atmosphere, orbiting at no higher than 2,000 kilometres (Riebeek 2009). In short, our contemporary infor-mational and surveillance orbits cling quite close to the planet. In contrast, the most intimate of the medieval heavenly bodies, the moon, orbits the earth at a distance of 384,000 kilometres. The other planets are many magnitudes further away, and the stars unfathomably distant. Yet it was to these heavenly agents that medieval magic confidently appealed. While talismans address the heavens, apps only address what early cosmic scientists called the sublunary sphere – and a very thin slice of it!

In addition, let me point out that digital apps do not work with true causality, but with statistical or quantitative quasi-causes that the designers select for their utility. They do not correspond to cosmic powers but, usually, to corporate or military interests. In contrast, talismans seek to harness the fundamental causal forces of the cosmos.

At this point a reader may be understandably sceptical about the actual powers of talismans. In what follows I will explain how medieval talismans functioned, and what conception of the cosmos made it possible for them to function. Then we will be able to test whether talismans can work now; whether, in our seemingly disenchanted times, it is still possible to re-fold the universe.

A Pliable Cosmos

The manifold cosmos of Leibniz, whose internal causality so fascinated Deleuze, is a closed, densely folded entity with a continuous inside surface and a continuous outside surface. In *The Fold*, Deleuze works to open up Leibniz's cosmos while maintaining the image of the universe as a vast, folded surface. Deleuze relates this concept of the manifold to the mathematical model for chaos within a contained system called the Baker's Transformation: a surface folded multiple times, like dough in the hands of a baker, until points that were adjacent become separated, while points that were far distant now press together, across a fold (Deleuze and Parnet 1996; Stivale 2000–11).[4] Félix Guattari, Deleuze's longtime collaborator, proposes that the cosmos is generated by way of two ontological foldings that generate first matter, then thought (Guattari 1995: 153; see also Goodchild 1996). These contemporary models of cosmoi appear to be chaotic, but folding allows them to maintain a fundamental order of connectivity.

The modern Western concept of the universe as manifold has one of its most important and least recognised origins in Islamic Neoplatonist cosmology, which developed in the Muslim world and spread to the Latin West in the medieval and early modern period. Neoplatonism conceives that all things emanate from God in a series of levels or hypostases, each of which has causal effects on the one below. The concept of emanation allows the cosmos to become multiple while retaining its unity: it is the unfolding of the one into the many. Islamic Neoplatonist texts combine Qur'anic teachings, Greek Neoplatonic cosmology, Aristotelian natural science, and in some cases Indian, Harrānian and other cosmologies in varied combinations, but generally they describe a cosmology of nested spheres (*aflāk*; singular *falak*), each of which is caused by the prior sphere and retains contact with it. At some point the transcendental spheres of (usually) First Cause (*al-Bārī*), Intelligence (*al-'Aql*) and Soul (*al-Nafs*) give way to the physically observable spheres of the heavens, the earth, and elements that compose earthly things. The French translators of the *Picatrix* note that it deploys by turns the hierarchical models of the eighth-century alchemist Jābir ibn Hayyān (see also Pingree 1980), the Ikhwān al-Safā' or Brotherhood of Purity, a tenth-century secret society based in Basra (see Netton 1982; Ikhwān al-Safā' 2011), and Pseudo-Empedocles, without seeking to reconcile them: what was important to the author of the *Picatrix* was that the source was God, and therefore the magic was legitimate (Bakhouche et al. 2003: 17). I wonder if this admixture of disparate sources is what allows Islamic Neoplatonist cosmology to map so directly on to astronomy, so that the divine world comes into contact with the physical world.

Diagramming the Islamic Neoplatonist cosmology involves a series of concentric circles. One can begin with God in the centre, emanating the universe; or one can place our earthly world at the centre in the sublunary (literally, below the moon) sphere, encircled by the celestial sphere, beyond which lies the divine sphere, with a variable number of other spheres in between. In Jābir's terms, the first sphere under the third hypostasis 'is the Supreme Luminous Sphere, namely the one which embraces the world in which we are' (qtd in Haq 1994: 54). For now I ask the reader to note that surface or membrane where the transcendental gives way to the physical, the divine makes contact with the sublunary.

The reader may remark a morphological difference between the Leibnizian and Neoplatonist cosmoi. While the manifold universe of Leibniz that Deleuze studies in *The Fold* consists of a single entity, body on the outside, spirit on the inside, the emanationist universe of the Neoplatonists consists of a series of concentric layers. The concern of these thinkers remains the same: to devise elegant solutions for how the universe can be simultaneously one and many. For the Islamic Neoplatonists, creation by emanation meets the Qur'anic criterion that there be nothing prior to or more powerful than God. The descending levels of the cosmos are caused by God and cannot exist independently of God; causality cascades down from one level to the next. Leibniz ingeniously reduced the number of layers to one, though he too argues for multiple kinds of causality whose final cause is God.

With this Neoplatonist model of a well-organised cosmos established, practices emerged to intervene in its order by *folding it differently*: astrology, alchemy and magic, in particular the making of talismans. The *talisman-image* intervenes in the order of the cosmos by folding it and drawing the folded points into contact with the body.

Talismanic magic in the Islamic Neoplatonist tradition allows the practitioner to manage the cosmos in miniature, folding the powers of planets and stars together with earthly people, places and objects to make things happen. Embodying not only entities distant in place and time but an entire cosmology that explains how they connect, in effect each talisman comes with a cosmological user's manual that not only allows it to intervene in the order of the universe but explains why it does. Talismanic magic builds on the older practice of fetishes, objects that establish a physical contact with some distant person or thing. Fetishes rely on sympathetic magic, the affinities among things that come into contact in the earthly realm. The talisman makers, however, in order to fend off accusations of devilry, insisted that they were doing celestial magic: calling on the influence of the stars and planets, which in turn answered to God's command.

Pictured here (Fig. 12.1) is an image from al-Ṭūsī Salmānī's *'Ajā'ib*

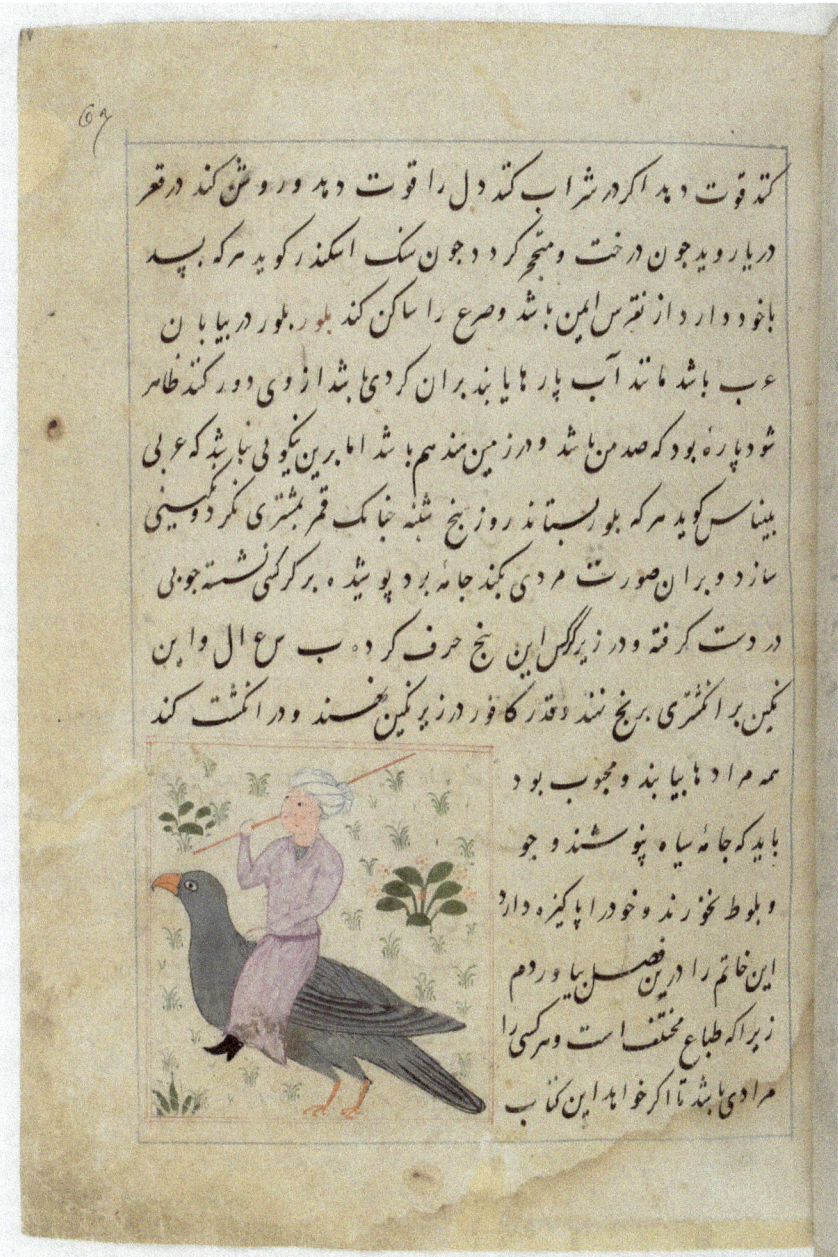

کنه قوت دید اکرد در شراب کند دل راقوت دهد و روشنی کند در قعر

دریا روید جون درخت و منجر کرد د جون سنگ اسکندرکو بید هرکه بسد

باخود دارد از نترس این با شد و صرع را ساکن کند بلوربلور در بیا بان

عرب باشد مانند آب پاره ها یا بند بر ان کرده ای بشد از وی دور کند ظاهر

شود پاره بود که صدمن با شد و در زمین هند هم با شد اما بر این نیکوی با نگاشته که عربی

بیناس کیدهرکه بلورسبتا ند روز نج شبه جناک قمر مشتری کرد و حسینی

سازد و بران صورت مردی کند جامه بربد پوشید و بر کرکسی نشسته جومی

در دست کرفته و در زیرگس این نج حرف کرد سب سع ال واین

نگین برا کنگری برنخ نند دقدر که نور در زیر نگین بنشند و در انگشت کند

مراد ها بیا بند و مجوب بود

باید که جامه بیا و پوشند و جو

و بلوط نخورند و خود را پاکیزه دارد

این خاتم را در این فصل بیا وردم

زیراکه طباع مختلف است و هرکسی را

مرادی با بند تاکر خوا هد این کتاب

Figure 12.1 Man riding a vulture: image to be inscribed on a crystal, from al-Ṭūsī Salmānī, '*Ajā'ib al-makhlūqāt*' [Marvellous discoveries and strange beings], 1388.
Courtesy of Bibliothèque nationale de France.

al-makhlūqāt wa ghāra'ib al-mawjūdāt' (Marvellous discoveries and strange beings, 1388), based on an instruction in the *Ghayāt al-ḥakīm*: a good-looking man in ample garments riding a vulture, to be inscribed on crystal when Jupiter is in the ascendant (*Picatrix* 2003: 145). The one who wears this useful talisman will be loved by officers and judges. This talisman would have been believed to draw down the powers of Jupiter to the hands of a political aspirant through the powers of *contact* between heavenly and earthly bodies; of *operational images*, by which the talisman connects to its planetary prototype; of *correspondence* between Jupiter and its earthly counterparts; of *passion*, which I will define as the suspension between heavenly and earthly realms; and of the *ceremonial body* of the magician. We will explore these below.

Using Deleuze's Leibnizian language, we can say talismans are special monads whose bodies, the folds that connect them to the cosmos, can be played like an instrument by the musician. Because talismans operate from an encrypted location known only to the magician, their perceptions are anamorphic: Baroque 'point of view as the secret of things' (Deleuze 1993: 22).

In fact, talismans in the Islamic Neoplatonist tradition are not just *like* Leibniz's monads, but, I am convinced, constitute one of the inspirations of Leibniz's monadic philosophy. Leibniz visited cabinets of curiosities and collections of wonders in Leipzig, Jena, Altdorf, Strasbourg, Paris, London, Braunschweig, Kassel, Frankfurt, Nuremberg, Florence, Bologna and Rome – this last curated by Jesuit priest Athanasius Kircher – as well as the comprehensive Wunderkammer of Olearius Worm in Gottorp (Bredekamp 2007: 212–13). There he would have seen innumerable objects that beg to be perceived as mini-monads: mechanical globes; astrolabes and other devices that model the heavens in miniature; natural objects that suggest a divine signature, like mandrake roots and agates; crystal balls; and talismans. Many of these objects have Islamic origins.

Leibniz would have found in the cabinets of curiosities exemplars of his monadic philosophy. These collections constitute the windowless upper floor of the monad's house, because each object within them maintains a spiritual connection to the cosmos from the monad's point of view (Deleuze 2003: 27). But the objects in the collections also embodied the monad's lower floor of *physical* connections to the cosmos.

A Bit of History

This vein of research into magic came as a complete surprise to me. For a long time I've been trying to unpack occulted Islamic sources of contemporary Western thought, especially the philosophers that inspired Deleuze, such as Leibniz, Spinoza and John Duns Scotus. I argued that a genealogy of Deleuze's conception of Being as a manifold, in which actual and virtual constitute unfolded and enfolded aspects of an infinite disjunctive unity, finds one of its most important sources in Islamic Neoplatonism. I demonstrated that Deleuze's conception of the univocity of being originated with the major philosopher Avicenna (Ibn Sīnā, c. 980–1037) (Marks 2013). More recently I've demonstrated the generative meeting between Deleuze's thought and that of Persian process philosopher Ṣadr al-Dīn Muhammad al-Shīrāzī (1571–1640) (Marks 2018). This chapter, however, pursues an even more 'minor' aspect of Deleuze's Islamic genealogy. Struck by the similarity between Leibniz's concept of the human as microcosm and that of the Ikhwān's al-Safā', but unable thus far to trace a connection between them in major or official philosophy, I fell into the deep, minor history of magic and the occult and began to learn how their texts and practices travelled from the Arab and Islamic world to the Latin West.

A history of magic always begins in the middle, and this chapter cannot do justice to the complex paths of transmission, synthesis and invention along which magical practices from Mesopotamia and India, Greece and Rome, Syria, Iran, the Nabateans and the Chaldeans travelled before they reached the Arab world in the ninth century. Scholars are working to disentangle these histories. As more details come into focus, the history takes ever more forking paths and becomes ever more minor, until it reaches an unwritable scale of fractal granularity. Therefore I will judiciously gloss.

Termed in Arabic *bāṭiniyya*, the search for inner secrets, the hermetic tradition[5] associated with Islamic Neoplatonism was developed by minorities within Islam or people working on the fringes of religious orthodoxy, including the non-Muslim Sabeans of Harrān, Shi'i Muslims and Sufis. (Sunni Islam rejected the Neoplatonist theory of creation through emanation, as it was incompatible with the indigenous Muslim concept of God (Netton 1982: 43), appeared to threaten the unity of God, and presumed knowledge of God's ways.) All these groups, especially the often-persecuted Shi'a, developed practices of secrecy, concealment and dissimulation to protect their communities and their doctrines. These practices shaped their cosmic knowledge into characteristic forms of secrecy, which I term manners of enfolding and unfolding (Marks 2010). Secret is *sirr* in Arabic, from the verb *sarra*. Ruqayya Yasmine Khan points out that two forms of the verb, *sarra* and *asarra*, connote both concealment and revelation: *asarra* means both 'he kept it secret' and 'he revealed it'. Khan argues this means *sirr* involves a dialectic: 'a secret is not a secret until it is revealed to someone, so secrecy invites revelation, and this revelation, in turn, may entail another concealment' (2000: 241). Secrets create relationships between those who share them, and their forms change, unfold and re-fold differently. Studying secrecy in the Shi'i community around imam Ja'far al-Sādiq (c. 699–765) in the hostile environment of late eighth-century Baghdad, Etan Kohlberg (1995) argues that *taqiyya* or strategic dissimulation involves two modes, prudential and non-prudential: the former protects oneself and one's friends from exposure, the latter protects the listener, for whom the secret knowledge may be unbearable.

But there were those who put secrets in writing, including the aforementioned alchemist Jābir ibn Hayyan and the Ikhwān al-Safā, as well as Maslama al-Qurtubī (d. 964), thought by some to be the author of the *Ghayāt al-ḥakīm* (Melvin-Koushki 2017; Saif 2017). Among other magical sciences, their texts explain how to appeal to the heavenly bodies at astrologically propitious times by fashioning talismans that would have specific effects.

Muslim practitioners of magic cultivated the persuasive theory that astrology works at God's command, and thus doesn't contradict monotheism. It would follow that using talismans to manipulate events is compatible with religious belief in divine causality, because talismans are natural, scientific phenomena and not idolatrous. This argument facilitated the movement of Arabic and Islamic talisman theory to the Latin, Christian West. Festooned with stern injunctions not to divulge their secrets to the unworthy, these texts circulated all across the Muslim world and, from the thirteenth century on, into Europe, where they became the basis of wildly popular 'books of secrets'. To give a few examples: the earliest Arabic book of magic translated into Latin may be the *Kitāb sirr al-khaliqa* (Book of the secrets of creation, 825) by Bālinās (Pseudo-Apollonius), which was translated by Hugo of Santalla in about 1145 as *Emerald Tablet* and attributed to Hermes Trismegistus. Another important text, the ninth-century *Kitāb sirr al-asrār* (Book of the secret of secrets), misattributed to Aristotle, compiled by Yahya ibn Batiq, was translated as *Secretum secretorum* in 1250. Al-Majrītī or al-Qurtubī bundled the chapters on magic from the *Rasa'il Ikhwān al-Safā'* (898) with the *Kitāb sirr al-asrār* and two chapters of Jābir into the *Ghayāt al-ḥakīm*. This work was translated into Castilian for Alfonso X in the thirteenth century and soon thereafter translated into Latin as the *Picatrix*, which was translated into all Romance languages and became a medieval best-seller. Everyone wanted to be a magus.

Within both the Muslim world and Europe, magic travelled by minor routes, considered suspect and disparaged in multiple ways. In the Muslim world magic was deemed suspect for its pagan origins and, by the Sunni majority, for its cultivation by Shiʻi groups. It was deemed suspect by both Islam and the Christian Church as idolatrous or demonic. Furthermore, Arabic texts on magic were not on the Latin Scholastics' curriculum, even if some Scholastics pursued it on the side. Magic was non-scholarly, popular knowledge. William Eamon argues that in bypassing the academy, this knowledge was proletarianised; magic and astrology were useful skills in the competitive world of the courts. The Shiʻi and Sufi concept of *bātiniyya*, the search for esoteric knowledge, resonated: 'The distinction between public knowledge and esoteric counsel was, in reality, the secret of power and advancement for late-medieval intellectuals' (Eamon 1994: 50). Magic also mingled with the suspect sources of women's and folk wisdom (Kieckhefer 1989).

Scholastic attacks on alchemy often used Avicenna's warning to alchemists in the meteorology in *Al-Shifa'* (The Healing, 1027), translated into Latin by Alfred of Sareshal in 1200. '*Sciant artifices*,' Avicenna writes; 'Let the artificers know' that art is inferior to nature and cannot change it. The characteristics of metals that determine their species (*na'u*) can't be known (Newman 1989). Basically, Avicenna is warning the alchemists that, because they don't understand all the variables involved, their data is worthless.

All manner of books of secrets circulated in late medieval and Renaissance Europe containing instructions on alchemy, astrology, mantic arts including geomancy and *'ilm al-kātif* or scapulimancy (divination from the shoulder blades of sheep, practised in many world cultures; Burnett 1996), recipes for medicine, perfumes, incendiary devices and many other useful arts. Each book contained a warning that echoes the Shi'i language of *taqiyya*, such as this in *Secretum secretorum* (based, you recall, on the Ikhwān al-Safā's *Rasa'īl*):

> I am revealing my secrets to you figuratively, speaking with enigmatic examples and signs, because I greatly fear that the present book might fall into the hands of infidels and arrogant powers, whereby they, whom God has deemed undeserving and unworthy, might arrive at that ultimate good and divine mystery. ... Know therefore that whoever betrays these secrets and reveals these mysteries to the unworthy shall not be safe from the misfortune that shall soon befall him. (Qtd in Eamon 1994: 47)

The enticing and flattering language of secrecy surely contributed to the secret books' cachet.

The thirteenth- and fourteenth-century European reception of Arabic texts eagerly applied the immediately useful aspects of magic, alchemy and astrology (which would develop into the sciences of chemistry and astronomy) less often than they evinced interest in their philosophical underpinnings (Eamon 1994; Gouk 1997: 234). An exception, Roger Bacon (c. 1219–92), based his own hermetic philosophy on the *Secretum secretorum*, though when he found out it was not by Aristotle he disavowed it like a hot potato. Only later in the Renaissance did European esoteric thinkers such as Nicolas of Cusa (1401–64), Cornelius Agrippa (1486–1535) and Giambattista della Porta (1535–1615) elaborate a full-blown Neoplatonist cosmology. By this time, the Arabic Muslim sources had already been partially effaced and replaced with more distant heritages in ancient Egypt, ancient Greece and Jewish mysticism.

This chapter focuses on the Islamic connection over better-documented Egyptian, Greek and Kabbalistic sources of the hermetic tradition in order to perform a historiographical unfolding. For, as often happens, the occulted Islamic elements of early modern European intellectual history remain neglected. Here lies my annoyance with Joshua Ramey's thrillingly original *The Hermetic Deleuze* (2012), which argues that certain of Deleuze's concepts derive from the Western hermetic tradition. In sympathy with Ramey's argument, I nevertheless regret that he repeats the Eurocentric error of ignoring the Islamic foundations of European hermeticism, instead jumping from the Greeks to the Renaissance as though eight centuries of civilisation did not occur in between.[6] I deepen the roots Ramey posits to identify some of their origins in Islamic esotericism: cosmology, astrology, alchemy, talismanic science and the arts of secrecy.

Another reason these occult historical connections between the Muslim world and Europe are so difficult to make manifest is a double standard in scholarship that indulges Western histories of the occult while censoring those histories in the Muslim world, in an effort to clean up after Orientalism. As Matthew Melvin-Koushki puts it, 'Reacting to the depredations of European colonialism, Orientalism's wellspring, the well-intentioned scholarly compulsion has been to exorcise Islamicate history and culture of "superstition" and "magic" in an effort to banish Orientalist stereotypes of cultural and scientific stagnation' (2017: 288). Historians of the Muslim world now focus on chemistry and astronomy and play down alchemy and astrology, even though in medieval times these constituted two sides of the same practice.

So let us turn to a media archaeology of the talismanic properties of *contact, operational image, correspondence, passion* and *ceremony*, the means by which magicians can fold the universe.

Magic by Contact: Al-Kindī's Ray Theory

The theory of affect or bodily causality popular in our time has some very deep roots, deeper still than Spinoza (1632–77), to whom Deleuze credits the concept. I'm talking about the theory of ray-based astral causation attributed to Yaqūb ibn Ishāq al-Kindī (801–73).[7]

Al-Kindī, a prolific scholar of mathematics, optics, medicine and cryptography, as well as philosophy, oversaw the lively translation industry at the Bayt al-Hikmeh (House of Wisdom) in Baghdad, the capital of the 'Abbasid caliphate. His *De radiis (On Rays)* proposes a universal theory of causality based on rays, a kind of wave-based physics. Al-Kindī argues that the heavenly bodies, at God's command, send out rays, which travel in straight lines in all directions and affect everything they touch. This argument is al-Kindī's interpretation of the Qur'anic verse 'The sun and moon revolve to a computation; And the grasses and the trees bow (to Him) in adoration' (Adamson 2007: 182; Ali 1993: 461). Since these rays differ according to their positions, distances and angles, they have infinitely varied effects. 'Because of this mutual condition of the rays,' al-Kindī writes, 'so much diversity comes about that hardly two or more things which actually exist in this world are found to be similar in all respects, even if human sensation cannot grasp the difference' (al-Kindī 2012: 222–5). (This will be why talismans tend to use redundant information: to get as many rays working together as possible, or to mitigate forces of certain rays.) Even if we cannot detect it, that is, the complexity and uniqueness of things on earth parallel those of the ever-changing heavens. Absorbing all those rays, 'each place in this world contains the rays of all the things that actually exist in it' (al-Kindī 2012: 226).

Earthly entities not only absorb rays but emit them in turn, al-Kindī continues. Sounds and colours emit rays. The emotional passions of the soul are the effect of rays and in turn send out their own rays. Imagination, too, or the inner capacity to make images, is the effect of rays, for the imagination absorbs the imprint of things and reproduces them in microcosm (Burnett 2009; Hanegraaff 2003: 363).

This ray-based physics synthesises several sources. The ray theory al-Kindī innovatively adapts from optics. The astral causality comes from the *Great Introduction to Astrology* by al-Kindī's colleague Abu Ma'shar al-Balkhī (d. 886), which argues that events in the terrestrial world are caused by movements in the celestial world. These movements are no mechanical clockwork but living forces, as Liana Saif points out, for Abu Ma'shar argues the stars and planets act 'through

their rational souls, by virtue of being alive, and through their natural movement
... by God's leave' (Saif 2017: 305). Al-Kindī attempted by a number of arguments to prove that the stars, with human-like psychology, did God's bidding by
free will, though he did not quite succeed (Adamson 2007: 183–5).

Thinking of the stars and planets as living, willing beings leads us to a third
ingredient in al-Kindī's ray theory, the fascinating figure Ṭābit ibn Qurrā (d. 901).
Ṭābit worked in Baghdad as a mathematician and translator, and was knowledge-
able in the production of talismans. He was not a Muslim but a Sabean of Harrān
in northwestern Mesopotamia, now southeastern Turkey. The Sabean religion
synthesised Greek, Syriac, Jewish, Persian and Indian sources. They worshipped
stars as representatives of a divine unity. Al-Kindī describes their basic tenet as:
'The world has a cause who has never ceased to be, who is one, not manifold,
who cannot be described by means of attributes which apply to the things caused'
(qtd in Pingree 2002: 19). The Sabeans carried out elaborate initiations in their
temple for equal numbers of female and male youths. Despite all this syncretism,
the Sabeans are mentioned in the Qur'an as people of the book.

From Ṭābit, al-Kindī adopted the Neoplatonist idea that God, as first cause, is
so high above us humans that we can only reach him through intermediaries, the
heavenly bodies (Burnett 1987: 87). Incorporating Abu Ma'shar's astrology with
Ṭābit's argument that the stars and planets enact God's will, al-Kindī is able to
argue that *all* events in this world are caused by the rays of the heavenly bodies,
at God's command.

In al-Kindī's cosmology the activity of every entity, down to the smallest blade
of grass, is the effect of the entire heavenly harmony (al-Kindī 2012: 225). If you
understand this harmony, he promises, you will know the past, the present and
the future. It is here that *On Rays* becomes a manual of talismanic magic: a set of
practices to bend celestial rays in order to influence earthly things.

Al-Kindī instructs the magician to make images of celestial bodies by carving
a figure into metal or stone or by moulding it. Judging by surviving talismans,
such as those illustrated by Emilie Savage-Smith (2003), the resulting image was
approximate. Tenth-century Iranian magicians inscribed figures of a scorpion,
rampant lion or dog, stars, and Arabic script on silver or base metal about two
centimetres across; Savage-Smith writes that these may have been intended to
ward off sudden death. The figures are very simple, but according to al-Kindī the
tactile impression of the specialist's ceremonial labour will send out rays. 'Every
actual figure, certainly every form impressed in elemental matter, produces rays
that cause some motion in all other things' (qtd in Page 2013: 91). This suggests
that effective images are not representations but physical indexes, that is, in
Charles Sanders Peirce's definition, signs that are caused by the object to which
they refer. In al-Kindī's account, talismans work in two directions, indexing both
source and destination. This theory that images are produced by contact resonates
not only with other arts of inscription and modelling but also with mechanical
media like photography, film and video.

Al-Kindī's ray theory was at the heart of Islamic and medieval Latin theories
that the heavenly bodies not only influence sublunary events but can be supplicated

to intervene in them. Six hundred years later, the Italian Neoplatonist Marsilio Ficino wrote in his manual on healing talismans adapted from the *Picatrix*, *Three Books on Life*:

> The Arabs say that when we fashion images [*imagines*] rightly [*rite*], our spirit, if it has been intent upon the work and upon the stars through imagination [*imaginatio*] and emotion [*affectus*], is joined [*coniunctum*] together with the very spirit of the world [*spiritus mundi*] and with the rays of the stars through which the world-spirit acts. And when our spirit has been so joined, it too becomes a cause why (from the world-spirit by way of the rays) a particular spirit of any given star, that is, a certain vital power [*virtus vivida*], is poured into the image – especially a power which is consistent with the spirit of the operator. (Ficino 1989: 3.20)

While significant differences exist, al-Kindī and Ficino both conceive of talismans as establishing a flow of power between the divine source, the practitioner and the image, which allows the image to carry out the practitioner's intentions.

We can see how al-Kindī's ray theory is a theory of causality by *contact*. Heavenly and earthly bodies affect one another, in infinitely diverse ways, by sending out and absorbing rays. I note a strong resemblance between al-Kindī's theory of stellar rays and Spinoza's theory of encounters among bodies that generate a great number of possible modifications, augmenting or restraining the body's power of acting (Spinoza 1901: Part III, prop. I). This theory is the basis of Deleuze's (1988) concept of affect. While I don't have evidence that Spinoza knew of the work of al-Kindī, al-Kindī's theory of astral causation by rays was well known in early modern European thought and was the basis of subsequent arguments about divine and earthly causality; thus it is possible to draw a conceptual genealogy of affect from al-Kindī to Spinoza to Deleuze and our contemporary theory of affect.[8]

What holds together those concentric spheres of the Neoplatonist cosmos, especially the celestial and sublunary spheres, the heavens and our world? A physical force? Natural correspondences? Spirits?

Operational Image: Diagrams of Force

Al-Kindī suggested that characters or engraved forms could augment the activity of planets, fixed stars and constellations. The *De radiis* is not illustrated. However, the magic text *Sirr al-asrār* of Pseudo-Aristotle, which as you recall is one of the sources of the *Ghayāt al-ḥakīm* and the Latin *Picatrix*, states that engraved forms channel astral influences into the talisman, thereby establishing the 'connection with the celestial bodies and the reception of their rays which enable you to achieve or destroy what you wish' (qtd in Saif 2017: 312). Thus at some point talisman makers began incorporating little symbols that appear to be based on al-Kindī's description of stellar rays. These little images of circles connected by lines condense the action of stellar rays into *diagrams*, or signs that represent relations among parts of a thing by analogous relations among their own parts (Peirce 1955: 105). They consist of two or more points or circles connected sometimes by straight lines, as one would expect of a diagram of rays, and sometimes by curving and path-like lines (Fig. 12.2). For example, five symbols in which straight or interlacing lines connect small, regular circles illustrate a spell in the *Picatrix*: 'So that a man of your choice runs to you (or wherever you want): Write these figures on a piece of linen on the day and hour of Venus. When the second decan of Taurus is in ascendant and Venus is there too, write his name on it; then set fire to the end of it' (*Picatrix* 2003: 139; my translation from French).

For the magicians and their clients, the stellar-ray diagrams act on their celestial target by diagramming its function. Diagrams draw forces into matter, Deleuze (2003) writes, describing how Francis Bacon begins a painting with a set of free marks. As Ramey writes, the diagram is 'a mark that potentially relates the known to the unknown' (2012: 162).

A later source of these diagrams is the esoteric works of the thirteenth-century Egyptian Sufi Ahmad al-Būnī (d. c. 1230), which are chock full of textual amulets employing magic squares, powerful letters (similar to the '*ilm al-hurūf* or science of letters of the Andalusian Sufi Ibn 'Arabi, 1165–1240) and stellar-ray diagrams. Al-Būnī's magic continued to be practised in North Africa: the early twentieth-century Moroccan magician Ibn al-Hajj combines stellar-ray diagrams with Arabic letters in his spells (Doutté 1909). Al-Būnī's magical books were taken up all across North Africa, the Levant and Persia. They were not translated into Latin or other European languages. However, as Noah Gardiner (2017) demonstrates, Jewish esotericist readers in Egypt studied al-Būnī's works. I speculate that they were additional conduits by which these diagrams of stellar efficacy found their way into Kabbalistic magic, and thence into European Renaissance esotericism.

Writing on medieval Latin books of magic, Sophie Page notes that they commonly hold that these astral signs faithfully represent 'the likeness of the countenance of the heavens', and that they were first made by wise men who named figures in the heavens that only they could understand (2013: 87). It is striking, then, that stellar-ray diagrams multiply and become more complex as later magicians devised their own private maps of cosmic forces, as though they are privy to new astral knowledge. Renaissance magicians such as Ficino, Agrippa, Nostradamus and John Dee seem to vie with each other to produce ever more singular astral signs.

The *Picatrix* describes how the talisman extends the power of the celestial rays that strike it across its surface, in a remarkably Deleuzian manner: 'The surface is the extension of the effect of the talisman in the place. When there is extension, there is necessarily surface; all that stretches out, up to the most subtle, is surface' (*Picatrix* 2003: 131; my translation from French). Deleuze emphasises in *The Fold*, *Difference and Repetition*, *The Logic of Sense* and other works that all meaning occurs on the surface of phenomena, rejecting the Platonic legacy of depth as a guarantee of significance. The *Picatrix*'s emphasis on surface allows us to consider that causation is physical; even very subtle causation is not metaphysical but simply requires a very refined perception, such as magicians cultivated.[9]

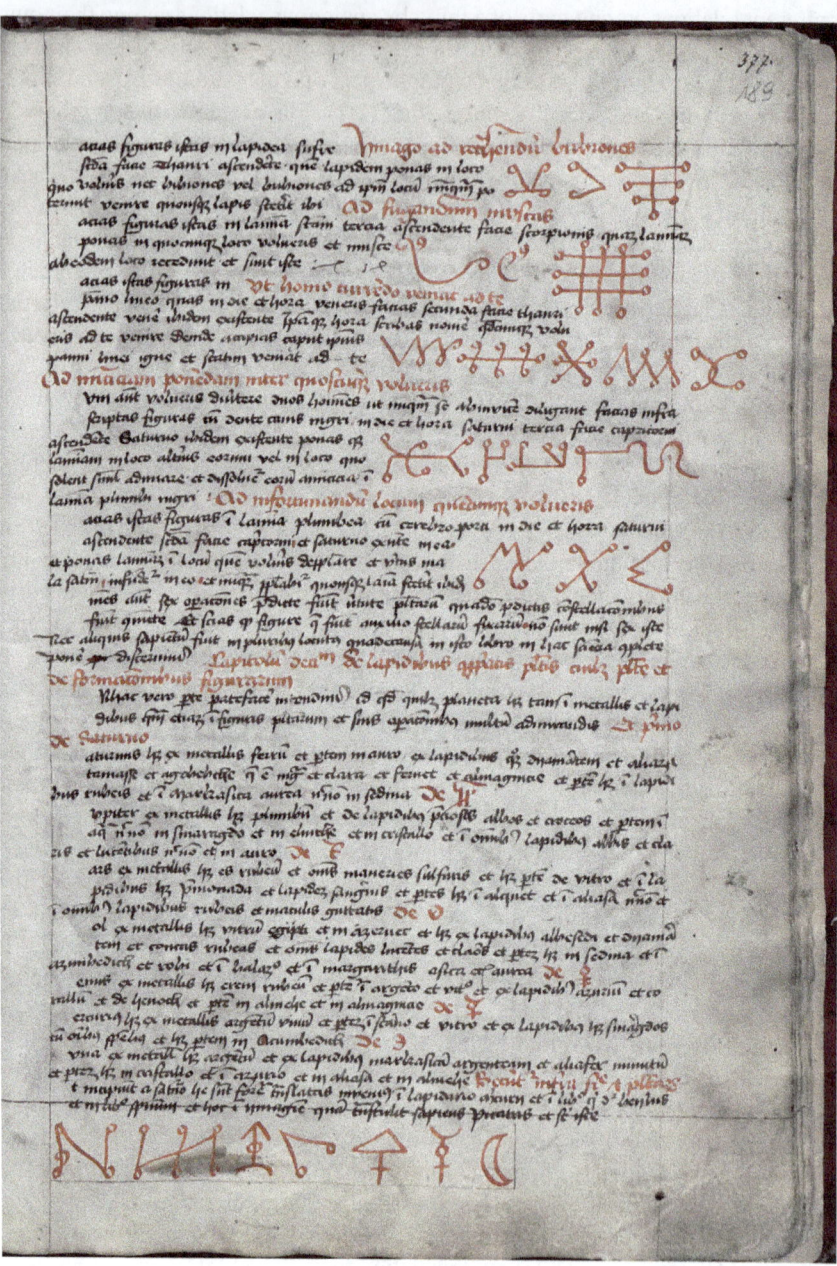

Figure 12.2 A page from *Picatrix Latinus* (1458–1459, f. 189ʳ). Courtesy of Biblioteka Jagiellońska, Kraków.

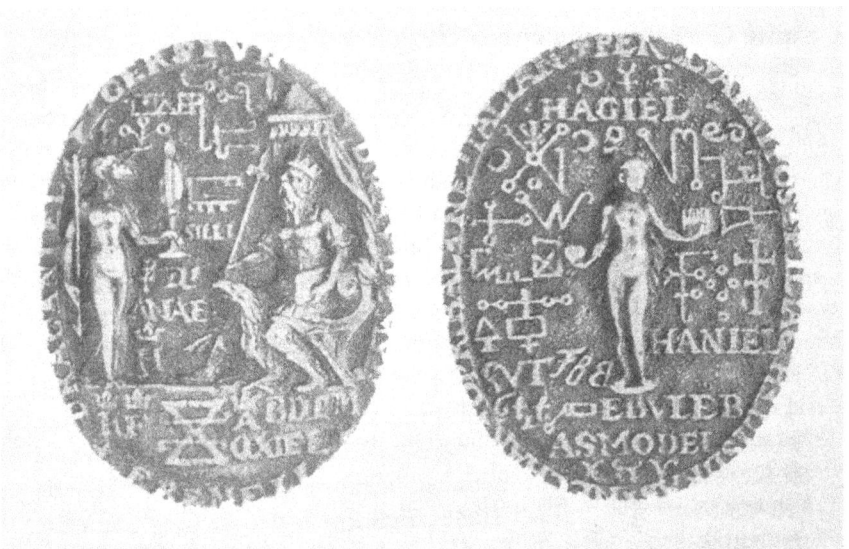

Figure 12.3 Talisman of Catherine de' Medici (in or before 1551). Drawing by Tancrède Abraham (1885). Courtesy of The Warburg Institute.

The talisman made (supposedly) by Nostradamus for Catherine de' Medici (1519–89) (Fig. 12.3) bears modelled figures of Venus and Jupiter, based on descriptions from the *Picatrix*, surrounded by Kabbalist names of angels that correspond to the decans that support these planets. With semiotic redundancy, Catherine's talisman is also densely covered with complex antenna-like diagrams, each line still bound at both ends by circles, that correspond to these heavenly bodies: these are Nostradamus' versions of the stellar-ray diagrams. Pierre Béhar's (1996) exhaustive analysis shows that this talisman, which Catherine wore at her bosom every day for the last thirty years of her life, was designed to ensure marital harmony and fruitfulness.

The stellar-ray diagrams are *operational images*, signs that 'do not represent an object, but rather are part of an operation' (Farocki 2004). The proprietary complexity of later stellar diagrams emphasises that this is an operation that only the magician understands. Like Félix Guattari's asignifying images, the stellar-ray diagrams act on things, bypassing the domain of representation (Celis Bueno 2017). More cautiously, we can define them as *agents*, in Alfred Gell's (1998) term: signs believed to act on the heavenly source by invoking its causal function.[10] Properly employed, the stellar-ray diagrams call down the forces of the stars, the planets and the spirits attending them. Magicians intend their diagrams of stellar rays to carry out specific effects, but they are facing unknown and potentially dangerous forces – hence the highly programmatic rituals and prayers that accompany talismanic magic.

Cosmic Correspondences

Like the Big Bang of physics, the emanated cosmology of Neoplatonism is created by a One/God that expands in all directions, producing the concentric spheres of the cosmos. As these spheres pull away, they maintain their connections to the source, all the way to the material realm of Earth. (This is where you mentally invert that diagram so that the earth, rather than the One or God, is at the centre.) Each heavenly body will maintain a connection with the earthly things that correspond to it, from stones to plants to personalities. Thus in Neoplatonic thought, sympathetic magic is the natural result of sympathy between entities that are separated but were once united. As Giovanni della Porta put it in his *Magia naturalis* (1551): 'The celestial intelligences, the stars, and the planets were thus links in a chain of multiple causation in which form, emanating from God, permeates the universe like the rays of the sun emanating from a central source' (qtd in Eamon 1994: 213).

Arabic uses several words for talisman. There's *tilsam*, from the Greek, and *nairanj*, from the Pahlavi word for magic. Other terms emphasise talismans' physical indexicality. *Al-qālib*, form or mould, is Ṭābit ibn Qurrā's term for the talisman, a sculpture of a human form. The Latin *Picatrix* translates this as *sigil*, seal. Though the terms are sometimes used interchangeably, they indicate two different kinds of talismanic magic, one, which we have seen, relying on contact, and one relying on resemblance (Weill-Parot 2011: 118–19). In fact, according to the Neoplatonist principle of similitude, resemblance is the result of contact, because things on earth resemble things in the cosmos with which they are connected. This is why in the Neoplatonist cosmos the world below, and in turn each human being, is considered to be a microcosm of the cosmos. Three times the *Picatrix* quotes Pseudo-Ptolemy, Abū Jaf'ar Ahmad ibn Yusuf ibn Ibrahīm: 'The faces of this age are subject to the faces of the stars', as well as Pythagoras' statement that heavenly figures are models of earthly ones (Weill-Parot 2011: 124).

Talismanic magic relies on this theory of causal connection by emanation, which builds on the ancient tradition of correspondences between earthly things and the seven planets and twelve zodiacal signs. For example, the *Ghayāt al-ḥakīm*'s list of correspondences for Mercury include sciences, geometry, writing and translation; the tongue, brain and heart; heterodox religions; linen; professions such as carpentry and sculpture; acrid flavours; streams and wells; mercury; reeds; medicinal plants like ginger; monkeys, wolves and other fast animals; and blue and mixtures of colours (*Picatrix* 2003: 181–2). The late sixteenth-century Ottoman *Matali' al-sa'ada* (Book of felicity), a book of astrology that belonged to Fatima, daughter of Sultan Murad III, is based on a text by Ja'far al-Sādiq, the sixth imam of Shi'i Islam. It includes several tables of correspondences beautifully illustrated by Nakkaş Osman, including a jolly chart of correspondences between planets and human personalities. Examples abound of methods to harmonise one's body with the cosmos by attending to correspondences. Correspondence charts are still commonly available on astrology and occult websites.[11]

Correspondence allows the talisman to transfer powers from superior to inferior forms. The thirteenth-century *Lapidario* or Book of Stones of Alfonso X, the first European book of magic based on an Arabic source, explains, with pictures, how to mine the stone or metal that corresponds to the heavenly body governing your target when the stars are propitiously aligned. The magician fashions the talisman when the planet or constellation pertaining to its nature is at its zenith, using a corresponding material, burning the corresponding fragrances, and eating the corresponding foods. All this allows the magician to incorporate the celestial body's powers. The contemporary sorcerer Clifford Hartleigh Low (2017) echoes the *Picatrix* when he writes on his blog, 'By consuming things that resonate with a particular planetary hierarchy, one harmonises with it and, in a sense, one's body gradually becomes similarly composed.' In correspondence theory we hear a strong resonance with Spinoza's concept of combining bodily powers.

In masterly research on talismanic functions in Islamic architecture, Persis Berlekamp (2016) points out that two forms of magic considered distinct by anthropologists like James Frazer and, following him, Michael Taussig and Alfred Gell, magic by similarity and magic by contact, are not separate in Islamic Neoplatonism. This is because, as we have just seen, the doctrine of creation by emanation posits that things are similar because they were once in contact (Berlekamp 2016: 85). I would say these two forms of magic are not redundant but overdetermined, a view that is useful for a time like ours when it is harder to argue that earthly things *resemble* the heavens, but still possible to argue that earthly things have had *contact* with the heavens.

A point about similitude I would like to mention here, without delving into detail, is that *abstract* images can also resemble the cosmic entities that caused them. Ornamentation produced by manual algorithmic processes, such as the geometric ornamentation on Islamic religious monuments, invites the viewer to cognitively and physically learn from it, as both Carol Bier (2008, 2012) and I (Marks 2010) have argued. In a magnificent analysis of the eleventh-century Seljuk tomb towers at Kharraqān, Iran, Bier argues that its inscriptions from the Qur'an's Light sura, 'these are the similitudes (or parables) which we offer for men to reflect' (Qur'an 59:21), refer to *amthāl*, the plural of *mithāl*, likeness or allegory, and relate to the concept of the imaginal realm, or realm of immaterial likenesses, *alam al-mithāl*. With such non-figurative images the connection from the divine source to the human recipient can be even greater, for as our eyes move over abstract images we physically embody their rhythms (Marks 2010, 2018). Such non-figurative motifs repeated over a surface give rise to haptic space, engendering an embodied and multisensory connection (Marks 1998, 2010). To the degree that they are a bit too complex to master cognitively, patterns give rise to a feeling of entanglement between beholder and object that Gell (1998) calls 'stickiness'. Bier suggests that the geometric patterns on the tower are *amthāl*, manifestations of the divine, so that the beholder reflects on the divine as their eyes move over the patterns; thus we can consider that such patterns in a religious context draw, or even 'stick', the beholder to their divine source.

Correspondence theory was eminently harmonious with religion, for it consisted of simply pointing to cosmic links that God had placed in matter. Albert the Great wrote in 1260 that 'the stars can impress an image on stones and certain marbles' (Grafton 2007: 192). The theory of correspondences would develop into the Renaissance doctrine of signatures, whereby outer marks correspond to inner natures (Grafton 2007: 185). Looking not to Arabic sources but to Ovid, Paracelsus von Hohenheim (1493/4–1541) devised a medicine based on the doctrine of signatures, in which ailments could be treated by ingesting natural analogues: walnuts for headache, but also fragrant, 'solar' plants like citrus for vision problems, since the eyes are ruled by the sun. Of course the demise of this universe of enchanted correspondences parallels the rise of modern science – but as Paula Findlen suggests more subtly, it marks 'another chapter in the exclusion of poetry from science' (1990: 518).

Passion: Mediating Spirits

In the Neoplatonist hierarchy of spirits, divine beings reside in the highest part of heaven; in the next sphere are the planetary rulers; and lingering in that ether between the celestial sphere and our world live spirits instructed to engage with humans (Page 2013: 199–200). For magicians, the most important surface in this series of embracing spheres is the membrane between the celestial and the sublunary, for this is where human intervention is possible. As I noted earlier, this is where the metaphysical and the physical worlds come into contact.

No Arabic texts by Ṭābit are known to survive, but a precious text by Fakhr al-Dīn al-Rāzī (1149–1209) relates a story by Ṭābit in which he uses talismans to call on the assistance of several different planets. Wrongly accused of some misdeed by the caliph al-Muwwafaq, he flees, his son still sleeping. The pursuers' torches go out and they do not recognise Ṭābit's son even as he moves among them.

Then I received the news that [the spirit] concealed him from the search . . . Then I questioned my spirit, saying 'Why did you not do the same for me as you did for my son?' They [the spirits] replied: 'Your *haylāğ* was in opposition to Mars and to a fixed star of Mars' complexion. So we did not feel secure in your case as we did in that of your son Sinān; for his *haylāğ* was safe from the malefics.'

Then I made a talisman and it overcame the enemy in 40 days. I got help against him [my enemy] from one of my brothers, over whom Mars was dominant, and he met with a dreadful end. Then my spirit was angry with me and punished me so that I feared for my life. So I apologised to her and told her: 'I thought you were too important to be concerned with affairs like those for which I was asking help from others.' I did not stop trying to placate her with sacrifice and prayer until she stopped harming my condition.

Then I asked him [the spirit of Saturn] to mend the heart of al-Muwaffaq toward me. But Saturn is a cold planet by nature and slow in movement, and so was taking a long time to deal with my case. So I asked Venus for help and made a sacrifice to her. At the same time I made a sacrifice to my spirit so that she should not harm me for asking for Venus' help. The aim was achieved and I was saved. (Burnett 2007: 13–14)

Notice how Ṭābit uses talismans and magic to fold the cosmos to his advantage, pulling in the powers first of Mars, then of Venus to influence his personal situation, adapting his energies to theirs with devoted supplication. Recalling al-Kindī's claims about the qualities of the heavenly bodies, 'rational' is not the first word I would use to characterise the planets with whom Ṭābit carries out his talismanic negotiations – more like capricious, sulky and vain – but there is no doubt that they possessed will.

Note that Ṭābit appeals both to various planets and to intervening spirits, both his personal spirit and the spirits of the planets. Many magicians rounded out their appeal to heavenly bodies with address to the spirits that attend them. Mediating between the celestial and the sublunary worlds, these spirits, angels or devils, are willing, desirous or forced to engage with humans. Arabic authors use the term *ruhāniyyāt* for the spirits associated with heavenly bodies. Saif argues that the *ruhāniyyāt* 'must be perceived as tools that impel volitional forces to facilitate natural processes for the benefit of the operator' (2017: 308). But at the same time, these Arabic authors, like medieval Latin authors, go to lengths to distinguish the heavenly powers associated with the planets from the lower powers of jinn and devils (Saif 2017: 308; Page 2013: chapter 5). Many of these are the decanic demons associated with each ten degrees of the zodiac. The *Picatrix* describes each one of these personified figures, which it attributes to Indian sources, and explains how to fashion talismans that appeal to them.

The Moroccan early twentieth-century magician Ibn al-Hajj practised a magic of correspondence that combined astrological, Islamic and indigenous North African beliefs. Ibn al-Hajj's spell to make yourself invisible relies on al-Būnī's recipe for a powerful burnt compound made by an impossibly long and complex process called *khankat'irya*. You must wrap your head in a cap of a gazelle skin inscribed with three characters, which his interlocutor Edmond Doutté illustrates, composed of lines tipped with circles – stellar-ray diagrams. You should invoke God with certain powerful names, and say, 'I beg you to submit to me one of the servers of your name who will do my will.' You deliver yourself to a long mortification exercise. You then throw some cinders of the *khankat'irya*, recite its spell seven times, and recite a certain invocation twice over a table inscribed with certain Arabic and rectilinear characters. Your shadow will disappear and you will become invisible and inaudible (Doutté 1909: 100–1).

Ibn al-Hajj asks for a helping spirit to descend. Those spirits who are suspended between the heavenly and earthly realms, right at the contact point, are considered more amenable to the magician's command. Interestingly, a Latin text argues the spirits are moved by *passion*. Medievalist Sophie Page translates from the thirteenth-century magic book in the Benedictine abbey of St Augustine's, the *Liber de essentia spirituum*: 'The lower the position, the more *passionate* the spirit and the more likely it is to interact willingly or unwillingly with human beings' (2013: 101; my emphasis). We saw that al-Kindī argued that the emotional passions of the soul send out rays, which may influence the things of the world, suggesting that passion is a powerful state that can affect others. Spinoza, in contrast, argues that passion is 'a state wherein the mind is passive', vulnerable to being affected by others (1901: Part III, definition 1). Deleuze, in his concept of the affection-image, would value passion more as a volatile suspension between passivity and activity (1986: chapter 6) – one of the differences between Spinozan and Deleuzian theories of affect.

The Church tried to repress these idolatrous practices. The 1277 Condemnations of Paris condemned the idea that higher intelligences can impress things on lower, and that intelligences imprint forms on matter via the heavenly bodies (Page 2013: 91). Albert the Great (d. 1280) wrote in *De minerabilis* that celestial magic, aimed at the immutable divine world, was acceptable, but condemned sympathetic magic that appeals to the sublunary demons with incantations or the burning of incense. In other words, the Church accepted natural magic that identifies correspondences between the earthly and the heavenly that can be accounted for by science. It outlawed destinative magic, that is, magic that seeks to make contact with a (possibly demonic) intelligence (Weill-Parot 2011: 130–2). The 1277 Condemnations also condemned suffumigation, or the burning of incense, presumably because a being that can smell incense must be sublunary, thus possibly demonic.

It follows that Albert would have criticised digital apps as demonic, for in their reliance on low to high Earth orbit satellites they appeal to the sublunary realm. At best, following Avicenna, digital apps are ignorant of real causality, as they confuse low-level effects, such as the weather, with causes. Let the artificers know!

The Ceremonial Body

For a talisman to function, the indexical, operational and passionate links between talisman and object are not enough: the talisman must be activated through ceremony. Talisman practitioners theorise some combination of desire, intention and bodily effect among *all* parties to the talismanic contract. Al-Kindī emphasises that both the operator and the recipient of image magic must have focus and right intention, and the magician must have imagination, desire and confidence/faith (*fides*). Pronouncing names 'with intention and proper ceremony' produces active rays – as though intention were a lens that focuses the rays' power (D'Alverny and Hudry 1974). Confidence and hope help the desire to produce an effect, he writes, just as scammony (bindweed) is a laxative (al-Kindī 2012: 233).

Arduous processes of study, asceticism, fasting and prayer match magicians' temporality to the temporality of the cosmos. In addition they must mine the stones, harvest the plants, make the talismans in stages according to the astrologically propitious moments, and write and pronounce very complicated spells. Commenting on the thirteenth-century Latin magic text the *Ars notoria*, Frank Klaassen points out that its program of fasting, contemplation, prayers and rituals would take several years to complete. He suggests that these practices could have brought about altered cognitive states. In particular, reading aloud long lists of *verba ignota*, unknown words, messes with your brain (2012: 46). These words, such as 'Semalfay, Craton, Anagil, Panthomagos, Tingen . . .' (2012: 47), look to me like the names of angels in different languages, suggesting that the initiate of the *Ars notoria* might truly have begun to hallucinate/perceive alternate worlds opening up in the cracks of this world.

Berlekamp argues persuasively that another way medieval Islamic magic was understood to be effective is 'efficacy by sensation': the senses were considered vulnerable conduits and needed special protection. Her analysis of zoomorphic bronze door knockers from thirteenth-century Anatolian mosques discovers several layers of apotropaic (that is, turning away harmful influences) significance. Figures of lions, coiled dragons and birds have protective qualities, according to astrological and hadith sources; the loud knocking would itself be apotropaic; the knocking effectively speaks the profession of faith inscribed on the door (2016: 90–8). Grasping the knocker, visually taking in its symbolic and tactile qualities, effecting and hearing the loud report of bronze upon bronze, believers at the mosque threshold would be channelling divinely sanctioned physical powers through their bodies and their senses.

Talismans also cultivate the intimate senses of touch and smell. In a beautiful essay Tanja Klemm emphasises that Marsilio Ficino's talismans operated not by representing but by performing the healing presences of the heavenly bodies, and were experienced in an embodied and multisensory way. Ficino's healing images worked best when they were of softer materials that could warm to the touch: 'If one rubs the *imago* on the skin, and thus warms it, the *virtus* of the image easily connects with the warm corporeal *spiritus vitalis*' (2016: 128).

Al-Kindī, the *Ghayāt al-ḥakīm* and other Arabic authors linked fragrances to each planet and constellation. Studying North African magic at the turn of the twentieth century, Doutté noted that every serious ceremony in which jinns are invoked begins with burning perfumes, each of which is especially effective at specific days and times (1909: 72). Doutté illustrates Ibn al-Hajj's mysterious olfactory magic square, whose letters correspond to a list of fifteen perfumes. Ibn al-Hajj states that if you burn all of these together and throw a little in the fire on the first night of the second half of the month, you will gain the force (via the appearance of a jinn) to carry out whatever conjuration you wish (Doutté 1909: 73). This magic square is a map of the spice routes; it includes no substance indigenous to Morocco but calls for spikenard (Nepal), sandalwood (India), mastic (Greece), frankincense (the Arabian peninsula or Somalia) and the rhizome of *Acorus calamus* or sweet flag (India), among other fragrant cargo.

'These perfumes will put the higher spirits in the service of those who nourish them with their smoke' (Doutté 1909: 73–4). The rising smoke of incense provides a visual and olfactory bridge between human and divine, as Susan Harvey observes (cited in Pentcheva 2006). Affective yet intangible, smell acts like a subtle body somewhere between material and immaterial. A combination of performance, mimesis, incense and disorientation can synaesthetically stage the presence of the divine, as Bissera Pentcheva (2006) writes of Byzantine ritual practices. Through all these rigorous and multisensory devotions, magic draws the heavens down to the earth and interweaves their powers with the senses and bodily practices of the magician. Magicians not only produce the talisman as microcosm but activate the Neoplatonic hierarchy of correspondences within themselves: the magician, through devotional practice, becomes a microcosm (Ramey 2012: 27).

Like certain experimental films, magic makes what Deleuze calls an 'irrational cut' into the perceptible world that may be able to discover primordial bodies, or bodies yet to come. Magic, like the cinema, 'affects the visible with a fundamental disturbance, and the world with a suspension, which contradicts all natural perception. What it produces in this way is the genesis of an "unknown body" which we have in the back of our heads, like the unthought in thought, the birth of the visible which is still hidden from view' (Deleuze 1989: 201). The magician fashions a ceremonial body that disconnects from everyday perception in order to make a fold that stretches from the body to the cosmos.

Talismans for the Disenchanted World

At the beginning of this chapter I heaped exaggerated scorn on digital apps and operational images that seek to control worldly events but lack real understanding of the cosmos. But there may exist some app-type media capable of bending the cosmos. They would need to be able to invest the user's body with ceremonial powers and link the user to cosmic events, which we have seen requires considerable devotion on the user's part.

Do there exist talismanic movies, movies that could fold the cosmos in order to carry out operations on it? There are plenty of movies that fold together distant times and spaces and make new discoveries; that *show* how the universe is interconnected. Other films fold together times and places that are incompossible, that is, that could not coexist in the same universe, and here a certain act of world-bending occurs. The incommensurable 'peaks of present' Deleuze observes in films like *Citizen Kane* are points where an image enfolds two or more planes of the past, each of which contracts the past differently (1989: 98–125; also see al-Saji 2004). The genre of incompossible-fold movies includes time-travel films, multiple-worlds films and documentaries about the interconnected world by filmmakers like Chris Marker, Mohamad Soueid and the Otolith Group. As I have written, 'To unfold or explicate the image requires retracing each of these pasts into histories that are incommensurable with each other. Thus to invite an intercessor into a film is to re-fold the sign according to their point of view, bringing out elements that were implicit and absorbing elements that were explicit' (Marks 2000: 202–3). That intercessor, given the knowledge and bodily discipline of a magician, might be capable of changing the present by drawing up a fold buried in the past.

Some films carry out *operations* on the universe: performative films, and fabulative documentaries, movies that make things happen (Hongisto 2015). Many movies, including some environmentalist films, activate sympathy among entities at different levels of the cosmos. A very few works make an *affective* fold that reaches all the way from the cosmos to your body, through delicate and risky processes of contact, correspondence, sympathy and passion. I save investigation of these media for another writing.

We have seen that talismanic magic relies on a tactile causality of encounters between bodies. Talismans operate in a cosmos in which all things are interconnected by *touch*. I consider al-Kindī's theory of rays to be a theory of indexicality. It, and later medieval philosophies, insist that signs don't just represent their object but are causally connected to it. I believe that everything is an index, in Peirce's sense: every sign is the expression of a causal relationship. We find such a tactile causality in Whitehead too: all prehensions are causal connections. We are constantly being pummelled by signs that do not *represent* their source but actually *transmit* it to us. This is my simple theory of how talismanic powers survive in our day.

But as we have seen, indexical links are not enough to make magic that folds the cosmos. Talismans pull in the most distant powers – the will of the stars – by appealing to interconnected cosmic levels of ceremony, passion, correspondence, operation and contact. I think it is possible to cultivate awareness of these interconnections and indeed to cultivate ourselves as microcosms. If I say I do not believe in magic, it is for the reason Avicenna gives in *Sciant artifices*. The universe is infinite; its inter-relationships are too complex for us to comprehend, let alone manipulate; we mistake causes by orders of magnitude or do not recognise them at all.

Modernity is thought to have broken the links between individuals and cosmos. The Copernican revolution cast the earth out from the centre of the cosmos, breaking the Islamic Neoplatonist cosmology that guarantees continuous contact from the divine to the heavens to the sublunary realm. However, after Latour (1991), I argue that we have never been modern. The apparent fragmentation of our world conceals profound continuities that we can grasp without recourse to mysticism. Here I am inspired by the work of architectural historian Samer Akkach, who demonstrates that certain classical Muslim architecture spatially articulates the link between the human body and the Neoplatonist emanated cosmos. Although the modern understanding of the universe has decentred humankind, Akkach proposes that the concept of 'cosmic habitat' would reassert humankind's responsibility in relation to the planet and the cosmos (2005: 209).

Like Akkach, I seek to recreate the premodern understanding that entities are linked in a web of cosmic connections. I argue that correspondences continue to exist, even in a cosmos that is no longer hierarchical, that is, a cosmos that dispenses with the Neoplatonic hypostases and even with the closed manifold of Leibniz's cosmology. That is because every mediation is a contact with the source, weaving every entity into long strands, chains, of quasi-tactile connection. Each of these chains of contact is unique, not exactly in the way al-Kindī's cosmic causality is unique (because rays strike surfaces in unique ways), but because no two entities are born of the same trajectory of causation. I do believe that distant sources can have powerful effects, even more powerful than what's close. Affect, in al-Kindī's and Spinoza's definitions, is a register of these relationships. When images make contact with us, we recognise that we are strung in webs of causality. By cultivating affective response and indexical awareness, we can draw the universe close, even rearrange it.

Leibniz's image of the universe as manifold descends from the Neoplatonic description of a divine order, lined at every juncture with devilish desire. We saw that Deleuze emphasises that in the course of folding, once-proximal points become separated. Elsewhere Deleuze and Guattari break down the connective tissue of the cosmos even further, admiring the way Riemannian space maintains the points of contact between neighbouring entities, without any wholes to hold them: it is an entirely tactile space (Deleuze and Guattari 1987: 485). It's not such a bad thing to end this chapter with those points of contact that embody an entire divine order even when the divine order is no longer in place – at the fingertips of the magician.[12]

Notes

1. This media archaeology follows the example of Siegfried Zielinski's (2006) anarchaeology, in that it perceives media of the past as more fascinating than those of the present, but it departs from Zielinski's approach in seeking precedents for contemporary algorithmic media in old sources (e.g. Cramer 2005; Link 2010; Parikka 2012) and demonstrating the cross-cultural travels that give rise to digital media (e.g. Cammann 1969; Küchler 2001; Eglash 1999; Bier 2004, 2008, 2012; Marks 2010).
2. This last could be achieved using a simple combination of Google Earth, Google Street View and Amazon.
3. That's why I prefer my Fairphone, an ethical, transparent, non-obsolescent, fully recyclable mobile phone. Fairphone works with its 103 suppliers, from assemblers in Suzhou to tantalum smelters in Turkey, to enfranchise workers, use recycled materials, avoid using conflict minerals, prevent pollution, and in other ways overcome the exploitation and nastiness coded into most smartphones.
4. I think Deleuze's use of this model is not completely apt, for the Baker's Transformation allows for *cutting* of the surface as well as folding (Shivamoggi 2014: 181–6).
5. I use this term broadly despite the warning of Kevin van Bladel in *The Arabic Hermes* (2009) that it should be confined to those movements that strictly follow the Greek Hermetic tradition, in order to acknowledge the contributions of Isma'ili and other Shi'i Muslim thinkers.
6. This mistake can be somewhat pardoned because many Arabic hermetic writers attributed their works to Aristotle, or to Aristotle's supposed teacher Hermes, to boost their credibility. See Burnett 1987: 87.
7. Some scholars dispute whether al-Kindī is the author of this text, given that the Arabic original is lost and that some works of astrology and magic are falsely attributed to him. See for example Burnett 2009.
8. Such a lineage from al-Kindī, or indeed the Sabeans of Harrān, to Spinoza might pass through Maimonides or Yehuda Halevi.
9. I refer in this chapter to the French translation of the *Picatrix*, but it is now available in an English translation by Dan Attrell and David Porreca.
10. Gell is circumspect about this causal relationship between agent and prototype: stellar-ray diagrams index their source *if* people believe them to be causally connected to it. 'What matters to me is only that people believe that the causal arrow is oriented

in the other way; they believe that the god, as agent, "caused" the image (index), as patient, to assume a particular appearance' (Gell 1998: 25). I relegate this circumspection to a note because I want to allow that talismanic magic, in the manifold practice I describe here, can actually work.

11. See for example 'Astrological Signs and Correspondences', *World Spirituality*, <https://www.worldspirituality.org/astrological-correspondences.html>; 'Zodiac Correspondences', *Sacred Wicca*, <https://www.sacredwicca.com/zodiac-correspondences> (both last accessed 24 March 2020).

12. Warm thanks to Radek Przedpełski and Steven Elliot Wilmer for inviting me to participate in this book and the stimulating conference that preceded it. I am deeply grateful to members of my secret society, the Substantial Motion Research Network (SMRN), who gave me invaluable suggestions on the work in progress, in particular Farshid Kazemi, and also Juan Castrillón, Tarek Elhaik, Azadeh Emadi and Kalpana Subramanian. Thanks to the wonderful students in my class 'A Deep History of Arts of the Secret', Department of Visual and Environmental Studies, Harvard, in autumn 2018. I also thank friends who invited me to present this research in progress and convened enthusiastic, quizzical and captive audiences: Jill Koyama of the Institute for LGBT Studies at the University of Arizona, Tucson; Sama Waham of PLASMA (Performances, Lectures and Screenings in Media Arts), SUNY Buffalo; Steven Chung for the 'Thinking Cinema' series at Princeton University; and Jack Halberstam and Patricia A. Dailey for the Columbia University Seminar on Affect Studies. And my supreme gratitude goes to Carol Bier, also a member of SMRN, for her extremely thoughtful and generous peer review.

References

Adamson, Peter (2007), *Al-Kindī*, Oxford: Oxford University Press.

Akkach, Samer (2005), *Cosmology and Architecture in Premodern Islam: An Architectural Reading of Mystical Ideas*, Buffalo: State University of New York Press.

Ali, Ahmed (1993), *Al-Qur'ān: A Contemporary Translation by Ahmed Ali*, Princeton: Princeton University Press.

Bakhouche, Béatrice, Frédéric Fauquier and Brigitte Pérez-Jean (2003), 'Introduction', in *Picatrix: Un traité de magie médiévale*, Turnhout: Brepols Publishers, pp. 5–38.

Béhar, Pierre (1996), *Les Langues occultes de la Renaissance: Essai sur la crise intellectuelle de l'Europe au XVIème siècle*, Paris: Éditions Desjonquères.

Berlekamp, Persis (2016), 'Symmetry, Sympathy, and Sensation: Talismanic Efficacy and Slippery Iconographies in Early Thirteenth-Century Iraq, Syria, and Anatolia', *Representations*, 133: 59–109.

Bier, Carol (2004), 'Pattern Power: Textiles and the Transmission of Mathematical Knowledge', in Inez Brooks-Myers, Susan Tselos and Carol Bier (eds), *Appropriation, Acculturation, Transformation: Textile Society of America 9th Annual Symposium 2004*, Middletown, DE: Textile Society of America, pp. 144–53.

Bier, Carol (2008), 'Art and Mithāl: Reading Geometry as Visual Commentary', *Journal of Iranian Studies*, 41(4): 491–509.

Bier, Carol (2012), 'The Decagonal Tomb Tower at Maragha and its Architectural Context: Lines of Mathematical Thought', *Nexus Network Journal*, 14(2), 251–73.

Bredekamp, Horst (2007), 'Leibniz's Theater of Nature and Art and the Idea of a Universal Picture Atlas', in Bernadette Bensaude-Vincent and William R. Newman (eds),

The Artificial and the Natural: An Evolving Polarity, Cambridge, MA: MIT Press, pp. 211–23.

Burnett, Charles (1987), 'Arabic, Greek, and Latin Works on Astrological Magic Attributed to Aristotle', in Jill Kraye, W. F. Ryan and C. B. Schmitt (eds), *Warburg Institute Surveys and Texts 11: Pseudo-Aristotle in the Middle Ages*, London: Warburg Institute, pp. 84–93.

Burnett, Charles (1996), *Magic and Divination in the Middle Ages: Texts and Techniques in the Islamic and Christian Worlds*, Aldershot: Variorum.

Burnett, Charles (2007), 'Ṭābit ibn Qurra the Ḥarrānian on Talismans and the Spirits of the Planets', *La corónica: A Journal of Medieval Hispanic Languages, Literatures, and Cultures*, 36(1): 13–40.

Burnett, Charles (2009), 'The Theory and Practice of Powerful Words in Medieval Magical Texts', in Tetsuro Shimizu and Charles Burnett (eds), *The Word in Medieval Logic, Theology and Psychology: Acts of the XIIIth International Colloquium of the Société Internationale pour l'Étude de la Philosophie Médiévale, Kyoto, 27 September–1 October 2005*, Turnhout: Brepols Publishers, pp. 215–31.

Cammann, Schuyler (1969), 'Islamic and Indian Magic Squares, Part I', *History of Religions*, 8(3): 181–209.

Celis Bueno, Claudio (2017), 'Harun Farocki's Asignifying Images', *triple C*, 15(2): 740–54.

Cramer, Florian (2005), *Words Made Flesh: Code, Culture, Imagination*, Rotterdam: Piet Zwart Institute.

D'Alverny, Marie-Thérèse and Françoise Hudry (1974), 'Al-Kindi. De radiis', *Archives d'histoire doctrinale et littéraire du moyen âge*, 49: 247–8.

Deleuze, Gilles (1986), *Cinema 1: The Movement-Image*, trans. Hugh Tomlinson and Barbara Habberjam, Minneapolis: University of Minnesota Press.

Deleuze, Gilles (1988), *Spinoza: Practical Philosophy*, trans. Robert Hurley, San Francisco: City Lights.

Deleuze, Gilles (1989), *Cinema 2: The Time-Image*, trans. Hugh Tomlinson and Robert Galeta, Minneapolis: University of Minnesota Press.

Deleuze, Gilles (1993), *The Fold: Leibniz and the Baroque*, trans. Tom Conley, Minneapolis: University of Minnesota Press.

Deleuze, Gilles (2003), *Francis Bacon: The Logic of Sensation*, trans. Daniel W. Smith, Minneapolis: University of Minnesota Press.

Deleuze, Gilles and Félix Guattari (1987), *A Thousand Plateaus: Capitalism and Schizophrenia*, trans. Brian Massumi, Minneapolis: University of Minnesota Press.

Deleuze, Gilles and Claire Parnet (1996), 'N comme neurologie', *L'abécédaire de Gilles Deleuze*, television programme, produced by Pierre-André Boutang in 1988–9.

Doutté, Edmond (1909), *Magie et réligion dans l'Afrique du Nord*, Algiers: Typographie Adolphe Jourdan.

Eamon, William (1994), *Science and the Secrets of Nature: Books of Secrets in Medieval and Early Modern Culture*, Princeton: Princeton University Press.

Eglash, Ron (1999), *African Fractals: Modern Computing and Indigenous Design*, New Brunswick, NJ: Rutgers University Press.

Farocki, Harun (2004), 'Phantom Images', trans. Brian Poole, *Public*, 29: 13–22.

Ficino, Marsilio (1989), *Three Books on Life* (bilingual Latin-English edition with introduction and notes), trans. Carol V. Kaske and John R. Clark, Binghamton: Proemium/Proem.

Findlen, Paula (1990), 'Empty Signs? Reading the Book of Nature in Renaissance Science', *Studies in the History of the Philosophy of Science*, 21(3): 511–18.

Gardiner, Noah (2017), 'Esotericist Reading Communities and the Early Circulation of the Sufi Occultist Aḥmad al-Būnī's Works', *Arabica*, 64: 405–41.

Gell, Alfred (1998), *Art and Agency: An Anthropological Theory*, Oxford: Clarendon.

Glucklich, Ariel (1997), *The End of Magic*, Oxford: Oxford University Press.

Goodchild, Philip (1996), 'Geophilosophy', in *Deleuze and Guattari: An Introduction to the Politics of Desire*, London: Sage, pp. 65–72.

Gouk, Penelope (1997), 'Natural Philosophy and Natural Magic', in Eliška Fučikova (ed.), *Rudolf II and Prague: The Court and the City*, London: Thames & Hudson, pp. 230–6.

Grafton, Anthony (2007), 'Renaissance Histories of Art and Nature', in Bernadette Bensaude-Vincent and William R. Newman (eds), *The Artificial and the Natural: An Evolving Polarity*, Cambridge, MA: MIT Press, pp. 185–210.

Guattari, Félix (1995), *Chaosmosis: An Ethico-Aesthetic Paradigm*, trans. Paul Bains and Julian Pefanis, Bloomington: Indiana University Press.

Hanegraaff, Wouter J. (2003), 'How Magic Survived the Disenchantment of the World', *Religion*, 33: 357–80.

Haq, Syed Nomanul (1994), *Names, Natures and Things: The Alchemist Jābir ibn Ḥayyān and his Kitāb al-Aḥjār (Book of Stones)*, Dordrecht: Kluwer Academic Publishers.

Hartleigh Low, Clifford (2017), 'Some Notes on Planetary Fragrances', *The Sorcerer's Blog*, 2 July 2017, <https://sorcerer.blog/2017/07/02/some-notes-on-planetary-fragrances/> (last accessed 23 March 2020).

Hongisto, Ilona (2015), *Soul of the Documentary: Framing, Expression, Ethics*, Amsterdam: Amsterdam University Press.

Ikhwān al-Safā' (Brethren of Purity) (2011), *On Magic: An Arabic Critical Edition and English Translation of Epistle 52a*, ed. and trans. Godefroid de Callataÿ and Bruno Halflants, Oxford: Oxford University Press.

Khan, Ruqayya Yasmine (2000), 'On the Significance of Secrecy in the Medieval Arabic Romances', *Journal of Arabic Literature*, 31(3): 238–53.

Kieckhefer, Richard (1989), *Magic in the Middle Ages*, Cambridge: Cambridge University Press.

al-Kindī, Yaqūb ibn Ishāq (2012), 'On Rays', in Peter Adamson and Peter E. Pormann (eds), *The Philosophical Works of al-Kindī*, Oxford: Oxford University Press, pp. 217–41.

Klaassen, Frank (2012), 'Subjective Experience and the Practice of Medieval Ritual Magic', *Magic, Ritual, and Witchcraft*, Summer: 19–51.

Klemm, Tanja (2016), 'Life from Within: Physiology and Talismanic Efficacy in Marsilio Ficino's De vita (1498)', *Representations*, 133: 110–29.

Kohlberg, Etan (1995), 'Taqiyya in Shi'i Theology and Religion', in Hans Gerhard Kippenberg and Guy G. Stroumsa (eds), *Secrecy and Concealment: Studies in the History of Mediterranean and Near Eastern Religions*, Leiden: Brill, pp. 345–80.

Küchler, Suzanne (2001), 'Why Knot? A Theory of Mathematics', in Christopher Pinney (ed.), *Beyond Aesthetics: Art and Enchantment*, Oxford: Berg, pp. 55–77.

Latour, Bruno (1991), *We Have Never Been Modern*, trans. Catherine Porter, Cambridge, MA: Harvard University Press.

Link, David (2010), 'Scrambling T-R-U-T-H: Rotating Letters as a Material Form of Thought', in Siegfried Zielinski and Eckhard Fürlus (eds), *Variantology 4*, Cologne: Verlag der Buchhandlung König, pp. 215–66.

Marks, Laura U. (1998), 'Video Haptics and Erotics', *Screen*, 39(4): 331–48.

Marks, Laura U. (2000), 'Signs of the Time: Deleuze, Peirce, and the Documentary Image', in Gregory Flaxman (ed.), *The Brain is the Screen: Deleuze and the Philosophy of Cinema*, Minneapolis: University of Minnesota Press, pp. 193–214.

Marks, Laura U. (2010), *Enfoldment and Infinity: An Islamic Genealogy of New Media Art*, Cambridge, MA: MIT Press.

Marks, Laura U. (2013), 'A Deleuzian *Ijtihad*: Unfolding Deleuze's Islamic Sources Occulted in the Ethnic Cleansing of Spain', in Arun Saldhana and Jason Michael Adams (eds), *Deleuze and Race*, Edinburgh: Edinburgh University Press, pp. 51–72.

Marks, Laura U. (2018), 'Lively Up Your Ontology: Bringing Deleuze into Ṣadrā's Modulated Universe', *Qui Parle*, 27(2): 321–54.

Melvin-Koushki, Matthew (2017), 'Introduction: De-Orienting the Study of Islamicate Occultism', *Arabica*, 64: 287–95.

Netton, I. R. (1982), *Muslim Neoplatonists: An Introduction to the Thought of the Brethren of Purity (*Ikhwān al-Safā'*)*, London: Allen & Unwin.

Newman, William R. (1989), 'Technology and Alchemical Debate in the Late Middle Ages', *Isis*, 80(3): 423–45.

Page, Sophie (2013), *Magic in the Cloister: Pious Motives, Illicit Interests, and Occult Approaches to the Medieval Universe*, University Park: Pennsylvania State University Press.

Parikka, Jussi (2012), *What Is Media Archaeology?*, Cambridge: Polity.

Peirce, Charles Sanders (1955), 'Logic as Semiotic: The Theory of Signs', in Justus Buchler (ed.), *Philosophical Writings of Peirce*, New York: Dover, pp. 98–119.

Pentcheva, Bissera (2006), 'The Performative Icon', *Art Bulletin*, 88(4): 631–55.

Peters, Francis F. (2004), 'Hermes and Harran: The Roots of Arabic-Islamic Occultism', in Emilie Savage-Smith (ed.), *Magic and Divination in Early Islam*, Aldershot: Ashgate, pp. 55–85.

Picatrix: Un traité de magie médiévale (2003), trans., intro. and notes by Béatrice Bakhouche, Frédéric Fauquier and Brigitte Pérez-Jean, Turnhout: Brepols Publishers.

Picatrix: A Treatise on Astral Magic (2019), trans. and intro. by Dan Attrell and David Porreca, University Park: Penn State University Press.

Pingree, David (1980), 'Some of the Sources of the *Ghāyat al-hakīm*', *Journal of the Warburg and Courtauld Institutes*, 43: 1–15.

Pingree, David (2002), 'The Sabians of Harran and the Classical Tradition', *International Journal of the Classical Tradition*, 9(1): 8–35.

Ramey, Joshua (2012), *The Hermetic Deleuze: Philosophy and Spiritual Ordeal*, Durham, NC, and London: Duke University Press.

Riebeek, Holli (2009), 'Catalog of Earth Satellite Orbits', NASA Earth Observatory, <https://earthobservatory.nasa.gov/features/OrbitsCatalog> (last accessed 23 March 2020).

Saif, Liana (2017), 'From *Ġāyat al-ḥakīm* to *Šams al-ma ʿārif*: Ways of Knowing and Paths of Power in Medieval Islam', *Arabica*, 64: 297–345.

al-Saji, Alia (2005), 'The Memory of Another Past: Bergson, Deleuze and a New Theory of Time', *Continental Philosophy Review*, 37: 203–39.

Savage-Smith, Emilie (2003), 'Islamic Magical Texts vs. Magical Artefacts', *Societas Magica Newsletter*, 11: 1–6.

Shivamoggi, Bhimsen K. (2014), *Nonlinear Dynamics and Chaotic Phenomena: An Introduction*, Dordrecht: Springer Netherlands.

Spinoza, Baruch (1901), *Improvement of the Understanding, Ethics and Correspondence of Benedict de Spinoza*, trans. R. H. M. Elwes, New York: Wiley.

Stafford, Barbara Maria and Frances Terpak (2001), *Devices of Wonder: From the World in a Box to Images on a Screen*, Los Angeles: Getty Publications.

Stivale, Charles (2000–11), Overview, '*L'Abécédaire de Gilles Deleuze, avec Claire*

Parnet (Gilles Deleuze's ABC Primer, with Claire Parnet)', directed by Pierre-André Boutang (1996), <http://www.langlab.wayne.edu/CStivale/D-G/ABC3.html> (last accessed 23 March 2020).

van Bladel, Kevin (2009), *The Arabic Hermes: From Pagan Sage to Prophet of Science*, Oxford: Oxford University Press.

Weill-Parot, Nicolas (2011), 'Images corporéiformes et *similitude* dans le Picatrix et dans le monde Latin médiévale', in Jean-Patrice Boudet, Anna Caiozzo and Nicolas Weill-Parot (eds), *Images et magie:* Picatrix *entre Orient et Occident*, pp. 117–35.

Zielinski, Siegfried (2006), *Deep Time of the Media: Toward an Archaeology of Hearing and Seeing by Technical Means*, Cambridge, MA and London: MIT Press.

Index

Page references in *italics* indicated illustrations.

EU representative:
Easy Access System Europe
Mustamäe tee 50, 10621 Tallinn, Estonia
Gpsr.requests@easproject.com

www.ingramcontent.com/pod-product-compliance
Lightning Source LLC
Chambersburg PA
CBHW051210170526
45166CB00005B/1836